"Jack Caputo is clearly on of the century. This archive will allow s important body of work." —Drucill.

"Caputo is one of our greatest philosophers of religion, and this monumental project makes the bulk of his work available to scholars, readers, and other interested souls who want to think about what matters most in the world." —Clayton Crockett, Professor of Religion, University of Central Arkansas

"John D. Caputo is one of the leading religious thinkers of the last 50 years, and these archives will be immensely valuable for scholars tracing the development of his thought and for those seeking to read him for the first time." —Neal DeRoo, Professor of Philosophy, Institute of Christian Studies (Toronto, Canada)

"The John D. Caputo Archives comprise an essential resource for all scholars working in contemporary European philosophy, especially Continental Philosophy of Religion." —Kevin Hart, Jo Rae Wright University Distinguished Professor, School of Divinity, Duke University

"The Caputo archive is an indispensable treasure trove of ideas for anyone interested in contemporary debates on the hermeneutics of religion and justice." —Richard Kearney, Charles B. Seelig Chair of Philosophy, Boston College

"John D. Caputo has been for the last forty years (and continues to be) one of the most important philosophers writing in the phenomenological tradition. His original works on religion have changed the way we conceive the relationship between philosophy and religion. Therefore, the formation of the 'John D. Caputo: Collected Philosophical and Theological Papers' archive is an essential undertaking, which I completely support." —Leonard Lawlor, Sparks Professor of Philosophy, Pennsylvania State University

"Professor John D. Caputo's monumental work in philosophy and theology is crucial to the mediation of contemporary European thought to a much wider readership." —Patrick Masterson, President Emeritus, Professor of Philosophy Emeritus, University College Dublin

"The 'John D. Caputo Archives' gathers together many of the works of one of the most original, influential, and uniquely American voices in continental philosophy and theology of the past fifty years. It is an invaluable resource for anyone wanting to know more about everything from phenomenology, hermeneutics, deconstruction, and negative theology to questions regarding the very future of philosophy and possibility of religion in our time." —Michael Naas, Professor of Philosophy, DePaul University

"The Collected Papers of John D Caputo is a valued resource. He is a wonderfully accomplished and creative philosopher/theologian in the Continental tradition, especially noted for his pioneering and influential work in the postmodern 'rethinking' of religion." —James Olthuis, Professor Emeritus of Philosophical Theology, Institute for Christian Studies (Toronto)

"The singular achievement of John D. Caputo's work has been to demonstrate that radical philosophy is so far from being a threat to Christian theology as to have been the means by which theology is directed to its own radical and therefore defining commitment to attend to the creative-recreative force of the insistent call that all things are possible. His is an exuberant path of thinking that dares to sit lightly to the conventional boundaries of the academy and is therefore able to confront us with what is most worth thinking about. The publication of his collected works will be a resource for both philosophy and theology for a long time to come." —George Pattison, Formerly Lady Margaret Professor of Divinity, University of Oxford; 1640 Professor of Divinity (retired), University of Glasgow

"John D. Caputo's extraordinary work from his earliest work on Eckhart, Heidegger and others to his later work on Derrida, and his contemporary philosophical theology have been a singular resource for all serious contemporary scholars. I heartily endorse this project." —David Tracy, Andrew Thomas Greeley and Grace McNichols Greeley Distinguished Service Professor Emeritus of Catholic Studies at the University of Chicago Divinity School

"Philosophers should not be allowed to have as much fun as Jack and I have had over the years debating what would make a truly radical hermeneutics. These writings are an important chapter in the development of 'continental' philosophy of religion as it has developed from Kierkegaard, Nietzsche, Heidegger, Derrida, and on into the present century." —Merold Westphal, Distinguished Professor of Philosophy Emeritus, Fordham University

John D. Caputo

The Collected Philosophical and Theological Papers

Volume 5: 2005–2007
Coming Out as a Theologian

Eric Weislogel, Editor

The John D. Caputo Archives

Copyright © 2024 John D. Caputo
Published by John D. Caputo Archives
All rights reserved.
ISBN: 978-1-7373127-5-8 [paperback]

TABLE OF CONTENTS

Introducing John D. Caputo Archives   iii

The Board of John D. Caputo Archives   v

Introduction to Volume 5 – *Coming Out as a Theologian*   1

POSTMODERNISM AND RELIGION

1. Atheism, A/Theology and the Postmodern Condition (2007)   9
2. Before Creation: Derrida's Memory of God (2006)   25
3. Theopoetic/Theopolitic (2007)   37
4. Hauntological Hermeneutics and The Interpretation of Christian Faith: On Being Dead Equal Before God (2006)   41
5. Bodies Still Unrisen, Events Still Unsaid (2007)   61
6. The Hyperbolization of Phenomenology: Two Possibilities for Religion in Recent Continental Philosophy (2007)   83
7. Beyond Sovereignty: Many Nations Under the Weakness of God (2006)   109
8. A Prolegomenon to Post-Secularism (2005)   123

POSTMODERN THEORY

9. Deconstruction (2005)   135
10. Temporal Transcendence: The Very Idea of "*à venir*" in Derrida (2007)   141
11. Of Hyper-Reality (2005)   159
12. In Praise of Ambiguity (2005)   167

DIALOGUES AND CONTROVERSIES

13. Beyond the Death of God: A Debate with T. J. J. Altizer (2005)   187
14. On Being Done with God: In Dialogue with Mark Taylor (2005)   201

15.	Laughing, Praying, Weeping Before God: A Response (2006)	211
16.	Towards An Idea of Danish Deconstruction: In the Wake of Louis Mackey (2005)	227
17.	Methodological Postmodernism: On Merold Westphal's Overcoming Onto-Theology (20XX)	241
18.	Jennings's Deconstruction of Christianity: On Paul and Derrida (2006)	257
19.	On Being Clear About Faith: A Response to Stephen Williams (2006)	265

BOOK REVIEWS

20.	Calvin Schrag, *God as Otherwise Than Being* (2005)	275
21.	Jean-Luc Marion, *Being Given: Toward A Phenomenology of Givenness* (2006)	279
22.	Jean-Luc Marion, *The Erotic Phenomenon* (2007)	285

INTERVIEWS

23.	Emmet Cole Interviews John D. Caputo (2005)	293

IN MEMORIAM

24.	Richard Rorty (1931-2007) (2007)	307
Acknowledgments		313
Previously Published		315

JOHN D. CAPUTO ARCHIVES

Eric Weislogel, General Editor

The mission of John D. Caputo Archives is to publish a series of volumes consisting of all of Professor Caputo's journal articles, book chapters, book reviews, interviews, and unpublished papers from 1969 to the present. Our aim is to make this body of work available in one place, handily and inexpensively. To that end, instead of working more traditionally with an academic press, we have chosen to publish the volumes that will comprise this series directly, both as e-books and in a print-on-demand format.

Under the general title, *John D. Caputo: Collected Philosophical and Theological Papers*, the plan is to publish at least seven volumes of papers over the next few years. In addition to these volumes, we intend to publish several of Professor Caputo's lecture courses as well as both his master's thesis and doctoral dissertation.

We have chosen to arrange the papers in chronological order rather than grouping them topically, reflecting the course of development of the main themes of Professor Caputo's work:

Volume 1. 1969–1985: *Aquinas, Eckhart, and Heidegger: Metaphysics, Mysticism, and Thought*
Volume 2. 1986–1996: *Hermeneutics and Deconstruction*
Volume 3. 1997–2000: *The Return of Religion*
Volume 4. 2001–2004: *Continental Philosophy of Religion*
Volume 5. 2005–2007: *Coming Out as a Theologian*
Volume 6. 2008–2012: TBA
Volume 7. 2013–2018: TBA

Readers interested in any specific topic or particular thinker with whom Professor Caputo has engaged can easily conduct a search in the e-book versions of the volumes. Each volume will contain a short introduction by Professor Caputo to provide some personal and historical context to the included papers. To facilitate the scholarly use of these volumes, full bibliographical information of the original publication is supplied at the beginning of each entry, and the page numbers of the original publication are inserted in square brackets in the body of the text.

Many of the essays in the *Collected Papers* originally appeared in edited books containing articles by various other authors. The reader is reminded when encountering references in our volumes to "essays appearing elsewhere in this book" and the like that this refers to the original publications and not to the present volume.

Note that certain previously published essays by Professor Caputo were incorporated into his books. When these essays were more or less substantially unchanged when included in published books – like the essays found in his *More Radical Hermeneutics, Demythologizing Heidegger* or, more recently, *In Search of Radical Theology* – we have chosen not to include them in this collection. But if the previously published essays were revised to any great extent for incorporation into books, then we believe there is something to be learned from consulting the original publication and the original context, and those essays are included in this series.

Beginning in April 2023, the papers, correspondence, notes, and library of Professor Caputo will be housed in the "John D. Caputo Archive" at the Simon Silverman Phenomenology Center, Duquesne University, Pittsburgh PA, and are available for scholarly consultation. To learn about the Center, visit: https://www.duq.edu/research/centers-and-institutes/simon-silverman-phenomenology-center/ .

John D. Caputo Archives Board

Linda Martin Alcoff
Drucilla Cornell †
Clayton Crockett
Neal DeRoo
Christina Gschwandtner
Kevin Hart
Richard Kearney
Catherine Keller
Leonard Lawlor
Patrick Masterson
Michael Naas
James Olthuis
George Pattison
B. Keith Putt
Jeffrey Robbins
David Tracy
Brian Trainor
Merold Westphal

Introduction to Volume 5

COMING OUT AS A THEOLOGIAN

When *The Weakness of God* appeared in 2006 Catherine Keller contributed a blurb on the back cover which read, "Caputo comes out of the closet as a theologian in this work." I laughed, but then I thought this is nothing to laugh at. In 2004, I had taken early retirement from Villanova University, where I spent most of my professional life. Forty years earlier I had done my Master's degree (1962–64, on Thomas Aquinas) and then, after taking my Ph.D. from Bryn Mawr College, I taught in the Philosophy Department for thirty-six years (1968–2004). I had decided to accept an appointment in the Religion Department at Syracuse University, where I would assume the Watson chair vacated by the untimely death of my friend and fellow conspirator in radical theology, Charlie Winquist.[1] That was not only a change of institutions but also a change of disciplines and it represented quite a change in my professional life. Not only was I able to use theological sources in my graduate courses, but my participation in professional associations, the speaking invitations I received, and my public profile shifted.

Of course, I never embraced the word "theologian" without a measured dose of legerdemain. For one thing, my academic training and teaching career were in philosophy and I made no pretense whatsoever to expertise in theology as a particular discipline. I have had a lifelong love of theology first launched in the years I spent in the De LaSalle Christian Brothers, a Catholic religious order which I had joined after graduating high school (1958–62), a love I have sustained ever since by the intense reading habits of an *amateur* in the literal sense. I would have described myself in 2004 not as a theologian but as someone working in the newly emerging movement of "continental philosophy of religion," and joining a religion department seemed to me like a philosopher of science joining a physics department. I was in the business of triangulating religion within phenomenology, hermeneutics, and deconstruction, which I thought, both then and now, offers a refreshing change of menu to the argument-based approaches found in analytic and Neo-Scholastic philosophy.

But Catherine Keller had a point which I cannot evade. *The Weakness of God* was different. It was about God, not Jacques Derrida (I do not confuse the two), and, strictly speaking, not even about religion. This book was not a contribution to the philosophy of religion, even of a continentalist variety. If it was about God, this was God-talk, theology, but it was *not* "confessional" theology, meaning the theologies we find in seminaries, the theologies of the various historical traditions and religious denominations. So I called it *weak* theology because I wanted to "weaken" the *logos* into a *poetics* and because I was advancing the notion that the name of God is not the name of an omnipotent being, not a creator *ex nihilo* of heaven and earth, but the name of what Derrida called an "event." This event I characterized as a "call," which calls upon us with the weak force of a solicitation, which leaves its realization to us. Whether what is going on in the name of God, whether whatever is calling there, comes about in reality depends upon us. Whether what "insists" in the name of God ever *exists* is our responsibility. I cultivated several ways of avoiding calling it theology, plain and simple, like naming it a theology of the event, or a theology of the insistence of God, or postmodern theology, or later on radical theology, or theopoetics. So the one qualification I would make on Catherine Keller's outing of me was that I never identified myself as a "theologian" with a straight face. I always had tongue in cheek, my fingers crossed behind my back. I always spoke with indirection, deflection, evasion, circumlocution, circumvention, never using the word without some kind of qualifier. When it comes to the charge or the compliment, the denomination or denunciation "theologian," my practice has been to be an artful dodger.

But why the fuss? Where's the mystery? Why does all this not fit neatly into a familiar academic category "philosophical" or "rational" or "natural" theology, as opposed to "supernatural" or "revealed" theology? That is the right question. It brings out a telling point. I intentionally *avoid* talking like that, in part, because that is pretty much what the analytic and Neo-Scholastic philosophers are doing when they speak of God, which is what Heidegger called "ontotheology," which we continentalists all solemnly swear to "overcome." As a matter of fact, that distinction is even maintained, quite militantly, in phenomenology itself by Jean-Luc Marion, when he distinguishes revelation, in the lower case, from Revelation, in the upper case, which brings me to the next point.

In weak theology, we weaken all upper-case pretentions into lower-case declensions, which is to say that this is a bad fit for me because I deny the distinction between *rational* and *revealed* theology. I take "revealed" theology to be a mystification, a reification, a literalization, an unwarranted capitalization. I treat "revelation" as the work of human authors doing the best they can to describe a human experience of something which they seek to bring to human words and images in and under the name (of) "God." I reject all supernatural interventions and supernal visitations. I have no time for trumping human experience with eternity. I will not tolerate attempts to go over the heads of other mortals. I will not tolerate claims of privileged information or be complicit in theological insider trading. I do not reject revelation. I reject its mystification. "Revelation" means for me a life-transforming "insight" into a "form of life," the sort of thing that is produced by a creative-poetic imagination and is cut to fit the cultural and historical tradition within which it takes place. There are as many "revelations" as there are forms of life. Nothing drops from the sky; everything emerges from our factical situatedness in that in which we live and move and have our being, which was set out so vividly in the young Heidegger's "hermeneutics of facticity."

So there is a genuine sense in which this *is* theology, but that word has to be used with asterisks, with extreme caution, with flashing signals, given that the word immediately suggests long robes and seminaries and accusations of heresy. That is why the lead essay in the present collection is my contribution to *The Cambridge Companion to Atheism*, where the question is raised of whether this weak or postmodern theology is theism or atheism or neither (chapter 1). Is it a death of God theology? Or does it come "after" the death of God? This is the question that is getting worked out here. Other essays in this first group ("Postmodernism and Religion") explore the unique relation of Derrida's work to "God" (chapter 2), whether weak theology is not theology but theopoetics (chapter 3), and how it plays out in Kierkegaard (chapter 4) and even in the question of the risen body (chapter 4). My dialogue with Ted Jennings's reading of Derrida and Paul could also have been placed in this section (chapter 17). I draw particular attention to the essay on the different, even opposed, "hyperbolic" interpretations of Husserl found in Marion and Derrida (chapter 6), since Marion is doing postmodern theology in a very premodern way.[2] In chapter 7, I propose imagining God without power but not without authority, as making an unconditional claim on us but outside the parameters of power, as a weak force, in order to find a new way to think about a "nation." The final essay in this section, previously unpublished, explains how, if what I am saying about God is neither theistic nor atheistic, then it is also neither religious nor secular but post-secular (chapter 8), a point also made in the response to Stephen Williams (chapter 19).

The second group ("Postmodern Theory") makes no special reference to religion. It begins with an encyclopedia entry on "deconstruction" (chapters 9). The analysis of the very idea of *à venir* in Derrida (chapter 10) I think is particularly important because it clarifies the difference between the to-come and any regulative ideal or Idea in the Kantian sense. Chapter 11 is a "Preface" to a book on Shakespeare and postmodernism, and chapter 12 defends the productive character of ambiguity over and against modernity's concern with univocal clarity.

In looking back over the work of these years I am struck by the large of number of "dialogues and controversies" – several of which are previously unpublished (chapters 13, 14, 16, 18) – in which I am trying to refine my position, for which neither classical theism nor death of God atheism is a good fit. On the one hand, when I am asked if I am an atheist, I respond that the

3

meaning of atheism is relative to what one means by *theos*. Like Paul Tillich, I am an atheist about the God of classical theism, the Supreme Being, the *deus omnipotens*, which for Merold Westphal is atheism pure and simple. To Merold's merry quip that my theology is "thin soup," I respond that his postmodernism is "postmodernism lite." I consider Westphal's version of postmodern theory strictly methodological, not substantive (chapter 17). Merold adopts a Kantian strategy with postmodern theory, using it to "deny knowledge," that is, to declare atheistic critiques of religion to be metaphysical excess, "in order to make room for faith" in a completely orthodox and classical theology, just as if there had never been any postmodern theory at all. I share Westphal's interest in the postmodernity of Kierkegaard (chapter 5), but I think he reads Kierkegaard in conjunction with Barth, whereas I read Kierkegaard in conjunction with not only with Tillich but also Derrida. The first and most impressive example of the Derridean approach to Kierkegaard of which I approve is found not in Mark Taylor but in Louis Mackey (chapter 16), whom I had invited to the first "Religion and Postmodernism" conference at Villanova, which he declined with great regret because of ill health. I also think that Jean-Luc Marion's work (chapters 6, 21, 22) bears an analogy to Barth, not directly, but through Barth's friend and compatriot Hans Urs von Balthasar, the Roman Catholic theologian of *Herrlichkeit*. I think the "saturated phenomenon" is at bottom a skillful phenomenological transcription of the transcendent "God without being" of Christian Neoplatonic beyond-being mystical theology,[3] drawing upon a *pre*modern and Patristic theology which goes hand in hand with an extremely conservative ecclesiology. The bottom-line result of the postmodernisms of Westphal and Marion is classical Christian theism, pure and simple.

On the other hand, I have never been comfortable with the atheism of the death of God theologians. I have disputed Mark Taylor's characterization of deconstruction as the hermeneutics of the death of God ever since I first read it in *Erring*.[4] I think his "a/theology" is ultimately indistinguishable from atheology, *without* the slash, so that his use of deconstruction is a methodological means to establish atheism pure and simple (chapter 14), hence a mirror image opposite of Westphal and of Westphal's Kierkegaard. I think Taylor's was led to this conclusion by reading the Derrida of the 1960s and 1970s. My own approach to Derrida, which adds in an account of the writings of the 1980s and 1990s, is that deconstruction is the hermeneutics not of the *death of God* but of the *desire of God*. For Derrida, nothing is ever completely dead, because even what is dead has its own presence or hauntological effect, which is why I am interested in Derrida's "memory of God" (chapter 2) and how deconstruction is a matter of prayers and tears (chapter 14). Just so, I think that while Altizer (chapter 13) associates himself with deconstruction, his argument that the death of God translates into "total presence" is anything but deconstruction. Altizer takes Hegel's critique of the transcendent God as an alienated being (which in Hegel represents only the first step on the way to the mediated presence of Spirit in the world) and reads Hegel through the lens of Nietzsche's death of God, where, once again, we are presented with atheism, pure and simple.

So it is clear, Keller is right. I am indeed working out a *theology*, a version or inflection of theology. But my view, my theology, is unorthodox and post-theistic, even as it is also post-atheistic, post-secular, coming, *after* the death of God, which is the way Jeffrey Robbins puts it in the book of that name which we did with Gianni Vattimo. That is why, in the Syracuse years, I went back and dusted off my collection of the works of Paul Tillich, one of the heroes of my youth back in the 1960s, and I began incorporating his work into my courses, which shows up here in my book review of Calvin Schrag, who had served as Tillich's assistant at Harvard (chapter 20). But even Tillich's view is too metaphysical for me, representing a kind of panentheistic metaphysics based in Schelling. My own theological view is neither theistic nor atheistic nor even panentheistic. It is best expressed – this is the subtitle of *The Weakness of God* – as a "theology of the event" harbored in the name (of) "God." With theism, I hold the name of God is sacred, but with atheism, I reject the notion that it is the name of a Supreme Being and, against panentheism, that it is the name of the ontological power and ground of being. It is the name of what Derrida calls the event, of the call of the event, of the event of the call, to which *we* should be the response.

The call can be specified as the call for the possibility of the impossible, for with God, even the impossible is possible. *The* impossible is not, however, an ontological impossibility but a phenomenological one, a shattering of our horizon of expectation, in which we give word to what we desire with a desire beyond desire, which is the event contained in the name (of) "God." That means that our talk about God takes the form of a poetics of the impossible, a poetics of our desire, a poetics of the event – which I would shortly start calling a *theo*poetics. While I had been speaking of "poetics" ever since *Against Ethics* (1993) the piece I coauthored here with Catherine Keller in 2007 (chapter 3) is the first time I find myself using the word "theopoetics." Because weak theology is focused on the event harbored in the name (of) "God," it takes classical theology seriously, but not straightforwardly, by searching for the event by which classical theology is inwardly inhabited and disturbed. Unlike classical theism, the name of God is the name of a possibility which may turn out badly, a theology of the "perhaps," of what Nietzsche would call the "dangerous perhaps." I take "religion" seriously, but this is a religion *without religion*. It is important to note that a theology of the event is not a rival theology or a rival religion but the inner disturbance inhabiting the existing religious traditions and their (confessional) theologies, a disturbance which shows up whenever confessional theologians begin digging deeply and asking questions, a sign of which is that they lose their jobs in confessional institutions.

After an interview by a Dublin philosopher about my reading of Derrida's reading of James Joyce (chapter 23), the collection ends with an *in memoriam*. Ever since I first met Richard Rorty in the mid-1970s, when we had invited him to speak at Villanova University, I have admired both the man and the work. I love, in particular, the boldness with which he defied the dogmas of the high church of analytic philosophy in the United States, just the way my weak theologians defy the ecclesiastical powers that be. Derrida died of pancreatic cancer in the fall semester I arrived at Syracuse and Rorty three years later, also of pancreatic cancer, about which Rorty quipped that it must come of reading too much Heidegger. My memorial tribute to him is a fitting conclusion to this volume (chapter 24).

John D. Caputo
Wayne, Pennsylvania
Summer 2024

---

[1] See "Charles Winquist (1944–2002): Desiring Theology as a Hermeneutics of the Desire for God," in *John D. Caputo: The Collected Philosophical and Theological Papers*, Volume 4, *2001–2004: Continental Philosophy of Religion*, ed. Eric Weislogel (John D. Caputo Archives, 2023), 451–63.

[2] See also John D. Caputo, "Derrida and Marion: Two Husserlian Revolutions," in *Religious Experience and the End of Metaphysics*, ed. Jeffrey Bloechl (Bloomington: Indiana University Press, 2003), 119–34; reprinted in *John D. Caputo: The Collected Philosophical and Theological Papers*, Volume 4, *2001–2004: Continental Philosophy of Religion*, Ed. Eric Weislogel (John D. Caputo Archives, 2023), 163–80.

[3] See also my study of Marion's *God without Being* "How to Avoid Speaking of God: The Violence of Natural Theology," in *The Prospects for Natural Theology*, ed. Eugene Long (Washington, D.C.: The Catholic University of America Press, 1992), 128–150; reprinted in *John D. Caputo: The Collected Philosophical and Theological Papers*, Volume 2, *1986–1996: Hermeneutics and Deconstruction*, ed. Eric Weislogel (John D. Caputo Archives, 2022), 287–320; and "God is Wholly Other – Almost: *Différance* and the Hyperbolic Excess of God," in *The Otherness of God*, ed. Orrin F. Summerell (Charlottesville: University of Virginia Press, 1998), 190–205, reprinted in *John D. Caputo: The Collected Philosophical and Theological Papers*, Volume 3, *1997–2000: The Return of Religion*, ed. Eric Weislogel (John D. Caputo Archives, 2021), 77–91.

[4] See my review of *Erring* in *Man and World*, 21 (1988), 107–14; reprinted in *John D. Caputo: The Collected Philosophical and Theological Papers*, Volume 2, *1986–1996: Hermeneutics and Deconstruction*, ed. Eric Weislogel (John D. Caputo Archives, 2022), 397–404.

POSTMODERNISM AND RELIGION

POSTMODERNISM IN SPORT

ATHEISM, A/THEOLOGY AND THE POSTMODERN CONDITION

[In *The Cambridge Companion to Atheism*, ed. Michael Martin (Cambridge: Cambridge University Press, 2007), 267–82]

[267] "Postmodernism" seems for all the world to religious believers as a continuation of Nietzsche by another means, the latest version of the idea that God is dead and everything is permitted. It has been vigorously attacked by the Christian right as a diabolical enemy of religion, a frivolous skepticism that undermines the possibility of any absolute – God, truth, or morality – and leaves us exposed to the wolves of relativism.[1] When Jean-François Lyotard described postmodernism as "incredulity toward grand narratives (*grands récits*),"[2] to take a famous example, he pitted it against the consolations of religious faith in divine providence, in a God who keeps an omnipotent and omniscient watch over the world, working all things wisely and to the good, which must surely be the grandest of the old grand narratives. We just do not believe that sort of thing anymore, Lyotard thinks; the old faith has become unbelievable.

But while it is perfectly true that in some of its incarnations postmodernism makes life difficult for traditional believers, it is no less true that it complicates the life of modern atheism. For, as Jacques Derrida says, we must keep a watchful eye for "theological prejudices" not only in theology, where they are overt, but no less in "metaphysics in its entirety, even when it professes to be atheist."[3] So Derrida warns us about the theologians of atheistic metaphysics! Theology reaches further than the divinity schools; it has to do with the very idea of a fixed center. That is why, upon closer examination, postmodernism turns out to be not a particularly friendly environment for atheism, either, not if atheism is a metaphysical or an otherwise fixed and decisive denial of God. Thus a version of postmodern thinking has emerged recently that unnerves the religious right and a lot of secularizing postmodernists alike, neither of whom saw it coming, one that identifies "modernity" with "secularization" and sees in "post-modernity" an opening to the "post-secular" and even to a "postmodern theology."

Those complex interweavings are what I hope to sort out in what follows.

[268] But first a word about the word – "postmodern." Originally coined in architecture to signify a mélange of modernism and historical citation, it was given philosophical currency by Lyotard in *The Postmodern Condition*. Derrida himself rejects the word both because it suggests an easy historical periodization and something *anti*-Enlightenment instead of a *new* Enlightenment, a continuation of the Enlightenment by another means.[4] For better or for worse the word has established itself, and while we can agree that it has been beaten senseless by overuse, we can for the purposes of this study locate its strictly philosophical content in a cluster of three ideas: (1) the affirmation of radical and irreducible pluralism (of what Lyotard calls "paganism"); (2) the rejection of an overarching, metaphysical or foundational schema (of what Lyotard calls "monotheism" and Derrida calls "theology"); (3) a suspicion of fixed binary categories that describe rigorously separable regions (typically characteristic of "structuralism").[5]

(1) Although the American historian and philosopher of science Thomas Kuhn had nothing to do personally with the movement, Kuhn's seminal idea of scientific change as a series of holistic switches among "incommensurable" paradigms that resist one-to-one comparison is highly congenial to postmodern ways of thinking. This shows up in the use of Kuhn's ideas by Richard Rorty,[6] the foremost American philosopher associated with the postmodern style of thinking. By the same token, Wittgenstein's theory of an irreducible complex of "language games," which is also important to Rorty, was also adapted by Lyotard. (Generally speaking, as a philosophical idea, French and Franco-American postmodern thought corresponds to what in Anglo-America is called "non-foundationalism.")

(2) Hegel is no doubt the high-water mark of modern "metaphysics" for postmodernists. Postmodernists share Hegel's critique of Enlightenment rationality as an abstract and ahistorical principle in favor of the complex, concrete rationality of social existence (*Sittlichkeit*); and they are (like Derrida) impressed enough by Hegel to look for ways to read Hegel against the grain. But in the end, they see the Hegelian critique of the Enlightenment as one form of modernism being criticized by another. Like Kierkegaard before them – in this regard Kierkegaard is the first postmodernist – they reject Hegel's idea of absolute knowledge, of history and nature as the unfolding of a single absolute principle making its way through time and space. From an epistemological point of view they are, as Lyotard says, "incredulous" about such an overreaching meta-narrative, but from an ethical point of view they view it as obscene, since it is implicated in finding some sort of rationale for "Auschwitz," taken both as the historical reality and an emblem for genocide, for any "unthinkable" evil.

[269] (3) Inasmuch as Hegelian metaphysics is premised upon a logic of opposition, of categories that contradict and mutually exclude each other (like "being" and "non-being"), the reconciliation of which generates the movement of dialectical logic ("becoming"), postmodern thinkers set about eroding such neat binary oppositions to begin with, thus preventing dialectical logic from ever engaging its gears of reconciliation in the first place. This strategy was put forth in 1962 by Gilles Deleuze in his *Nietzsche* book. Deleuze, seeing that simply to oppose Hegel is grist for the mill of dialectics, which turns on a logic of opposition,[7] formulated a logic of difference. The model for this is found in de Saussure's account of linguistic difference. Signifiers function just in virtue of the discernible difference, the phonic and graphic "space" or "play" between "signifiers." Thus the differences among ring/sing/king are discernible and significant, but not binary or contradictory, and neither require nor inspire any reconciliation.

While the postmodern critique of these assumptions produces results that are very antagonistic to traditional religious beliefs, the results are no less damaging for the atheistic critique of religion, which is why Derrida warns us about the theology of atheistic metaphysics. In fact, classical atheism comes under fire on all three points. (1) Given a plurality of incommensurable discourses, there is nothing to stop religious discourse from reasserting its rights as an irreducible discursive form against nineteenth century modernist critiques of religion, a point made by Wittgenstein among others.[8] (2) Given the demise of sweeping metaphysical meta-narratives, the simple atheistic dissolution or dogmatic reduction of religion to one big idea like the sigh of the oppressed (Marx), a psychotic fantasy (Freud) or the resentment of the weak against the strong (Nietzsche) is sheer overreaching. (3) Finally, the doubt thrown by postmodernists upon binary pairs, which affects theological oppositions like God/world, soul/body, or eternity/time, has no less an erosive effect upon any clean distinction between theism and atheism or the religious and the secular. The characteristic postmodern move is made in what Mark C. Taylor calls "a/theology," something situated on the slash between theism and atheism, in a space of undecidability before things are definitively settled one way or the other, in the milieu in which any such decision can be made.[9]

Whence the dilemma of theism/atheism in a postmodern setting. "Modernity" is marked by a strict sense of boundaries – the rigorous discriminations in Kant's three critiques are exemplary of modernity in this regard – in which religious faith is cordoned off as something subjective, not objective, private not public, and finally reduced to something irrational or devoid of cognitive worth, the effect of which is summarized under the notion of "secularization," the disenchantment [270] of the world, in Max Weber's phrase. But the post-modern view of things is to distrust such neat borders. So if modernity culminates in a decisive "death of God," in "the end of an illusion," then post-modernists expose the "illusion of the end," the end of big stories about the end, the death of the death of God. But then the question is, if postmodernists make trouble for both religious belief and antireligious disbelief, where does that leave us?

* * *

The place to start in any account of the fortunes of God in postmodern thought is Friedrich Nietzsche's notion of the "death of God,"[10] for Nietzsche more than anyone else is responsible for the atheistic side of postmodern thought. In the narrowest sense, Nietzsche was referring to what Kierkegaard complained about under the term "Christendom:" in the increasingly secular and bourgeois world of the nineteenth century, religious faith had become, or was fast becoming – the statement was as much predictive as descriptive – moribund. Kierkegaard and Nietzsche are the two nineteenth century background figures of contemporary postmodern thought, which is why it (like Existentialism before it) has both religious and antireligious versions. Of this great event Nietzsche will have been the prophet. But as with most prophecies, the results have been uneven. While something like that might be happening in western Europe, nothing of the sort has happened in the United States, not to mention South America, the middle east, Asia, Africa or in the post-Soviet Eastern Bloc. Sociologists who wrote about the "secularization" of America in the 1960s were soon sent scurrying back to the drawing board to write about its "desecularization."[11]

More broadly, the death of God meant the demise of the "ascetical ideal," of belief in any sort of absolute center or unshakable foundation. This ideal includes not only theology but also metaphysics, and not only metaphysics but also physics, which is also an "interpretation," and even grammar (we shall not be rid of God until we are rid of grammar).[12] That is what Derrida meant when he spoke of the "theology" of atheistic metaphysics, which turns on the "theological" idea of an absolute center – even if the center is physics or grammar, both of which are menaced by a thinly disguised theological absolutism. To be sure, this very Nietzschean critique of God (of metaphysical theology) provides an opening for post-metaphysical religion, for by denying metaphysical knowledge, Nietzsche (like Kant) unavoidably makes room for faith. In the place of anything absolute and a priori Nietzsche himself put a kind of animal faith in fictions (hypotheses) that we produce to promote and enhance life, to push the drive to life (*conatus essendi*), the "will-to-power," to ever new heights. Each thing has its own drive or local force – its "perspective" – and the world is a multiplicity of competing perspectives. Ideas do not have "truth" but "value," that is, an [271] effectiveness that is measured by their capacity to enhance life. The idea of "God" is a spent perspective, an idea once vital – it played a role in disciplining the will – that has turned inward and become destructive ("bad conscience"), life-denying, a longing for death and another world outside the strife of time and corporeality.

Insofar as we fail to recognize that the Platonic-Christian idea of God is a decadent perspective, a value that has lost all value, nihilism (the devaluation of all values) reigns. Nietzsche's prescription is an active nihilism, the active destruction of the preachers of death, in order to permit the joyous affirmation of becoming and bodily life in the very face of its mutability. Nietzsche is indeed a strident "atheist" and a prophet of the death of God, if that means the God of Paul and Augustine, of Luther and Calvin, which are morbid expressions of death and decay. But as a perspectivist he is not an atheist about the gods of Greek and Roman mythology, or even about a warlike tribal Yahweh, which are for him so many healthy fictions, ways that ancient poets have invented to honor the earth and give thanks for life. Indeed Nietzsche's entire thought is emblematized under the name of a god – Dionysus – whom he opposes to "The Crucified."

Nietzsche's point about God, grammar and the ascetic ideal may be seen in the work of Gilles Deleuze's philosophy of sheer becoming, of the "plane of immanence." When we say "it's raining" do not be seduced by grammar into positing some "it" that is the subject of the action; do not separate the doer from the deed. To adhere rigorously to the plane of immanence thus is to affirm the "univocity of being" (Scotus) as a play of differences (Nietzsche) of infinitely varying intensities, of surfaces without depth. Philosophy must avoid the illusion of positing some transcendent point beneath difference that stabilizes becoming, like a substance, or above difference which imposes difference upon some indifferent substrate below, like God, or that produces differences as mental constructs, as in epistemological representationalism, or as systemic effects of the opposing signifiers, as in structuralism. Those are just so many variations on the idea of a stabilizing center. Becoming demands not transcendent explanations, like God or mind, but transcendental ones, cultivated immanently from within the "events" or differences themselves. However, Deleuze adds a twist: we can willingly embrace the illusionary link of God and grammar with our eyes wide open, miming it and enjoying the play of simulacra. Our age has "discovered theology" as "the science of non-existing entities" which animate language and give our lives a buzz or glow, like reading *Alice in Wonderland*.[13]

* * *

The pivotal figure for any discussion of God in the twentieth century continental thought is Martin Heidegger, whose project of "overcoming [272] metaphysics" stakes out the space within which twentieth century continental thought takes place. In his early writings, culminating in *Being and Time* (1927), Heidegger constructed an existential ontology which is a "formalization" of both Aristotle's man of practical wisdom (*Nicomachean Ethics*) and the early Christian experience of time contained in the Pauline letters. In this ontology, Heidegger said, we must practice a "methodological atheism,"[14] a systematic suspension or *epoche* of the data of revelation and faith in God, in order to isolate the formal structure of the "factical life" of Dasein. While the account of "authentic Dasein" in *Being and Time* is drawn from a reading of Paul, Augustine and Kierkegaard, Heidegger insists that it is methodologically neutral, providing an existential ontological ground on whose basis one may make the "ontic" choice either for or against God, or immortality, or a particular ethical ideal. The latter are matters to be decided by each existing individual, not by a formal ontology.

In his later writings, Heidegger shifts to the point of view of what he calls the "history of Being." Being was originarily illuminated for but a moment in the "early Greek" (Presocratic) experience embodied in words of elemental power like *logos*, *physis* and *aletheia* and then gradually occluded by the rising tide of metaphysics. In metaphysics, the "subject" represents an "object" (*Gegenstand*), which is a latent tendency of Greek and medieval metaphysics that awoke explicitly in Descartes and modernity. Accordingly, eighteenth century "onto-theo-logic," a science of God as the *causa sui* (like Pascal's "the God of the philosophers"), is a typically modern creation in which God is already as good as dead. Metaphysics is finally unleashed in all its fury in the essence of contemporary technology, in which the world and human being itself have become the raw material (*Bestand*) for the technological domination of the earth. Technology brings to completion what Nietzsche's called the "death of God" and "nihilism," now redefined as the time of need in which Being has been emptied of its true power. To this state of extreme depletion and oblivion, Heidegger opposes the possibility of another beginning. This he characterizes in terms of a new coming of the "holy" and the gods, so that an "atheism" about the God of onto-theo-logic (metaphysics) is in fact closer to the "truly divine God," by which he means dwelling poetically as mortals, upon the earth, under the skies and before the gods, a portrait drawn chiefly from the poetry of Hölderlin.[15]

By the death of God, then, Heidegger understands the technological darkening of the earth, and by the return of the holy a purely poetic experience that is closer to German Romanticism than to biblical faith. About the God of the Jewish and Christian Scriptures one could [273] observe a perfect "atheism" were one so minded, declaring this God to be part and parcel of the history of metaphysical oblivion, as secular Heideggerians do. But by the same token, what the later Heidegger says about language, meditative thinking, the holy, and overcoming onto-theology, is so evocative that Derrida was able to construct a fictional dialogue of Christian theologians with the later Heidegger, in which the theologians confess that this is just what they have been saying all along.[16]

* * *

Heidegger's most strident critic is Emmanuel Levinas, whose thought is mobilized around a massive critique of "ontology," the paradigmatic representatives of which are Hegel and Heidegger. Levinas's critique is cast— contra Heidegger – in language that has such an unmistakably biblical resonance that it occasioned Dominique Janicaud to complain about the "theological turn" it precipitated in French phenomenology.[17] By ontology Levinas understood a thinking that remains "riveted" to Being, trapped inside the categories of being, almost claustrophobically, against which he posed the necessity to "escape" by thinking what is "otherwise than being."[18] "Being" means the brutal order of reality, the way things are done in the world (paganism), what he and Nietzsche following Spinoza called the *conatus essendi*. But what is "otherwise than Being" is the Good, *epekeinas tes ousias*, although definitely not in the strictly Platonic sense of an eternal transcendent metaphysical structure, in a world beyond this world, about which Levinas was as atheistic as Nietzsche.

By the Good he means something rather more Kantian than Platonic, the ought rather than the is; but all this is developed with a markedly Biblical tone. Because God hides his face from us, we are turned to the face of the neighbor, which is marked by the trace of the withdrawn God, who is said to be "wholly other" (*tout autre*). Now the perplexing thing about Levinas is how closely his thought approaches what might be called a "death of God theology."[19] Like Kant's Enlightenment critique of religion, Levinas thinks that religion is ethics and the rest is superstition.[20] God is nothing more than the very order that orders us to the neighbor. To turn to God is to be returned to the neighbor. God is the law, the moral order of things, a kind of *ordo ordinans,* but not a being outside time and space, lest God be "contaminated" by being. God is an imperative issued from the depths of the face of the neighbor, but God is neither being itself nor some sort of higher being or person beyond the persons and beings we encounter in reality (being). Our being turned to God (*à-Dieu*) is our being returned to the neighbor, and that is all the God there is. God commands but God does not exist. About the separate and supreme being of classical theology, Levinas (the most [274] theological resource of postmodern thinkers) is no less than Nietzsche (their most anti-theological resource) an atheist.

* * *

Things certainly do not get less complicated with Jacques Derrida, who is to all appearances a secularized Jew, a leftist intellectual, who thinks that religion is a neurosis, and who says of himself that he "rightly passes for an atheist."[21] But it is in Derrida, more than in any other postmodern figure, that the undecidability between theism and atheism is the most intense and the distinction the most porous and unstable. For Derrida says that he prays all the time; he speaks of his faith in the pure "messianic" and of a "religion without religion;" and he adds that, while he "rightly passes" for an atheist, he has no way to know if he really *is* one.

In his earlier writings Derrida criticized the idea of God as a dream of plenitude, of "presence without difference" that brings the "play of signifiers" to rest in an absolute foundation, as an attempt to find refuge in "the encyclopedic protection of theology." All this seems to implicate his critique of the "metaphysics of presence" in religious skepticism and perhaps outright atheism.[22] At the very same time, Derrida was being accused of (or congratulated for) being a negative theologian. When he described *différance* as itself neither a word nor a concept, but the quasi-transcendental condition of possibility of words and concepts, that sounded to some a lot like the *deus absconditus* of negative theology. Both implications are incorrect. *Différance* withdraws from view not because it is a being beyond being (*hyperousios*), or a Godhead beyond God, in the manner of classical negative theology.[23] It is elusive not because it is transcendent but because it is a transcendental condition of possibility, a *Bedingung* not a *Ding*, a *quo* not a *quod,* a neutral condition which makes it possible either to affirm, deny or withhold judgment about a God. But please note, it is a *quasi*-transcendental (not a new metaphysical center), which means it makes these things possible in just such a way as to see to it that whatever we say on behalf of or against God, we may have to unsay. Hence, our atheism may be inhabited from within by theological assurances and our theology may be a disguised form of atheism. In short, there is no negative ontological argument against God implied in *différance* nor is *différance* to be confused with God.

In his later writings, in which Derrida spoke of the affirmation of the "undeconstructible," deconstruction began to look like itself a certain kind of a/theological religion. In a now famous 1989 talk at the Cardozo Law School he made a distinction between the law, which is a contingent, positive, historical construction and hence deconstructible (revisable, repealable), and justice in itself, which, if there is a such a [275] thing, is not deconstructible.[24] Without this revisability, the law would be an unyielding tyrant. So being able to deconstruct a law is a condition of its justice while justice is that undeconstructible affirmative something in the light of which laws get deconstructed. Justice if there is such a thing (*s'il y en a*) is not deconstructible. In a sense, there never *is* justice, since whatever *is*, is a conditioned positive law, and justice is what we desire, not what exists. Like Levinas's God, justice calls but justice does (quite) exist, except insofar as it acquires the force of law in those deconstructible things we call more-or-less-just (positive) laws.

After 1989, Derrida analyzed a series of undeconstructible structures: the gift and forgiveness, hospitality and friendship, and most notably the "democracy to come." Furthermore, the name of God, hitherto criticized as a "theological" term, the absolute center, the show-stopper that arrests the play of signifiers and brings discourse to a full stop, a full presence, a "transcendental signified,"[25] is taken as the name of a desire beyond desire, of a memory and a promise, a self-effacing name that tries to erase its own trace, and is as such precisely un-arrestable. The name of God evokes endless substitution and translation and is caught up in ineradicable undecidability. When the Scripture says that God is love, we will never know whether that means that love is the best name we have for God or that God is the best name we have for love, the latter being the "atheistic" position taken by Luce Irigaray, who often casts her accounts of love in the attributes of religion and divinity.[26]

When Derrida was asked why he says he "rightly passes" for an atheist instead of (simply!) saying "I am" an atheist, he said it is because he does not know.[27] By this he did not mean that he is personally confused about what he thinks. He meant, first of all, that there is always a number of competing voices within the self that says "I" believe or "I" do not believe, some of which are unconscious, so that we never achieve that kind of self-identity and self-transparency required by a simple egological assertion. We never know to what extent our belief or disbelief is a disguised form either of its opposite or of some third thing. But beyond that point of self-questioning, he meant that the object of radical affirmation, the undeconstructible, is subject to an undecidable fluctuation and an open-ended future, a certain promise/threat in virtue of which we have no way to monitor the real distance between an "atheist" who affirms the justice to come and a religious believer who affirms the coming of a messianic age. Derrida distinguished the structural "messianic," an indeterminate affirmation of the "to come" (*à venir*), from the determinate belief systems of the concrete messianisms, like Christianity, which awaits the second coming of Jesus. The structural messianic is built into deconstruction as the affirmation of the [276] undeconstructible, which gives deconstruction the formal structure of a certain religion without (concrete, confessional) religion. The operative distinction therefore in deconstruction is not between theism and atheism, but between determinate and indeterminate objects of affirmation, the words "theism" or "atheism" being rather too simple to describe what is going on.[28] That is why, when asked about the "death of God," Derrida said he does not believe in the simple death of anything.[29]

* * *

The permutations of which postmodern thought is capable are also strikingly illustrated by the paradox of the *theological* form atheism assumed in the 1960s and thereafter, principally in the Anglo-American world.[30] In "death of God *theology*," in which we recognize a certain continuation of Feuerbach's "transformational criticism" of Hegel, the perplexing idea is to produce, not a simple atheism in the manner of a David Hume or Bertrand Russell, but an atheistic theology, one with historical roots in theology itself. By this was meant an analysis of how the transcendence of God had become immanent in the world, so that the secular world could be sounded in terms of echoes left behind by the "dead" or immanentized God, for which one would require a theological ear.

The British version of the movement was marked by the appearance of Bishop John Robinson's best seller *Honest to God*, which begins with citations of Paul Tillich, Dietrich Bonhoeffer, and Rudolph Bultmann. For Robinson, following Tillich, the Christian is today called upon to recognized that God is neither a being "up there" (pre-Copernican astronomy) nor something "out there" (metaphysical transcendence). God is here amidst the joys and trials of human life, in the very ground of our being, the only real atheist being one who denies that life has depth and seriousness.[31] The movement's most sophisticated philosophical expression is the "theological non-realism" of Don Cupitt. For Cupitt, the word "God" does not pick out either Tillich's ground of being or some entity in reality who answers to that name but instead constitutes a "*focus imaginarius*," as George Pattison puts it, around which the strictly human project of autonomously configuring our spiritual values may be organized. In his later writings, under the influence of Derrida, Cupitt gravitated away from the language of an autonomous human subject as too modernist a formulation and adopted instead the postmodern, deconstructionist idea of a disseminated subject.[32]

The same shift from a modernist to a postmodernist version of death of God theology, again under the influence of Derrida, can also be found in the United States. The best known of the older atheistic theologies in the United States is Thomas J. J. Altizer's *The Gospel of Christian Atheism*,[33] which follows Hegel's view that the Jewish God is an alien and pure being (the religion of the Father) which is first negated [277] by the Incarnation (the Religion of the Son) and then superseded when the empirical reality of the Son (Jesus) breaks up (the Crucifixion) in order that the divine principle may be distributed among everyone (the post-Easter religion of the Spirit). While Hegel regarded Christianity as a picture story (*Vorstellung*), like a series of stained-glass windows, of a conceptual truth that could be stated only in the metaphysics of absolute idealism, Altizer holds in some more literal way that in an act of divine self-sacrifice, God abdicated transcendence, became flesh in Christ and died on the cross, making purchase upon an unspecified "apocalyptic future." The baffling thing is that Altizer rejects both the Hegelian explanation that Christianity is simply a picture story needing to be demythologized by philosophy and the distinctions introduced by orthodox theology that the Son underwent a death in his human but not in his divine nature.

Altizer's position was criticized and reworked by Mark C. Taylor in the light of deconstruction. Taylor argued that Altizer was serving up another version of the metaphysics of presence, a dialectical presence/absence system in which everything is either simply dead or alive, simply absent or present, in which total death is the purchase price of "total presence." In *Erring: An A/theology* (1984), the book that was for many the first introduction of the work of Derrida into theology, Taylor describes deconstruction as the "hermeneutics of the death of God," by which he meant not the black-or-white modernist dialectics of Altizer but the nuanced undecidability of the "a/theological," in which the clean distinction between the theological and the atheistic is disrupted. Taylor's critique of Altizer is a parallel to the way a Deleuzian would describe as still too theological (or modernist) Robinson's Tillichian affirmation of the depth or ground of being, where even if God is no longer transcendent, God is still being deployed as a way to stabilize becoming, as a grounding center of our being.

But Taylor was in turn criticized for failing to adhere rigorously to the demands of an "a/theological" program, for not maintaining the slash, or undecidability, between theology and atheism, and for simply allowing the theological to dissipate without remainder in a world of random play and bottomless chessboards.[34] Taylor has gone on to write creatively about art, architecture, and the revolution in information technologies, about everything it seems except religion (since, on his thesis, religion is present where it is not) and consequently to be read less and less by people who are interested in religion where it actually is present. Taylor's use of deconstruction in theology was guided largely by a certain reading of Derrida that was dominant in the United States in the 1960s and 1970s, whereas recent work on deconstruction and religion takes its lead from Derrida's writings in the last two decades of his life. There deconstruction is described in terms not of the endless play of signifiers but of [278] an affirmation of the impossible, of a desire beyond desire for the undeconstructible, so that deconstruction is structured like a certain faith or religion without religion.[35]

The "secular theology" of Charles Winquist was associated with the early death of God movement, but in seizing upon the idea of "theological desire" in his later writings Winquist entered into an interesting alliance with Deleuze and the later post-*Erring* deployment of deconstruction in theology.[36] Gianni Vattimo, who earlier had been tracing the hermeneutics of nihilism or of the death of God, in his recent writings has come to see in the breakup of the God of the old ontotheology a new life for Christianity as the religion of love, peace and justice on earth, on the basis of which Vattimo has entered into a dialogue with Rorty's idea of democratic hope.[37]

* * *

The most recent chapter in the story of postmodern atheism is found in a reaction against the specific postmodern tendencies I have singled out. Slavoj Žižek complains that postmodernism is a kind of permissiveness in which anything is possible under the rubrics of identity politics, political correctness, liberalism or capitalism. One of its most deplorable developments, he says, is the return of religion – not only fundamentalist religion and New Age religion, but even the religion without religion to be found within deconstruction itself and hence the whole idea of "post-secularism" that we have been discussing.[38] As an atheist, a Leninist and a Lacanian, Žižek warns that the best way to combat all this obscurantism (religion) is not to attack it frontally but to employ the kind of Trojan horse strategy found in Alain Badiou's reading of St. Paul, which infiltrates the religious camp and boldly affirms the lineage from Christianity to Marxism. Žižek sees Badiou's defense of Christianity against its postmodern corruptions as a model for the radical left, which must defend a hardy and radical Marxist-Leninism against its wimpish liberal humanist corruption. Badiou's St. Paul exhibits, albeit in a strictly formal way, all the marks of a militant Marxist: personally galvanized by a singular life-transforming event, Paul sets out with apostolic zeal to declare its truth, undertaking a worldwide mission to turn that singular event into a universal truth. For whatever is true is true for everyone, Greek or Jew, master or slave, male or female. Of course, Badiou's point is that Paul's truth (the Resurrection) is a pure fable, that Paul is telling the (Marxist) truth in a mystified manner. In his own work Žižek dialogues with Christian orthodoxy, both the older one of G. K. Chesterton and the more recent "radical orthodoxy" of John Milbank. Militant Christian orthodoxy is vastly to be preferred to deconstruction's religion without religion, as decision is to be preferred to undecidability, as substance to froth, as firmly affirmed truth to historical relativism, as real faith to [279] skeptical dilly-dallying. As in Hegel and Feuerbach, Christianity is the real truth but in mythological form, and it needs only to clear its head with a few sessions on the couch with Lacan and a stirring speech by Lenin about the need to be hard, with whose help the theistic myth can be demythologized into concrete social truth. But as critical of postmodernism and deconstruction as Badiou and Žižek are, they do not challenge the postmodernist claim that religion and atheism communicate with each other and share a common form of life.

* * *

Taken in strictly philosophical terms, postmodernism is a sustained attempt to displace a fixed categorial opposition of theism and atheism, to make trouble for both traditional religious faith and modern atheism. Postmodernists identify the ways these opposites turn on a common structure and explore the possibility of a certain region or even an affirmation that is indifferent to the difference between the theistic and the atheistic, or the religious and the secular. If critics like Žižek think this arises from an anemic refusal to make decisions, thinkers like Derrida seem inspired by a kind of "learned ignorance," believing that we are not hard-wired to some metaphysical verity, hesitating – in the name of peace – before making determinate and militant declarations of belief or unbelief. They are moved, I think, by a hope or suspicion that there might be some other possibility (Derrida's "perhaps," *peut-être*), something a/theological, beneath or beyond this dichotomy, some hidden future that is concealed from all of us today.[39]

Notes

[1] See Brian Ingraffia, *Postmodern Theory and Biblical Theology* (Cambridge: Cambridge University Press, 1995) and Douglas Groothuis, *Truth Decay: Defending Christianity Against the Challenges of Postmodernism* (Downers Grove, Ill: InterVarsity Press, 2000) for rather strident evangelical critiques of postmodern thought. Brian D. McLaren—see especially *A New Kind of Christian* (San Francisco: Jossey-Bass, 2001) —is an astute defender of the positive implications of postmodernism for evangelical faith.

[2] Jean-François Lyotard, *The Postmodern Condition*, trans. Geoff Bennington and Brian Massumi (Minneapolis: University of Minnesota Press, 1984), xxiii-xxv; this is the most well-known philosophical definition of postmodernism.

[3] Jacques Derrida, *Of Grammatology*, corrected edition, trans. Gayatri Spivak (Baltimore: Johns Hopkins University Press, 1997), 323n3.

[4] Jacques Derrida, *Points...Interviews, 1974-94*, ed. Elisabeth Weber, trans. Peggy Kamuf (Stanford: Stanford University Press, 1995), 428. For a commentary, see John D. Caputo, *Deconstruction in a Nutshell: A Conversation with Jacques Derrida*, edited with a commentary (New York: Fordham University Press, 1997), 50–60.

[280] [5] That is why it would be more accurate to call the core philosophical idea "post-structuralism."

[6] For the sake of economy I refer only to Richard Rorty, *Contingency, Irony and Solidarity* (Cambridge: Cambridge University Press, 1989) as the most representative.

[7] Gilles Deleuze, *Nietzsche and Philosophy*, trans. Hugh Tomlinson (New York: Columbia University 1983).

[8] See D. Z. Philips, *Wittgenstein and Religion* (New York: Palgrave Macmillan, 1984).

[9] Mark C. Taylor, *Erring: A Postmodern A/theology* (Chicago: University of Chicago Press, 1984), 12.

[10] See Friedrich Nietzsche, *The Gay Science,* trans. Walter Kaufmann (New York: Vintage Books, 1974), sections 125, 343.

[11] Both Peter Berger, *The Desecularization of the World: Resurgent Religion and World Politics* (Grand Rapids: Eerdmanns, 1999) and Harvey Cox, *Religion in a Secular City: Toward a Postmodern Theology* (New York: Simon and Shuster, 1984) have been forced by the facts to recast their earlier pronouncements on secularization and the secular city.

[12] Friedrich Nietzsche, *Beyond Good and Evil*, trans. Walter Kaufmann (New York: Vintage Books, 1989).

[13] Gilles Deleuze, *The Logic of Sense*, trans. Mark Lester (New York: Columbia University Press, 1990), 281. Among his many works, Gilles Deleuze (with Felix Guattari), *What is Philosophy?*, trans. Hugh Tomlinson and G. Burchill (London: Verso, 1994) is not a bad place to start.

[14] Martin Heidegger, *Being and Time*, trans. John Macquarrie and Edward Robinson (New York: Harper & Row, 1962); see Istvan Feher, "Heidegger's Understanding of the Atheism of Philosophy," *American Catholic Philosophical Quarterly*, 64 (May 1995): 189–228.

[15] A great deal of this argument can be found in the essays collected in *Martin Heidegger: Basic Writings*, ed. David F. Krell, 2nd. ed. (New York: Harper & Row, 1993) and in the crucial essay "The Onto-Theological Constitution of Metaphysics" in Martin Heidegger *Identity and Difference*, trans. Joan Stambaugh (New York: Harper & Row, 1969). Heidegger gives a brilliant account of

his later view of the genesis of modernity in *The Principle of Reason*, trans. Reginald Lilly (Bloomington: Indiana University Press, 1991).

[16] Jacques Derrida, *Of Spirit: Heidegger and the Question*, trans. Geoffrey Bennington and Rachel Bowlby (Chicago: University of Chicago Press, 1989), 109–13. See John D. Caputo, "Heidegger and Theology," *The Cambridge Companion to Heidegger*, ed. Charles Guignon (Cambridge: Cambridge University Press, 1993), 270–288.

[17] *Phenomenology and the "Theological Turn:" The French Debate*, eds. Dominique Janicaud et al. (New York: Fordham University Press, 2000).

[18] The problem that Levinas first poses to himself in 1935 in *On Escape*, trans. Bettina Bergo (Stanford: Stanford University Press, 2003) reaches its highest resolution in the 1970s in *Otherwise than Being or Beyond Essence*, trans. Alphonso Lingis (Pittsburgh: Duquesne University Press, 1998).

[19] See the interesting "Annotations" by Jacques Rolland in *On Escape*, no. 10, pages 89–90.

[281] [20] Merold Westphal, "Levinas's Teleological Suspension of the Religious," in *Ethics as First Philosophy: The Significance of Emmanuel Levinas for Philosophy, Literature, and Religion*, ed. Adriaan T. Peperzak, (London/New York: Routledge, 1995), 151–160

[21] Jacques Derrida, "Circumfession: Fifty-nine Periods and Periphrases" in Geoffrey Bennington and Jacques Derrida, *Jacques Derrida*, trans. Geoffrey Bennington (Chicago: University of Chicago Press, 1993), 155.

[22] Derrida, *Of Grammatology*, 18; see also 47, 84, 131, 135, 139.

[23] See Jacques Derrida, "How to Avoid Speaking: Denials," in *Derrida and Negative Theology*, eds. Howard Coward and Toby Foshay (Albany: SUNY Press, 1992), 73–142.

[24] "The Force of Law: 'The Mystical Foundation of Authority,'" trans. Mary Quantaince, in *Deconstruction and the Possibility of Justice*, ed. Drucilla Cornell et al. (New York: Routledge, 1992), 68–91.

[25] Derrida, *Of Grammatology*, 71.

[26] Luce Irigaray, *An Ethics of Sexual Difference*, trans. Carolyn Burke and Gillian C. Gill (Ithaca, New York: Cornell University Press, 1993); "Belief Itself" in *Sexes and Genealogies* (New York: Columbia University Press, 1993). For a commentary, see Grace Jantzen, *Becoming Divine: Towards a Feminist Philosophy of Religion* (Manchester University Press and Indiana University Press, 1998).

[27] See Jacques Derrida, "The Becoming Possible of the Impossible: An Interview with Jacques Derrida," in *A Passion for the Impossible: John D. Caputo in Focus*, ed. Mark Dooley (Albany: SUNY Press, 2003), 21–33.

[28] While Michel Foucault appears to reduce religion to a set of confessional and disciplinary practices that constitute the religious subject, there is a growing and comparable interest in finding his religious side. See *Michel Foucault and Theology: The Politics of Religious Experience*, eds. James Bernauer and Jeremy Carrette (Burlington, VT: Ashgate, 2004).

[29] Jacques Derrida, *Positions*, trans. Alan Bass (Chicago: University of Chicago Press, 1972), 6. See Hugh Rayment-Pickard, *Impossible God: Derrida's Theology* (Hampshire, England: Ashgate, 2003), 18–19, 134–43.

[30] This is the atheistic form of theology as opposed to the theological (dogmatic, metaphysical) form of atheism.

[31] John Robinson, *Honest to God* (London: SCM Press, 1963), p.22.

[32] Don Cupitt, *Taking Leave of God* (London: SCM Press, 1980); *Is Nothing Sacred?* (New York: Fordham University Press, 2002). For a good commentary on the British movement, see George Pattison, *Thinking About God in an Age of Technology* (Oxford: Oxford University Press, 2005), chap. 1 "The Long Goodbye."

[33] Thomas J. J. Altizer, *The Gospel of Christian Atheism* (Philadelphia: Westminster Press, 1966); *The New Gospel of Christian Atheism*, rev. ed. (Aurora, CO: The Davies Publishing Group, 2002);

T. J. J. Altizer and William Hamilton, *Radical Theology and the Death of God* (Indianapolis: Bobbs-Merrill Press, 1966).

[34] See my review of *Erring* in *Man and World*, 21 (1988): 108-26. reprinted in *John D. Caputo: The Collected Philosophical and Theological Papers*, Volume 2, *1986–1996: Hermeneutics and Deconstruction*, ed. Eric Weislogel (John D. Caputo Archives, 2022), 397–404.

[35] John D. Caputo, *The Prayers and Tears of Jacques Derrida: Religion without Religion* (Bloomington: Indiana University Press, 1997); Hent de Vries, *Philosophy and the Turn to Religion* (Baltimore: Johns Hopkins University [282] Press, 1999); Kevin Hart, *The Trespass of the Sign* (New York: Fordham University Press, 2000); Richard Kearney, *The God Who May Be* (Bloomington: Indiana University Press, 2001).

[36] Charles Winquist, *Desiring Theology* (Chicago: University of Chicago Press, 1995).

[37] Gianni Vattimo, *Belief*, trans. Luca D'Isanto and David Webb (Stanford: Stanford University Press, 1999); Richard Rorty and Gianni Vattimo, *The Future of Religion* (New York: Columbia University Press, 2005).

[38] Alain Badiou, *Saint Paul: the Foundations of Universalism*, trans. Roy Brassier (Stanford: Stanford University Press, 2003); Slavoj Žižek, *The Fragile Absolute* (New York and London: Verso Books, 2000); Giorgio Agamben, *A Time that Remains: A Commentary on the Letter to the Romans*, trans. Patricia Dailey, (Stanford: Stanford University Press, 2005).

[39] See Gavin Hyman's suggestive chapter in this volume, which demonstrates both the inner link between modernity and atheism and the relativity of atheism to the theism it is denying. If modern atheism is the rejection of a modern God, as Hyman says, then the delimitation of modernity opens up another possibility, less the resuscitation of premodern theism than the chance of something beyond both the theism and the atheism of modernity.

2

BEFORE CREATION: DERRIDA'S MEMORY OF GOD

[In *Mosaic: A Journal for the Interdisciplinary Study of Literature*, 39:3 (September 2006): 91-102; also translated into French: "*Avant la création: le souvenir de dieu de Derrida,*" trans. Patrick Dimascio, in *Derrida pour les temps à venir*, ed. René Major (Paris: Editions Stock, 2007), 140-58]

[91] Imagine this unimaginable scene: Jacques Derrida – a man of prayers and tears, on his knees, on a *prie-dieu*, like a weepy Augustine, *coram deo*, or like a woman blinded by tears weeping at the foot of the Cross.

Imagine this: Derrida: the least and last of the Jews, a Jew in virtue of an alliance never kept yet never broken, a Jew without quite being Jewish enough, who only learned enough Hebrew to get through his bar-mitzvah; always at least as much a Jewgreek or a Greekjew, or rather someone who situates himself in the distance between the Greek and the Jew, not to mention the Arab also. Derrida: the author of an odd sort of Jewish Augustinian confession that is neither Jewish nor Augustinian, a man of faith who affirms a messianic but without a Messiah, who practices a secret religion about which no one knows anything, not even his beloved mother, who should have known something about it, a religion without religion according to the strange grammar of the *sans*.

[92] I have always been fond of tracing the ambiguous traces and distorted memories of the religious tropes and figures that play back and forth across his texts. I am not saying that *he* himself always remembers them – he played hooky from Hebrew school too often to have studied them closely. Perhaps they are remembered for him by Levinas, or sometimes perhaps by Benjamin or Blanchot or many others.

I have long been interested in his tears. He is famous for his laughter, for outraging the academic establishment with his playful spirit, but I am held captive by his tears. Why is he weeping? Over what? Is he perhaps laughing through his tears? And why is Derrida, who rightly passes for an atheist, praying? What is he praying for? And to whom? Could it be that there is a memory of God inscribed in deconstruction, whether or not he himself remembers?

In the approach I make to Derrida, the odd way he spells *différance* does not spell the death of God or the destruction of religion but a certain repetition of religion, a re-invention of a certain religion. How could it be otherwise? For deconstruction, which is in the business of opening up things – beliefs and practices, texts and institutions – and of releasing their future, does not spell the simple death of anything. Derrida knows very well that the dead have a peculiar way of living on. Above all, God, who is one of the most famous and holiest ghosts the West has known, with a well-known capacity for burying his own grave diggers, with a long line of resurrections and returnings from the dead to his credit, is especially difficult to kill off, almost impossible. ("God is dead" –Nietzsche. "Nietzsche is dead" –God.) Indeed deconstruction does not kill things off but engages them in a spectral, hauntological interplay. It weaves back and forth between our most hallowed spirits and ancient memories and the most open-ended affirmation of what is coming, its "come" (*viens*) coming as it does in the middle of the exchange that is always taking place between the *revenant* and the *arrivant*, between mourning and messianic expectation.

So it is not surprising to find in Derrida's texts the regular, almost rhythmic appearance of certain versions or unusual adaptations, certain memories, of the most classical biblical figures – like hospitality and forgiveness, for example, or the prophetic call for justice, or the Messiah and the promise, or prayer, or the name of God, of course.

Or *khora*, which will be my example here, which may not seem to be an obvious candidate for this list. I will sketch here how Derrida's reinscription of *khora* into deconstruction is, as often happens, not a purely Greek operation but a Jewgreek one, and how the khoral picture of things that emerges in deconstruction has accordingly an oddly biblical flavor. When he says *khora*, he is not simply drawing upon the *Timaeus*, which is the manifest reference, but there is also, for anyone with the ears to hear, an allusion being made to the opening verses of Genesis. My contention is that [93] there is a desert scene – a biblical desert, but then a desert within the desert – that presides over everything in deconstruction, and provides the setting for his prayers and tears. My contention is that everything in deconstruction is marked by a memory of the primal scene of creation, whether or nor Derrida remembers. Let that, then, be the strange hypothesis of this modest tribute to Derrida's massive contribution to contemporary thought, a little gift we proffer which, however modest, means to touch a nerve, a more or less Jewish or more broadly biblical or quasi-biblical nerve, in deconstruction.

Bereshit bara elohim

Bereshit, in the beginning, it was already there. Before creation, mute and wordless, not yet good or evil, more innocent than any innocent becoming dreamt of by Nietzsche. Not a wicked chaos threatening to swallow us. Not a monster out to devour us. Not a rival god out to challenge Elohim. It was just there, without saying a thing and without threatening anyone, a kind of null state that yet was not nothing. The only noise one could have heard, were there anyone to hear, would have been the rustling of the wind as it swept across the deep.

Bereshit, in the beginning, *bara elohim*, when Elohim began to create the world, things had evidently already begun. Upon closer examination, this famous beginning turns out to be a non-original origin, a beginning which, like every beginning, begins where one already is, the absolute origin having already receded from view in a time out of mind. The act of creation is inscribed in something that received the creative operation. So if we want to say that in this narrative Elohim is the *arche*, the beginning, the one who begins to create, then we must also add that there is something there with Elohim, his everlasting companion, just as old as Elohim, something anarchically and anarchivally old and equi-primordial. Over and above Elohim, or below him, or beside him, it is there, its presence there being given or taken for granted, no more in need of further explanation than is Elohim. We would say, in the language of philosophy, it is "necessarily" there, which means it requires no further explanation for being there.

In Genesis, creation is not a pure act without a patient, like a pure dance without a partner, not a pure perfect exinihilatory performance, an absolute act carried out entirely in a sphere all its own. It is nothing of the sort. *Creatio ex nihilo* is a creation of metaphysics, a fantasy of power and clean pure acts, a creature that was not formed in Genesis but much later. There was indeed a *there* there, if I may beg to differ with Gertrude Stein, something to receive the act, to respond to the call, like a sleeper being [94] called to wake. The creative act is inscribed, or spoken, in a context or a container, in a receptive medium, received by a receiver, which is not a pure space, exactly, as in the *Timaeus,* nor an absolutely indeterminate *apeiron* as in Anaximander, but an expanse of barren and lifeless elements, which Elohim stirs or enlivens or awakens with a word. In the beginning, we are told in Genesis 1, when God began to create:

(1) The earth was a *tohu wa-bohu*. (1:2) This has come to mean the "chaos" but it does not precisely mean chaos. In its most concrete sense, it actually means something barren and desolate and often signified a desert, a wasteland, an arid, barren and

uninhabited expanse. Taken in a more general sense, it could mean a void or an emptiness and so it is translated in the New Revised Standard Version as "formless void," but it is formless not because it is chaotic but because it is a void, devoid of life, desolate.[1] It would be a desert indeed but for the fact that it seems to be covered by the waters from which (v. 9) it must be separated off.

(2) Darkness covered the face of the deep, the *tehom*. The *tehom* is the waters, the churning salty sea, a great watery womb, a uterine beginning, the primal marine belly of life, like the stuff of which Luce Irigaray writes. But it was, in the beginning, a barren womb, empty of life, devoid of fish or whales. There it was, just there, its face or surface tossed by the wind. And all this took place in a dark more primal than night because, in the beginning, there was no day or night. A darkness older than the dark, a lifelessness older than death.

(3) And a wind from God, a *ruach Elohim*, swept over the deep, the mighty wind that God is, the Spirit of God, or more likely the wind God sent, because it, too, was just there, sweeping across the face of the deep.

This is the mute but majestic scene with which Genesis opens, the null point of creation, the first picture taken of the world, which Levinas calls a "muffled rustling" (*sourd bruissement*), which is the inspiration for his own phenomenology of the *il y a*, of an elemental "there is," which even terrifies Levinas a little, which is perhaps how this haunting picture gets into Derrida's pen.[2] The scene is simple: upon a barren sea bottom rests a lifeless watery deep, over whose surface a mighty wind sweeps, and it is darker than dark. More elemental than any phenomenal element, a certain proto-earth, proto-sea, proto-wind, proto-sky – all poised and waiting for the event, waiting for the call. The scene is tranquil. There is no *Chaoskampf* here, no war with chaos, no Heraclitean *polemos*, the war that is the father of us all. This was rather more a mother than a father, more uterine. There are no monsters here to be slain, nor anything like Karl Barth's account of a menacing nothingness, *das* [95] *Nichtige*, which is perhaps an all too masculine fear of uterine encapsulation. Just a vast sea, its waves tossed by the wind, and all quite lifeless and wordless.

With Elohim, who was the everlasting comrade of the elements, not their cause or explanation.

That is why the rabbis like to point out that Genesis does not begin with the first letter of the alphabet, aleph, but with the second, with bet or beta, *bereshit*, in the beginning. That signifies that in the beginning something was always already there. There is no alpha-arche, no alpha-absolute, no pure beginning, no pure first.

(The idea of *creatio ex nihilo* does not gain currency until the second half of the second century when Christian metaphysical theologians, in debate with Neoplatonic philosophers, reject the idea of any preexistent matter, like the *khora*, in favor of a pure act of unlimited and perfect paternal power, an unconditional expenditure of solitary exnihilatory omnipotence!)

After separating them, Elohim brings these barren spaces to life, and then he blesses them: good, good – five times – and then, in sum, *very good. Oui, oui* – for, as Franz Rosenzweig points out, this "good" can also be understood to mean "yes." So the idea behind biblical creation is not to bring something out of nothing but to make the barren spaces live. Creation is not a movement from non-being to being, but from being to good, from the inanimate and desolate to the lushness of life. What the philosophers call "being," on the other hand, was just there, always there, and the narrative has no notion that this deserves further comment.

What significance are we to attach to the elemental materials of creation which never made it into the theology books, which metaphysics expelled from the official story and literally reduced to nothing? The elements are not evil but the very makings of the very world that is called very good. Evil can arise only after creation, after Elohim has formed things and breathed life into them, and Cain slays Abel, which reverses and contradicts Elohim's life-giving work. But there was no murder back in the *tohu wa-bohu*, which, with the *ruach* and *tehom* was a neutral, tranquil, non-combatant, the simple innocent stuff of things, the sheer there-ness of the world. The elements do not explain the evil in the world – that is something lodged deep in the heart of humankind, in the dark heart of the children of Cain – but they do account for its contingency, its chanciness, its riskiness, its shaky uncertainty. They are the reason why whatever is done can come undone. The world is woven of unstable and slippery stuff, of water that will always finds its own level, of wind that blows where it will, of earth, which explains why things have feet of clay. Creation is thus a risky business, a bit of a chance, and – contrary to Herr Professor Einstein – quite precisely a roll of the dice. According to an old rabbinic story:[3]

> [96] Twenty-six attempts preceded the present genesis, all of which were destined to fail. The world of man has arisen out of the chaotic heart of the preceding debris; he too is exposed to the risk of failure, and the return to nothing. 'Let us hope it works' (*Halway Sheyaamod*) exclaimed God as he created the

world, and this hope, which has accompanied the subsequent history of the world and mankind, has emphasized right from the outset that this history is branded with the mark of radical uncertainty.

So creation is a risk, but a good one, a *beau risque*, according to Levinas; it is worth the risk. The world is formed of deformable and reformable structures, etched and shaped and sculpted this way rather than that, yet ever liable to come undone, not altogether unlike the famous scene of the "annihilation" of the world that Husserl described in *Ideas I*, in which the contingent unity of the world is exposed to an almost Kafkaesque decomposition or deconstitution.

"Good, good…very good," said Elohim.

And then he added, "But let's hope it works."

Khora

Deconstruction, too, is inhabited by the memory of an uninhabitable desert. Everything is inscribed in the primal scene of a desert within the desert, more deserted than any historical desert, a place more elemental than anything that takes place within it. The desert is not a chaos or a radical evil, but an elemental spacing that is neither good nor evil and this because it provides the space between the two, between any two or more than two. The archi-desert is a third thing, a *triton genos*, which tries to preserve a kind of radical neutrality – *ne uter* – although it constantly verges on becoming uterine – "ne-uterine." The figure, called *khora*, is in the first place clearly borrowed from the *Timaeus*, but it is congenial to the imagination of the religions of the Book, congruent with the opening verses of Genesis, with which Plato's *khora* happily co-habited until the second half of the second century C. E. Indeed, Derrida himself draws the biblical analogy for us. In a commentary on Angelus Silesius, referring to what he calls "the test of *khora*," Derrida asks:[4]

> Is this place created by God? Is it part of the play? Or else is it God himself? Or even what precedes, in order to make them possible, both God and his Play? It remains to be known…if it is "older" than the time of creation, than time itself, than narrative, word, etc…if it remains impassively foreign, like *Khora*, to everything that takes its place and replaces itself and plays within this place, including what is named God.

[97] For Derrida, *khora*, which is a surname for *différance*, means the very spacing in which historical names like the biblical "desert," or "God," or "creation" are forged, khora is indeed older than all of them, by which he means it is their quasi-transcendental condition.

But what – or who – is *khora*? What is Derrida's desert, his version of the *il y a*? Is it a kind of kin of the *tohu wa-bohu*, a *cousin/cousine* of *tehom*?

The reinscription of *khora* in Derrida's texts is not, as his critics suppose, a nihilistic exercise which jettisons all sense and signification in a wasteland or a semantic waste bin and exposes us to a monstrous abyss. It is rather in no small part the legacy of a biblical imaginary, an exercise of a biblical and creational imagination – not the conceptuality of the metaphysics of *creatio ex nihilo* to be sure but the imaginary of the Genesis narrative. It is another case of Derrida's complicated biblical memory, another image from his childhood, or from Levinas, or Levinas reminding him of his childhood, coursing its way through his texts whether or not he himself is monitoring these memories. There are no clean margins around the world for Derrida, no well demarcated beginning or end, no absolute *arche*, no tidy *telos*. Things are always already inscribed in *différance*, woven from its spacing, inscribed in a differential matrix, caught up in the inescapable condition of an ancient archi-spacing, in an ancient non-originary condition that is as old as time, an archi- space from time out of mind. For Derrida, what exists – the distinct and particular things that make up our world, the narratives that constitute our histories – is inscribed in a medium or milieu or desert place that is older than the world or life, older than nature or history, that is older than time and eternity, older than Europe or philosophy or science, or Judaism and Christianity. That is what he is calling *khora*.

Khora describes the irreducible condition of our lives, the inescapability of living always under the conditions of this elemental spacing. Then is everything we do condemned to conditionality and can we do nothing but trade one condition for another? Is there nothing *un*conditional? The *un*conditional is such stuff as dreams as made of, the stuff of prayers and tears. The *un*conditional is always to-come, for what does indeed actually come, what really exists, can only come subject to this khoral condition. Derrida is not against the unconditional, just as he is not against praying and weeping. On the contrary, he prays all the time and is not ashamed to kiss his tallith every night. *Viens, oui, oui* – that is his prayer and he is praying for the coming of something unconditional. That indeed is what "deconstruction" – a very imperfect word for what he is doing – "is," if it is, *s'il y en a*, viz., a prayer and a tear for the coming of the event, of unconditional hospitality, of the unconditional gift, which is impossible, *the* impossible, for which he prays and sighs like weepy Augustine on his knees throughout the *Confessions* or like a saintly anchorite out in the desert or like a rabbi at the Weeping Wall praying for the coming of the Messiah.

[98] But what does *khora* do? *Khora* does not pray or weep, or desire anything, or give anything, but it makes praying and weeping, desiring and giving both possible and impossible by providing them with their element or condition. *Khora* does not take place but it is what makes it possible for something to take place – or to lose its place. *Khora/différance* is more withdrawn than even the God of the most negative of negative theologies, older than the Bible and revelation and theology. It does not make these things possible in an active sense, like the *agathon*, which gathers all things to itself as to their goal and good, but, rather more like what Plato himself calls the *khora* in the *Timaeus*, by receiving them and containing, by letting them be inscribed in its space. It does not make these things possible in an active sense, as does Elohim, by calling them out of the abyss by the word of its mouth. *Khora* is rather more like the *tehom* or the *tohu wa-bohu*, like that condition or container to which and in which Elohim speaks, like the receptacle or the receiver of the divine action, like those empty and desolate places that Elohim fills with life.

Khora is our inescapable condition, not a terrible tragic fate, which is too Greek a way to think and one that is lacking in biblical hope, but a first, last and constant condition, a quasi-transcendental condition. It is in that sense Derrida can say, adapting a remark of Plato's, that *khora/différance* is marked by a certain "necessity," not the upper, eternal necessity of the forms, but the lower necessity of the necessary condition that *khora* imposes on sensible things. For things must always be inscribed in its space, which is then prior to or independent of either the supersensible form or the sensible things by providing a medium for sensible things to come to be and pass away like figures in a mirror or lines in the sand. In deconstruction, *khora* provides an allegory of or a figure for the necessity that every unity of meaning – from the highest to the lowest – is under to be inscribed within *différance*, by which it is conditioned and precontained as are all the oppositions that are inscribed within it. Conditioned by and inscribed in *différance* such unities are both constituted and deconstituable, both formed and reformable or deformable, both constructed and deconstructible, deconstructible because constructed.

What then does *khora* do? A provision is made in both the *Timaeus* and the Book of Genesis for an elemental necessity, an inescapable condition, an ineluctable "in-which" or "from-which" or "with-which" that is "before creation," that is always already imposed upon us, that we are always already coping with, an inoriginate medium or milieu, without truth or falsity, without good or evil, a kind of non-originary origin, a groundless ground that is an almost mocking counterpart to its more prestigious paternal partner – the *agathon* or Elohim. For like the maternal nurse *khora*, the uterine *tehom* and mother earth can hardly maintain their neutrality; they constantly [99] verge on maternal figures over and against the imposing and erect fathers with which they are juxtaposed. Both texts provide for a kind of inescapable anarchivable anarche below the level of truth, below both being and the good, the effect of which is to insure the fundamental contingency of our lives, the risk, the chance, the shakiness, the *ébranler*, the flux, that sees to it that creation, contra Einstein, is indeed a dicey business, a *beau risque*. A risk for us, to be sure, but also for the Lord God, who by Chapter 6 of Genesis had come to regret the day he ever made these creatures. So he opened up the floodgates that held back the primal sea, thus starting creation all over again with Noah, which shows that creation too is a repetition. That is the point of that Talmudic story that says that after failing twenty-six times, the Lord God finally got the thing to hold together and then, crossing his divine fingers, said, with a certain amount of divine trepidation, "let's hope it works."

Deconstruction, like the creation story, is describing a risky business, indeed a dangerous world, but it does not lose its faith that it is a good risk and it does not descend into tragic complaint. For just as in Genesis, creation bears the stamp of Elohim's judgment, "good," and just as in the *Timaeus*, everything is run by the Good, so in deconstruction everything is driven by the impossible, by the promise, by the desire beyond desire for the coming of something unconditional, something I know not what, let us say, by a prayer for the justice or democracy or hospitality to come, in a word, in an ancient biblical figure, the expectation of the Messiah. Everything in deconstruction happens *by* the impossible, which is why Derrida spends some time in a desert, like a certain an-khora-ite, praying and weeping for the coming of *the* impossible, for the coming of what cannot in fact actually show up. The very prospect of its "coming" or "in-coming," the very expectation of the impossible is what makes things happen, makes the "event" possible, which is what deconstruction is all about.

There is a certain *anarche* in Derrida, which issues not in a street-corner anarchism or violent lawlessness, but in a radical and creative anarchy that preserves the memory of the opening scene of Genesis. Our lives are inscribed within a non-originary origin, a groundless ground, a bottomlessness that no theoretical eye can fathom, in virtue of which we are always already exposed to time and tide and chance, just as in Genesis the elements, which are Elohim's everlasting companion, constitute our inescapable condition. Derrida does not thereby consign our lives to evil or violence or a monstrous abyss that will swallow us whole, or surrender to a tragic fated necessity. Rather, existence for him is inscribed within an aleatory element, exposed to an unavoidable chance and inescapable contingency which keeps the future open and unfinished, while we long for the coming of something unconditional, for the coming of the unconditional gift. As a spacing, which is necessarily a disjointedness, the figure of *khora* is a [100] way to concede that what is built up can be unbuilt, which is why things contain their own auto-deconstructibility. That is not nihilism but the condition of our lives, the condition of being created.

Nor is it bad news, because it provides the occasion for the call that invokes the coming of the unconditional. It even provides the makings of a kind of politics of *khora* (could there by a politics of the *tehom*?) For by reminding us of the fragility of our institutions and our doctrines, we are reminded to proceed with caution, both with a certain faith in what is coming and a salutary skepticism about what is currently passing itself off as the sovereign good or true. This is not nihilism but an odd mix of biblical faith and rabbinic pragmatism, which keeps its finger crossed. The much vaunted "deconstruction of the metaphysics of presence" is more closely considered an old idea, not unlike the ancient biblical caution to beware of idols. For we are forged from fragile stuff, from earth and wind and water, all with a will of their own, all liable at any moment to leak through our mortal frame or throw us to the wind or expose our feet of clay. This loosely joined and fragile condition, the play within the joints that join us, makes for maximum flexibility and reinventability, even as it exposes us to the worst.

Why then is Derrida weeping?

He is, like Walter Benjamin, weeping over the dead, the lives long lost, whose shadowy figures haunt our days, even as he is weeping for the coming of the Messiah, of the gift, of justice, of the democracy to come, for the coming of the unconditional amidst these constraining mortal conditions. But he is not simply a man of prayers and tears, for there is always a twinkle in his eye, a devilishness, a kind of rabbinic risibility, a Reb Rida, who is constantly laughing through his tears.

There has been a twinkle in eyes all along. We saw it for the first time when he started to sort out the sense of contingency, of being forged or constituted from a certain flux – the infamous "play of signifiers," deconstruction's first *succès de scandale* – that he stressed in his early studies of Husserl. We have seen it lately in his sense of the future, of a formable and reformable future, of a future to come, of messianic expectation that defines the work of the last two decades. They both belong to Derrida's quasi-biblical imagination, or to the biblical side of his multi-sided imagination, which Derrida exercises like an impish rabbi, with a fondness for humor in the midst of the most grave-like deathly conditions, like a heretical rabbi who rightly passes for an atheist.

Deconstruction springs in part from an ancient anarchivable memory, from a time out of mind, of an ancient desert condition, of an archi-aleatory state that is older than time, antedating creation. Deconstruction springs from a memory that our [101] lives and limbs have been woven from a fragile stuff and that we are ever exposed to time and tide and the hazards of fortune. But it never fails to keep alive the gleam of expectation and of hope. Things are ever astir with the chance of the gift, the gift of chance, with the grace of a gift, the gift of a grace. In deconstruction an ancient aleatory benediction hovers over the risky business of life, almost as if Derrida is thinking back on an Elohim who pronounces things "good" all the while keeping his fingers crossed.

Derrida is possessed of (or by) not exactly a comic-tragic sense but rather let us say a Talmudic sense of humor that is laughing through his tears, like an eccentric rabbi praying like mad to the Lord God, blessed be his name, and trusting in his mercy, for the coming of the messianic age, but all the while wondering secretly to himself (as if he could keep something from God!) about just how things were actually going to turn out.

When Derrida says *viens, oui, oui,* does that conjure up the memory of a desert scene that he hardly remembers, having been remiss as a youngster about his duties at Hebrew school? Does he remember without remembering a certain Elohim, who, in the beginning, when he created the world, said, good, good, very good, and then added, since this was his twenty-seventh try, "let's hope it works."

When Derrida says *viens, oui, oui,* when he hopes against hope with a desire beyond desire, is he remembering God?

Notes

[1] See David Toshio Tsumura, *The Earth and the Waters in Genesis 1 and 2: A Linguistic Investigation* (Sheffield, England: JSOT Press, Supplement Series 83, 1989), 43; see 17–43.

[2] Immanuel Lévinas, *Totalité et l'infini*, 2nd. ed. (The Hague: Martinus Nijhof, 1965), 117, 120.

[3] I follow the English translation of this text in Ilya Prigogine and Isabelle Stengers, *Order out of Chaos* (Boulder: New Science Library, 1984), 313. I first found this text in Catherine Keller, *The Face of the Deep: A Theology of Becoming* (London: Routledge, 2003), 193–94, which is itself a powerful feminist theology of creation.

[4] Jacques Derrida, *Sauf le nom* (Paris: Galilée, 1993), 94–95; Eng. trans. *On the Name*, ed. Thomas Dutoit (Stanford: Stanford University Press, 1995), 75–76.

THEOPOETIC/THEOPOLITIC

[In *CrossCurrents*, Vol. 56, No 4 (Winter 2007): 105–07]

At the November 2006 American Academy of Religion convention in Washington DC, a number of religious scholars joined in a panel conversation with Jim Wallis, the well-known author of *God's Politics*. Although the conversation explored many aspects of contemporary experiments in political theology, I found theopoetic and theopolitical explorations of Jack Caputo and Catherine Keller especially engaging. Caputo and Keller are two of the most interesting philosophical theologians writing today, and thus we offer their constructive thoughts on religion and politics, the first from Caputo, followed by Keller.
—Scott Holland, Editor, CrossCurrents.

[Note: The original article was a composite of two papers. The first was by Caputo, which we present here; the second was by Keller.]

[105] Have we not learned by now to keep theology out of politics? Do not the sacred oils of religion fuel the fires raging in the Middle East? Must we not clear our heads of theology and so liberate politics from the distortions of the political order for which religion is responsible?

My hypothesis is the opposite, that theology goes all the way down, that there are always lingering or unavowed theological presuppositions in what we say or do, and hence, as Heidegger said a long time ago, it is not a question of getting free of our presuppositions but rather of entering into them all the more primordially. Consciously or not, avowedly or not, the political order has theological roots; whenever we order political space we also and inevitably have God on our mind. In a view that I have developed elsewhere, thinking cannot be insulated from the event that is invoked under the name of God, which means that thinking is always a certain proto- or primal faith, whatever may be our particular or concrete beliefs, be they confessional or even secular. We always move about in the space of an archi-theology, whatever the particulars of our theology or anti-theology may be. In the same way, thinking is always a certain proto- [106] or primal desire beyond desire, whatever our particular desires may be, which means we are always asking what we love when we love (our) God. Consequently, on my proposal, a reformation of political thought would require not ridding ourselves of theology but rather reexamining our theological presuppositions and learning to think about theology differently, which means to think about God otherwise, to reimagine God. In the context of the present discussion, that means that any renewal of the political order requires a renewal of theology, which in turn requires us to consider the unavowed theology of the politics that are all around us, whose psychical and symbolic center is the war over Jerusalem.

There is no straight line from the Biblical imagination to any concrete political structure or public policy, but that does not mean there is no line or connection at all. Rather we are called upon to imagine the Kingdom of God in the concrete political structures of the day, and that requires political imagination and judgment. The Kingdom provides a *politica negativa*, a critical voice rather like the voice of a prophet against the king, like Amos railing against Jeroboam, calling for the invention of justice, and which in turn requires, in addition to prophets, the hard work of concrete political invention, the cleverness of inventive political structures.

What would a political order look like, were the Kingdom able to be reinvented and transformed into a political structure? What would it be like if there really were a politics of the bodies of flesh that proliferate in the New Testament, a politics of mercy and compassion, of lifting up the weakest and most defenseless people at home, a politics of welcoming the stranger and of loving one's enemies abroad? What would it be like were there a politics of and for the children, who are the future; a politics not of sovereignty, of top-down power, but a politics that builds from the bottom up, where *ta me onta* (1 Cor 1:28) enjoy pride of place and a special privilege? What would a political order look like if the last were first, if everything turned on lifting up the lowliest instead of letting relief trickle down from the top? What would it look like if there were a politics of loving one's enemies, not of war, let alone, God forbid, of preemptive war?

Would it not be in almost every respect the opposite of the politics that presently passes itself off under the name of Jesus? Are not the figures who publicly parade their self-righteousness, their love of power, and their hatred of the other under the name of Jesus singled out in advance by Jesus under the name of the whited sepulchers and long robes whose fathers killed the [107] prophets? In this connection, it would be amusing – were it not so tragic – to recall that the question, "What Would Jesus Do?", which provides a cover for the arrogance, militancy, greed, and hatred of the Christian Right, is taken from an immensely popular book written in 1896 by Charles Sheldon entitled *In His Steps: "What Would Jesus Do?"* Sheldon was an early leader of the Social Gospel movement, and his answer to this question was, in brief, that Jesus would be found in the worst neighbors in the poorest cities serving the wretched of the earth. To do what Jesus would do, would mean to make everything turn on peace not war, forgiveness not retribution, on loving one's enemies not a preemptive war, on all the paradoxes and reversals that can be summarized under the name of "radical democracy."

A politics of the Kingdom would be marked by madness of forgiveness, generosity, mercy and hospitality. The dangerous memory of the crucified body of Jesus poses a threat to a world organized around the disastrous concept of power, something that is reflected today in the widespread critique of the concept of "sovereignty" – of the sovereignty of autonomous subjects and the sovereignty of nations powerful enough to get away with acting unilaterally and in their own self-interests. The call that issues from the Cross threatens what Derrida calls the "unavowed theologism" of the political concept of sovereignty by returning us to its root, to its understanding of God, to its underlying or archi-theology. The crucified body of Jesus proposes not that we keep theology out of politics, but that we think theology otherwise, by way of another paradigm, another theology, requiring us to think of God otherwise, as an unconditional claim or solicitation without power, as a weak force or power of powerlessness, as opposed to the theology of omnipotence that underlies sovereignty.

Still, the weakness of God is not the last word but the first, coming as a call or provocation that solicits our response, our witness to the call, which is what comes next, like an "amen" or a second yes. For it is *we* who have mountains to move by our faith and *we* who have enemies to move by our love. It is *we* who have to make the weakness of God stronger than the power of the world.

4

HAUNTOLOGICAL HERMENEUTICS AND THE INTERPRETATION OF CHRISTIAN FAITH: ON BEING DEAD EQUAL BEFORE GOD

[In *Hermeneutics at the Crossroads*, ed. Kevin Vanhoozer, James K. A. Smith, and Bruce Ellis Benson (Bloomington: Indiana University Press, 2006), 95–111]

> "We dance round in a ring and suppose,
> But the Secret sits in the middle and knows."
> Robert Frost

[95] In what follows I will advocate a theory of interpretation as a conversation with the dead. By this I do not mean reading the works of dead white European males, but simply conversing with the dead, with the ones you would meet (or not quite meet) in any graveyard. So if the theme of our deliberations here is hermeneutics at the crossroads, then think of this as a discourse on hermeneutics at the cemetery, as if in coming upon the cross in the road we were to find a cemetery. I will maintain that the creative conflict of interpretations arises from the ambiguity of this conversation, from the difficulty we have in making out just what the dead are saying, for their voice is ever soft and low, almost absolutely silent. One might say, if one were of a mind to say such things, that only as "hauntology" – to deploy an impish Derrideanism – is hermeneutics possible.[1] It is in this general hauntological hermeneutical framework that I will insert in particular the interpretation of Christian faith. I offer thus a contextualization of Christian faith such that the [96] inspiration that comes from the Holy Ghost is itself breathed upon by another ghostly aspiration.

Conversations in a Danish Church Yard

Kierkegaard and his pseudonyms liked to stress that before God, *coram deo*, we are all equal. When it comes to the God relationship, which is the absolute relationship to the absolute, no one has an inside track, a privileged angle, special access. You can't buy yourself "access" and "influence" with God by way of big contributions to the church, the way big contributors to presidential campaigns get to sleep in the Lincoln Bedroom in the White House, while the rest of us middling contributors sleep in our own humble beds at home. Nor is the absolute relationship to the absolute a matter of good luck, as if the God relationship depends upon having the good fortune to be standing in the right place at the right time just as the divine motorcade goes speeding by so that you catch a glimpse of the God not afforded other unfortunate chaps who were not around at the time. The *coram deo* is a great white light, an absolute and punishing leveler of human differences and human advantages, which mercilessly exposes the various masks and costumes that are donned in time and relativity. In divine matters, there are no lucky breaks, no inside traders, no special discounts for members of the family of the owner. Those are the corrupt ways things are done in the world, in a market economy, in a market town. Kierkegaard continually chided the residents of "*Koben-havn,*" the "merchant harbor town," who like the Dutch love nothing more than a bargain, with the thought that you cannot cut a special deal with God. God does not offer special discounts; the God relationship cannot be had on the cheap. When it comes to the absolute relationship to the absolute, all dealings are on the absolute up and up.

For example, in the *Philosophical Fragments*, Johannes Climacus spends a good deal of time arguing that, vis a vis the Paradox, there is no special advantage in belonging to the generation that was contemporary with the God/Man and no special disadvantage in coming along 2003 years later (well, he said 1843 years, but that 160 years ago).[2] True, the contemporary generation had the advantage of seeing the man in the flesh, of hearing his words, of knowing the apostles and his family. But whatever advantage there was in that was offset by a terrifying disadvantage, by the "jolt," that is, the stunning, unthinkable and to a Jewish mind blasphemous thought that this man of temporal flesh and bone was the Eternal one come into time. That jolt was revolting; it repelled and repulsed the contemporary generation, constituting a stumbling block to some and a scandal to others. We later generations have enjoyed the "consequences," the interlude of the intervening 2003 years. We have had the history of theology and the church, the history of Christian art and literature, excellent sermons, comfortable, padded pews and well appointed churches, a flood of musical compositions and even a Hollywood film or two to ease the jolt and tease us into the idea. But that advantage of ease is exactly our disadvantage, for we have lost the difficulty and taken [97] the idea for granted. We are all convinced that we are Christian because we most certainly are not Moslems, Hindus, or Zen Buddhists. The point is, Climacus said, in whatever generation we were born, we each bear the same infinite responsibility to make the movements of faith, to intensify existence to the point of absolute pathos, to reach the point of infinitely passionate existence. Before God, *coram deo,* we are all equally in need of maintaining an absolute passion for the absolute telos and a relative passion for any merely relative telos.

When it comes to the *unum necessarium,* the one thing necessary, which is the one-to-one relationship with God, we are all dead equal. If you doubt it, he says in the "Work of Love in Recollecting One Who Is Dead," near the end of *Works of Love,* take a trip to the cemetery and consult with those silent, still, and steady fellows lying just below the sod. They will not lie to you; a false word will never cross their lips. They are steadfast chaps and true, to a man. Kierkegaard spent a lot of time hanging around the lovely cemetery outside the nineteenth century city limits, which was a deeply autonymic operation for him. His very name was funereal, *Kirke + gaard,* church yard, cemetery. While other fellows took their girlfriends there for a picnic, Kierkegaard went there to be alone and commune with these silent, solitary shades. To be a Kierke-gaardian then is to be a Church-Yardian, to adopt the view, not from nowhere, but from the "no more." No thinker can think life through like these fellows, he says, those "masterful thinkers" who cut right to the chase. They see through every illusion and offer the shortest and most succinct summary of life. If you are dazzled by all the different paths life may take, go the cemetery, "where all paths meet" and finally end up. If you are dizzied by all the dissimilarities in life, then go out and talk to these dead folk, where all men are equal, just as the political theorists say. In life we may deny that we are all of one blood, but in death we cannot deny the kinship of clay. Best of all, he urges us, go there in the morning, when the birds are chirping and the garden is lush and beautiful, when "the profusion of life out there almost makes you forget" all those chaps lying quietly six feet under the surface. Then you will see that only there do we actually attain "equal distribution" – Kierkegaard was writing this in the midst of the revolutions of 1848 – where each family ends up with about the same square footage and share of the sun. Of course it is true that the plot of the wealthier families is about a foot or a half a foot bigger, and death's summary would not be accurate if it did not reflect that. The dead are deadly honest brokers. They tell us succinctly, in their wry and taciturn but loving way, in "an earnest jest," that this is all worldly advantage amounts to – about half a foot. Here, Søren Churchyard says, the prolixity of life is brilliantly and briefly summarized. In the view from the churchyard, we are all equal. Dead equal.[3]

In another place in the *Works of Love,* he makes the same point about absolute equality by way of the parable of the wedding feast. Suppose a man had a banquet and invited the lame and the beggars but not his friends? The world would call that not a banquet but an act of charity. Yet that is just what Jesus said to do, so that in the kingdom the banquet is given precisely for the "neighbor," for love (*agape*) of the neighbor – which means, for each and every one, as opposed to a [98] dinner for a short list of one's closest friends (*philia*) or to an intimate dinner date with one's lover (*eros*). To be sure, the world would laugh at such a banquet; it would be madder than the mad hatter's party. But that is because the world can only see the worldly "dissimilarities" but cannot see the "neighbor" in each man, which is the essentially human and the essentially equal. After all, he says, these earthly differences among people are like the roles actors play, while the real person behind the role is the neighbor. When the curtain goes down, the one who plays the king and struts about the stage ordering everyone hither and yon, and the one who plays the beggar pleading for a morsel of bread, are just a couple of actors who remove their costumes and go out together for a drink. We would think these fellows mad if they started believing they really were in actuality His Royal Highness or the Emperor of Japan. So, Kierkegaard says, do not lace "the outer garments of dissimilarity" too tightly lest you cannot remove them when the play is over. In the play, we are entertained by the illusion and do not want to see the person beneath the role; acting is the art of deception. But Eternity – or God or death – is not deceived. Thus, if dissimilarity is temporality's mark, equality is the mark of eternity.[4]

We are indeed all equal, he says elsewhere in *Works of Love*, but not all the same.[5] The essentially human, the species-wide difference that sets us above the animals but a little lower than the angels, is not the highest. For beyond the universally human there is also what is most often forgotten, that within the species, each individual is essentially different. If one upright individual cannot do the opposite of what another upright individual would do under the same circumstances, then the God relationship – which is one-to-one – would be abolished. If every human being would be judged by a universal criterion, then everything would be completed in our public secular social life. Then everything would be easy and empty, having removed the depth that comes of the one-to-one relation with God. We are all equal, but all equally different, before God, like so many points on the circumference of a circle, all equidistant from the center, yet each point with its own defining, singularizing, uniquely proper one-to-one radius to the center.

But to whom, then, are the *Works of Love* addressed? To the Danes? To all Christendom? If they are to be themselves a work of love, as Kierkegaard plainly suggests,[6] and if the works of love concern the neighbor *in* each and everyone of us, then not are they only *about* the neighbor, about defining this concept as a central idea of love, but they must also be addressed *to* the neighbor: that means, to everyone without order of rank, not simply to a closed circle of friends on the invitation list. *The Works of Love* is a word of love sent out to Copenhagen and beyond, to all Christendom; to all Christendom and beyond, to everyone, that is, to the neighbor, with the unconditional and universal word that before God we are all equal, dead equal, and equally worthy of love.

That is the surprisingly cosmopolitan view from a relatively provincial church yard of a merchant harbor town[7] — and this provides the setting for my cosmopolitan hermeneutics at the cemetery.

[99] Before the Secret

What I am going to call "hauntological hermeneutics" owes a thing or two to Jacques Derrida, which is, let us say, its guardian angel or Dutch uncle.[8] To be sure, the name "Derrida" is the name of the devil himself in certain quarters, of the devil of "relativism" and other forms of Franco-American postmodern *décadence*. This demonizing of Derrida is the issue of a deep-seated fear of difference and of an insecurity about the absolutist stance his critics have adopted, which is a matter I cannot take up now. Here I hope only to make it plain that, far from being a form of relativism, this hauntological hermeneutics he inspires in fact reproduces the religious structure of the absolute relationship to the absolute, or an absolute passion for the absolute, a passion for "the impossible." An absolute relationship to the absolute "transforms the whole existence of the existing person," Climacus says,[9] as opposed to a merely aesthetic pathos, in which one would be perfectly content to have a "correct idea" but without having to do anything about it. Having one's existence transformed all the way down is just about what Derrida means by having an "experience of the impossible," whereas those who are content to play within the domain of the possible have to content themselves with a merely relative *pathos*.

So my quasi-Derridean hauntological hermeneutics shares this Church Yard wisdom, this word from the dead who can be trusted never to let a false word cross their lips and to steadfastly abide by their views. We might even regard this hermeneutics as a post card from the dead to the living, as a way to recollect the dead, to mourn their death, and in so doing to ensure that we all remain dead equal before God. Dead equal before God or death. Before God or death or eternity. These three limit structures — God and death and eternity — are, from a hauntological and structural point of view, the same — an aside that itself stands as worthy of a fuller investigation. But suffice it to say for the present purposes that what God and death and eternity have in common is a certain intractable, irrefragable unknowability, a certain coincidence of irreducible elusiveness. They are slippery fellows all, representing as they do the *passage aux frontières*, a passage to the limit. God and death and eternity dwell just outside our reach and just beyond our grasp, ever so slightly but infinitely on the other shore. Death lies just across the line of life, eternity just over the edge of time, God just beyond the border of the world, even as together they all lie just across the boundary of language. Impossible experiences, experiences of the impossible. *Le pas au-delà.*

That is why we can briefly but without injustice succinctly summarize all three under the name of the "secret," the secret that we have no secret access to the secret, and why we ourselves can be defined in terms of having to maintain an absolute relation to the absolute secret, which is what Climacus would call our highest passion. Think of the secret as a shroud placed over things that conceals our view. Before the secret, we are all dead equal, the secret for which "God" and "death" and "eternity" are among our most venerable and prestigious names. Here we are all equally at a disadvantage, all at an equal remove. No one is hardwired to the secret; no one has secret or privileged access to it. If *they* know it, they are [100] not saying, they who lie there calmly, hands crossed, in solemn silence, unwilling to impart a hint or trace of what they know or do not know, unwilling to give anyone a special advantage. If they know it, we have not yet found a language in which we can communicate with them about it. For while the Babelian multiplicity of languages has there been stilled, and while there is but one common tongue there, it is a dead language that we cannot decipher. Indeed the dead can almost be defined by their reticence on the subject of the secret, as the ones who know but do not say, while *we* who visit them of a sunny Sunday afternoon, who stroll about on the grass above their heads, are really walking around in the dark. We lack both the vocabulary and the grammar of the secret, as we lack the language of the dead. Our hauntological hermeneutics is as convinced as any Christian spiritual writer that all temporal differences belong to the "garments of dissimilarity" that are donned in mundane life but are doffed at death, where our common nudity before the secret is exposed. But in this hermeneutics the white light of death, the funereal leveler of differences, the knight of absolute equality, goes under the name of the secret.

But do not despair. For the secret does not paralyze us but provokes us; it does not dispirit us but animates us. Indeed it inspires a dance, a ring dance, which is of course to move in circles. "We dance round in a ring and suppose," the poet says, "the Secret sits in the middle and knows."[10] The secret sends us scurrying about in circles, drawing hermeneutic rings around its center, while it sits calmly in the middle and knows. The secret does not reduce us to silence but provokes interpretation, evoking multiple and conflicting interpretations, a flood of discourses, a multiplicity of poetic, religious and philosophic discourses. Before the secret we are like those loquacious mystical preachers and prolific negative theologians who cannot manage to say enough about the ineffable, unspeakable mystery of God. For the nameless secret has many names, too many. The *deus innominabile*, said Meister Eckhart, is *omninominabile*. The unnameable is omni-nameable. If there will never be enough names to name God or death, that is because we do not know their name. The condition brought on by the secret is not the lack of names but the excess, not the defect of names but the surplus. We cannot stop up this excess; we cannot staunch the flow of names which flow like blood from an open wound. For in the end, the silence of the dead, like every silence, is ambiguous; we cannot quite make out what they are or are not saying. Hauntological hermeneutics takes up residence in this excess, in the polynymic, polymorphic overflow, in the uncontainable stream of names, which represents a condition of unstoppable translatability and inexpungeable unknowability. We never reach the high ground from which to survey the whole; never attain the authority to pronounce the final word, the master name that stills the play of names that surges from the hidden depths of the secret sitting in the center. The secret is imperturbably dark and deep, like a tomb. It lies there calmly, silently, aswarm in the endless swell of interpretations that sweep over it up above, the subject of endless disputes, to which it never replies except with the ironic smile of the dead, itself the creation of a funereal art.

[101] The secret provokes us with a bottomless undecidability, which constitutes a bottomless hermeneutical provocation. Whence the origin of hermeneutics in the cemetery, where endless interpretations of these matters of ultimate concern, as Tillich called them, flit about like ghosts on All Hallows Eve. The secret is the source of the multiplicity of interpretations, of interpretation itself, for if we knew the secret, there would only be one interpretation, and if there were only one interpretation, there would not be any interpretations but only one uninterpreted fact of the matter, one uninterpreted absolute truth, which would also be the name of absolute terror. If we knew the secret – and this is to make the same point – with whom could we entrust it?

The Messiah

Driven on as it is by the secret, hauntological hermeneutics is therefore not despair but hope, not negation but affirmation, indeed, infinite, absolute, unconditional affirmation, yes, yes. But it subjects this unconditional and unlimited affirmation to certain limits, to certain conditions. It feels compelled to tip its hat to the undecidability in things, confessing in a certain Augustinian spirit that it does not quite know what it affirms, or what it desires, or what it loves, which is always inscribed within the secret. It loves with an everlasting love (almost) something, it does not know quite what. Even as it loves what it seeks, it is always seeking what it loves. So just as the pseudonyms enjoin maintaining an absolute relation to the absolute telos and a strictly relative relationship to a merely relative telos, so a certain pseudonymous "Jacques" – that is not his name, it's all a jest, but an earnest jest – insists on an absolute and unconditional affirmation of the undeconstructible, of something I do know quite know what, while making a strictly relative affirmation of everything deconstructible. That is the structure of what, following Johannes Climacus, we might call a certain religious *pathos* in deconstruction, what Derrida called a religion without religion.[11] For our hearts are restless and they will not rest in whatever makes itself known and present, which is deconstructible – we look on these things and they say *ipse fecit nos*,[12] which means they have been constructed. Our hearts will not rest until they rest in the undeconstructible, *s'il y en a*, which is the object of a desire beyond desire, which is neither known nor present. Our hearts rise up or surge past what is given and presented in the phenomenological field. What is given is not it, not the impossible secret, which lies just on the other side of knowledge and the impossible. What is given and present is deconstructible in the dark light of the unknowable and unrepresentable secret, which is never given, because the dead won't give it up.

Now if we locate the heart of a certain religious desire in the desire for the coming of the Messiah, in the dream of the coming of the messianic age,[13] then from a hauntological point of view what else can one say but *viens, oui, oui*? What else can we do but engage this passion absolutely, to allow one's existence to be entirely transformed by this affirmation? Entirely, unconditionally, infinitely, absolutely – but with one little proviso or condition. That is, one must make room for a certain [102] coefficient of undecidability, which means, tip one's hat to the secret, *memento mori*. Remember the word from the dead who silently observe all the fuss up above, who remember well all life's passion and agitation but who now take a cooler and more dispassionate look at things, practicing a colder hermeneutics. That reminder is observed by offering a modest little distinction, which we might take as a word to the wise, as a word from the dead, who know whereof they do not speak. This accommodation is made by introducing a distinction, small, lame and wooden though it is, between absolute passion, let us say, the "messianic" passion itself, if there is such a thing, in which we love and affirm unconditionally, and the various ways this absolute passion is given flesh and blood, brought down to earth in one place or the other, incarnated in one or another historical language and tradition (the "concrete messianisms"). That is, we are introducing a distinction between an undeconstructible and absolute relation to the undeconstructible (the impossible) and a relative and deconstructible relation to the deconstructible (possible). To observe that distinction is to do no more than recollect the dead, which is a work of love, for the dead have their eye on us. *They* know that *we* do not know the master name, certainly not the way *they* do.

In hauntological hermeneutics undecidability and undeconstructibility go hand in hand. Think of it as all slightly Jewish, arising from a deeply Jewish distrust of idols.[14] So from a strictly hauntological point of view, the Messiah is a shady character, slipping like a shade among various concrete messianic traditions, showing up here, deferring his presence there, taking different messianic forms, never settling on just one shape, the multiplicity of which keeps the figure of the Messiah in play, alive, in the world, but none of which stills the undecidable messianic dance, for the mysterious figure of the Messiah is likewise involved in a hermeneutic dance around the center. The Messiah is the figure of the *à venir*, of what is always and essentially to come, the *arrivant*, whom we affirm unconditionally, absolutely, undeconstructibly, while everything presently passing itself off as concrete messianic goods is deconstructible. Do not confuse the coming (*venue*) of the Messiah with his *présence*, with his real givenness or actual presence, for the Messiah is the very structure of hope and expectation, of the future, wherever there is a future. That is why even where it is believed the Messiah has already come, in Christianity, what is desired if not a repetition, the hope and expectation that he will come *again*? That is what it means to have a history? Christianity, the history of Christianity, which is a redundancy – for "Christianity" *is* the history that resulted from the deferral of the second coming. The earliest Christians did not expect to *have* a history. The history of Christianity is lived out in the *différance* between two comings, which is why the interpretation of Christian faith is inscribed within *différance* and undecidability. History is always a history of deferred presence, of what is groaning to come into presence, but any history worthy of its name is inwardly disturbed by the coming into presence of something unforeseeable, unpresentable, unrepresentable. Whatever is historically given is deconstructible, strained to the breaking point to bring forth the undeconstructible, *s'il y en a*, something I do not know quite what. *Memento mori*. If in love we recollect the dead, [103] who are watching us, and if we do not forget the secret, before which we are all dead equal, the dead will return our love by reminding us that we do not have access to the final word or master name for what we desire, that even the name of the Messiah is the name of something whose name we do not quite know.

The various concrete messianisms are all "inhabited" by the Messiah, animated by his spirit, and one might even say – and this is the way I prefer to put it here – that they are spooked by his (holy) ghost.[15] That is why I am positing another not as holy ghost which haunts the Holy Ghost, a spirit spooking the Holy Spirit. To be haunted by a holy ghost is on the whole a holy and wholesome thing, a salutary reminder from the dead that we do not know the secret, although we have many interpretations. Only as hauntology is a holy hermeneutics possible. On the one hand, the pure messianic without the messianisms is a spook, a bodiless, ghostly, disincarnate specter. But on the other hand, if the concrete messianisms are not spooked by the messianic ghost, they become a danger to themselves and to others, a menace constantly exposed to the terror of absolute truth, the deadly terror that springs from the death of interpretation. The messianic and the messianisms interlace chiasmically, the messianisms giving the messianic flesh, the messianic keeping the messianisms on the move. The messianic disturbs the sleep of the concrete messianisms by whispering ghostly thoughts in their ear that all paths end in the silence of the Church Yard, that before the Secret we are all equal, all equidistant from the secret that sits silently in the center and will not say what it knows. For we are all equally one-to-one with God, with death, with eternity. The messianic reminds the messianisms that if one individual cannot do the opposite of what another good individual would do in the same circumstances, the God relationship is abolished, for the God relationship is one to one, which is why there is more than one concrete messianism.

The Weak Messianic

Now let us see what this hauntological model means in the concrete, in the flesh, if I may say so, what effect it has on those of us who inhabit one of the concrete messianisms. The thing that characterizes inhabiting one of the concrete messianisms, or so it should, is that you believe them with all or heart and you cannot be half hearted about it. Being half heartedly in love with something has all the makings of what Johannes Climacus called a mediocre fellow.[16] The whole idea is to have a full-throated, whole-hearted, red-blooded living faith. But the very idea of a ghost is to haunt all that living vitality with an uncanny thought or two that comes to us in a church yard. So the messianic specter disturbs the concrete messianisms with the spectral thought that they are an historical garment, each its own way of naming the secret that has no name, since the dead won't give it up. It is all about the historical point of departure for eternal happiness, just as Johannes Climacus said. Were we born in another time, another place, another world, we would inevitably believe and hope and love something different, giving our messianic passion another form, or maybe even giving passion another form than [104] messianic, or maybe even in another way than desire, and this with no disadvantage to our absolute relation to the absolute secret. There are many ways to actualize the passion of existence and God does not play favorites. The God-relationship is not a matter of being in the right place at the right time, just when the divine motorcade is passing by.

To haunt the concrete messianisms with this disturbing thought is to bedevil them, to make productive trouble for them, not to destroy or to disable them, but to prevent them from circling in upon themselves, from setting themselves up as closed circles, to prevent their sleeping soundly at night. It is to force them to continue to dance in a ring on the edge and not to think that they have somehow found a way to slip surreptitiously into the center when no one else was looking. This spectral thought roams about the houses of the concrete messianisms and spooks them, keeping them up at night worrying about the contingency of their vocabularies, of their circumstance, of their time and place and language and historical setting. Or, to switch to another figure who is important for Kierkegaard, the Messiah is a kind of a Jewish gadfly, like a Socrates who speaks Yiddish, who keeps the concrete messianisms in question, loose, unnerved, and open-ended, on their messianic toes, reminding them of their contingency of their birth and circumstance, reminding them that before the secret, we are all equal and no one enjoys special privileges. The pure messianic fills the concrete messianisms with fear and trembling, reminding them that the invitation to the heavenly banquet is not sent out to the special friends of God, to those inside God's inner circle with whom God has cut a special deal, but to the "neighbor," that is, to everyone, which includes, indeed which *refers especially* to the outsiders. *Tout autre est tout autre.*

To be a Christian is to believe Christianity with all one's heart, but to believe is to say I do not know; *il faut croire.* The limitation does not lie in Christianity, which one believes entirely, but in belief.[17] Believing with your whole heart is only half the story, not all there is to it. It does not close down the undecidability; indeed, believing depends upon and presupposes the undecidability, otherwise it would not be believing but knowledge. Many different people believe different things with all their heart, and to suppress that is to suppress the one-to-one God-relationship. Believing with all your heart does not touch the cold and heartless heart of the secret. The secret is the seat of the undecidability and the undecidability is irreducible, which is why the other half of believing with your whole heart is to acknowledge the undecidability. The undecidability sits silently in the center, while believing with all your heart is a ring dance around the edge. After all, believing with all your heart does not get a rise out of the dead, does not move those unmoved movers so far removed from us, though they lie but six feet away. Believing with all your heart does not break their silence, cause them to rise to their feet and speak their mind. Nothing does. They remain unmoved. Like a tomb.

The pure messianic floats or hovers over the concrete messianisms, coming from beyond or otherwise than being – like a ghost. The messianic specter is not more than being but less, a half or demi-being. It differs from the concrete messianisms as the weak – Benjamin had spoken of a "weak messianic power" – differs [105] from the strong.[18] That is because the concrete messianisms are hale and healthy beings, living, thriving confessional faiths with determinate and proper names, historical languages and institutions, sacred places, sacred texts, sacred languages, theological traditions, national and international headquarters, conference centers, hymnals, liturgies, candles, hearses and official pallbearers, and even – here is an advantage not to be denied – silver collection plates and professional bookkeepers. But the pure messianic has not the wherewithal to lay down its head and wanders in ankhoral night, like a desert nomad dependent upon the hospitality of those who will take it in. The concrete messianisms are strong and robust, full-bodied presences, while the messianic is a ghost of a thought, a ghost of a chance, at best a demi-being who disturbs our sleep.

A Quasi-Transcendental Ghost

On this hauntological model, the pure messianic haunts but it does not judge; it spooks but it does not command. Far from supposing that in virtue of its pure messianicity the messianic exerts a transcendental authority over the concrete messianisms, as if it were a transcendental monitor or judge, as if it were an *Aufklärer* passing judgment on them from above, the most the pure messianic can do is to exercises a spectral, haunting, graveyard function. The pure messianic is a voice from the dead, a voice in the dark not the light of the Enlightenment or some sort of religion of pure reason, which looks down upon historical Christianity as an instance or token of the pure ahistorical messianic type and therefore as entirely governed by a priori laws set forth from on high. The pure messianic is more like that Swedenborgian *Geist*/ghost that Kant was worried about than the pure reason he defended. Do not mistake the conceptual status of the "messianic" as a strong Enlightenment universal rather than as a weak or minimalist hauntological shade, as a strong transcendental condition rather than as a poor, weak quasi-transcendental ghost. The pure messianic is just a demi-being, and it is neither a concrete historical presence, a full blooded living being like Christianity or Judaism or Islam, nor is it a pure transcendental form. It arises from and confesses our common weakness and poverty, avowing our blindness and powerlessness before the secret. It is a hauntological confession, without ontological or transcendental pretension. It does not take the form of a formal a priori that professes a transcendental ideal but of a confession that I do not know the secret.

If we want to give this hauntological structure an ontological account, then we should say that it is not a true universal in the logical sense but rather more like a "formal indication" in the Heideggerian sense,[19] which can do no more than point to something, I do not know quite what, something that assumes flesh and blood in living individuals and living traditions. The ghostly formality of this desert-like messianicity does not transcend the concrete messianisms but falls short of them; it does not surpass the concrete messianisms but does get that far. The concrete messianisms go where the messianic does not go. The messianic is not a formal abstraction of which the concrete messianisms are material instances. A formal universal contains its subalternates under it, the way the universal "dog" contains the various subspecies of dogs within it. But a "formal indication" is not a transcendental form but a kind of weak schematic and indeterminate pointing in the direction of certain concrete actualizations which can only be realized *in actu exercitu*, that is, in the realizing acts in which they are taken up in the concrete by concrete individuals or communities. The messianic is not as sure footed as the messianisms, but more lost; it is not as reflectively clear about itself as the messianisms, but more befuddled by the cloud of unknowing. The pure messianic has no history of its theology or defenders of the faith, so saints or apostles, no official publications, and no vestments, hearses or hymnals.

Accordingly, like any ghost worthy of the name, the pure messianic needs a house to haunt, or, to revert to an earlier Derridean figure, the pure messianic is like a parasite which requires a living body to inhabit, but not in such a way as to make them ill and lay them low, but just in order to keep them on their toes, on the *qui vive*. So by thus haunting or inhabiting the concrete messianisms, the messianic thereby acquires a certain concretion or incarnation for itself. It is perfectly true that all our prayers and desires and our faith require content; they must, in virtue of the law of intentionality, intend something, which means, be *for* or *of* or *in* something.[20] They must, in virtue of their facticity, belong to and draw upon the founding narratives of their traditions. Messianic passion must always have content. In what I would like to call *the first messianic movement*, the messianic always initially takes the form of a desire for or faith in something relatively determinate and nameable – for a democracy or justice to come, a gift or a forgiveness to come, a hospitality or a friendship to come. These are the topics of Derrida's later seminars, which turn on what are for Derrida tremendously evocative words, words that are very much like what Heidegger would call "the force of the most elemental words in which Dasein expresses itself,"[21] all of which are words that we have inherited from our traditions. Derrida does not affirm an oligarchy or a National Socialism or an anti-Semitism to come,[22] although it is true that he is haunted by their menace, disturbed that that is what may indeed come, kept awake by the nightmare that what will come will be not the Messiah but the Monster, not the messianic age but the catastrophe. He is haunted by the fear that such will be the upshot of all our promises, but that is not what he desires and affirms.

Messianic passion always has a concrete, historical *terminus a quo*. We begin where we are; where else could we begin? But the *second messianic movement* is to circumcise this content, to cut it open in order to give it a future, to keep the future open to something coming, I do not know quite what, something indeterminate, an open-ended *terminus ad quem*. Remember the dead, who remind us that *we* do not know what *they* know and hence that we do not know the name of what we desire. This second messianic movement is thus a work of carrying to an unforeseeable infinity the movement of what is astir in these words. For these are the least bad words we have *today* for something shrouded by the deathly secret, something *to come*, something unforeseeable, something that cannot be contained by those words that we use in the present to name justice or the gift. The second messianic movement evokes the spectral possibilities that haunt but also animate these words, like a good spirit or a guardian angel or a holy ghost, or even like a devilish fellow who prods these words and gives them no rest. "Democracy" and "justice" are words that invoke an open-ended future rather than describe the present, words of unconditional passion for which there are all around us only contingent and conditional realizations. *Inquietum est cor nostrum*, our hearts are restless with an infinite restlessness that is not quenched by anything that is present.

The relationship of the messianic to the concrete messianisms is not *logical* but *hauntological*. It is not a matter of the formal relationship of the universal to the particular, or the superalternate to the subalternate, of the pure to the empirical, which are the categories of formal or transcendental logic, but rather as a hauntological difference between a living presence and the specters by which it is inhabited. We might also put say that the relationship between them is not logical but *confessional* or better *circumfessional*, where we would distinguish between a more strictly Augustinian confession, which is also a confession that professes, and a confession that circum-fesses but without a profession. For the concrete messianisms have proper names to profess, untranslatable names, names that are above every other name, at the sound of which everyone's knees are to bend, names that they believe with their whole heart. But in the weak, ghostly circumfessional messianic ones gives up the idea that there is a final vocabulary for its desire, that there are final unrevisable, untranslatable terms in which my absolute passion can be cast. The weak messianic confession is a confession of its weakness. So the messianic is only a quasi-Augustinian confession, where I am always asking what I love when I love my god and I am always in the dark about the answer, because the dead won't give it up. Here I am haunted by the idea that in the name of God, or of the love of God, or of the God of love, two good people may be do opposite things, might believe with all their heart opposite things. So one might well argue that this weaker messianic confession is an even greater confession, for it has more to confess, is more at a loss, is more radically cut and adrift, more radically a question unto itself than in the confessional confessions, where one has all the benefits of churches and synagogues, hymnals and long robes, canons of orthodoxy and honorary degrees, by observing which professional clerics can earn a profitable living professing with a unnerving certainty what they profess not to know but to believe, while holding suspect those who believe differently. To suspect a good man who does the opposite of another good man is to abolish the God-relationship – in the name of God! It was ever thus.

A Haunting Conclusion

I have called upon a hauntological hermeneutics to contextualize Christian faith. I have not engaged in a contest between deconstruction and Christianity, which makes no sense, since deconstruction is not a position to take but a certain way of having a position (or de-position), Christian or otherwise. I have not chosen Derrida over Kierkegaard, because it is not a matter of choosing between them. But I have invoked the hauntological structure of undecidability as the framework or context in which the leap of faith, Christian faith to be sure, but any faith, takes place. I have thus allowed the Holy Ghost to be disturbed by another ghost, a spectral figure of the secret, a ghost who prowls about in a deathly shroud trying to unsettle everyone. I have done all this not out of impishness or impudence or impiety but in the name of God, or in the name of the absolute equality of each individual before God. Before God, or death, or the absolute secret, before which we are equal, dead equal. God does not cut inside deals with favorites, does not engage in insider trading. God's covenant is a fair deal, on the up and up, and if a banquet is thrown in the mad hatter, topsy-turvy kingdom of God, then it is one in which the outsiders are in and insiders are out. That means God's covenant is cut with everybody. Or else "God" is an idol, a narcissistic image we project in the name not of love of the neighbor but of self-love, which is the very opposite of the love advocated in the *Works of Love*. When the invitations go out to what is called the "neighbor" in the *Works of Loves*, that means they go out to *everyone*, which means the other, *tout autre*, not to a short list of insiders and special friends, which means the same.

In hauntological hermeneutics, the "before God," *coram deo*, shades off into before death, *coram morte*. We are all equal before God or death, which means, all equi-distant from the secret, absolutely related to and removed from the absolute secret, equally deprived of transcendental credentials, cut off and circum-cised from the secret which sits in the middle and knows. We are dead equal, equally driven by a passion for the undeconstructible, equally haunted by the hope of things to come, equally disturbed by the midnight thought that, were we born at another time, in another place, in another language, we would have formulated our absolute passion relatively differently, and with no absolute disadvantage before God.

Remember the secret. It does not paralyze us or reduce us to silence. On the contrary, it multiplies interpretations, sending out round and round the ring of interpretation. It multiplies discourses, so that names fly up like sparks in the cold night air of the secret. Let there by many dances, many names for God, omni-nameable, or death, God or death, so long as all of them are true.

Remember what Kierkegaard said in the *Works of Love*, that if one good individual cannot do the opposite of what another good person would do in the same circumstances, the God-relationship is abolished and everything is reduced to the public and the universal and the same. That is because for both individuals, the question is raised about what they love when they love their God and for both in absolute passion.

Remember that are many ways to have an absolute passion for the absolute, and a relative passion for the relative. Let there by many ways to actualize the absolute passion for the absolute, many ways to charge existence to infinity, so long as all of them are true. Let there be many ways to transform our whole existence, inside and outside Christianity, many ways to bend our knee in absolute passion, so long as all of them are true.

Above all, remember the dead. Nothing moves them to speak out, or causes them to intervene in our disputes, or motivates them to take a stand in our endless interpretations of the secret, which we may assume they would surely do were one of us up above to hit upon the secret which they know but will not say. We cannot but wonder what is running through their minds as they lie there, calmly listening to the bustle and buzz overhead. They well remember all the passion of the ring dance up above. They well remember the diverse and colorful garments of dissimilarities they wore on the stage of life. They cannot but smile when they recall this fellow Hans, a few plots over, who strutted about like quite a prosperous fellow up there, and that poor chap Nielson, several plots down, who could never make ends meet up above. A man here, a woman there; a rich man here, a poor man there; a famous judge here, a humble pastor there; a very ardent Christian here, an equally passionate Moslem there. But down here, down below, they are all equal and they are all neighbors, of common kin and clay. These masterful thinkers teach us, in the succinct and silent seminar they conduct down below, that we are all equal, all equally removed from the secret by the small but infinite distance of six feet of earth.

Meanwhile, back in the cemetery, Magister Kierkegaard, the Church Yard philosopher, that master of conversations with the dead, can be found concealed behind a tree on a sunny summer morning, while all the birds are chirping, making notes for a new upbuilding discourse. In it, he intends to remind all of Copenhagen, nay, all of Christendom, nay, everyone, the whole world, *urbi et orbi*, for we are all neighbors, everyone without exception, that before God, *coram deo*, we are all equal.

Dead equal.

Notes

[1] I am borrowing the figures of the "specter" and of a "hauntology" from Jacques Derrida, *Specters of Marx: The State of the Debt, the Work of Mourning, and the New International*, trans. Peggy Kamuf (New York: Routledge, 1994).

[2] See *Kierkegaard's Writings*, VII, *Philosophical Fragments, or A Fragment of Philosophy and Johannes Climacus, or De Omnibus dubitandum est*, trans. and ed. Howard and Edna Hong (Princeton: Princeton University Press, 1985), chs. 4 and 6.

[3] *Kierkegaard's Writings*, XVI, *Works of Love*, trans. and ed. Howard and Edna Hong (Princeton: Princeton University Press, 1995), 345-346.

[4] *Works of Love*, 81-89.

[5] *Works of Love*, 230.

[6] *Works of Love*, 359 ff.

[7] A final note on Kierkegaard: the motif of the absolute equality of each individual before God in Kierkegaard and the pseudonyms competes with and disrupts his Christo-centrism, that is, his central motif that only before Paradox of the God/man, and hence only in Christianity, can existence achieve absolute passion. But this Christo-centrism privileges Christians over non-Christians in a way that is disturbed by the theme of absolute equality, for the God-relationship would be destroyed if two men could not achieve absolute passion by doing the opposite of one

another (*Works of Love*, 230), that is, the one being Christian, the other not. For a penetrating account of the universally human in *Works of Love* and the upbuilding discourses, see George Pattison, *Kierkegaard's Upbuilding Discourses: Philosophy, Literature and Theology* (London & New York: Routledge, 2002).

[8] Here, as always, I argue that although Derrida is a critic of the word "hermeneutics," which he takes to mean decoding or deciphering a master meaning, deconstruction has in fact all the makings of a hermeneutics more radically conceived

[9] *Kierkegaard's Writings*, XII.1, *Concluding Unscientific Postscript to "Philosophical Fragments,"* trans. and ed. Howard and Edna Hong (Princeton: Princeton University Press, 1992), 387.

[10] Robert Frost, "The Secret Sits," in *Poetry of Robert Frost*, ed. Edward Connery Lathem (New York: Vintage Books, 2001), 362.

[11] Derrida, *The Gift of Death*, trans. David Wills (Chicago: University of Chicago Press, 1995), 49.

[12] Augustine, *Confessiones*, X, 6.

[13] Messianic desire would apply to the "religions of the Book," to the three great monotheisms. How to identify religious desire outside these religions is a more difficult problem and may perhaps involve something other than passion or desire, e.g., the passion or desire to detach oneself from passion or desire. There is no one thing called "religion," which is a western, Latin word for something, I do not quite know what.

[14] That is a motif which has been nicely improvised upon in Bruce Benson, *Graven Ideologies: Nietzsche, Derrida & Marion on Modern Idolatry* (Downers Grove, IL: Inter-Varsity Press, 2002).

[15] Christianity for Derrida is one of the "concrete messianisms," one of the historical garbs assumed by the figure of the Messiah. He mentions several such messianisms, both religious and philosophical: the three great religions of the Book, Judaism, Christianity and Islam, and the three great philosophical eschatologies of Hegel, Marx, and Heidegger. The messianic or messianicity, on the other hand, is a pure, formal, open-end hope, a hope not in some determinate outcome to history, like the hope in the second coming of Jesus in Christianity, or the repetition of the first Greek beginning in Heidegger, or the Absolute's return to itself in pure self-knowledge, but a hope in the future itself, in the very idea of the *à venir*. The *venue*, the coming of the Messiah, is thus to be distinguished from the historically given ways in which the messianic figure is concretely represented. The real and actual history of the concrete messianisms are so many ways for the Messiah to come, so many ways the Messiah enters time and history. These matters are discussed in some detail, with extensive references to their textal sources in, *Deconstruction in Nutshell: A Conversation with Jacques Derrida* (New York: Fordham University Press, 1977), ch. 6. Climacus was flirting with something like this distinction when he spoke about the relationship between the *Fragments* and the *Postscript*. In the *Fragments* he was describing the formal structure of the relationship to the Teacher, but in the *Postscript* he gave that nude and formal structure its concrete "historical costume" (*Postscript*, 10), fleshed it out in all of historical particularity. The *Fragments* were describing a ghost of a possibility, an ethereal thing, and were all about "the god," which does not exist, while Christianity is its concrete and historical embodiment.

[16] *Fragments*, 37.

[17] If I know something to be true, I also believe it. But from the fact that I believe something, it does not follow that I know it to be true; it is that sense that I speak of belief, which is a faith not a knowledge

[18] The Messiah is a figure Derrida clearly inherited from the religions of the book, but the immediate source from which Derrida borrowed the idea was Walter Benjamin, for whom the figure was not only a figure for the future but also a figure of memory and mourning, thus containing a reference to the dead. On Benjamin's use of the idea, we today are the messianic

generation whom the dead awaited, whom they were expecting to right the world's wrongs, so that we bear an infinite responsibility to them to bring about the messianic age. See Walter Benjamin, "Theses on the Philosophy of History," in *Illuminations: Essays and Reflections*, trans. Harry Zohn, ed. Hannah Arendt (New York: Schocken Books, 1969), 253-64; cf. Derrida, *Specters*, 180-181 n2.

[19] See Martin Heidegger, *Phänomenologische Interpretationen zu Aristoteles. Einführung in die phänomenologische Forschung*, WS 1921/22, *Gesamtausgabe*, Vol. 61, Hg. W. Bröcker and K. Bröcker-Oltmanns (Frankfurt/Main: Klostermann, 1985), 33-34, 60-61, et passim. See Daniel O. Dahlstrom, "Heidegger's Method: Philosophical Concepts as Formal Indications," *Review of Metaphysics*, 47 (1994): 775-795; and John van Buren, *The Young Heidegger* (Bloomington: Indiana University Press, 1994).

[20] However, intentionality does not guarantee a determinate object. Husserl points out that it is possible for an intentional act to be directed towards an indeterminate object, in which case indeterminacy is what specifically or determinately characterizes the essence of the act. See Edmund Husserl, *The Shorter Logical Investigations*, trans. J. N. Findlay, ed. Dermot Moran (London & New York: Routledge, 2001), 228. In Heidegger and Kierkegaard, the feeling of anxiety is determinately differentiated from fear precisely by the indeterminacy of its object.

[21] Martin Heidegger, *Being and Time*, trans. Edward Robinson and John Macquarie (New York: Harper & Row, 1962), 262.

[22] See "De l'antisémitisme à venir," in Jacques Derrida and Elisabeth Roudinesco, *De quoi demain...Dialogue* (Paris: Fayard/Galilée, 2001), 175 ff.

5

BODIES STILL UNRISEN, EVENTS STILL UNSAID

[In *Angelaki: Journal of Theoretical Humanities*, Vol. 12, No. 1 (April 2007): 73–86. A revised version of this article was published in *Apophatic Bodies: Negative Theology, Incarnation, and Relationality*, eds. Chris Boesel and Catherine Keller (New York: Fordham University Press, 2009), 94–116, and is sufficiently different to warrant being reproduced in *Collected Philosophical and Theological Papers*, Volume 6]

[73] In what follows, I identify the apophatic element in the body by way of a distinction between bodies and the events harbored by bodies, and by taking the phenomenon of the "risen body" in the New Testament as a focal body.

Bodies in the New Testament

The New Testament is all about bodies – bodies that are paralyzed, fevered, lame, leprous, blind, deaf and dumb, bodies that are seized by demons, tortured, crucified and dead bodies. It is no less about bodies that are miraculously healed, bodies from which demons are driven out, bodies that pass through walls, walk on water, the maternal body of a virgin, a babe born under heavenly signs, about bodies that glow with a white glory in a transfigured state, about resuscitated and even risen bodies. As I have pointed out elsewhere, all of this represents a missed opportunity for Gilles Deleuze, who was otherwise attentive to texts like this. For here is a world that is every bit the match for anything produced by Lewis Carroll, at least as unusual as any rabbit with a pocket watch or the telescopic changes in size undergone by Alice's body after falling down the rabbit hole. Here was a perfect illustration of what Deleuze meant by the "event" of "sense" and by the origin of sense in non-sense by which he meant a kind of neutral or proto-sense. What Deleuze meant by sense is what Averroes called an "absolute nature," that is a meaning, form or structure that in and of itself is neither universal, particular nor individuated, neither abstract nor concrete, but is of itself absolved and set loose from all the conditions of mind (logical classes) or of existence (individuals). The eventiveness of the event lies in its ability to migrate freely between these spheres, heedless of the laws of logic that govern classes and of the laws of physics that govern real bodies. Curiously, that structure prior to or liberated from the conditions of logic and physics is also part of what Husserl called a pure *Sinn*.[1]

The event is a kind of epistemic free radical that can migrate through many strata, the analysis of which reveals to us a sphere of the absolutely possible, of hitherto suppressed possibilities, previously undisclosed openings, and unimagined, unrealized unsuspected futures. While this is the sphere of hopes and dreams, it is no less the sphere of monsters and nightmares, [74] since nothing guarantees that the unsuspected or undreamt of will not be unexpectedly terrible. To put all this in the terms of Jacques Derrida – in whom there is a no less potent account of the event than in Deleuze, one that has taken on a certain messianic tone – the event describes the sphere of the unforeseeable coming, of *the* impossible beyond the possible and foreseeable, which is both a promise and a threat. This is aptly put by Paul who describes the event that is harbored by the name of God in terms of the coming of what eye has not seen nor ear heard (1 Cor 2:9).

When Hamlet says that there are more things on heaven and earth, Horatio, than are dreamt of in our philosophies, that suggests a shortage of philosophers who dream, or who sigh and weep, praying for "*the* impossible," which is a technical term in deconstruction. Its sense is not logical but phenomenological, or at least quasi- or counter-phenomenological. In phenomenology, all experience is structured by a horizon of expectation which defines the possible, and in this counter-phenomenology the impossible is that which shatters that horizon.

The course cut by the event as it circulates through words and things traces out a general phenomenological or hermeneutic field for interpretation. In the case of the New Testament, I have described this as a *metanoetic event* which circulates throughout a general metanoetic field.[2]

The metanoetic event moves back and forth between bodies and spirits, crossing and crisscrossing with all the freedom of the event. In this way the metanoetic event constitutes a field of general transformations and transfigurations, in which bodily healings go hand in hand with a change of heart (*metanoia*), of which they are also a symbol and with which they form a symbolic counterpart. Jesus came teaching and healing (Matt. 4: 23–25), offering a *therapeutic* for the body and a *didactic* for the spirit, mending hearts and healing lepers, curing bodies and preaching the forgiveness of sin, which together constituted what he called the coming of the "Kingdom of God." The Kingdom of God is the realm in which the metanoetic event reigns, the realm through which it freely circulates, whereas in the "world" it is tightly bound and confined. In a way that precisely parallels making the lame to walk, Jesus was also the site of the forgiveness of sin. The Greek and Latin root of forgiveness (*aphiemi*, *dimittere*), unlike our Anglo-Saxon root (*geben*, giving) meant to release, to set free from sin. So Jesus is a man who releases limbs that are paralyzed just as he releases hearts that are bound up by sin. In Jesus, all the forces of freedom and releasement are concentrated and organized so that his words and deeds reverberate with metanoetic effects. By the Kingdom of God Jesus meant the twin effect that is produced on our hearts and bodies when God rules. In Deleuzian-Derridean terms the Kingdom of God means that things are charged, transfixed, and transfigured by the event that is astir within the rule of God. It never (or hardly ever) occurred to Deleuze to ask, what if by the "event" we meant the effects or the potencies that stir within the name of "God" or the "rule of God," what effect is produced by the eventiveness of God? Deleuze had an eye for the event that takes place in literary texts but not in sacred texts. But that is precisely the field or domain of events that is explored in the New Testament, in which the Kingdom of God is from start to finish populated with bodies that tremble with the event, with bodies that are thoroughly transformed even to the point that they rise from the dead. That generalized effect, that phenomenological or counter-phenomenological field or hermeneutic horizon is what St. Paul called the new being, the new creation, in which life – of the body and the heart – is raised to a new order of vigor and energy, in which the event is taken to a new level of events hitherto and still unsaid.

Given this context, what can we say of the meaning of the body in the Kingdom, that is, what sorts of events in particular circulate through the various bodies in such a world? The focal bodies in the New Testament, and to some extent in the Jewish and Christian Scriptures generally, the ones upon which attention is centered, tend to take the form of what I will call "flesh." By flesh I mean a body reduced from action to passion, from an agile agent body, which is the ordinary subject of the phenomenology of the body, to a body patient, a body that suffers from disease or malformation or finally even [75] death, even as it is a body transformed and lifted up by pleasure. The hand that swings a hammer and drives a nail is part of a body agent, the hand that caresses or is nailed to a cross is flesh. The flesh is simultaneously a site of vulnerability and of pleasure, of bodies that so pulsate with sensation that their acting in the world is suspended and the flesh itself becomes all the world there is. These are bodies that are saturated with themselves, scenes of "auto-affection," as Michel Henry puts it.

So there is nothing masochistic or hopeless about these suffering bodies in the New Testament. On the contrary, Jesus comes eating and drinking and his body is the site of hope, providing the setting for the events that will transform the flesh of those laid low by suffering.

Jesus is the center and agent par excellence of these events. Even his garments exude power. His body is the locus, the subject, the site, the scene, the agent of transformation and transfiguration. He transforms other bodies even as he is himself transfigured (Luke 9:28–36). He heals in the most bodily ways, by spitting in the dirt and using the spittle as a curative, which could not be more earthly (John 9:6). The New Testament is marked by what theology and metaphysics calls "miracles," which means the releasing of the event, the exercise of religious-mythic power, just as the events in *Alice in Wonderland* are astir with a literary-magic power – magic playing cards, foods, etc. Divine mythic power and literary magic have in common that they are each scenes of the event, exercises in freedom in which the human imagination breaks the bonds of logic and physics and dreams of being otherwise and of what is otherwise than being. However differently motivated, each represents what, in the language of philosophy, is called an agent or efficient cause, a cause of motion or of being, unrestrained by the laws of causality; they both actualize the possibilities of the event with a special freedom from ordinary causal law. They have causal powers that are released from the constraints of actuality, like making inanimate physical objects move with a mere word. They thus provide the opportunity to put the potencies of the event on full display, to release the powers of the possible, the possibility of the impossible, the im/possibilities of the "absolute event." Released from the constraints of causality and actuality, they each employ a certain *epoche*, which is the defining operation of and entrance door to phenomenology, of which they are the literary counterparts, upon which works of religious literature and works of fantasy and magic depend.

The difference between them is that in the New Testament "miracles" are always tied to the service of suffering, to the transformation of suffering bodies and even of death itself, to the sphere of "flesh," and to its eventive correlate, the transformation of the heart. In *Alice in Wonderland*, the literary magic is a way to put on display the events that circulate through certain verbal, mathematical and logical problems. In *Alice* events are too light-hearted to be concerned with a deep change of heart. Deleuze comes closest to appreciating the events we find in the New Testament, to its suffering bodies and tormented spirits, when he turns from Lewis Carroll to Artaud's account of the schizophrenic body. Then he finds himself called upon to defend Carroll from some extremely unfavorable criticisms of Carroll as an English don who takes suffering lightly.[3]

Clearly, being raised from the dead is the most extreme transformation possible for this body of flesh, the most radical movement imaginable, the event in which the body is pushed to the limits, to what Derrida would call the impossible. This happens three times, in each one of which Jesus is centrally involved, twice as the agent of God, in the raising of Lazarus and of the daughter of Jairus, which prefigure his own raising, when he is a patient or subject of God's agency. Raising the dead is the paradigmatic or exemplary transformation, of which every other transformation is an imperfect approximation. To cure blindness is to restore the life of the eye, to cure the paralytic is to restore the life of the limb, but to raise the dead body is to restore life itself, the life of the whole body. Raising the dead is both a figure and the substance of utter transformation, of rebirth, of the new being, new life, new creation to which Paul refers. Jesus announced the coming of the Kingdom, when all things would be made new by the rule of God. Paul and the New Testament made Jesus into the locus and [76] the vehicle, the medium and the substance, of the new being, so that one puts on the new humanity or the new being not by living by the Torah but by living in Jesus. Jesus became the mystical source of the very event of the Kingdom he came to announce; the messenger became the message, the announcer of the event became the event itself. Either way, the event announced by Jesus (the Kingdom), or the event that is Jesus (the new being brought by living in Jesus) is given its most incandescent expression in this event that exceeds every other event, this preeminent event of which every other event is a partial prefiguration. On this point of the risen body in particular, the debate about the difference between the historical Jesus and Christianity is not a focal issue because they both affirmed the resurrection of the body. While Jesus taught the resurrection of every body, Christianity reorganizes this same event around the resurrection of the body of Jesus. The latter is not the miracle that proves the truth of Christianity but the "firstborn of creation" (Col. 1:15), the first body in a chain of bodies to undergo such transformation that is set in motion by the body of Jesus. If it does not start with Jesus, it will not keep going.

Theology and Transcendental Suspicion

What the New Testament calls the risen body (or the new creation) is not itself the event but it harbors or contains the event. Maintaining a distinction between an event and its embodiment or expression is the defining feature of what I will call *transcendental suspicion*. An event – because it is a potency, impulse, and freely migrating sense — cannot occur in some definitive form. There could not be a final event that decisively closes the history of the event, since the event is the event of history's ongoing process. So the event that is astir in the "risen body" cannot take a final form; it cannot be enclosed within a conclusive and definitive form like a final resurrection that supersedes the apparent finality of death. What is called the "resurrection of the body" in theology and religious discourse would always be a figure in which the event takes place, a narrative in which the event is expressed. As long as there is life, there will always be the possibility of new life, of rebirth and resurrection — that is the event. Life is a process of constant renewal, which depends upon the influx of new being, upon getting a new start, of birth and rebirth. In a theology of the event, that is, in a theology mindful of transcendental criticism, we distinguish the miracle stories, above all the focal miracle of the risen body, of rebirth and resurrection, from the events which constitute them, from which they are woven, out of which they are forged. The event is a *dynamis*, the virtuality of a power, potentiality, possibility, the capacity to develop and unfold. The event is an impulse that is expressed in words or realized in things which are constituted by a state of perpetual dissatisfaction, a restlessness and discontent with themselves that propels them forward. There will always be risen bodies and bodies still unrisen.

To be sure, nothing prevents someone from affirming the literal embodiment or purported fact, over and beyond the event which it harbors, like the raising of Lazarus — except a certain transcendental suspicion that keeps an eye out for the distinction that obtains in principle between the event and its expression, actualization or instantiation. I speak of "suspicion" rather than "criticism," because criticism comes from on high, speaking from a higher-critical standpoint, while "suspicion" is practiced from below, exercising a cautionary dubiousness. The event is what we desire, what we hope and pray for, in all that is happening around us, even as our ethico-religious task is to make ourselves worthy of the event, as Deleuze says.[4]

So we can never underestimate the extent to which we need to see the event realized and embodied, and consequently never underestimate the temptation we feel to affirm that here at last the event has happened, has been actualized in some exemplary or paradigmatic way. But events do not happen; they stir and disturb what happens, are astir in what happens so that what happens is never finished. But there is a difference in principle between a fact or state of affairs and the event, the appreciation and articulation of which is what we mean by transcendental suspicion. The life and death of Jesus, what he said and did, in which an event [77] clearly transpires, is one thing, and that becomes the stuff out of which the New Testament was woven, but the event that is harbored in the name of "Jesus" is another. An event, something eventful, happens in Jesus, as everything we know about Jesus confirms, but that does not authorize us to say that Jesus *is* the event. The theological doctrine of the Incarnation means that Jesus incarnates the event, but that does not imply that the event is exhausted there and nothing authorizes us to say that Jesus is *the* event Incarnate. If that is the very definition of Christian theology or Christian orthodoxy then orthodoxy and theology are too "strong." They need to be reformulated in terms of a "weak theology," that is, one that shows some appreciation for the event and the multiplicity of ways – both religious and non-religious – in which it can be embodied. The very idea or representation of the Event Incarnate is best read as the exercise of a religious-literary imagination, comparable to the personification of Justice or Mercy as characters in a philosophical dialogue, all of which depends upon the priority of the event.

That the whole world is not Christian is testimony to transcendental suspicion. There is always a difference between the event and the facts, cultures, traditions, institutions, and doctrines in which events are expressed and embodied. The New Testament evolved into a literary form with a narrative structure. It grew out of sayings gospels, which collect the words in which Jesus announces the good news about the Kingdom, into the form of gospel narratives, stories about Jesus, in which Jesus becomes the good news. That tends to collapse the distinction between the event and the fact or state of affairs in which the event transpires. It gives birth to strong theology, whereas weak theology is defined by its fidelity to this distinction.

Such a collapse would do injury to the concept of truth cultivated in transcendental suspicion. Events have to be embodied and expressed or else they lie fallow in their potentiality, inactive, ineffective and unrealized and consequently unsaid, and their truth is a dead letter. Questioning is a way of staying underway to the truth and events are what keep the question open, what keeps questioning alive, for it is by virtue of the events they harbor that words and things are continually provocative and find it impossible to settle finally in place. For that reason, events are closely tied to the notion of truth. The idea that events are defined as a process of constant becoming does not undermine the truth but compels us to redescribe truth in terms of process. It just means that events are always on the way to truth, attempting to work out the truth, to make it happen, to bring it about in words and things. In the perspective we are taking in this paper, the "risen body" represents an effort to express the *truth* of the body, what the body desires, not as a fixed state, however, but as the very becoming of the body, the becoming true of the body. The body is a vital force, a force of life and more life, at the heart of life's rhythms, of life ascending and declining and then re-ascending or rising again, the body rising and rising again. In virtue of the event the body is a process of continually coming true, in process toward what the body would become. Rising is a figure for endless becoming, the endless coming of more life, so that life gives birth to more life, in an endless movement of self-overcoming. The truth of the body is not an ideal state or term that it would attain, which is quite literally a terminal condition, because life is interminable even as it is interwoven with death. There is no final truth to the body other than its interminable becoming. Every "term" is but a nodal point of transition to another level, condition or state. Every termination is the occasion for new life – for the child, the new day, the new beginning, the new life, the new being, the new creation. The new creation is the truth of the body, but that is not a defined condition or final state but the process of becoming true. Seen in these terms, form, essence, and definition are figures of stasis, of death and untruth, while transformation, existence, and infinition are figures of life and truth. Staying underway is the truth, which is why the *way* is the truth and the life. The name of God, the event harbored in the name of God, is an important case in point, and in theology it is the point itself, of transcendental suspicion. There can be no event of all events, as if all events are monitored and supervised by a single event, let us say some hyper-event, since [78] the very idea of the event is to twist free from any such hierarchical embrace. The event as such is anarchical, not hierarchical, as I will shortly explain. But the classical idea of God in western metaphysical theology is the idea of a being who is the realization or actualization of the event of all events, the idea of a being (which cannot therefore be simply *a* being) in which all being is summarily concentrated and realized. In this idea of God the event and the being that realizes the event are identical. *Essentia dei et suum esse sunt idem.* Because the event is linked to sense it is close to the classical idea of essence, although it is crucially different and no less a nomadic, nominalistic non-essence, an essence without essence. An event is an impulse of which an essence is the cinematic still or frozen representation.

Transcendental suspicion, which patrols the distinction between event and being, is crucial to keeping theology, that is, the question of God, open. In a theology of the event, the question of God cannot be closed off atheistically even as it cannot be brought to a conclusion in some theological dogma or religious doctrine. The challenge to non-religious thinkers – the question put to non-religion by the event – is not to dismiss or close off the event that takes place in the name of God, not to preclude the possibility that the names held dear in non-religion can be translated into the name of God. The challenge to the religious thinker – the question put to religion by the event – is not to dismiss or close off the expression or realization of the event under other names than God and in other places and times, not to preclude that the name of God is translatable into other names. In a theology of the event the name of God is not the name of an ordered hierarchical super-being but the locus of a complex of events, of interwoven and open-ended events that keep "the question of God" open in an open-ended chain of substitution. In a theology of the event, the name of God contains an event that lays claim to us without saying or gainsaying that something exists in which that event, or complex of events, exists.

The event is the basis of a religious discourse about the love of God. The love of God is the love of what we desire with a desire beyond desire. The name of God is the name of what we desire just because it contains or shelters the event of what we desire. The name of God is an elemental part of all human life, whether or not one is "religious." There is even a sense in which we can say that the love of God is an elemental part of life itself and, beyond that, of all things, living or non-living. In that sense, the love of God is an inextinguishable energy that drives all creation, what things everywhere and in multiple ways are in search of. We might even say that, if things are what they seek, the love of God is what defines them. The body is a manifestation of the love of God, for what else is the body than life and what else is life than the love of more life, of the increase of life, of sensations more intense, more extensive, or of feeling more delicate and sensitive, of passions more profound, more pervasive, of tranquility and rest as also of exhilarating exertion. Go and multiply yourselves, for life seeks to multiply life, to extend itself in every direction and by every indirection, in degree, intensity and number. To live in order to live even more.

Bodies without Flesh

The risen body is a distinct phenomenon that should not be confused with other related phenomena. The risen body is not the same as the immortality of the soul, where immortality is gained by separating oneself from the mortal and corruptible body. The risen body is the refusal to separate oneself from the material body. It is the refusal to abdicate the body and an insistence on the reinstatement of the body even after death and in such a way as to transcend death. The risen body is not a resuscitated body – Lazarus and the daughter of Jairus are resuscitated, but they do not have risen bodies. Rather, in being brought back to life, they reacquire their mortal or corruptible bodies, subject all over again to suffering and to death at a later date. Snatched from death once, their final death is but deferred. The risen body is not a matter of reincarnation, in which an imperishable soul migrates from one corruptible body to another. The risen body is not matter of eternal recurrence, in which one passes through the cycle of birth and death, [79] living this same corruptible life over and over again, being born and dying over and over again.

The risen body refers to the rising again from the dead in such a way to put all mortality and corruptibility behind it once and for all. The body that is risen, reinstated and resurrected is "imperishable" or incorruptible (1 Cor 15: 35–54), released from suffering and death. It is presumably blocked from sensual pleasures, since pain and pleasure are seated alike in self-feeling. That makes for a quite unusual body, which is why it provides an inviting and suggestive occasion for the exploration of the event. The risen body is a body without bodily limitations. It is able to pass through walls, to appear instantly in distant places and just as instantly to disappear (Luke 24: 31; John 20: 19–29), which is effectively to have no containing place and to show no signs of being limited by temporal conditions. Such a body effectively contradicts the central features of embodiment, of spatio-temporal limitation, which is why it has the look of a body that is no less a soul than the soul, that seeks to separate itself from the body no less than does the soul.

In the risen body, the distinction between the soul that has escaped its body and the body it escapes begins to weaken, without being entirely eliminated, and it raises the question of the extent to which the notion of the risen body is a repudiation of the body, which it both is and is not.

In one sense the risen body certainly does not repudiate the body. The risen body is visible and recognizable; it is not supposed to be a soul that has escaped its body and been set free to lead a purely immaterial life, as in the *Phaedo*. Nor is it a ghost, as in *Hamlet*, which means a body that is still quite dead but with still unfinished business on earth which requires that a replica or simulacrum of itself be sent back to tidy up its affairs. A soul is not a body at all and a ghost is a bodily remnant or afterglow, whereas the risen body is a completion or perfection of the body. The risen body is the body itself restored and extended to perfection. One is reminded of the medieval Franciscans who explained angelic life by means of an "immaterial matter," a kind of prime matter that when given form issues not in a material substance but an immaterial one, which was a lighter, thinner, more light-suffused, airy, aerial, ethereal stuff, capable of a kind of absolute velocity and of passing through solid substances (passability). The risen body is something like these Franciscans angels, or like the angels in Fra Angelico's murals in San Marco, the Dominican friary at Florence, with their wispy transparency. One is also reminded of some medieval accounts of the body of Mary, which shared in these properties. Not only was she penetrated by the power of the Holy Spirit, which required a Spirit to pass through her bodily walls without damage to her virginity, but even in some of these accounts the newborn baby Jesus was able to traverse the birth canal without rupturing the hymeneal membrane. The risen body is the restoration of the body but this time possessed of the power to be freed of bodily limitations, marked by passability, absolute mobility, luminosity and – above all – "incorruptibility" (Paul). The risen body is a body (not an angel, soul, or ghost) without the horizon of death or mortality. In this way the body is not only restored to its status in the second Genesis myth, where our mortal bodies were not supposed to die but incurred mortality by sin, but raised to a higher and more ethereal life.

If the idea of the risen body closely skirts the outright rejection of the body – by rejecting bodily limitations – it cannot be simply reduced to it, otherwise the construction would simply have been abandoned in favor of a soul freed from the body. The risen body is not so much the rejection of the body as its projection, the body carried to idealization or completion, just as in a transcendental illusion, when an empirical concept is brought to its limit or carried out to its idealized conclusion. The risen body is not a soul without a body but a body without corruptibility. Of course, it is to that extent unavoidably and importantly also a rejection of the body. One need only recall the Nietzschean affirmation of the body in which the test of affirmation, of the yea-sayer, is whether we are prepared to affirm the entire circle or cycle of life – of suffering no less than pleasure, of sorrow no less than joy, of the midnight darkness no less than the high noons. To affirm life one-sidedly, trying to extract the joy without paying the price of sorrow, trying to extract life without its partner and attendant death, is the very definition of the nihilism of belief in the Christian afterlife. If there is to be any myth of afterlife at all for Zarathustra it is the myth of the eternal recurrence of the very lives we have, which [80] means not only living but also suffering and dying an infinite number of times. The doctrine of the risen body is thus an affirmation of the body, of incarnation, but in rather a half-hearted and qualified sense, rather like a feint-hearted friend. The doctrine affirms bodily life just so long as it is to our advantage but rejects the body when the going gets rough. It affirms life, not the body, and the body just insofar as it is a vehicle of life and not a living thing as such, one that also corrupts and dies. That is not *the* impossible that we dream of but the simply impossible, because it breaks the tension between the possible and the impossible. It is not a body exposed to the possibility of the unimaginable but a simply impossible body.

The risen body is at best a *figure* of the event where the event is the event of life and life more abundantly. That is why I practice transcendental suspicion. On my accounting, the risen body, held suspect as a literal fact, is an attempt to release the *event* that stirs within the body, to release the sense, or at least a sense, of the body. The risen body is an idealization of the empirical body which is trying to express the truth of the body, the event that takes in the body – as an event of mobility, velocity, light, power, and incorruptibility. Empirical bodies, immortal souls, ghosts, and risen bodies are so many ways to actualize or instantiate events, in words and things that are variously material or immaterial, hauntological, literary or religious. The difference between the empirical body and risen body does not lie in the event but in the mode of realization of the event; in the one case, subject to bodily limitations, in the other not. In the one case, under duller, heavier, more plodding and difficult conditions, in the other more brilliantly and unencumbered.

The risen body rises above the limitations of space and time, illness, weariness, frailty, aging, injury and finally death itself. It is a body from which all real risk and vulnerability have been removed. In short, the very "flesh" that defines the bodies that so massively populate the New Testament vanishes in the risen body. The risen body of Jesus at the end of the gospels is the opposite of the blind, lame, leprous, and paralyzed bodies with which it opens. The risen body of Jesus is the "first born," the first of the bodies to be transformed by the event, which other bodies, our bodies, are to follow. The sparks the agent body gives off, the surge of power, agility, mobility, the sway and swagger of being on the move are all magnified, intensified and concentrated in a single entity whose characteristic status is to be neither mere matter nor spirit, neither soul nor mere body, neither/nor, and thus to be the slash between the two. The risen body signals the event which is expressed in words and realized in things as a kind of non-thing or no-thing of particular brilliance and effulgence. Nothing more perfectly betokens the event than a no-thing that cannot find a firm place on the side of either souls or bodies. It is a construction peculiarly tailored to embody the event whose proper place is nowhere, whose time is always to come or lodged long ago in the irrecuperable past, whose power is the power of the impossible, of the unthought of, undreamt of, unimaginable bodies still to come.

Deleuze undertook his study of *Alice* unencumbered by any background problem of the search for the historical Alice or by an institution hovering in the background monitoring the interpretation of the text and armed with the disciplinary weapons of excommunication. Deleuze was not trying to establish the empirical probability of the things that occur in Wonderland but to explore the range of the event, the free-floating character of the exercise of the event of sense, to examine how the event is released in an exemplary text, one in which events were set free in a special way. Without in any way conflating the nature and the intentions of these texts, the New Testament displays the workings of the event in a suggestively parallel way. In both texts, bodies are emancipated from the laws of physics and meaning is emancipated from the laws of signification. In the New Testament, the result is a phenomenology of the body as a thing of beauty, power, and incorruptibility, marked by qualities of shining whiteness and glowing incandescence.

This is brought out clearly by one of the more interesting episodes of the risen body of Jesus, when he eats a piece of broiled fish to allay the doubts of Thomas (Luke 24: 36–43). [81] There is an episode that surely requires a gloss. If it is left to stand as it is, its implications would overwhelm the narratives of the risen body. It would imply a functioning digestive tract and consequently the production of waste products, a heavenly food industry, requiring farms, a favorable climate and a waste management industry, to put it all rather circumspectly. What is foolish or amusing about this, of course, is that we have literalized and reified an event, conflated an event with some sort of heavenly or otherworldly fact of the matter. That would be the equivalent of taking seriously what sort of housing, food supply and waste management system would be required to accommodate Alice's surprising change of size in Wonderland, or where the Mad Hatter purchases his tea. The mistake here is what the logicians call *ignoratio elenchii*, missing the point. It would be like the disorder Merleau-Ponty reports was suffered by Schneider, who did not know how to take a metaphor, so that if someone said to Schneider that the events of the day caused him to eat his hat, Schneider would be puzzled and wonder whether the hat were cooked or eaten in the raw. What has gone wrong here is that a kind of category mistake has been committed in which one fails to pick up on the event that is on display and is distracted instead by the particular manner of presentation. The same thing is going on in the metaphysical debate about the composition of angelic being, where the literary function of a messenger charged with delivering a surprising communication from on high is hypostasized as a kind of immaterial entity.

If Deleuze could speak of the body of a schizophrenic as a body without organs, we might offer a parallel hypothesis of the risen body as a body without flesh, a body without the physics of density and volume, without the biochemistry of organic functions, and without the deep structure of vulnerability and mortality. This is a body that is all function, all action and agency, without flesh, vulnerability, wound, passivity. The story of eating fish illustrates this point graphically, because in order to avoid the unwieldy implications referred to above we have to assume that the risen body of Jesus totally assimilated this fish without remainder, that the risen body Jesus was not hungry and did not produce waste, but totally transmuted the fish into his transfigured ethereal body. When food is normally consumed it is assimilated into flesh and blood and generates waste materials, which is what could not have happened here. No more than the body of Jesus could have been cut by the knife with which the fish was cut, no more than he could have bled from this cut, or would have had to brush his teeth after eating. His body could not suffer hunger or take nourishment, no more than it could be cut or wounded or grow weary or need exercise. It is a body without flesh.

The transfigured body is woven from or a construction made out of events. It imaginatively projects a body that represents the crowning triumph over the body that was crowned with thorns, that is now invulnerable to Roman swords and Roman nails and the blows of the soldiers. If the prelapsarian body of Adam is innocent and uninjured, if the fallen body is wounded and mortal, and if the crucified body of Jesus is almost all flesh, then the risen body is a triumphant flash of power and beauty without flesh. It does not get exhausted, sweaty, constipated, hungry, erotic, senescent or stuck in traffic jams; it does not have a blood pressure or temperature; it is not lowering the risk of high cholesterol by eating fish or running the risk of getting overweight with a bad diet. It does not sink back in happy exhaustion, unable to move a limb, after a strenuous but exhilarating physical exertion. It cannot sink like a rock into bed at night. It does need a bed or house at all, or umbrellas to protect it from the rain, where in fact it does not need to rain, etc. It is a life without work or rest, sleep or dreaming, without food, shelter, or clothing, marrying or divorcing (Luke 20:35), virtually without everything we know as life – except the powers of relocation and intelligence. The risen body is all agency without flesh, all action without vulnerability, all function without substance, all form without the material conditions of matter, all play without work, all light without density and weight, all life without death. The risen body is freedom from this body of flesh and death. Thus the risen body of Jesus eats without any possibility of being eaten – whether by a hungry animal or merely bitten by an insect or losing blood to a leech. It is a body whose powers of agency have been extended or allowed to run to completion beyond all the [82] limitations imposed by flesh. It instantiates the event of agency, the agency of the event, without restriction, in a body of pure action, vision, light, intelligence and power, in which these qualities, the qualities of these events, are released or put on display, allowed free play in exemplary fashion.

We today cannot avoid noticing how much the risen body attempts to imagine the possibilities for the body that to a certain extent and within limits have been and will be progressively realized by medical science and contemporary bionics and bio-technology – the possibility of moving through the air in flight, curing disease, straightening even replacing limbs and organs. It imagines the body beyond the present, beyond the actual, beyond the possible. It imagines impossible bodies. The point of the multiple bodies that populate the New Testament is the event they harbor, and the event they harbor on my accounting is summarized under the name *metanoetics*, that is, the transformability of body and heart. The risen body, the transformed heart, are symbols of life in the Kingdom, of hearts and bodies that have come under the event of God's rule. They are symbols of a new life, a new being, a new creation, ways of dreaming of a transformed life, of reimagining the event that unfolds in life itself, in bodies still unrisen, in events still unsaid.

Grammatological and Sacred Anarchy

The phenomenology of the risen body is the work of a religious imagination that is structurally parallel to the literary imagination of Lewis Carroll. It visualizes a body that has suffered the event of the divine, a sacred or sacralized body, in the same way that Carroll tries to imagine a body that has been drawn into a world of logical paradoxes, that has suffered the blow of the logical dilemma. It visualizes, embodies, incarnates, or incorporates the effect of this preternatural or extra-natural force upon bodily life, not as way of predicting that such is what could or would actually happen, but as a way to write large, to visualize or illustrate, the events harbored by the body. *Alice* and the New Testament embody events that are there released, magnified, and visualized, the way a Venn diagram visualizes logical relationship of class inclusion and exclusion. When Alice grows alternately taller and shorter she embodies the relativity built into "longer than" and "shorter than" which express the "event" (sense) of magnitude or extension, just the way a "half cup of tea" exploits the ambiguities of language. Carroll's events belong to the logical and grammatological anarchy of words and meaning. They put on visual and narratival display all of the ambiguity, paradoxes, dilemmas, disseminations and undecidabilities of language and logic. The goal is not to make a mockery of language and logic, no more than it is to suggest that this is a world that would or could come about. It is rather to suggest the ambiance of life and language, the ambience of the event. It suggests the flexibility, the undecidability, or what Derrida calls the unprogrammability of life. The rule that logic and language exert over us is not tyrannical, absolute, rigid, or deterministic. It does not close our lives off, determine or predetermine them, or bind them in. On the contrary, it harbors the possibility of the surprise, of the unforeseen twist, of what would otherwise have seemed impossible.

To the logical and grammatological anarchy of Lewis Carroll there corresponds the sacred anarchy of the New Testament, which depicts a world of bodies undergoing no less marvelous metamorphoses. Seen in terms of the event, the point is not to determine whether such bodies enjoyed factual existence or could come about in the future, but to keep the horizon open, to keep open the hope of what is coming, when things will come under the rule of God, which is a Kingdom not of magic but of miracles. Its point is to imagine the ambiance of the life of grace, of God's rule, of life that flows under the rule of God. Then – in the Kingdom – we shall be as if we are angels or risen bodies. We shall pass through solid substances, glow with God's light, move with God's power, see as if with God's eye, act but not suffer, love but not die. Our bodies will be all light, all agency, all action, all power. This is what we envision it is like when God rules. That is what the new time, the new creation, the new being will be like. In a theology of the event, this is not a physical or metaphysical description of what [83] things may be like at some point in the future or some possible future course that things may take. This is not a prediction of future but a portrait of the events that stir and simmer within the name of God. The name of God is not the name of a separate substance, without relation to space and time, but the name of a promise. It is a name that harbors events that are manifest in the body of Jesus, events of unfathomable suffering on the cross, events of weakness, of the power of powerlessness, as well as events of transforming glory, of grace-filled and Spirit-filled life, of light and joy and free play. There, in the rule of God, the events are sacred and the world is one of sacred anarchy, which is summarized under the name of the "Kingdom of God."

What the New Testament and Lewis Carroll describe in common is a certain free play of paradoxical events, of play without weariness or work. In the case of Carroll the events are primarily cast in terms of humor and incongruity while one has to look hard to find any humor in the New Testament. That is perhaps a function of the limits of the imagination of the evangelists or of the historical information we have about Jesus. It is easy to imagine that Jesus who, from all we can tell, could turn a sharp and memorable phrase, would also have been capable of a considerable wit and that he would have used that wit to advantage in his critique of religious authorities. After all, he was criticizing hypocrites and what better weapon for that than satire and wit? Be that as it may, the free play of paradox in the Kingdom is not the play of humor but the play of grace, the grace of marvelous bodily transformations and the grace of love beyond rigid prescriptions, of prodigious mercy and forgiveness.

If the operative figure of forgiveness is release from sin, and if the first bodily figure in which this release of the spirit is displayed is release from paralysis and disease, then its final figure is the risen body, which is release from the deepest and darkest limitation of the flesh. First the frailties of the flesh are mended and healed, then they are abolished altogether, removed in principle. First we are healed, then we are set free from all possible sickness. The risen body restores and even exceeds the pre-lapsarian body. It is the higher counterpart to the mythic bodies of Adam and Eve, which never would have incurred death and illness at all but for their fatal fall, their fateful disobedience. Religious myth describes a condition in which the event is released, and where everything about the name of God is meant to be the occasion of the releasing the event. The risen body is a way to imagine the event even while, in the real world, the only one there is, we must work and suffer, grow ill, and die. Our bodies are frail bearers of the event. The name of God is the name of an event. The Kingdom of God is the name of that scene in which the events that name contains have been released and set free, which is what I have called a sacred anarchy.

Apophasis

The apophatic element inscribed in the body is a function of the event. The event is intrinsically apophatic, or has an intrinsically apophatic element, because the event is inexhaustible, possessed of an unforeseeable future, an inner restlessness and dynamic, in virtue of which the event is never given a final expression in words and never reaches a final realization in things. Whatever is in any way apophatic is so in virtue of the event. If a word or a thing lacked the event, it would instantly volatilize into a completely transparent surface. The opposite of the apophatic is not precisely the overt or manifest but the spent, the exhausted, the used up, something whose string has run out, that has exhausted all its possibilities, whose life is over, even if it is not actually dead. For example, a word in a dead language is a word that only has a past and no future metaphoric deployments, reinvention, and transferences. One could completely spell out its meaning if one had a record of all its past occurrences. A word without an event, where there is no more unused event, is a word that will no longer be redeployed in new and unprecedented circumstances. Or it would be like an extinct species whose evolutionary string has run out. The opposite of the apophatic is whatever is spent, deprived of the future, deprived of the event, deprived of "truth" in the sense of its becoming true.

The event is the ongoing process of becoming – or it is nothing and there is no event. The event [84] is the incessant unfolding or taking shape in words and things – or there is no event. The event has a future; the event is the future; the future of the event is the event of the future – or there is no event.

There is a future I can foresee and plan for and a future I cannot. I can and should plan for my own future, or that of my family, and that is called the future present. This is the future I can reasonably predict – for example, the need to plan for anticipated expenses for my children's education or for my retirement – the future that it is only a matter of time until it becomes present. I would be foolish, improvident, and short-sighted if I did not see this future coming; it is the future that savings banks and life insurance companies depend upon to turn a profit. Here the event follows a more or less predictable course, the future of things that were all along quite possible, and possible to the point of probable, and probable to the point of inevitable, and I am expected to make provisions.

But there is also a future that is radically unforeseeable, that takes me by surprise, that I could not have seen coming, for which I could not have prepared. That is called the "absolute" future, meaning that it is absolved or detached from the ordinary course of things, more free floating and spontaneous, the sphere of improbability, unpredictability, chance – or grace. Whether it be chance or grace the insurance companies call it an "act of God," by which they do not mean to express their piety but to say they do not want to pay for it. This is the sphere in which when something happens we are astonished, reduced to asking, "How was that possible?" The absolute future is *the* impossible, something that shatters the horizon of expectation, of what was assumed to be at all possible.

The absolute future emerges from the deeper recesses of the event, from its most unforeseeable possibilities or, alternately, from the most unforeseeable concatenations of events, where it enters into combinations that are entirely unpredictable. The absolute future arises from the defining feature of the event, its potentiality, its simmering possibilities, its restlessness and stirring, its *dynamis*. Exposure to the absolute future is beyond preparation and exceeds all possible readiness. This radical exposure is well described in James Joyce's neologism "chaosmic." In a chaosmos the event is sustained by the tension between chaos and cosmos, order, and disorder, *arche* and *anarche*, where neither one nor the other can get the upper hand. In a chaosmos, the future is kept open.

The risen body is an apophatic figure, indeed, a figure of the apophatic, a way to imagine or depict it. One of the defining and uncircumventable features of the figure of the risen body is its unrepresentability, its unintelligibility. Every attempt to make sense of the risen body soon enough breaks down, throws up its hands and quickly has recourse to "mystery," one of strong theology's most treasured methodological resources for the conundrums it weaves. The mystery runs afoul of foolishness or simple unintelligibility by trying to transliterate or reify the event into a literally embodied figure. The figure of the risen body is a figure of the unimaginable future. That is why my attention is directed to the event that takes place in this figure and I invoke the principle of transcendental suspicion, which respects the distinction between the event and any literal embodiment of the event, which suspects any identification of the event with a proper name or privileged incarnation.

The apophasis of the body is what the future holds for the body, what it withholds from the body, what the body is capable of, the future we cannot possibly know, foresee or imagine. The final and most radical veil in life, and the scene of the most radical apophasis, is death. Death is at once completely foreseeable, one of our most elemental certitudes, and yet the very definition of the absolutely unforeseeable. It is a common and everyday occurrence, and yet nothing is more unknowable, more unimaginable, more apophatic. This event of absolute unimaginability, the absolute apophatic unimaginability of this event, is the most basic overlapping feature shared by "God" and "death."

In just the way that words have a history, undergo metaphoric transformation and a history of meaning, so bodies have a future and a history. The *risen* body is a figure not of a relative future but an absolute one; it imagines not the restoration of life in this or that order, but the absolute restoration and transformation of life. The risen body attempts the step/not beyond, to [85] go where we cannot go, to make the movement beyond the grave, to pierce the absolutely impenetrable veil, to imagine the future of a body that has no future. In this sense, there is no more perfect and thoroughgoing figure of *the* impossible, of going where you cannot go, of seeing what you cannot see, than the risen body. There is no more striking or powerful apophatic figure, or figure of apophasis, no more powerful way to imagine the possibility of the impossible, than the risen body. It is a concept of the inconceivable, a representation of the unrepresentable, an icon of transcendence. The defining feature of transcendence is movement beyond a horizon or line of sight. The notion of absolute transcendence *stricto sensu* makes no sense since one would always have to specify transcendence beyond *what*. Absolute transcendence makes no more sense than saying "absolutely longer." It is always a relative term, relative to the corresponding sphere of immanence. Transcendence is a movement beyond that is relative to what is not beyond, beyond the known toward the unknown. The transcendent element of bodily life is the extension of the body that we know to a dimension presently forbidden and unknown. It is a figure of the bodily life we can only dream of, for which we pray and weep (or which we fear). "Death" is the absolute barrier, the line beyond which we cannot, dare not cross, from which no one ever returns or reports back – at least, not without some controversy about the reliability of the reports. Just as the many relative limits we face are summarized, recapitulated and absolutized in the limit that is death, so the many versions of transcendence we seek are concentrated, summarized and absolutized in the transcendence of death. Just as life is a movement of transcendence, of rising above the many daily deaths with which we must deal, the transcendence of death itself hovers before us like a ghost, a specter, a spirit – or the dream of a risen body.

In the risen body, relatively accessible and empirical figures of rising again are brought to completion, allowed to run to the end beyond any empirical fulfillment, like a transcendental illusion. There are several figures in which the body "rises" not absolutely but relatively, not from death but from something death-like. The body "rises" each morning from sleep as from a certain sweet and transient death, especially from a deep sleep, untroubled by disturbing dreams or restlessness, when one was "dead to the world." One rises, refreshed, ready for a new day, in a kind of quotidian resurrection from a sleeping non-death. Death is like a deep sleep; a deep sleep is like death. The morning itself, the rising sun, is such a figure for every rising again. The early morning hour combines the quiet of a night that has not yet been disturbed with the light of a new day; it is as quiet as the night, but blessed by the light of day; it is a moment when there is light but we are temporarily spared the assault of daily action, allowed a moment for quiet reflection or silent contemplation. One rises again – from a sick bed, which is a kind of death, which even threatens death, and one says one has one's life back; life has been restored after having been taken away. In a larger sense, we rise again from defeat, from stunning set backs, which are a kind of death, when everything says the cause is dead, but we refuse to give up. We rise from the death of the other, the *dimidium animae meae,* the death of the better half of our souls, when the better half of us dies with the beloved, and we think ourselves quite dead but then must find some way to come back to life. The body rises from the dead when someone dies but we refuse to let their work or their cause die with them, when we resolve to let them live again in us, who have resolved to carry on their work, and everyone who engages in this work can feel the breath of their spirit.

The risen body is a figure of rebirth in the most unqualified and radical sense and as such the figure of the absolute future, which is fundamentally apophatic. The risen body is the most radical way to imagine metamorphosis, *metanoia,* and rebirth. It is the most fundamental way to image a new life, a new creation, a new being, which means to carry the event to a new level of actuality, vitality, energy, and life.

The future is the horizon of new possibilities yet unrealized. As a living being, the body is always rising, again and again, in an upward trajectory turned toward the future, toward rebirth and resurrection. Before it is the name of a purported episode in history, some occurrence confirmed or [86] unconfirmed that is submitted as evidence in apologetics, the risen body is an event, or harbors an event, of rebirth. The future is the horizon of possibilities yet unrealized, of events for which we lack the vocabulary and the grammar, of apophatic bodies, whose comings and overcomings are as yet unimagined. The event is the absolute power of the to-come, of the open-endedness of the future. The risen body is the figure of the step/not beyond, of surpassing the unsurpassable, of surviving death itself, of living on, even though there is death all around. The absolute future stretches out before us like an infinite expanse, beyond the horizon, projecting an unimaginable future. The risen body is a figure of an unfigurable future, of impossible bodies, of the event of the future, of the future of the event, of bodies still unrisen, of events still unsaid.

Notes

[1] See Gilles Deleuze, *The Logic of Sense*, eds. and trans. Mark Lester and Constantine Boundas (New York: Columbia UP, 1990) 28–35.

[2] John D. Caputo, *The Weakness of God: A Theology of the Event* (Bloomington: Indiana UP, 2006) 127–54.

[3] See Deleuze, *The Logic of Sense* 82–93.

[4] Ibid. 149.

6

THE HYPERBOLIZATION OF PHENOMENOLOGY: TWO POSSIBILITIES FOR RELIGION IN RECENT CONTINENTAL PHILOSOPHY

[In *Counter-Experiences: Reading Jean-Luc Marion*, ed. Kevin Hart (Notre Dame: University of Notre Dame Press, 2007), 67–93]

Two Transgressions of Phenomenology

[67] What is phenomenology? Of what is phenomenology capable? Is God, who exceeds all our powers and possibilities, one of phenomenology's possibilities? Is phenomenology capable of including the transcendence of God in the field of phenomenological immanence, of encompassing one who is by definition incomprehensible and unencompassable? Or is that impossible? Alternately, is God, for whom all things are possible, capable of making himself manifest, capable of pitching his tent in the field of phenomenological immanence, or are we prepared to deny God that power in advance? Would the entrance of God into phenomenology be the ultimate transgression, exploding its claim to rigor and violating its philosophical integrity? Or does phenomenology itself, however paradoxically, require transgression in order to be true to itself?

My hypothesis in this essay is that phenomenology has recently become religious and it has become so by a series of transgressions that I identify as movements of "hyperbolization." By this I mean that the religious element enters phenomenology in the form of a transgression or a passage to the limits (*passage aux frontières*), precisely in order to open phenomenology to God, who exceeds its limits. Such a claim leads us inevitably back to Husserl, who first staked out the rigorous limits and scientific possibility of phenomenology, which this process of becoming religious directly threatens, even as it leads forward to the transgressions, which are ways of radicalizing phenomenology and driving it to excess. The idea behind the excess is to pry phenomenology [68] open, even if in opposing directions – to push it beyond itself, but always in such a way as to force it to be true to itself; for left to itself, to its traditional form, phenomenology cannot be what it wants to be. To radicalize it in the name of God in order to be true to God – that is the surprising thing. The excess and the madness are divine, and the violence against phenomenology religious.

I have in mind two transgressions of phenomenology. The first is represented by the work of Derrida, which I will describe here as a "hyperbolization of desire," while the second is represented by the work of what might be called generically the "new phenomenology" in France, spearheaded by Jean-Luc Marion, but including Jean-Louis Chrétien, François Courtine, Michel Henry, and Jean-Yves Lacoste, which constitutes a "hyperbolization of givenness." Both Marion and Derrida think that it is impossible to avoid Husserl even as it is impossible to avoid exceeding Husserl, to avoid going where Husserl dared not go. Far from simply shutting down phenomenology, both regard this impossible excess as positive and constitutive of a more radical phenomenology or post-phenomenology of the impossible. What I am calling Derrida's "hyperbolic desire" I trace back to what Husserl called "intention" carried to infinity, passing to its limits, pushed beyond its limits to an impossible desire beyond any possible fulfillment. In Marion and the new phenomenologists, we see an almost perfectly opposite movement, where the process of what Husserl called fulfillment or givenness is carried to infinity, pushed beyond its limits, to an impossible givenness beyond any possible intention. Here the excess of fulfillment, or the frustration of fulfillment by excess, reveals the defect of intention, which is its tendency to short circuit givenness in advance. Two hyperboles, two transgressions, two ways that God has recently found a voice in continental philosophy: in the one by means of a desire beyond desire for a phenomenon without phenomenality, an appearance constituted by its non-appearance, and in the other, by means of a saturating event, a phenomenon beyond phenomenality, which is constituted by a hyperbole of givenness.

Deconstruction, thus, on my telling, is not irreligious. On the contrary, its hyperbolic desire issues in a poor and naked religion, a certain religion without religion, making a confession without confessional or doctrinal content of the name of God. In the new phenomenology, on the other hand, we encounter a robustly religious and theological religion that makes no apologies about introducing phenomenology to phenomena of an unmistakably confessional, doctrinal or dogmatic-theological kind. Deconstruction circum-fesses its blindness [69] and poverty, while the new phenomenology moves in vicinity of a concrete confessional faith, a determinate and sacramental Christian faith.

Thus, if deconstruction has taken a "religious" turn, this is a religion without theology, representing, let us say, a religious but "a-theological turn," so long as atheology is not confused with atheism and irreligion, while the new phenomenology has taken a decidedly "theological turn," an expression coined by the late Dominique Janicaud as a criticism of the new phenomenology. Janicaud attacks the second but not the first hyperbolization, the transgression of Husserl's stated methodological constraints to be found in the new phenomenology. Janicaud charged that Levinas, Marion and the new phenomenologists violate the strictures of phenomenological method by trying to bootleg the transcendence of God into the immanence of phenomenology. For Janicaud, phenomenology first strayed from the narrow path of phenomenological method in Levinas, who overwhelmed Husserl not with Being (Heidegger) but with the Good and the transcendence of God.[1] What Levinas produced is not a "negative phenomenology" but a baldly metaphysical phenomenology that describes the grey on grey of a *tout autre*, a notion that violates the neutrality of phenomenology towards all matters theological and metaphysical.[2] If in *God without Being*[3] Marion was unapologetically theological, Janicaud concedes that Marion has become more circumspect in his later writings. Thus in *Reduction and Givenness*[4] Marion puts on the airs of having methodological rigor by miming the very idea of a "phenomenological reduction." For Janicaud, Marion describes a pseudo-reduction that culminates in the trick move of the "pure call," where he finally tries to make phenomenology what it cannot be, and to do so under the guise of a rigorous method, for the purely "interlocuted" is too thin and meager a thing to have phenomenological substance.[5] With his confession of confusion and surprise in the experience of the pure call Marion bids farewell to both common sense and phenomenology. The dice of phenomenology are loaded further by Jean-Louis Chrétien,[6] whose search for a body fully manifest and without secret – like a dancer whose body reveals not only its visibility but its invisible soul – culminates in the confession that the body cannot fully reveal itself here on earth, but only in eternity as the resurrected body. That represents a phenomenology which, however edifying, is clearly only for Christians, for no one else can find phenomenology there.[7] It constitutes a phenomenology that is no more phenomenological than Marion's mystifying musings on the "call." These later developments of phenomenology confirm that Husserl did not bracket [70] the transcendence of "God" arbitrarily. In sum, Janicaud concludes, phenomenology and theology are two different things: phenomenology, which has to do with seeing, must recognize its limits within experience and confess that faith, as Luther said, consists in giving oneself over to things we do not see.[8]

Janicaud's critique, which is directed at the transgressions of the new phenomenology, not at Derrida, helps us to focus the issues, which have to do with the nature and extent of the transgressions in which the recent turn to religion is implicated. Are these hyperbolizations necessary, unavoidable, inevitable extensions of phenomenology? Or do they represent a kind of perversion of philosophical inquiry by the perpetual menace of hidden (or not so hidden) theological presuppositions?

Derrida's Hyperbolic Desire for God

If it seems scandalous to link Derrida's name with the name of God, there are also many who will be scandalized by linking him with Husserl and phenomenology. Derrida's early work on Husserl was mistaken as simply a criticism of Husserl's phenomenology, an attempt to debunk phenomenology as something hidebound to the "metaphysics of presence." As usual, nothing is simple in deconstruction and if Derrida was indeed effecting a critical delimitation of Husserl, his intentions were entirely affirmative and productive of something that can pass beyond Husserl only if it first passes through Husserl. Derrida criticized Husserl for concealing what he revealed. That is, Husserl's valorization of presence occludes what Derrida calls an "irreducible non-presence as having a constituting value" which, Derrida maintained, Husserl himself had discovered.[9] So Derrida meant to criticize the metaphysical side of Husserl just in order to emancipate Husserl's more critical, radical and transcendental side, and Derrida's restlessness with phenomenological presence turned out, in the end, to go hand in hand with a deeply religious aspiration for an excess beyond presence. This delimitation centered on four points in which Husserl could be seen to be resisting his own discoveries, repressing or suppressing what he himself had released.

(1) Having shown that "experience" was the naively lived effect of prior and anonymous transcendental syntheses, Husserl remain attached, nonetheless, to an ideal of pure and primordial experience that provides the founding substratum for all conscious life. When Derrida said that there never was such a [71] thing as "perception"[10] and when he voiced his suspicion about "experience," he gave voice to a widespread recognition of a residual naivete in Husserl, an innocence about the structures – linguistic, social, and so on – that lay more deeply imbedded within experience and are constituted as effects of a still more anonymous transcendental, or quasi-transcendental, "field" or operation called *différance*. Perception and experience, Derrida was maintaining, are mediated all the way down, or they are not possible at all.

(2) Although Husserl had unearthed the radical principle of constitution, which means that every unity is the effect of a prior synthesis,[11] and hence that every presence was the effect of a certain re-presenting, reproduction, or

repetition, he nonetheless treated ideal unities of meaning as having an independent priority and validity, a *Geltung*, of their own and on their own. So when Derrida said that repetition produces what it repeats,[12] including ideal objects, where the scope of repetition was widest of all, he was not doing anything other than holding Husserl's hand to the fire of his own discoveries, of just the sort Husserl made in the "Origin of Geometry" when Husserl showed the constitutive role played by language in the production of geometric ideality.[13]

(3) Husserl introduced a fruitful distinction between intention and fulfillment, but he did so in such a way as to subordinate intention to fulfillment, so that fulfillment is the aim and telos of every intention. But this was again to repress what Husserl had discovered, Derrida maintained, which is the capacity of signifiers (intentions) to function in the absence of the signified (fulfillment), for it is the very idea of a signifier that it can get along by itself when what it signifies is not on hand. His "most audacious" reduction, Derrida says, lies in "putting out of play, as 'non-essential components' of expression, the acts of intuitive cognition which fulfill meaning."[14] When it comes to signs, the whole idea of an intention is to function in the absence of fulfillment, and this Derrida applied to intentions generally. Husserl had liberated signifiers from the rule of intuition, unfettered them from the regime of givenness, and given them a new freedom in which they were able to leap ahead where the leaden feet of intuition and fulfillment could not follow, to produce new effects of which fulfillment and intuition could only dream.

(4) Finally, and here Derrida is simply repeating Husserl with a slight difference, Derrida, in the wake of Levinas, seized upon Husserl's description of the analogical apperception of the other ego in the *Fifth Cartesian Meditation*, the constitution of the *tout autre* which Levinas mistakenly rejected because Levinas had confused "constitution" with creation and did not see that here "constitution" [72] here simply means the "confession" that the other is the shore that I cannot reach. The other for Husserl is not one of my possibilities, as Levinas charged, but one of my impossibilities, not a part of my powers but the heart of my powerlessness. What interested Derrida here was once again that Husserl had put his finger on the constitutive value of non-presence and had identified in a paradigmatic way an appearance that was constituted by its non-appearance. For here was an appearance – the other person – who was precisely and in principle constituted by its refusal of appearance. Were the mental life, the "secret" life of the other, on display, were it phenomenalizable, even in principle and as an ideal or "Idea" in the Kantian sense, then the very appearance of the other would disappear and its very phenomenality would

evaporate under the glare of the sun of knowledge, like the moon or the stars at high noon.[15]

The deeply affirmative point of Derrida's critical delimitation of Husserl was lost on all but the most careful readers. For Derrida's public persona was swallowed up by the tempest over the "free play of signifiers" and over the notorious saying that "there is nothing outside the text," which grabbed all the headlines. But that point became unmistakable in Derrida's later writings when he saw fit to characterize deconstruction by resurrecting the word "experience," not of pedestrian presence, but an experience of "the impossible," of an unforeseeable and unimaginable event called the "coming" or "in-coming of the other"(*l'invention de l'autre*). What became clear in the later writings, as I argued in 1997, is that deconstruction is structured like a religion, albeit a religion without religion.[16] The errant play of signifiers is not the last word on deconstruction, or the last move deconstruction has to make, as Mark C. Taylor seemed to think in *Erring*,[17] but only its first word or preliminary move, a preamble to its leap of faith. Like Kant, Derrida has found it necessary to detain the heady rush of knowledge in order to make room for the risky movements of faith, to defer the day of knowledge in order to make room for the anxious (k)night of faith. That is what structures the "desire" of deconstruction and allows the name of God to gain entrance into phenomenology.

What emerged from Derrida's delimitation of Husserl – not to mention of Heidegger, Levinas, and Nietzsche, of Plato and Christian Neoplatonism, and of quite a few others – was a certain quasi-phenomenology of the "messianic," a more austere and minimalist post-phenomenology, turning on the structure of the "to come." Derrida was arguing that phenomenology cannot be what it wants to be, a philosophy of fulfilling intuition and givenness, because any such fulfilling presence turns out to be a function of a constitutive non-presence. [73] But that is not a result that Derrida viewed with nostalgia or regret; it is not a criticism or a negative result at all. By insinuating the constitutive value of the cut of non-presence into what phenomenology called "perception," "presence," and "experience," Derrida meant to cut open phenomenology, and philosophy itself, to the future, to reinscribe phenomenology in a framework of messianic expectation and hope in what is always and structurally to come.

We can read Derrida to be saying that phenomenology can only be true to itself by *confessing* the cut of this desire, by confessing or "circum-fessing,"[18] that it desires what cannot be present, and hence that phenomenology cannot be what it wants to be. This confession opens its horizons by cutting or circumcising them, by turning phenomenology, or "thought" – in a sense that is at least as Kantian as it is Heideggerian – toward the unthinkable to-come.

Deconstruction has to do not with the given or fulfillment but with the cut of what is never-given and which is, however, ever-to-come. In deconstruction, the Messiah is never actually present, never actually comes, and, according to one of the old rabbinic traditions, is never going to show up just because the Messiah represents the very structure of hope and expectation.[19] Deconstruction is structurally advenient or invenient – in the liturgical calendar of its religion it is always advent: always turned towards what is coming, not confined to what is present, with the result that nothing that presents itself in the present can ever measure up to our hope and expectation. The deconstruction of the metaphysics of presence, therefore, belongs not to some sort of skeptical or relativist project of "anything goes," but to an ancient Jewish critique of idols. If in deconstruction one philosophizes with a hammer, it is with the hammer that Moses took to Aaron's golden calf, where the intent is not simply destructive but aimed at inscribing a zone of absolute respect around the *tout autre*. If Derrida underlined the primacy of intentions over givenness, and the capacity of intentions to function in the absence of fulfillment, he did so not out a nihilist love of emptiness but precisely in the name of messianic expectation, which is structurally turned toward what is to come. The religious turn taken in deconstruction turns on this messianic turn, which is turned toward what is always and ever to come, which should never be confused with what is present now or in the future. It has to do not with something that will be present at some distant point in the future, but with the very structure of expectation and hope. The messianic structure of the to come, of the democracy or the justice to come, for example, has a prophetic character, not in the sense that it somehow forecasts something that will be present (as a meteorologist might do), but in the sense that [74] it announces a justice to come that denounces the injustice in what at present calls itself justice or democracy. Like Socrates, it does not know what justice is, but only that nothing present can lay claim to justice. Thus, the effect of the call to come is not to *predict* anything coming but to *intensify* our desire.

That is why I would say that the religious turn taken in deconstruction represents a kind of Jewish Augustinianism, a post-phenomenology of quasi-Augustinian desire, which is the source of my discontent with the way the "atheological" turn is worked out in Mark C. Taylor's *Erring*. Taylor catches the cut of errancy and atheology in Derrida but he misses the messianic desire, the religion without theology, the Jewish-Augustinian man of prayers and tears who kisses his tallith before bed every night. He focuses instead on Derrida's critique of the idols of presence which I take to be purely propaedeutic to what is affirmed in deconstruction. Deconstruction is not the hermeneutics of the death of God, as Taylor claimed, or at least it is not simply that, but rather the hermeneutics of the desire for God. Taylor is an avant-garde thinker who championed deconstruction as atheology but lost interest in this more religious Derrida. He thinks that we should all be analyzing Las Vegas right now and forget Derrida. But this reading of Derrida cuts off in advance a more genuinely religious but non-theological turn Derrida was taking just as *Erring* was published more than twenty years ago now. My *Prayers and Tears* was intended in part to displace this death of God reading of Derrida and replace it with a more religious reading, albeit a religion without religion, based on a much more careful reading of what has been published since the appearance of *Erring*. Taylor would, I suspect, not deny but rather regret the "religious turn" that we are discussing today because he would see this return as a regression. The difference between us is that if Taylor thinks that God is dead, I think that God is the name of what we desire, which is how it functions in Derrida.[20]

On the model I defend, deconstruction is structured as a desire beyond desire, as a desire for God, a *cor inquietum*, a restless heart that desires we do not know quite what, where the name of God is the name of our desire even as it is the best name we have for what we do not know. Contrary to the Heideggerian dogma that the name of God puts questioning to sleep, for Derrida the name of God makes everything questionable, makes everything tremble, for we cannot say what we love when we love our God. *Quid ergo amo cum deum (meum) amo?* (*Conf.* X, 6-7). Whenever we love anything we love our God, but what do we love when we love our God? If indeed we say that God is love, does that mean that love is the best name we have for God, which is what the Scriptures [75] mean, or that God is the best name we have for love, which is what a more secularizing theology might say? Or if we say that God is justice, does that mean that justice is the best name we have for God, which is what the prophets say, or that God is the best name we have for justice, which is what a more secularizing theology might say? In deconstruction there is no resolution of this undecidability. Where would it get the authority to bring that endless fluctuation and translatability to halt? Who would authorize it to make such a pronouncement? Where would one be standing when that resolution was pronounced? In what place or time, speaking in which natural language? The task of deconstruction is not to bring that undecidability to a halt but to maintain it and keep it alive because that is the very condition of a decision, of faith, in which what Climacus called the "poor existing individual" decides in the midst of undecidability. The opposite of undecidability is not a decision, but programmability, which obviates decision by reducing decision to the conclusion of a set of premises.

The religious turn in deconstruction is to make everything turn on desire, and to make desire turn on faith, on what Derrida calls the "passion of non-knowing," which is a movement of a desire for I know not what. True, there is much to be said for a desire that knows what it desires, and for a faith that knows what it believes. We should not underestimate the inestimable roles such faith and such desire play in life. But such faith and desire belong to the realm of what Derrida calls the "future present," the foreseeable and plannable future, which once it rolls around brings us joy by bringing us what we were waiting for and could foresee. But if that is all that life brings, if our life is entirely circumscribed by the foreseeable and plannable, then by and large for Derrida life has been without "event," without a radical surprise, that is to say, by and large life has passed us by. The more radical quest, the more radical desire, the more radical faith is for Derrida the more radically open-ended one in which we do not know what we desire. Not knowing what we desire is constitutive of desire in its deepest sense. If I set out in search of something that I know, I am not lost. But if I cannot say what I desire then I am truly en route. I do not know what I desire even when I say that what I desire is justice, democracy or the gift, for these are but the least bad names at my present disposal for what I desire, the least bad words that have been handed down to me from a past that was never present, from a polyphonic and polyvocal complex that I call by the vast and oversimplifying shorthand name of "tradition." Something stirs in these words, something is astir, something is *promised* in them that [76] is not delivered by them, like intentions that intend more than they give us to see. Our best words are empty intentions, promises that have not and cannot be kept, words that we cherish because of the promises they make but do not quite keep. They are what they are if and only if they are what Husserl calls "inadequate" to themselves, not themselves, not yet, never really, but restless with becoming what they can never be.[21] There is a longing in these words – evoked by what Heidegger would call "the force of the most elemental words in which Dasein expresses itself"[22] – that stretches out beyond their fulfillment in the present and even beyond their intention, since I cannot even be sure that what I desire when I affirm the "democracy to come" will even bear the name of democracy. When some future historian writes the history of what I desire when I speak of a "democracy to come," it will turn out that what we called democracy today was the name of some antecedent state that is linked by a series of historical transformations to successor states for which we have today neither the name nor the concept.

The religious turn taken in deconstruction is the name of the covenant between desire and the promise of what is to come. But who is making that promise? What is her or his or its name? And what is being promised? If I could say that, if I could answer that, that would compromise the promise; it would represent a lack of fidelity to the faith, of loyalty to the desire, of dedication to the quest. It would be already to know or see in advance what is to come, to maintain one's bearings. There is thus in deconstruction a purer faith, a more perfect prayer. But it is purer not because it is more sublime or uncontaminated but because it is more penurious, more at a loss, more distressed, more wounded, more cut and circumcised and less consoled by what Kierkegaard called the "comforts of the universal," the consolation of the "millions" who congratulate themselves on their common confessional faiths. Derrida's "ankhoral" faith or desire arise in the desert of *khōra*, where the name of God is the name of what I desire, where the desire for God is the desire for I do not know quite what.[23]

Hyperbolic Phenomenology

If Derrida's radicalizing reappropriation of Husserl moves in a messianic direction, which maximizes desire and expectation, Marion and the new phenomenologists move Husserl in an equally radical but almost perfectly contrary direction, evolving a phenomenology of an impossible of an almost perfectly [77] opposite kind. Derrida had complained that Husserl's distinction between the empty intending of an object and its fulfilling intuition or givenness turned on an implicit valorizing of fulfillment as the telos of intention, and that needed to be overturned in order to release Husserl's discovery of the virtually unlimited capacity of intention to operate in the absence of fulfillment. But Marion makes the opposite complaint, that Husserl's distinction between the empty intention of an object and its fulfilling intuition or givenness turned on an implicit valorizing of intention which is allowed to set the standards for givenness, and that needs to be overturned in order to release Husserl's discovery of the virtually unlimited power of givenness from its subordination to intention.[24] For Husserl, intention sets the parameters of fulfillment, its standard or high water mark, such that the rush of givenness can rise in principle and at the most to the level of the intention. We intend the whole object but not wholly, *totum non totaliter*, so that the complete fulfillment of the intention is regarded as an Idea in the Kantian sense. Givenness is always the givenness of what is previously intended and there will always be something about what is intended that is not given, a certain excess in the intention that givenness can never reach. But for Marion this ideal limit represents a law for only one class, and that a restricted class, of poor pedestrian phenomena, purely formal or scientific phenomena or the sort of medium sized and quotidian things of everyday experience. If allowed a universal scope or application, Husserl's account would compromise the full power of his own principle of givenness as Husserl stated it in the principle of all principles (*Ideas I, §24*), which is to take what is given just insofar as it is given and in just the way that it is given, and to do so without prescribing any limits for it in advance. Hence Marion explores the provocative and ingenious post-Husserlian possibility of a hyperbolic givenness that exceeds intention, that overflows the high water mark of intention, or as Marion says that "saturates" the intention with a flood of givenness.[25] I think that we will see that what is also — dare I say ultimately? — at stake for Marion is a theological issue, nothing less than a non-correlational *theo*logy such as one finds in Barth and von Balthasar, where God is allowed to be God on God's own terms, without submitting God to prior conditions of possibility, where *theo*logy is confessed to be *God*'s word about God, not our word (theo*logy*). Thus these two possibilities for religion in recent phenomenology also represent two possibilities for theology.

That makes for two alternate and even contrary phenomenologies — or two post- or quasi-phenomenologies — of the impossible. In deconstruction, the [78] experience of the impossible means that we have maximized intention and unfettered it from fulfillment, allowing intention an infinite reach, beyond the possible to the unforeseeable *tout autre*. Deconstruction turns on an intention that can never be fulfilled, on a gift that never can be given, where presence, intuition and givenness are constantly being deferred and detained, where intention is permanently haunted by an ungivable givenness. That does not frustrate desire but it is constitutive of the very structure of desire. The very idea of this intention is that it intends what will never be given, *can* never be given, its givenness being impossible, *the* impossible, which we always intend and never meet, which we always desire but never have.[26] For Marion, on the other hand, Husserl is pushed in the direction of a hyperbolic givenness. Here the impossible is the givenness that saturates intention,[27] where what is intended is never adequate to what is given, where the horizon of intentional expectation is not fulfilled, not from defect but from excess, because it is shattered or breached. Fulfillment is frustrated not because intention is cut off from intuition but because intention is flooded with a givenness that it cannot contain or intend. Here, *the* impossible is the unimaginable, unforeseeable, inconceivable, uncontainable givenness with which we are actually visited, where the best that the understanding can report of its experience is to produce in a stammer the halting concept of that than which no greater can be conceived.[28] Hence instead of the desert and the blindness of faith, Marion speaks of the brilliance of transfiguration, the blindness of bedazzling glory, and instead of messianic desire Marion describes the gift of messianic advent, the flesh of the Messiah, the Christ, the Anointed One, whose coming among us is described in the Scriptures.

Marion describes a two-fold process of saturation, where saturation is said to be a process of maximization, of raising the level of givenness to a "maximum" or "apex."[29] In contrast to the "poor" or common place phenomena described in conventional Husserlian phenomenology, where the measure of givenness is taken by intention or signification and givenness never measures up to the intention, the saturated phenomenon of the first order reverses the process and floods intention with a givenness that the intention cannot accommodate. Marion describes four types or classes of such phenomena – events, flesh, the idol and the icon – a categorization that he has come up with by way of a rather imaginative stretch of the four classes of categories of the understanding in Kant's first *Critique*. On Marion's view, the subject is inundated in four ways by a flood of givenness that the intentional act cannot contain: (1) When it is caught up in the midst of an uncontainable and [79] incomprehensible historical event (e.g., September 11), one that is so latent with sense that there is no privileged perspective from which it can be seen or put in perspective; (2) in the movements of pleasure or the suffering of the flesh (a recent work is entitled *The Erotic Phenomenon*)[30] where, as in the extremes of pain or of pleasure, our conceptual powers are inundated; (3) in the work of art whose color, sound or form overwhelms the subject like an idol; (4) in the invisible face of the visible other, which reverses the intentional gaze.[31]

But over and beyond these saturated phenomena of the first order, Marion posits – in a certain sense he hypothesizes – a higher order of saturation, in which a phenomenon gives itself by revealing itself, which is the saturated phenomenon of "revelation." This is said to be saturation raised to the second degree, where the saturation is re-saturated. The phenomenon of revelation, or second order saturation, is defined by the confluence or concentration of all four kinds of first order saturation (quantity, quality, modality and relation; event, idol, flesh and icon) in one single phenomenon, thereby constituting a fifth form of saturation, a saturation of saturation, a parodox of paradoxes, the possibility of the impossible.[32] In an important footnote that seems like it belongs in the text, this is described as "revelation" with a small "r," as a mere phenomenological possibility: were there to be a revelation, it would be of just this sort (*quid sit*). But it is not the province of phenomenology to say whether there is an actual fact of "Revelation," an historically actual Revelation (*an sit*), where this time the word is capitalized.[33] Phenomenology has to do with essence; theology with existence. For example, if God reveals or has revealed himself – let us say, in history or in mystical experience – it would be by means of a saturated phenomenon of the second order. But this is a matter for theology alone to determine and strictly in the terms of theology. But that does not mean for just any theology, but rather for rigorously non-correlational theologies, like that of Karl Barth and Hans Urs von Balthasar, which are better at finding the fact of Revelation, but not for correlational theologies like Rahner and Bultmann, which compromise the revelatory in Revelation by prescribing antecedent conditions for the hearing of the Word.

As an example of such a pure possibility, he chooses the phenomenon of Christ revealed in the New Testament. It is worth noting that, in principle, other phenomena could have been chosen – the life of the Buddha, say, or perhaps literary phenomena – because the requirement is purely formal, viz., that in a saturated phenomenon of the second order all four features are combined in one.[34] The Christ is, according to quantity the surprising [80] "event" or astonishing advent of the one who is to come; according to quality, he overwhelms what the phenomenological gaze can bear – "his clothes became resplendent, excessively white" (Mark 9:3). In terms of relation, the Christ is an "absolute" phenomenon, because the flesh of Christ annuls every mundane horizon of containment and expectation; and finally, in terms of modality, the Christ is an irregardable icon, the counter-gaze which inverts my gaze, who regards me and constitutes me as witness and disciple, while I am unable to constitute him.

All this is said within the framework of a phenomenological hypothesis or sketch, an uncapitalized *r*evelation as a pure phenomenological possibility. Phenomenological intuition – like historical or scholarly research – does not have the resources or the authority to determine whether there are any transfigured bodies or bodies risen from the dead, the phenomena described in the New Testament, as matters of historical *fact*, in *actuality*. Phenomenology is restricted to "the reduced immanence of givenness," and cannot "judge its actual manifestation or ontic status."[35] Thus Revelation has to do with being, actuality, ontic status – a surprising intrusion of the language of *being* into the saturated phenomenon *par excellence*, where one is supposedly sovereignly free from the conditions of being. In the most classically Husserlian terms, phenomenology brackets existence in order to intuit essence.

The shift to existence, to actual Revelation, is made by shifting from a phenomenological to a theological attitude, from the field of immanent givenness to that of faith. But this precaution, which prevents the transformation of phenomenology into theology, is not without another danger: not the theologization of phenomenology (of which Janicaud warns), but the phenomenologization of theology.[36] In the end, one is struck by the effect of this analysis not so much on phenomenology but on theology, which, having been loosened from its moorings in speculative metaphysics or dogmatic onto-theology, is then transformed from a speculative to a phenomenological discipline. Uncapitalized revelation is the province of a properly philosophical phenomenology, which, unable to experience the actuality of the risen Christ, which is off limits to it, can at least delineate its essential possibility. Were there to be a Resurrection or a Transfiguration, Marion is saying, it would have to be of the following sort: certain transfiguring and hyperbolic events would occur that would intensify the structures of quantity, quality, relation and modality, and concentrate them into a single phenomenon, raising them up to a second level of just this sort. First order phenomenology then leads up to the possibility of second order saturated phenomenon on strictly phenomenological grounds. One [81] is thereby led by the hand of phenomenology to the threshold of theology, which can be crossed only by faith and would represent, if confirmed in actuality, an existential and theological "crowning" of phenomenology by actualizing an essential possibility of which phenomenology itself is not capable. Theology would be what phenomenology wants to be but cannot attain. Without confusing itself with theology, and modestly confessing its own limits, phenomenological revelation points to the possibility of a theological Revelation. Without confusing itself with a purely natural phenomenology, a Revealed theology would take over the controls of phenomenology and describe phenomena of maximum paradoxicality and hyper-phenomenality. One might think of Marion as having written, in effect, a kind of phenomenological counterpart to Maritain's classic *Les dégrées du savoir,* which charted an analogous course from (Thomistic) metaphysics to mysticism to the beatific vision. But with Marion the first philosophy is phenomenology, not metaphysics, and the concern is not with the degrees of knowledge but with the degrees of givenness, *Les dégrées de la donation.*

On Marion's telling, Revealed theology has to do not with an essential but with an existential order, with phenomena of an ontically actual Revelation, e.g., the hyper-experiences the apostles have of the transfigured body of Jesus or the post-Easter appearances of the risen Jesus. To be dazzled by the brilliance of Van Gogh is already an excess, but to be dazzled by the brilliance of the transfigured Jesus, is to bedazzle that bedazzlement all over again, to exceed that excess, representing a kind of saturation of saturation. One thus "exceeds the very concept of maximum" to a "givenness without reserve."[37] This would mean, for example, that beyond the saturation undergone in contemplating a great painting, vision is further saturated and pushed beyond itself to the point of a breakdown of vision, to what we might call a kind of hyper-blindness, a hyperbolic blindness from excess not defect, becoming a sight that cannot see because it is blinded by a dazzling light that exceeds its limits. There is no object given to a subject to see or intuit, no being given to Dasein to be comprehended within the horizon of Being, but rather an excess of givenness that pushes us past intuition, past the subject and past Dasein. Indeed, so true is this that the very idea of such a phenomenon would be undone if it were *not* bedazzling, for its very idea is to be that than which nothing more manifest can be given.

In the language of traditional philosophy, one is reminded of the allegory of the cave, where one moves, to pursue an analogy, from the common law [82] phenomena of sensible things, to the saturating phenomena of the pure forms, to the excess of the good, beyond being, which cannot be beheld directly but only in its effects, where there is a kind of hyperbolic blindness in the hyper-vision of the *hyperousios,* in which the eminence of the forms is concentrated. But the more pertinent comparison is to the language of traditional theology, where the transition from the pure phenomenological possibility of revelation to the actuality of Revelation seems to correspond to the natural and supernatural orders. Uncapitalized revelation is accessible in principle to all without the aid of grace and functions as a kind of preamble to faith, while Revelation is accessible only in and through the gift of supernatural faith, which is a special grace given by God. As grace crowns and perfects nature, grace perfects phenomenology; the wounded vision of phenomenology is perfected by the aid of supernatural faith.

Then what are we to make of Janicaud's objections? They are largely unjustified once one takes into account Marion's precautions about revelation as a possibility and Revelation as an actuality. When indeed Marion does tread upon ground that phenomenology as such and of itself dare not approach – the transfigured body of Christ, resurrected bodies, etc. – he does so with methodological consciousness of the limits of unaided phenomenological experience, knowing full well that phenomenology and theology belong to two different orders, which meets Janicaud's objections. Nor as a phenomenological matter is there anything improper about the confession of confusion and bedazzlement that Marion makes in his phenomenology of the saturated phenomenon. There are comparable phenomena of confusion in phenomenology's history – the account of the nothingness of *Angst* in *Being and Time*, or of nausea in Sartre, or of the *il y a* in Levinas, or even, for that matter, of the destructability (the de-constitutability) of the natural world in *Ideas I*. The commitment of phenomenology to the clear description of phenomena does not guarantee that all the phenomena to be described are clear. One can clearly articulate how something is unclear, in which case the unclarity would be essential to the act.

I do not think that it is phenomenology but rather theology that is at stake here. As I have said, and as Marion himself says in that important footnote mentioned above, the non-correlational theologies of Barth and von Balthasar are closer to *theo*logical Revelation than those of Bultmann and Rahner, where a correlational theo*logy* submits Revelation to anterior conditions. I do not find what Janicaud finds, that phenomenology has been hi-jacked by theology, [83] but almost the contrary, that theology has been invaded by phenomenology and that it is theology that suffers a distortion. Now Marion recognizes that the phenomenological turn of theology, rather than Janicaud's fear about the theological turn of phenomenology, is the truer "danger" in all this.[38] The danger is that theology would be taken over by a certain sort of phenomenology, one that has itself been overrun by a principle of givenness that has gone out of control. I say this for the following reason.

Marion thinks that one must either admit the paradox of the saturated phenomenon, or one cuts off the possibility of Revelation in advance on the basis of preconceived philosophical conditions or prejudices – e.g., naturalistic and reductionistic ideas about what is possible – about the limits of phenomenality. What would be more astonishing, Marion asks, that God would have the right to inscribe himself within phenomenality or that we should stubbornly refuse God this right?[39] Capitalized Revelation means that God can enter the world unconditionally and on his own terms. So one is either for the saturated phenomenon or against God's Revelation. (One detects a certain imposition of conditions here in the manner of correlational theology: were there to be a Revelation, it would have to be of just this sort; the condition is that it be unconditionally given.) But there is a third possibility, that one might be just as enthusiastic about Revelation as Marion but have a rather different idea of it than he does, viz., a correlationist idea rather than an ultra-conservative literalism about the text of the New Testament. So the real either/or is to be cast as a choice not between the saturated phenomenon and God, but between two ways of doing theology, either for Barth/von Balthasar or for Bultmann/Rahner – or someone like Schillebeeckx.)

One does not have far to look to see what sort of scriptural hermeneutics lies behind Marion's position, which appears committed to a kind of historical literalism about the events of the New Testament. Events that many, dare I say most, New Testament scholars – like Schillebeeckz, a decidedly correlationalist theologian – regard as "later theological reflections" or expressions of faith by a later community of faith – namely, that God was with Jesus in a preeminent way – are treated by Marion as having *onto-phenomenological status*, as if they were literal, actual and ontical occurrences that true believers would have witnessed. Suddenly the language of *sans l'être* becomes quite *ontic* and existential. In the classical manner of negative theology, these phenomena beyond or without being thus acquire a kind of *hyper-entitative* or *hyper-ousiological* status. Thus the hyperbolization of givenness is implicated in a hyperbolization [84] of being, in an historically actual or ontical Revelation of certain existential hyper-events. This is rather like, indeed it is exactly like, giving angels ontical or hyper-ontical – and therefore an onto-phenomenological – status, instead of treating them as literary vehicles. Rather than treating angels as elements of a narrative, one treats them as entities or hyper-entities, forcing theology to come up with some sort of hyper-phenomenology of angelic visitations that would account for the possibility of close encounters of a phenomenological kind, experiences of hyper-beings of dazzling phenomenality sent to us on divine missions. In an ultra-traditional manner, Marion regards narratives written by non-eye witnesses many years after the death of Jesus in order to give expression to their faith as if they described historical actualities, hyper-entities, that were experienced as hyper-events by the faithful.[40]

Let us consider more closely what sort of phenomena they would be. In the Transfiguration narrative, the apostles experienced the unbleachable "whiteness" of the clothes worn by the transfigured body of Christ (Mark 9:3). This is not the normally visible white of the order of commonplace phenomena like a white sheet but a white of surpassing intensity. Nor could this white have been recorded by a high tech video camera whose lenses could tolerate higher intensities than can the human eye, had one been available at the time, because a mechanical instrument cannot be outfitted with theological faith. No more than the heavenly voice that says "This is my beloved son" (Luke 9:34-35) could have been detected by a super-sensitive microphone. Such devices would experience only static, however high tech they may be. If the whiteness of the garment worn by the transfigured Christ is neither the white of commonplace phenomena nor of measurable scientific objects, neither is it the exquisite use of white by a master painter who uses a white that seems to be not of this world to portray the risen Christ's Resurrection,[41] which is a saturated phenomenon of the first order. It is rather a white that dazzles and confuses the senses in a still higher order, where all four features of saturated phenomena of the first order are concentrated in one phenomenon, a white of such extreme and "unbearable" intensity that the eye is blinded by the excess and brilliance of light,[42] so that one sees without sight. Intuition and fulfillment break down, breached by saturation. These are phenomena beyond phenomena, hyperbolic phenomenological events, that leave phenomenology bedazzled and brought to a halt, having reached the *ne plus ultra* of its own order of natural revelation.

At this point, phenomenology passes the baton to faith; only faith can go farther; only the eyes of faith can interpret. Here, then, Marion introduces a [85] theological hermeneutic action, let us say, a theologico-hermeneutical "as" in virtue of which an otherwise confusing phenomenon is taken as an event of Revelation. But it is at just this point, I think, that Marion's account is overtaken by a kind of theological magical realism (a *theo*logical magical realism). By this I mean a method that treats sacred narratives and narrative vehicles as intensified and bedazzling hyper-realities that have acquired existential onto-phenomenological status. This theological magical realism intensifies narratival elements into super-events, with the result that commonplace realities like garments and voices are transformed into a bedazzling hyper-realities. The result is a kind of mythological onto-phenomenology of transfigured bodies, risen bodies, dazzling garments and the like phenomena taken from the extraordinary narratives of the New Testament. I am reminded of Kierkegaard's warning that there would be nothing in the smile of the knight of faith, no "bit of heterogeneous optical telegraphy" that would betray the infinite, no "crack through which the infinite would peek."[43] It would be paganism to think that the divinity of Jesus would have been detectible, as if there were something in the bearing of Jesus, or the look in his eye, that suggests the divinity. The Revelation is revelation *that* Jesus is the anointed one, not a Revelation *of* the divinity, which no one can see and still live. The divinity is a matter of faith. By faith, we are given to believe *that* Jesus is divine, to intend Jesus as divine, but the divinity is not itself *given*. Even if you were standing right beside Jesus you would not see the divinity unless you believed it; and if you believed it, that is because you would not see it. You would believe it even though, indeed in spite of the fact, that you did not see it, which is what faith means. Events like the early Christian experience of the resurrection belong to a phenomenology not of the saturated phenomena but to that of invisible *credibility*, to the sphere of what eye has not seen nor ear heard.

Let us pursue this point by distinguishing, in Kierkegaardian fashion, the experience of the first generation, the first followers of "The Way," and the experience of later generations. The first generation must have had an experience of the risen Jesus, which can alone explain what got "the Way" underway. If so, this experience admits and demands a phenomenology. But this would surely be a phenomenology of the Spirit, not in the Hegelian sense, but in the sense of being filled with the Holy Spirit, which means of being filled with faith in one who is in some sense still appearing although he has disappeared, who in some sense still lives on in spite of his dying, who is present somehow in spite of his absence. Such filling is not the fulfillment of givenness but the [86] fullness of the living faith/intention. As the disciples reassembled after the crucifixion they began to experience the Spirit in their midst, wherever two or three were gathered together in his name, and a community of faith was gathered together, nourished by the faith that God somehow lived in Jesus even as Jesus now somehow lives with God, which they expressed in the form of the sacred narratives. The narratives would then express what the community came to believe later about who Jesus was before his death; they would express what the first followers came to believe, how they came to interpret his life and death, in retrospect, after his life and death among them had transpired. Presumably anyone who met Jesus in the flesh would have been touched by his presence in a special way; but that is a saturated phenomenon of a purely natural order, viz., of human charisma, at most an iconic experience, but not of divinity. The elevation of that purely human experience to an experience of Revelation would not transpire *on the level of saturating givenness but rather on the level of faith*, of a messianic affirmation of Jesus who was born, had died and who would come again, an affirmation made in the interim time, in a sphere where givenness gives out, for this is revealed, not by "flesh and blood" but by the Father in heaven (Matt. 16:17).

The subsequent generations do not experience Jesus in the flesh, but they experience the memory of Jesus preserved in these narratives and in the *ecclesia* gathered around them. The narratives of the extraordinary events do indeed have a saturating element – as *narratives*. These are profound and moving narratives in world literature for anyone who can read, which is a saturated phenomenon of a literary order, which exhausts their intuitive content. But if they touch the lives of those who belong to the community of believers, those for whom these are the founding narratives, in a special or higher way, they do so *just because and only because of the community's faith, not because of their phenomenal content*. The sacred stories are actualized or fulfilled when they are repeated for the faithful in a life transforming way in the context of faithful preaching and reading. But that existential actualization is not to be confused with the hyperbolic givenness of the narratival elements in higher order saturated phenomena.

The narrative of the transfigured body of Christ can transfigure the lives of the believers who accept it, or who at least accept its point, on faith. New Testament scholars like Schillebeeckx treat the story of the transfigured body of Christ as a later narratival expression of a faith in the preeminent and transfiguring way God was with Jesus during his lifetime. The great religious

[87] narratives, Christian and non-Christian, are what Gadamer would call "classics" of the world religions and as such they represent saturated phenomenon of world literature, that is, stories for which we have no adequate concept. There are many such classics in many different traditions. But to be raised beyond that to the level of an actual religious Revelation, requires *faith* in what the narrative is getting at, which is something over and over and above their intuitive or saturating content, which would be the same for believers and non-believers. In faith, the sacred narrative is read or heard and made one's own in a special way that goes beyond what is given. Faith supplies a particular hermeneutic take, an interpretive slant, an *Auffassung*, that allows the believer to intend something that is precisely *not* given, not properly or strictly *given*, but taken on faith. But the hermeneutic reading does not remove the veil of faith in the point of the narrative, which is an intention without givenness.

The first generation stood shoulder to shoulder with Jesus but they accepted him only through faith; the later generation has preserved his memory in the gospels and the church, but they too accepted him only through faith. As Climacus says, both are on equal ground. Neither has the advantage. Both face the same decision; both must effect the same absolute relation, which turns on faith.[44] Now there is a phenomenology here, even a hyberbolic phenomenology, but it is a phenomenology of *faith*, which is an excess in the order of *intention* beyond fulfillment, of how to take or mean something which is only given in part, and not one of saturating *givenness*, which is the same for believers and non-believers, otherwise it is not a phenomenological datum. Doubting Thomas is taken to task precisely for taking his stand with givenness and not being content with unfulfilled intentions. There is, to be sure, a phenomenological *surplus* in faith, but the surplus is to affirm more than one is given to see, to affirm what one is not given to see, which is what makes faith blessed. Jesus opposes the *oligopistoi* – those of *little faith* – not to those who see much but to those whose *faith* is great. The excess and the greatness belong to the gift of faith, which is a matter of believing, which is a matter of intending *without* givenness.

To a certain extent Marion concedes this point, just when he introduces the hermeneutic of faith in order to make room for treating saturated phenomena of the second order as matters of Revelation. But at that point his analysis finds itself resubmitted to the most classical Husserlian constraints in which givenness falls short of intention and swings him over to the side of the hyperbolization of intention. Put in Husserlian terms, the gift of faith is a gift that [88] belongs not to the order of givenness but to the order of intention, for the believers are given to believe what they are not given to see, what they cannot see, which is not given but believed. Not every gift has to do with givenness; for faith is a gift in the order of intention, meaning or signification. The hermeneutic slant provided by faith supplies what Husserl would call an "*Auffassung*" [taking up (as)], an interpretive reading or a grasping of something given as such and such, one that is not fully or adequately confirmed but only "in part [*ek merous*]" (I Cor.13:9) or, as Husserl would say, inadequately given. What is given as a saturated phenomenon is bedazzling and not intended clearly; what is intended through the hermeneutic act of faith is the divinity, which is not given or confirmed but believed. Something is given, I know not what, that is intended *as* a presence of the risen Jesus in the community; it could also be intended *as* an hallucination, if one does not have faith or has a different faith. In terms of givenness, faith is an unfulfilled or only partially fulfilled intention, which is why the faith-intention will be given up later on when it is completely filled and passes over into knowledge. As Paul says to the Corinthians, what is seen by faith is seen only "in part," through a veil and darkly; "but when the complete (*to telion*) comes, the partial will come to an end" (I Cor. 13:8-13). Then faith will be no more. *Faith is not a saturated givenness but an intending that ventures out beyond the given to take the given as something that it is not fully given as.*

Marion has successfully described saturated phenomena on the natural order, but he has failed to establish that the phenomena of Revelation are marked by an excess of givenness beyond intention instead of intention beyond givenness. Revelation turns on the interpretive act of faith, of an intensification of the interpretive intention, not on an intensified or redoubled saturation of givenness. The movement to Revelation is effected by means of an interpretive intention, which outstrips what is strictly given. If it belongs anywhere, what Marion calls the "event of Revelation" as a saturated phenomenon belongs to a theology of glory, "when the complete comes," which is what medieval theology calls the beatific vision. But here and now, *in hoc statu vitae*, there is faith, not glory, and faith means being ready, stretching out intentionally toward a completion that is not yet given, that has not yet come. In my view, the hyperbolic phenomenology of the saturated phenomenon par excellence is a brilliant but failed experiment or, at least, let us say, it is a hasty or precipitous one. It is perhaps a suitable way to explain how things will be *then*, when faith is no more, not *now*, when things are given only in part, through a [89] glass and darkly. It is an hypothesis better fit for explaining the possibility not of historical Revelation but of post-historical, supra-historical life in eternity. But in the meantime, on the way from here to eternity, we are compelled to make a more circumspect use of phenomenology *in theology*. The excess in faith is not that of phenomena saturated or doubly saturated with plenitudinous givenness but of venturing out beyond the limits of givenness into deeper and uncharted seas, out upon the sixty thousand fathoms as Kierkegaard used to say. Blessed are those who believe what they do not see, who hope against hope when all seems hopeless, and who love those who do not seem lovable, which from a Husserlian point of view means blessed are those can sustain their intentional acts of faith and hope and love, which are only fulfilled in part while waiting for them to be filled completely, which is akin to what Derrida calls "desire beyond desire."

Conclusions, Confessions

If at the crucial point, in the transition to the order of Revelation, the phenomenology of saturated phenomena has recourse to faith, and if faith belongs to the order of intention not of givenness, what then finally is the difference between the hyperbole of desire and the hyperbole of givenness? What is the difference between Derrida's hyperbolic faith, his more desert like and pure messianic circumfessional faith, and Marion's more robustly biblical confession of faith, if both confessions in the end turn on faith, and faith is an intention that is short on fulfillment? I have not differentiated these two hyperbolizations of phenomenology as religious and anti-religious, but as two forms of religion, two ways for phenomenology to become religious, two different possibilities for religion latent in phenomenology. In Derrida's case we have to do with a more indeterminate and a destinerrant faith, a quest more open-ended and lost, a more desert-like "ankhoral" desire, while in Marion faith is nourished in the lush growth of determinate tradition, more anchored than ankhoral. This is the difference between the faith and desire of what in Derrida's own vocabulary is called an indeterminate messianicity and the faith and desire of a concrete messianism.

We might even risk saying that it comes down to the difference between a *theological* and an *atheological* religion, which are to be construed as two different possibilities for *religion* in phenomenology today, the one with and the [90] other without attachment to a determinate theological tradition. The hyperbolization of phenomenology undertaken in Marion's affirmation of the impossible is nourished by an identifiable, historical theology, highly sacramental and incarnational and very non-correlational. But Derrida's is a religion without religion, that is, a religious desire without a theology, a religious desire whose terms cannot be fixed within the framework of a determinate and historical theological tradition, a radical quest and questioning for something, it does not know quite what. Marion's confession is deeply confessional, rooted in a Catholic-Christian profession of faith, in a community and a liturgy, in sacred texts and a *traditio*. Derrida's is deeply circum-fessional, cut off from determinate professions of faith, wary of community, somewhat more lost, so that Derrida does not quite know what he professes when he circum-fesses his faith. Derrida's words are more cut and wounded, which does not count against his religion, for that, according to Jean-Louis Chrétien, is the very definition of a prayer, and prayer is the very stuff of religion.[45]

Derrida says of himself that "I quite rightly pass for an atheist."[46] When asked why he does not just say he *is* an atheist, he responds that he does not *know* whether he is one, whether he is *one*, for there are several voices within him and they do not give one another any rest. That, I think, is also a fitting formula for the believer. Did not Johannes Climacus decline to say that he *is* a Christian, on the ground that he could at most lay claim to *becoming* one? To quite rightly pass for this or that, while acknowledging the incessant *sic et non* that goes on within us all – what is that if not the very heart of faith, the very heart of the Augustinian *cor inquietum* that, in several different forms, is echoing down the corridors of continental philosophy today?

* * *

The first version of this paper was delivered at a December 2002 symposium of the American Philosophical Association at the invitation of Professor Merold Westphal, and it has profited greatly from the criticisms Merold has made of it – on the sound phenomenological principle he follows that no good deed should go unpunished. See Merold Westphal, "Transfiguration as Saturated Phenomenon," *Journal of Philosophy and Scripture* 1, no. 1 (Fall 2003). Available at www.philosophyandscripture.org

Notes

[1] Dominique Janicaud, "The Theological Turn of French Phenomenology," in *Phenomenology and the "Theological Turn": The French Debate*, ed Jean-François Courtine, trans. Bernard G. Prusak (New York: Fordham University Press, 2000), 39. This is an extremely useful volume for our purposes as it contains papers by Marion, [91] Jean-Louis Chrétien, Michel Henry, and Paul Ricoeur, all of which address Janicaud's critique, directly or indirectly.

[2] Janicaud, 46.

[3] Jean-Luc Marion, *God Without Being*, trans. Thomas A. Carlson (Chicago: University of Chicago Press, 1991).

[4] Jean-Luc Marion, *Reduction and Givenness: Investigations of Husserl, Heidegger, and Phenomenology*, trans. Thomas A. Carlson (Evanston: Northwestern University Press, 1998).

[5] Janicaud, "Theological Turn of French Phenomenology," 62.

[6] See Jean-Louis Chrétien, "The Wounded Word," in *Phenomenology and the "Theological Turn,"* 147–75; *The Unforgettable and the Unhoped For*, trans. Jeffrey Bloechl (New York: Fordham University Press, 2002); *Hand to Hand*, trans. Stephen Lewis (New York: Fordham University

Press, 2003); *The Call and the Response*, trans. Anne Davenport (New York: Fordham University Press, 2004).
   [7] Janicaud, "Theological Turn of French Phenomenology," 101-103.
   [8] Ibid., 66–68.
   [9] Jacques Derrida, *Speech and Phenomena and Other Essays on Husserl's Theory of Signs*, trans. David Allison (Evanston: Northwestern University Press, 1973), 6.
   [10] Ibid., 103.
   [11] Edmund Husserl, *Cartesian Mediations: An Introduction to Phenomenology*, trans. Dorian Cairns (Dordrecht: Kluwer Academic Publishers, 1995), 40–41.
   [12] Derrida, Speech and Phenomena, 52.
   [13] Edmund Husserl, "The Origin of Geometry," in *The Crisis of European Sciences and Transcendental: An Introduction to Phenomenological Philosophy*, trans. David Carr (Evanston: Northwestern University Press, 1970).
   [14] Derrida, *Speech and Phenomena*, 90.
   [15] See Jacques Derrida, "Violence and Metaphysics," in *Writing and Difference*, trans. Alan Bass (Chicago: University of Chicago Press, 1978). Derrida sided with Husserl against Levinas on this point but he criticized both for their "humanism," that is for not seeing that *tout autre est tout autre*, that every other enjoys such singularity and transcendence, which is a phenomenon that Duns Scotus had called *haecceitas*.
   [16] See John D. Caputo, *The Prayers and Tears of Jacques Derrida: Religion without Religion*, (Bloomington: Indiana University Press, 1997) for a more detailed and patient unpacking of a certain religious – if atheological – turn in deconstruction.
   [17] Mark C. Taylor, *Erring: A Postmodern A/Theology* (Chicago: University of Chicago Press, Chicago, 1984).
   [18] I will make use throughout of Derrida's quasi-Jewish adaptation of Augustine's "confessions" as a circumcisional "circum-fession." See "Circumfession: Fifty-nine Periods and Periphrases," in Geoffrey Bennington and Jacques Derrida, *Jacques Derrida* (Chicago: University of Chicago Press, 1993). See Caputo, *Prayers and Tears*, 281ff.
   [19] For a fuller account of the messianic, see *Deconstruction in a Nutshell: A Conversation with Jacques Derrida*, ed. with a commentary by John D. Caputo (New York: Fordham University Press, 1997), chap. 6.
   [92] [20] See Caputo, *Prayers and Tears*, 14; and see my review of *Erring* in *Man and World*, 21 (1988): 107–14. Reproduced in John D. Caputo, *Collected Philosophical and Theological Papers*, Volume 2, *1986–1996: Hermeneutics and Deconstruction*, 397–404.
   [21] See Jacques Derrida, *Voyous* (Paris: Galilée, 2003), 62–63.
   [22] Martin Heidegger, *Being and Time*, trans. Edward Robinson and John Macquarie (New York: Harper & Row, 1962), 262.
   [23] For a fuller account of Derrida's experience of faith and desire, see my treatment of his "prayer" in "Shedding Tears Beyond Being: Derrida's Experience of Prayer," *Augustine and Post modernism: Confessions and Circumfession*, eds. John D. Caputo and Michael Scanlon (Bloomington: Indiana University Press, 2005), 95–114.
   [24] That is the argument of *Reduction and Givenness*.
   [25] See Marion, "The Saturated Phenomenon," in *Phenomenology and the "Theological Turn*," 176–216.
   [26] One proceeds along a shattered horizon of expectation and foreseeability, where the horizon of the future-present, of the "possible" has been breached. Here one reaches the limits of *voir, avoir, savoir, s'avoir* – let us say, of seeing, securing, savvy and self-possession – in a movement that confesses its cut, that circum-fesses its "blindness" and need for faith, *il faut croire*.

²⁷ See Marion, "The Saturated Phenomenon," *Phenomenology and the "Theological Turn,"* 76–216.

²⁸ In Derrida, we have no concept that allows us to have a foreconception of what is to come; in Marion, we have no concept for what is given, which is that than which no greater can be given or conceived.

²⁹ Jean-Luc Marion, *Being Given: Toward a Phenomenology of Givenness*, trans. Jeffrey L. Kosky (Stanford: Stanford University Press, 2002), 28–29, 196–197, 225–226.

³⁰ Jean-Luc Marion, *Le phénomène érotique* (Paris: Grasset, 2003). *The Erotic Phenomenon*, trans. Stephen E. Lewis (Chicago: University of Chicago Press, 2007).

³¹ See Jean-Luc Marion, *Being Given*, §§19–24; *In Excess: Studies of Saturated Phenomena*, trans. Robyn Horner and Vincent Berraud (New York: Fordham University Press, 2002). Marion devotes a chapter to each type of saturated phenomenon: Chapter 2 describes the event; chapter 3 describes the idol and the painting; chapter 4 describes the flesh; chapter 5, the icon.

³² Marion, *Being Given*, 235–36.

³³ Ibid., 367 n. 90.

³⁴ Every case of theological Revelation would be a phenomenological revelation, but not every phenomenological revelation would be a theological Revelation.

³⁵ Marion, *Being Given*, 236.

³⁶ Ibid., *Being Given*, 243.

³⁷ Ibid., *Being Given*, 241.

³⁸ Ibid., *Being Given*, 243.

³⁹ Ibid., *Being Given*, pp. 242–44.

⁴⁰ I am not a New Testament scholar, but in these matters I follow the account of Edward Schillebeeckx, *Jesus: An Experiment in Christology*, trans. Hubert Hoskins (New York: Crossroad, 1985), 516–72. That is not just more modernist Enlightenment, more secularist reductionism, which would be an unhappy fate to visit upon me – I [93] who have made a profitable living out of selling post-modernist ideas. To tell a long story briefly, there are three possibilities here. The first (premodern, before the period of historical criticism), is to simply believe that these are historical accounts. The second (modernist, the stance of the *Aufklärer* and the result of historical critical research), is to simply jettison them as the inventions of superstitious believers. The third is the middle (post-critical, postmodern) position taken by Schillebeeckx. That involves taking seriously the work of modern historical research – and not to do so is I think simply intellectual suicide. It is one thing to have one's horizons shattered, another to simply allow one's mind to be shattered. As Thomas Aquinas said, you get nowhere demeaning the world, or the human minds, that God has created. Otherwise, one has to treat the two Genesis creation myths as a (single) physical hypothesis about the origin of the physical world, to imagine that there really was an Adam and Eve, Jonah's whale, and so on. It gets us nowhere to say if you do not think these are literal events, you are just another *Aufklärer*, as there surely is something between literalism and reductionism. This third option does not, in *aufklärisch* style, reduce the New Testament narratives to fiction or superstition, but treats them as narratives linked to some historical core = *x*, employing inherited Jewish tropes and Jewish models that express and give shape to a growing faith about Jesus, a faith that one would say, in faith, is prompted by the Holy Spirit. When Jesus asks, "Who do men say that I am?" it is the community of faith asking itself that question and clarifying its faith to itself. This is not an ultra-conservative evangelical but a liberal-Catholic, a liberal-Christian way to think about one's faith, with emphasis on *thinking* about one's faith. See my *More Radical Hermeneutics* (Bloomington: Indiana University Press, 2001), chap. 9.

⁴¹ Marion, *In Excess*, 65 n. 14.

42 Marion, *Being Given*, 238.
43 *Kierkegaard's Writings*, vol. 6, *Fear and Trembling* and *Repetition,* trans. and ed. Howard and Edna Hong (Princeton: Princeton University Press, 1983), 39.
44 See Kierkegaard's Writings, vol. 7, *Philosophical Fragments, or A Fragment of Philosophy and Johannes Climacus, or De Omnibus dubitandum est*, trans. and ed. Howard and Edna Hong (Princeton: Princeton University Press, 1985), chaps. 4 and 6.
45 Chrétien, "The Wounded Word," in *Phenomenology and the "Theological Turn,"* 147.
46 Derrida, "Circumfession," 155.

7

BEYOND SOVEREIGNTY: MANY NATIONS UNDER THE WEAKNESS OF GOD

[In *Soundings* 89:1–2 (Spring-Summer, 2006): 21–35]

[21] I address the question of religion and the nation by taking up what Jacques Derrida calls the "un-avowed theologism"[1] behind the notion of sovereignty. By this Derrida means an implicit theological paradigm that nourishes and provides the model for the idea of sovereignty. So if, as Derrida maintains, the idea of God lies in the background of our idea of sovereignty, and if sovereignty goes to the heart of the modern idea of the nation, that would mean that one way to disturb the sovereign rule of sovereignty and of sovereign nations would be to return to theology and reimagine God. The challenge I am posing in particular is to move beyond the traditional schemata of power and omnipotence, to imagine God without power, even if this is, as I concede, a bit heretical. In my defense I would add that I am saying without power, but not without authority, for these are different matters. But is it possible to think about God without thinking of God in terms of power? Is it possible to think the authority of God without power? Is it possible to think of God as at best a "weak force," or at most as a kind of "power of powerlessness?" Would it be possible to think of God as something unconditional but outside the parameters of power and force?

Name and Event

To speak of "the weakness of God" is to adopt the language not of Derrida but of Saint Paul. I have extracted the phrase from the opening chapter of First Corinthians, which is rich with wonderful reversals and surprising metaphors about how the great ones of this world are laid low by the lowliness of the cross [22] (1 Cor 1:25). I am now prepared to admit that what I am doing here is theology, a term I used to avoid, albeit of a heterodox sort. In the past, I was more inclined to speak of "religion" than of theology, because I associated theology with institutional power, and to say that I was undertaking a philosophical – a deconstructive or hermeneutical – analysis of religious beliefs and practices. But now I am coming out of the closet and confessing that I cannot avoid speaking of God, or, more precisely, of the name of God, which is after all what we mean by theology. I once heard a speaker who did not like Jacques Derrida ask (or rather intone somewhat angrily, to be more precise), "Can God be deconstructed?" I replied that while I was not prepared to speak for God, I was prepared to say that the *name* of God can be deconstructed, and that we have no access to God except through language, except through that name. So I offer here, in all modesty, a certain deconstructive and radical hermeneutical but nonetheless theological analysis, one that is akin to Christian theology if not part and parcel of it. If my account is bound to Christianity in a particular way, I do not think it is inextricably so bound. It is bound mostly through my ignorance, for I simply do not know enough about anything other than the Christian tradition and its Judaic predecessor or parent to speak about it with confidence. But my hypothesis is that what I am saying cuts across several religious and cultural traditions and would make sense there as well.

I propose that we reflect upon the name of God, or more precisely, upon the event that stirs within this name. When I say "event" I am drawing upon a considerable continental philosophical tradition – Jacques Derrida, Gilles Deleuze, and Martin Heidegger in particular. But I am going to assume responsibility for this discourse myself and not blame anything on these philosophers (unless I get in trouble). Everything turns on this distinction between the name and the event that stirs within the name of God. What is the difference between name and event? The name is a coded, finite, element in a natural language. By natural I mean historical, real languages – English or French or German – or families of language. The event is, let us say, an impulse or an energy or a potentiality that stirs in that name, which seeks nominal expression in that name. Names have a certain kind of contingency, replaceability, and substitutability. They can be [23] translated from one language to another. No given name is the unique or exclusive way – and the richer the name, the more likely this is to be the case – to articulate the event. It might be that the event surges, moves, provokes, tries to eventuate in several names and in several ways.[2]

The name is always de-literalizable, which means I am taking an approach that is the extreme opposite of fundamentalism and of literalism. In distinguishing between the name and the event, I seek to avoid reducing the name to its literal embodiment, which is always deconstructible. Names are contingent unities that hold together for a little while, but the event they contain is more interesting. To de-literalize the name is to feel about or massage the name to see what event is stirring there within its literal boundaries. There is always a certain excess in the name, because it contains the event. One way to put it, and this is a nice way to define deconstruction by the way, is to say that names contain what they cannot contain, that they contain something uncontainable. What is deconstruction in a nutshell? It is the theory that any structure or element contains something uncontainable, which is why it tends to break open. That is why we do not want to put the lid on too tightly on anything, including names. We need a lid, a relatively stable and pragmatic unity of meaning that will help us make it through the day. But we want to keep things open, to be able to be reconfigured and to move on.

That also explains my predilection for heresies. The name will always appear as a lid, or a set of guardrails, and heresies do not first appear as names but as events that tend to break open established names. We have established names for things, an established vocabulary and conceptuality which tend to settle in place. But the event that stirs within the name is unsettling, disruptive, playing at the limits of these established borders and so it tends to cause trouble. It might surface in an anomalous way, as in Thomas Kuhn's theory of paradigm shifts, where the key is the anomaly, the scientific heresy. If we ever rule out the anomaly in science – the heresy relative to the prevailing paradigm – on Kuhn's account, we rule out scientific progress and we foreclose scientific revolution. The best science is ever ready for the anomalous. The anomalous in Kuhn is what I am calling the event, so that Kuhn, Derrida, and Deleuze all fit together in this schema.

[24] Finally we can say that the event is the truth of the name. It is the truth not in the sense of a classical correspondence theory, nor even in Heidegger's sense of unconcealment, but the truth in the sense of what's really happening, what's really going on in the name, the disturbing truth that we find inconvenient, uncomfortable and difficult to bear. In my view, the name of God requires us to put a lot of our deepest and most heartfelt notions on hold and to expose ourselves to the question of a radical truth.

My hypothesis is that the event that is contained within the name of God has been systematically distorted by philosophy and theology, by metaphysical theology, by "high" or "strong" dogmatic theology in particular, distorted, that is, because it has been treated as the name of power and omnipotence, and hence of sovereignty. As a result, we have been led down several false paths and drawn into several wrong-headed debates. I will single out two such debates in particular.

Against Omnipotence

The first wrong-headed debate we get drawn into when thinking about God in terms of power is a question that emerges in the history of metaphysical theology again and again – "Can God do anything God wills?" Is not God the very one who can do whatever God wants? In its most extreme versions of this position in the voluntaristic tradition, the Franciscan and Augustinian traditions of the middle ages, and in the Cartesian tradition in modernity, God can make two and two to be five – if God is of a mind to do so. God may not want to; it may not be a good idea; but God could do it. We see this in Kierkegaard's interpretation of the story of Abraham and Isaac in *Fear and Trembling*. There is a deep division between eternity and time in Kierkegaard, and whenever the two face off the temporal always loses. When the command of God comes up against the human law, the law that you should love your son more than you love yourself, the human law loses. The command of God is unconditional. God can command the death of Isaac, God can torture Job and his family half to death, or anything else God pleases. Peter Damian in the eleventh century went so far as to say that God can change the past. God can make it to be that Rome was not founded, even though it was. Now Peter Damian said that in a [25] good cause. Damian's heart was in the right place, because he was talking about making sinners whole. As long as it is good, God can do it. If it is evil, God would not want to do it. Now in that schema God ends up looking something like a mad Roman Emperor. God can do anything, so it is best not to defy him. We can hear the theological imperialism that resonates here. God, theology, revelation all set their own terms, for which everyone else should make way. By God we mean the unconditional power to do whatever God wants. What is the foundation of ethics? God commanded it. If God changes his mind, then ethics changes. While there are more moderate senses of God, of course, I think that what is always wrong with this approach is the idea of divine power from which it proceeds.

The second, even more important but no less wrong-headed path we are drawn down has to do with the problem of evil. Why does not God prevent evil? Why does God let certain things happen? The book of Job is the most famous case in point. Job is in the right throughout that book and everyone else, God and Job's friends included, are wrong – until at the very end, Job blinks. God's ultimate response to Job's objections is to ask, to thunder, really, "Where were you when I created the world?" That is, how dare you ask a question of me? How dare you point out that I am wrong?" As Catherine Keller says, "If that's the answer what was the question?" It's the classic case of the *argumentum ad baculum*, the argument from the stick, from force or violence. It is the sort of thing we tell our children when we are sick of their questions: "If you ask me that again you'll be sorry." That's the argument of the Book of Job, at least the beginning and the end of the book, which are the parts that grab the theological headlines without regard to the twenty-four intervening and very beautiful chapters on the splendor of the world. God is baldly trying to change the subject. As James Kugel, of the Harvard Divinity School, says in reference to this kind of thing, God's record in terms of intervening on behalf of the wretched and the oppressed is so bad that you wonder why theologians keep bringing it up.[3]

The problem has always been there. In the Hebrew Scriptures God is almighty, the mightiest one. But this notion underwent a dramatic sea change when Christians began arguing in the second century that God creates *ex nihilo*. When the terms of that debate are examined closely, we see that *creatio ex nihilo* was, at [26] that moment, unorthodox; that was heresy, at that point in the second century. Everyone thought that God created "out of the deep" – that there were the originary elements, water and wind, sea and land, to which God gave form and life. In the second century Christian theologians worried that such a view sounded too much like Plato's *Timaeus,* and they wanted the Christian God to do better than that. So they advanced the idea of *creatio ex nihilo*, which arose in connection with a philosophical debate with the Gnostics – although, in fact, the Gnostics were the first ones to say it. It is interesting to see that the arguments advanced against the proposal centered on the problem of evil. The opponents of the new idea argued that if God is responsible for everything *ex nihilo*, there will be no way to extricate God from responsibility for evil. If God is responsible for the world all the way down, then we will have implicated God in evil and established a notion of God as infinite power. And if power corrupts, infinite power corrupts infinitely.[4]

In terms of our subject, the paradigm of sovereign divine power is ethically, politically, and socially a dangerous road to follow. It established the idea that at the heart of things there is unconditional, absolute, unquestionable sovereignty. It creates a figure of power as top-down subjection, of a hierarchical order of power and of authority that works its way down the system. At the top of the scale is God, in whose place stands the King and just beneath the King, the "man" – as when we think of man and woman, or man and animal, or man and earth. The background idea of every order of subjection is the theological paradigm of divine sovereignty. The idea also structures our way of thinking about the self. What is the self, *ipse*? In this word *ipse* the Indo-European root *"ps"* is related to the Latin words *posse, potentia,* power. The self is a being whose action begins and ends within itself – the circle or circuit of power that constitutes the self. I am the origin of my action, and my action comes back to me. The self is *dominus sui actus,* says Saint Thomas, "the lord of his action," like the lord of an estate. It even shows up in Heidegger's *Being and Time,* when Heidegger says that the very Being of Dasein (human being) is to be concerned about its being, that its Being is for the sake of itself. The same paradigm is preserved in the modern idea of democracy as formulated by one of our heroes, Abraham Lincoln, who speaks of an order of democracy as [27] a government of the people, by the people, and for the people – beginning and ending with the people. Two possibilities open up at that point. The first is to speak of a particular people – *das Deutsche Volk,* God Bless America, "hail to the Queen," *vive la France* – where a given people, this people, is sovereign. But the second more promising possibility is to ask ourselves, how about *all* the people, not just French, German, American, and English people, but the poorest and most unrepresented people, third world people, old people, children, women, *everyone*?

What does sovereignty mean? I confess that I am giving it a slightly critical, even a slightly cynical definition. It might be possible to define it another way – and this just because of my distinction between name and event. Sovereignty is deconstructible and if something is deconstructible there is something going on there that can always be re-described. But, for the moment, in order to make this argument work, I want to think about sovereignty in a relatively well-received way which comes out of the German conservative jurist and theologian Carl Schmitt who defined it as the power to make an exception, to create an exception. The sovereign individual is the one with the power to make an exception, to suspend the law, the one who says, "Well, the law holds all the times that I say it holds, but there are times when I can say it doesn't hold, and I can do that because I am sovereign (or the President)." In a nation, sovereignty is the power to operate unilaterally in the face of international law. A nation will cooperate with other nations when it is to its advantage, and when it is not, it operates unilaterally, that is, it reserves the right to suspend international law. That is what sovereignty means, and the idea behind it is ultimately a theological one.

The Figure of Jesus

How, then, to think of God differently? My recommendation is that we turn for light to the idea of God in the New Testament. Suppose we treat Jesus as the icon of the living God, the one in whom we can find a model or image of God. I am fully prepared to say that there are many such images or icons in many traditions about which I am not going to say much, mostly because of my ignorance. So if I do not speak of alternative icons, it is not because of their poverty but because of mine. But my hypothesis is that if you analyze the great compassion in Buddhism, the [28] prophetic tradition in Judaism, in short, the real depths of other religious traditions, you will get comparable results. The doctrine of "the Incarnation" is not unusual. The notion of a being born of a heavenly father and an earthly mother is a common one in antiquity, found in many mythologies, and not unique to Christianity. But Jesus is unique, because Jesus is not a typical super-hero, not a typical mythological power who slays things and crushes his enemies with his power. What is most interesting about Jesus is that the icon of God we encounter in Jesus is a man defeated, executed and abandoned, whose symbol is the cross and whose message is peace. Of course, Jesus also says that he comes to bring the sword and not peace, so the picture is more complicated than I am presently admitting. The narratives of Jesus in the New Testament are of a man who shows a preferential concern for the poor, a concern with healing the lepers and the lame, preoccupied with the outcasts, the outsiders. But above all else, probably first and foremost, something that no one familiar with the scholarly literature on the historical Jesus would question, he seemed to be saying something controversial about God's forgiveness.[5] That very likely had a great deal to do with why he got into trouble. Were he simply repeating the standard Jewish doctrine on *teshuva*, he would not have attracted any attention. He was saying something different. Perhaps he suggested that the sinner is forgiven in some kind of unconditional way. That is why the notion that his death was a sacrificial exchange to make satisfaction for our sin seems to me to be another perversion of the icon of God that we find in Jesus. One of Jesus's "last words" on the cross, one that is central to our memory of Jesus, is his word of forgiveness of those who executed him. Even if we have no reason to believe it is an historical citation, those words have the ring of Jesus. Think of him as genuinely nailed there, unable to move, unable to escape. Forget the magical images of him, that all he had to do was blink and those Roman soldiers would have been hurled through the air and smashed against a rock. Forget the opinion of Thomas Aquinas that he was intimately conjoined with the beatific vision at that moment, which offered him infinite relief from suffering. If we forget all that and think of Jesus as the icon of God who really is crucified, and who feels abandoned, then the icon of God we find in Jesus on the cross is not an icon of power but of powerlessness.

[29] But is this not the classical doctrine of *kenosis* – that God freely enters into human history, empties himself, and assumes our weakness? My reservations about the classical view is that it is what the retailers call "bait and

switch." It is not an account of the weakness of God all the way down but of the weakness of God as a form that he assumes freely out of his even *greater* power of sovereignty. *Kenosis* enhances God's power; it is a strategy. If we go back and look at the texts in which St. Paul talks about the weakness of God, we see that it is clearly a strategy for Paul, too. The weakness of God is *greater* than the strength of man; the foolishness of God is wiser than the foolishness of men. So, just wait, bide your time, and you will see that, behind all this talk of weakness and *kenosis*, the true and lasting power is God's.

That classical doctrine of *kenosis* is just what I reject. Suppose the event contained within the name of God is an event of weakness, of which the cross would be its best emblem, but the weakness goes all the way down? What rises up in majesty from the cross? Not power but forgiveness; not power but a protest against the unjust execution of a just man, a great divine "no" to injustice and persecution. So I regard the cross as a prophetic rather than a sacrificial death and I think the power of the cross is a power without power, the power of a weak force. There were no armies, human or angelic to rescue Jesus. Nonetheless, something unconditional happened there, something of unconditional value happens in that weakness – something unconditional but without sovereign power.

To make this more concrete let me offer you an example. Let us take the idea of justice as an example of something unconditional without power or of what we can also call the power of powerlessness. To do this, consider the distinction between justice and the law. If we transgress the law, the law bites back, but justice does not have teeth. What is justice? A dream? A call? There's something unconditional about justice but it has no army. The law has the army – the courts, the institutions, the jails, the police. Laws can be good or bad, which is why it is necessary to continually revise – or deconstruct – laws. But justice is unrevisable, undeconstructible, unconditionally binding – but without any power of itself to enforce its commands. For enforcement, we need the law, just laws. The law without justice is a tyrant, and justice without the law is a dream.

[30] Now, on this way of thinking, if justice is a name for God, one of the oldest and most venerable names, then we are not thinking of God as the highest *being* or most powerful *thing* who can outdo and outwit other beings. Nor are we even adopting the position of Paul Tillich, who said that God is not a particular being but rather the deep ground of being, the inner substance, the source and basis of beings, from which all things emerge, and which in some mysterious and unique way guides them forward. That is no less a theory of divine power and omnipotence, even though it is not the power of an entity.

Tillich advances not a theory of ontical or entitative power but of ontological power, Being's power, not the power of a being. But in my way of thinking, God is neither a being nor being itself but a kind of unconditional claim beyond being.

Nor when I say "beyond being" am I adopting the position of Plato in the *Republic* when he defines the Good as beyond being. There the Good is so eminent that it cannot be called being. At most, being may be said to be one of its effects. We cannot call the Good being because it is the source of being beyond being, even as it is the source of truth beyond truth. The Good is a hyper-eminent, super- or ultra-being. That is no less a theory of power – a higher greater ultra-power. That is why the ones who get to know the Good, to get that far up the ladder of dialectics in Plato's Republic, get to be the King, get the power, and everyone else down the ladder should be grateful to have the enlightened ones in charge. The ones who know this Good beyond being are alone fit to rule. That is why negative theology, which is inspired by this Platonic paradigm, is an even higher, even more eminent affirmation of the being and power of God, and it is also why the politics of Neo-Platonic mystical groups turned on the distinction between the esoteric (insiders who are in the know) and exoteric (outsiders who are in the dark), a schema that is quite the contrary of that found in the New Testament.

The Structure of the Call

What then – to make a more complicated story a little too simple – do I mean by the unconditionality of the event that is contained in the name of God, and why is this an unconditionality without power? Let me give you a tripartite answer.

[31] (1) The name of God is the name of an unconditional promise; it has the structure of an open-ended future, of what is to come. This notion, which we find in Derrida, has clearly been borrowed from Judaism, which is why Derrida calls it the pure messianic. He has in mind an idea of a Messiah who never shows up, which goes back to an old Rabbinic tradition cited by Maurice Blanchot. In a sense, as the very structure of the future, of hope, of expectation, the Messiah would ruin everything if he ever actually appeared in the flesh. As long as we live in time, in history, we need to be sustained by hope, by expectation, so that the "Messiah" is the figure of what is always coming. This even obtains in Christianity, which turns on the idea that the Messiah has actually come. For even here, in Christianity, we want him to come *again*. The structure of Christianity is the hope of a *second* coming. In this context one would say not so much that "God is" as that "God promises." The messianic

structure is openness to the future. The chair is always set for Elijah. He may come knocking at our door and we must always be ready. We must never let the present close. The present must always be split wide open with expectation. Derrida's critique of the metaphysics of presence – a notion that discomforts both the Christian right and also the secular left – is actually just good old Jewish theology. It is nothing less than the critique of idols: we never want to identify the present with the Messiah. The Messianic age is never here. So if ever we are inclined to identify the nation where we live, the language that we speak, the constitution under which we are ruled, any of the political structures presently in place, with messianic peace, that would be idolatry. Messianic peace is always coming, always promised.

(2) The name of God is also the name of an unconditional memory. At this point I am invoking the work of Walter Benjamin, whose work was taken up by the German theologian Johann Baptist Metz, who spoke of "the dangerous memory of suffering," which means the disturbing memory of the dead, the memory of the unjustly persecuted dead. Benjamin has an interesting theory of the Messiah. He does not speak of the Messiah as someone who never shows up; rather Benjamin claims that we are the messianic beings, we are the ones whom the dead were waiting for, the ones called upon to save the dead. We are the messianic beings. In this context, we want to say not that God is, but [32] that God recalls. God calls us back and asks us to remember the dead. And in the case of Christian theology, in the case of Metz, Christian theology is founded on the dangerous memory of the suffering and death of Jesus, the danger in this memory being the danger that it poses to every power and principality that oppresses and kills.

(3) Finally, the name of God is the name of an unconditional call, or solicitation, in the present. We live every moment under a provocation or (in the most literal sense) have been given a vocation, which makes of us the people of the call, the people who have been called, gathered, solicited, disturbed, addressed, and even, in some sense, accused. We are, here and now, summoned by what is happening in and under the name of God. We are responsible, which means that our being is to respond. Now it is just at this point that we can see that power comes into play, direct or actual power. For it is our business, our responsibility, to respond, to make God happen in the world, to actualize and instantiate God. God is not some supernatural agent who intervenes and fixes things, who stops earthquakes in their tracks or averts tsunamis from the mainland. God addresses us and we are the ones who are responsible. We bring God into existence. We bring God's power to bear on the earth, here and now. You will notice that this tripartite structure bears the very structure of time,

or temporality, and so constitutes my own weak version of the Trinity, a "trinity" of temporal relationships. The call summons us toward the future, from time immemorial, in the now. However futural, justice is here and now, because justice that is only deferred and only to come is justice denied. Justice has always to be deferred but this deferral is only part of the story; it cannot *simply* be deferred. So in Blanchot's story, the Messiah does show up one day, dressed in rags, and someone in the crowd who recognizes him goes up to him and he asks, "When will you come?" There are many interesting ways to gloss that old rabbinic story. In one sense it means that waiting for the Messiah is like waiting for the verdict of a jury. You really want to know what the verdict is but on the other hand, you do not, not if the verdict goes against you. The Messiah is a lot like that: we want him to come, but then again we don't. So there is an element of that in this story. But the Benjaminian twist is this: Every day is the day in which the Messiah comes. So [33] the meaning of the temporality of the unconditional promise is that of a calling forth (promising) and a recalling (memorializing) that calls us to action in the present, addresses us here and now.[6]

Many Nations Under God

Let us now, after this long propaedeutic, take up the question around which this conference is organized, the question of the nation. By rethinking God on the model of something unconditional without power, we would be forced to rethink the nation's sovereignty, but can the idea of sovereignty be saved or reinscribed in this new framework? If the sovereignty of the nation is a dangerous notion and a platform for unilateralism, can we re-think sovereignty or should we give it up? Suppose we imagine the sovereignty of *all* the people of the earth? Then would we not feel free to kill all the animals if we needed? And what would we do to the environment?

Perhaps we might think of a sovereignty in which each and everything would be "sovereign," not in the sense that each thing was free to act unilaterally, but in the sense that everything would command its own respect, be respected for its value. Then we would think of ourselves as addressed by everyone and everything, by all of God's creatures. I can think of no objection to that. But notice what has happened on this version: we have switched from *my* sovereignty, or *our* sovereignty, to the sovereignty of the *other*, and we have switched from thinking of ourselves as sovereign to thinking of ourselves as *responsible* to the other. That is a clue, I think, that the idea of sovereignty is on its last legs – in our "theory," at least; it is alive and well on the streets – and it needs to be replaced by something new, as in a more radical notion of democracy, in which each and every person, each and every thing, is included in the process. What has happened is that we have found that sovereignty is at bottom a figure of autonomy and that what is required is a figure of heteronomy, of responsibility to the unconditional appeal coming from the other, to the call by which we are all called. To think of a nation without sovereignty is to think of a nation marked not by autonomy but responsibility, a nation that belongs to an international constellation of nations with a sense of being called – by the weakest and most defenseless among us, by the majesty of the earth and all its living things, by the dead and by the children. A nation without sovereignty is a [34] nation with a vocation or a calling, a nation *under* God, one of *many* nations under God, where the name of God is the name of a call that is issued by the victims of injustice, by the weakest and most defenseless people on the globe, where the icon in whom we imagine God is the figure of man unjustly executed by might of imperial Roman power.

Rather than the autonomy of sovereignty, I would think of the nation in terms of the heteronomy of hospitality. Hospitality represents a very interesting combination of power and powerlessness. Once again, we can hear the "*potens*" or "*posse*", the "power," in hospitality (*hostis* + *posse*). I cannot invite the other to your house. Hospitality means that the host is the master of the house, that he or she owns the premises, and that means the host has to have some kind of power, but this is a power that makes itself vulnerable to the other. It is power interrupted by the call of the other. Just as hospitality is asked of the individual and of the community, it is also required of the nation. A nation cannot be without borders, but those borders can be very porous. One might even imagine a nation that posted a statue at its borders that said, "Give me your tired, your poor, Your huddled masses." What an idea that would be! Who knows, maybe someday there will be a nation like that, one that would show hospitality to the stranger. Not one that acts unilaterally but a multi-lateralist, one that does not retaliate but forgives. Could there be a politics of hospitality and forgiveness? What would such a politics look like? Is there any political power on earth with the power to forgive? We can easily enough imagine hospitality and forgiveness and loving one's enemy as a kind of personal ethic. But what would it look like as a form of politics?

The event that stirs in the name of God under the provocative Pauline expression I have taken as my motif – the "weakness of God" – is an imperative to re-imagine God, to turn our thinking about God around or upside down. Allow me to conclude by citing a text from Derrida that has inspired this entire reflection:

In speaking of an onto-theology of sovereignty, I refer, under the name of God, of the One God, to the determination of a sovereign and hence indivisible omnipotence. But when the name of God would give us something else to think, for example a vulnerable non-sovereignty, suffering and divisible, mortal even, capable of contradicting himself, of regret (a thought which is neither impossible nor without example), that would be a wholly other story and [35] perhaps even the story of a god who would be deconstructed even in his ipseity.[7]

What calls, what is calling, what is called for is the weakness of God, the coming of a God who does not have the wherewithal to lay down his head, whose only power is the power of a powerless but unconditional appeal.

Notes

[1] Jacques Derrida, *Rogues: Two Essays on Reason*, trans. Pascale-Anne Brault and Michael Naas (Stanford: Stanford University Press, 2005), 110. For my reading of this text, see "Without Sovereignty, Without Being: Unconditionality, the Coming God and Derrida's Democracy to Come," *Journal of Cultural and Religious Theory*, Vol 4, No. 3 (August 2003). www.jcrt.org.

[2] This distinction, along with just about everything else I say in this paper, is developed with more detail and documentation in *The Weakness of God: A Theology of the Event* (Bloomington: Indiana University Press, 2006), of which it is a kind of summary presentation.

[3] James L. Kugel, *The God of Old: Inside the Lost World of the Bible* (New York: The Free Press, 2003), 125–36; Catherine Keller, *The Face of the Deep: A Theology of Becoming* (London: Routledge, 2003), 124–40.

[4] See Gerhard May's *Creatio ex nihilo: The Doctrine of 'Creation out of Nothing" in Early Christian Thought,* trans. A. S. Worrall (Edinburgh: T & T Clark, 1994); Keller, *Face of the Deep*, 41–99.

[5] See E. P. Sanders, *Jesus and Judaism* (Philadelphia: Fortress Press, 1985) for a superb account of Jesus's position on forgiving sin, which I am following here.

[6] For more on this, see *The Weakness of God*, 253–57.

[7] Derrida, *Rogues*, 157.

8

A PROLEGOMENON TO POST-SECULARISM

[Unpublished paper delivered November 4, 2004: Plenary Address at "Eye to Eye: A Global Conference on Cultural Relations," sponsored by the British Council (London); revised 2005]

My thesis is that the present age is best characterized as a "post-secular time." By "secularism" I mean the conceit that the secular order is all in all, that every possibility is enclosed within the horizon of the world and can be reduced to the terms of a world in which God is dead. By the post-secular, I mean the notion that the secular order contains what it cannot contain, that it is inwardly disturbed by something that exceeds the world, which gives the secular order no rest, and that this something goes under the name of God (even while one concedes that there are other names). The post-secular is not pre-secular but late secular, having passed through secularism in which it emerges as its late stage, as its breakup, and as the transition to something else, neither secular nor anti-secular. Post-secularism is a post-critical effect, which means it works its way through the critical closure effected by secularist modernity and allows the naivete of a pre-critical religious faith to resurface in a new and post-critical way.

What I am arguing here can be condensed into a tripartite claim: (1) Our lives are structured by the desire for God (which is a pre-critical religious aspiration); (2) by the desire for the event that is stirring in the name of God (which is a critical intervention on this name); (3) by the desire for something, I know not what, that calls to me as if from beyond the world, something for which I can lived unreservedly (which is a post-critical, post-secular faith).

Post-secularism

On can now safely say that the "death of God" movement of the 1960s has proven to be an anachronism. At the time, it looked like a bold affirmation of the ultimate implications of modernity, a courageous theological movement with the audacity to embrace the atheistic result to which all modern philosophy seemed to be inevitably rushing. It looked like a band of theologians honest enough – "honest to God," as Bishop Robinson put it years ago – to say that the time had come to see that God had come down to earth once and for all, with no heavenly remainder. But a funny thing happened on the way to the funeral: "death of God" theology ended up as a resurfacing in the middle of the twentieth century of an essentially nineteenth century idea. Within a decade or so after the movement, we witnessed an unprecedented wave of religious fervor. That sent the sociologists of religion back to their drawing boards to revise their recent declarations of the "secularization" of American society, forcing the best among them, like Peter Berger, to declare instead the unexpected "de-secularization" of the United States, with a chastened sense of the limits of sociological prediction. Today, Christian evangelicals are a potent social and political force with which every candidate for elected office must reckon. Indeed popular religious movements have since swept over South America and Africa. Almost immediately after being declared dead, God made a stunning comeback everywhere – except in the faculty clubs! It is almost as if the movement had gotten up the divine dander. For better or worse, religion is everywhere today, north and south, east and west.

I say for better or worse, because a good deal of the rise of popular religious sentiment has been for the worst, consisting as it does in a reactionary, dogmatic, intolerant fundamentalism which is, from a theological point of view, a flatly idolatrous fetishizing of the Bible. It ignores the work of historical critical research and makes an idol out of a text even as it confuses God with the church and makes an idol out of ecclesiastical authority. Inasmuch as such idolatry has little to do with the living God, one could say that God is dead without resurrection in this wave of reactionary religion and world-wide religious violence. But it would be too simple to reduce all religious sentiment today to fundamentalism and violence.

Indeed, the lesson to be learned from the recent American presidential election [Editor's note: 2004 election in which George W. Bush defeated John Kerry] is that it has become increasingly difficult, and perhaps impossible, to elect a secular liberal to national office. It may well be that if a liberal democrat is to be elected president he or she must emerge from a religious left, that is, from someone of unmistakable religious sentiments for whom religion means social solidarity and uplifting the poorest and most defenseless members of society, a respect for life that includes a love of peace, not war-mongering, and a respect for the natural world God has created. As Rabbi Michael Lerner wrote[1] after the recent election:

> For years, the Democrats have been telling themselves "it's the economy, stupid." Yet consistently for dozens of years millions

of middle income Americans have voted against their economic interests to support Republicans who have tapped a deeper set of needs. Tens of millions of Americans feel betrayed by a society that seems to place materialism and selfishness above moral values.

Yet liberals, trapped in a long-standing disdain for religion and tone-deaf to the spiritual needs that underlie the move to the Right, have been unable to engage these voters in a serious dialogue. Rightly angry at the way that some religious communities have been mired in authoritarianism, racism, sexism and homophobia, the liberal world has developed such a knee-jerk hostility to religion that it has both marginalized those many people on the Left who actually do have spiritual yearnings and simultaneously refused to acknowledge that many who move to the Right have legitimate complaints about the ethos of selfishness in American life.

Imagine if John Kerry had been able to counter George Bush by insisting that a serious religious person would never turn his back on the suffering of the poor, that the Bible's injunction to love one's neighbor required us to provide health care for all, and that the New Testament's command to "turn the other cheek" should give us a predisposition against responding to violence with violence.

Imagine a Democratic Party that could talk about the strength that comes from love and generosity and applied that to foreign policy and homeland security.

Imagine a Democratic Party that could talk of a New Bottom Line, so that American institutions get judged efficient, rational, and productive not only to the extent that they maximize money and power, but also to the extent that they maximize people's capacities to be loving and caring, ethically and ecologically sensitive, and capable of responding to the universe with awe and wonder.

What interests me here is the fact that the death of God has proven to be an anachronism to secular intellectuals, who have also turned their attention to God and pointed out the untapped riches of the religious paradigm for purely secular reflection. Secular philosophers like the late Jacques Derrida, figures at the forefront of *post*-modernity, have turned anew to religious paradigms to understand personal and public life, writing provocative interpretations of St. Augustine and St. Paul, among others.

Philosophically, it turned out, it was not God who was dead but the old Enlightenment and the secularism and reductionism that it implied. Completely secular philosophers had for completely secular reasons in the meantime become suspicious of Enlightenment suspicion, critical of Enlightenment critique, and were in search of a new Enlightenment, one is which the pretense of the old one was made questionable. In this new postmodern, post-critical Enlightenment, it was stressed that there are many varieties of rationality – scientific, poetic, philosophical and, one cannot avoid this, religious or theological rationality. Sweeping overarching narratives that told us that some one thing called "religion" is "nothing other than" some one thing called resentment (Nietzsche) or displaced libidinal desire (Freud) simply lost their credibility. Thoroughly secular philosophers ended up ushering in a post-critical "post-secular" point of view.

The Name of God

Let us then feel free to speak of God. Let us say that the name of God is the name of our salvation, and that the saving effect of the name of God is to make the secular order – the "world" – questionable, to give us leverage on the world, to loosen up the grip of the world, which threatens to be all in all. This flies in the face of the commonplace idea that the name of God shuts thinking down and closes us off from real questions by supplying a ready-made answer to everything, a dogmatic or theological explanation. Let us say that the name of God is the name of an open-ended exposure to the future as well as of an act of recalling a time out of mind, and hence of an infinitely subversive turn in things which destabilizes the present. To think theologically is to break up the presence of the world and of the world at present, to prevent it from closing over and sealing itself off, and thereby to expose the world to an event that the world cannot contain.

On this account, to think theologically is to be saved, but to be saved in a very frustrating way, since such salvation does not bring the sigh of peace but the sword of turbulence. For here being saved does not mean being made safe but being shaken to the core, inwardly rocked, traumatized, unhinged by the name of God, exposed to an abyss that will not close over, suffering from a wound that will not heal. For after theological questioning has irrupted, nothing is the same again. One cannot go on as if this irruption had not occurred, even if from outer appearances one looks as hale and whole as the next chap. One has been snared by the infinite, shaken by a relation to an unconditional claim, completely unhinged by an absolute relationship with the absolute, rocked by an infinite trauma, shaken by exposure to an abyss, even if one strolls about town with all the equilibrium of a computer programmer!

To put this post-secular point of view in the terms supplied by theologian Paul Tillich one would say that while busy with many matters of immediate interest, one is inwardly disturbed by an exposure to the questions of "ultimate concern." The opposite would be to be tranquilized and lacking this concern. There would be a peace here, but it would be a somnambulant peace. One would not be stirred by deep theological unrest, having confined one's attention to preliminary, proximate and superficial matters, raising only finite, determinate and particular questions, while never noticing the event contained within the name of God, the event that provokes thinking and desiring, sending them tumbling down endless and labyrinthine paths. To be saved is to be saved from a somnambulant life and to be awakened to the event.

But in this post-secular condition, which passes through modernist critique and which emerges as a late stage within it, we must also confess the ambiguity and endless translatability of the name of God. We make no claim that this is a universal name or that it has a universally received meaning, or that the name of God is not translatable into other names, or that it belongs to some final and unsurpassable vocabulary. Every historically determinate name is bound by time and tide and circumstance, and no name is or could ever be impartially accessible to everyone or uniformly desirable by everyone. I am simply proffering here the modest proposal that this is arguably one of the most prestigious names that have been handed down to us, one of the most assuring and intimidating, most comforting and haunting, most promising and threatening names we know or do not know, where by "we" or "us" I mean Westerners who have descended from a long line of prolific, polyvalent and polymorphic monotheists and polytheistic Greco-Romans.

This name has come to us from our mother's breast, from the dark waters of the womb, from our unconscious, from the hidden depths of our language, from our most ordinary language, as opposed to a formal or contrived one, from the lost roots of our multiple histories, all the forces of which have been run together in a massive simplification and concentrated shorthand called "God." This name is made to bear the weight of that history, which it cannot bear, and to carry the torch of our desire, which it cannot carry, and to contain an event that it cannot contain. We partisans of post-secularism advance the hypothesis that theology has the interrogatory force to awaken questioning and to stir thought and this just because the name of God is the name of our desire, or one of those names. To proclaim the death of God, as Nietzsche realized better than anyone, is to proclaim a stunning and mind-numbing event, compared to which the death of anything else would receive only passing notice, at most two columns in the obituary section, for the death of God would signal the death of our desire.

Consider the catastrophe that would result were the event that simmers within this name suppressed or closed off. The result would be the free reign of the superficiality of the "profane." The *profane* is the unbroken rule of the "world," of overbearing being, the harsh economy of giving and taking in return, where there are no gifts, where everything has a price, where nothing is given for free. The *profane* is the degradation of the sacred into acquisitiveness, the truncating of human experience into consumption, leaving us to wander the shopping malls in search of what we desire and relegating us to reality TV to search for what is real. The profane shrinks human life into the surface of the accumulation of as many things as possible, reducing love to sexuality, history to nostalgia, politics to power, religion to self-righteousness. The profane is trafficking with the brutal for the sake of a profit and allowing the poorest people in our society to fend for themselves, even though they are defenseless. The profane takes what is sacred and debases it, puts it on vulgar display, robbing it of its powers. On the plane of the profane, the highest quest of which we are capable is a good bargain. The profane life is flat and thoughtless, short-sighted and mean-spirited, like people living on top of an earthquake who do not hear the first tremors because their computer games are playing too loud. The profane life is passionless, the half-life, the demi-life, of what Kierkegaard's Johannes Climacus called a mediocre fellow, by which he meant a lover without passion, a mercantile soul.

The opposite of the profane is the sacred, which is the anarchic effect produced by the interruption of secularism, by piercing its closure by means of the event that stirs within the name of God, which is what save us. By the "*secular*" world or order I simply mean the condition in which we all live today, believers and non-believers, believers in this and believers in that, apothecaries, apostles, and large animal veterinarians alike. Modernity simply tries to be tidy about the distinction between the sacred and the secular, private and public. But by "*secularism*" I mean the *rule* of the world, the *regime* of the profane, which represents an assault on the event, a reductionistic attack on the excess of the sacred, a failed attempt to disenchant the world in virtue of which God, and everything we mean by God, is reduced to the economy of the *saeculum*, where everything has a market price and nothing is free.

But by "post-secular" thinking I mean a thinking that abides within the secular order and works its way through secularism and the death of God and comes out the other end on the grounds that it has become obvious that the event harbored by the name of God cannot be contained by the "world" (*saeculum*). The death of God is the defining feature of "secularism," and deconstruction, Mark Taylor famously said, is the hermeneutics of the death of God. I myself regard this as too downbeat a view of deconstruction, which for me is a religion (without religion). The religious dimension in deconstruction is to make big totalizing projects like secularism look incredible on the grounds that a genuine event cannot be contained within closed borders. Deconstruction gives faith and the spirit of God room to breathe. The post-secular is a celebration of the event contained in the name of God, of an excess or transgression of the world by the event of that name. Post-secularism means that the name of God is too much for the world to contain. We advocates of a post-secular theology have found the death of God to be a dead end. We are subscribers to a *new* Enlightenment, one that is enlightened about Enlightenment, which comes *after* secularization springs a leak, breaks down or breaks open, in a world that is torn open by the desire for God. The death of God *simpliciter* would spell the death of desire. The death of God *simpliciter* would mean the death of every possible God, the death of the unconditional event that is contained in the name of God, in a name like God. That would spell the death of what we love and desire with a desire beyond desire, the death of everything that makes our beliefs and practices tremble, making them open up like an abyss whenever they come in contact with it, with something, I know not what.

The sacred scrambles the lines of force in the world and gives the ordinary surface of things their glow, like the lilies of the field, which is how it is possible to be superficial out of depth. The sacred today is the anarchic effect produced by re-sacralizing the settled secular order, disturbing and disordering the disenchanted "world," producing an anarchic "chaosmos" of odd, brilliant disturbances, of gifts that spring up like magic in the midst of scrambled economies, like sparks given off when wires cross, filling the air with brilliant elliptical, parabolic and paradoxical effects. The name of God then turns out to be a poetic and parabolic celebration of the blessed event of the foundering of the "world," of the excess and open-ended shock that is delivered to the world by the name of God. The name of God triggers the potencies that stir in things, releasing their pent-up charges of divinity, rocking the world with the trauma of the divine. The result is the grace, the graciousness, the aleatory gratuitousness of the gift, the madness of the "Kingdom," the divine sparks of a sacred anarchy.

The Undecidability of the Call

Post-secular thinking is interested in the way a seemingly secular world is inhabited by unexpressed and implicit theological structures. It investigates the way the world is inwardly disturbed by traditional religious structures, by the structures of transcendence and prayer, by the hope for a Messiah and messianic peace, which it treats as irreducible. In post-secularism the name of God is the name of the future, of the promise, of the desire beyond desire for what is coming, while for secularism the future is refused the name of God, for God has been offered up in a sacrificial death for this future.

In post-secularist thinking, we would not say that God is dead but that the name of God is deconstructible, which means that it is structurally exposed to substitution, and that its future wavers in undecidability. For me, the name of God is the name of what I desire with a desire beyond desire, harboring an event that is undeconstructible, for which one of our best names is the name of God, while for secularism the name of God belongs to death and the past. While I expose the name of God to deconstructibility – every name is deconstructible just in virtue of the event it harbors, of what is to come, which is undeconstructible – I do not hand it over in sacrificial death.

In post-secularism, the name of God is the name of something irreducibly futural, of something that solicits us from up ahead, that interrupts the world, which puts it into question. Without the event harbored in this name, without the theological disturbance that is stirring in this name, we would all be barbarians, pagans caught up in the world, where the world is all in all. For the all-encompassing grip of the "world" is broken by a messianic call, which comes, as if from beyond the world, to call the world to terms, to call it what it is, to call for an age of peace and justice, for which we pray and weep. *But the identity of the call, of the caller in the call, is a secret and remains forever undecidable.* How would one be able to say in any final and decisive way either that it is God who calls or that God is dead? For it is quite beyond us – it belongs to the sphere of the secret – to decide whether there is or is not some Transcendent Super-being outside space and beyond time overseeing the whole and calling us beyond ourselves, or whether that Transcendent Super-Being has come down to earth and died away in the world. Those are the tall tales of an overreaching metaphysical imagination. Like Kierkegaard's Johannes de Silentio, we wish the great omnibus of metaphysics well but we confess we have no head for the progress of the Absolute Spirit through time or the place of India in the History of Being.

By speaking of the death of God, by engaging in a metaphysical conceit that says that God has come down from heaven and died away into the world, we deprive ourselves of the theological resources harbored by this name. We insulate ourselves against its disturbance. We would do considerably better to speak of the irreducibly religious character of even the most secular experience, and to recognize that there is no clean cut between religious and secular, that the secular contains what it cannot contain, to concede that irreducibly un-secular or anti-secular impulses stir within the world (*saeculum*), that the world is made restless with an irreducibly religious desire or aspiration, let us say, which haunts and disturbs the world from within. Haunts, like a ghost, neither present nor absent, neither purely alive nor merely dead. Our lives do not easily settle into one side of the secular/religious divide, but we are endlessly tossed about by the undecidability of these motifs, the fluctuation between them, and the impossibility of resolving in some decisive way what event is stirring in this name.

But what calls us *as if* from beyond the world? Is it some unknown power of the unconscious, some biological instinct? Or is it some better angel of our nature? God only knows. That means that it belongs to the essential realm of the secret, about which we have no inside information. But the question we raise, one that fluctuates in endless undecidability, has to do with a fundamental structure of our existence, with a structure of desire or affirmation, with an event that is so elemental that it cuts beneath the names of theism and atheism, hence undercutting black and white distinctions between the secular and the religious, and cuts to the core of our wounded hearts. We have been wounded by an invisible wound, cut by a desire for something I know not what, driven by a passion of non-knowing, which is all at once a source of our dignity and our unrest, of our nobility and our unhappiness, which is the passion of our lives. *Inquietum est cor nostrum*, St. Augustine said: our hearts are restless with the restless desire for what Augustine called "you," *te*, by which he meant God, restless with a desire for something for which he used the name of God, which was the best name he had.

The name of God is the name of a desire for something unconditional, something that we can unconditionally affirm, something that we desire with a desire beyond desire, with a hope against hope, something for which we ceaselessly pray and weep, for which we can live unreservedly, while everything around us is deconstructible, including the name of God. That is why Meister Eckhart, in an exquisitely perfect deconstructive formulation, prays God to rid him of God, which is in the end a prayer, a prayer to what is alive in the name of God, a prayer for an event and an event of prayer.

Notes

[1] Nov. 3, 2004, http://www.tikkun.org

POSTMODERN THEORY

9

DECONSTRUCTION

[In *Encyclopedia of Religion, Second Edition,* Vol. 4, ed. Lindsay Jones (New York: Thomson Gale, Macmillan Reference USA, 2005), 2245–48. Also available at Gale eBooks]

[2245] The word "deconstruction" was coined by French philosopher Jacques Derrida with whom the movement of that same name is identified. Derrida rejects the classical anthropological model of language according to which the speaking subject gives verbal expression to inner thoughts which are subsequently written down. In such a model, writing is a sign of speaking; speaking is a sign of thinking; thinking is a sign of being. Instead, Derrida follows the "structuralist" thesis of Swiss linguist Ferdinand de Saussure (1857–1913) that language is to be understood scientifically as a purely formal system of signs (*langue*) internally related to one another (like a dictionary in which one word is defined by other words) and underlying the utterances of speaking subjects (*parole*), thus eliminating both the subjective-psychological and objective-metaphysical factors. In Saussure's model, *signifiers* are arbitrary (the word *king* has no natural likeness to a real king) and differential (they differ by the "space" between, say, *king* and *ring*). The *signified* is the effect produced by the rule-governed use of signifiers. Derrida's thought is *post-structuralist*; it criticizes Saussure for privileging speech over writing, in violation of the arbitrariness of the linguistic sign, and for treating linguistic strings as a closed system of fixed structures. Metaphors and word play illustrate the uncontainable capacity of linguistic chains to network out indefinitely in new directions, pushing endlessly against the limits imposed by the rules. Derrida encapsulated his adaptation of Saussure in the neologism *différance,* French philosophy's [2246] most famous misspelling. The idea is to keep networks open-ended, to resist their tendencies to closure, in order to allow new and unforeseen effects.

Deconstruction is not a settled body of substantive theses or positions but a style of thinking that applies in any field of inquiry, theoretical or practical, in virtue of which any present set of beliefs or practices is held to be indefinitely revisable (deconstructible) in the light of something unrevisable (undeconstructible). Inasmuch as the undeconstructible is never actually present or realized, the undeconstructible is also said to be "the impossible." According to Derrida, the least bad definition of deconstruction is the "experience of the impossible." "Least bad" because, in deconstruction, which is resolutely anti-essentialist (nominalistic), words have only a relatively stable unity of meaning, ever shifting histories of use, and no fixed or defined borders. Derrida uses the word *experience* in the sense not of empirical data gathering but of running up against something unexpected, even traumatic. "The impossible" does not mean a simple logical contradiction, such as (p & $\sim p$), but something that shatters the horizon of expectation, that is not accountable for (or possible) under prevailing presuppositions.

The same sense is conveyed when Derrida describes deconstruction as the "invention of the other." "Invention" has the more literal sense of "coming upon" and even of "in-coming," (Latin *in-veniens*) running up against something that comes in upon or comes over us, overwhelming our powers of anticipation. By the "other" Derrida means not the relatively other – that is, new evidence confirming an existing horizon – but the "wholly other" (*tout autre*), a phrase he borrows from the Jewish ethicist Emmanuel Levinas, meaning something unforeseeable, unrepresentable, for which we have no concept. A deconstructive analysis thus prepares the way for or explores "the possibility of the impossible." Jean-François Lyotard makes a comparable distinction between making a new move in an old game (the possible or relatively other) and inventing a new game altogether (the impossible or wholly other). That in turn invites comparison with Thomas Kuhn's distinction between normal science, which makes new discoveries within an existing paradigm, and revolutionary science, when an anomaly forces a fundamental reconfiguration of the current schema or a "paradigm shift."

Derrida has recourse to a family of *venir* words picked up in English in both Latinate (invention) and Anglo-Saxon forms (coming). Deconstruction is turned to the "in-coming," the invention or the advent, of the "event," which is a unique and "singular" happening, not an instance or example of a universal (his idea of "singularity" is derived from Soren Kierkegaard, Martin Heidegger and Levinas). The event defies convention, where everything is regularized and routinized. Deconstructive thinking is guided by the invocation "come" (*viens*), which Derrida has not hesitated to call a certain "prayer," by which he means a deep desire or love of the event to come, which is not without anxiety since the future is also an absolute risk. The motif of the "come" clearly has messianic overtones that Derrida has acknowledged in later more autobiographical essays like "Circumfession," where he reflects on his birth as a Jew and on his early family life in a Jewish family in French Algeria. The motifs of love and desire have overtones of Augustine's *cor inquietum*, of what Derrida calls the "prayers and tears of Augustine," which also surfaces in these same essays about his life in the Franco-Christian colony which is the historic land of Augustine.

The word "deconstruction," which has the predominantly negative sense of disassembling something, is clearly not the best word for this deeply affirmative mode of thinking. Coined by Derrida as a translation of Heidegger's *Destruktion*, and used by him to characterize his own work, it owes its currency just as much to commentators who seized upon it. Heidegger himself was very likely referring back to Martin Luther's use of *destructio*, which itself goes back to 1 Corinthians 1:19. Just as for Luther, destroying the wisdom of the wise meant nothing destructive but rather the recovery of the original sense of scripture by breaking through the crust of Scholastic theology; and just as Heidegger did not mean anything negative but rather the recovery of the unthought sense of Being hidden in the history of metaphysics, so Derrida does not mean anything negative but rather the releasing of the possibility of the impossible, or the coming of the event, that threatens to be closed off by conventional interpretation and practices. While the word has entered the general vocabulary (e.g., "deconstructing Woody Allen") with the negative sense of knocking down and exposing faults, to deconstruct something in Derrida's sense is not to ruin it but to give it a history, to open it up to a future. Something that is insulated from deconstruction is not protected but petrified, having hardened over into a dogma, like a law that could never be reformed or repealed. The word enjoyed, or suffered from, a *succès de scandale*, particularly in American literary theory circles in the 1970s, where it seemed to invite a kind of interpretive anarchy that licensed any interpretation, however bizarre. When Derrida protested against such interpretations, critics thought him involved in the self-contradiction of insisting that his own texts should be interpreted carefully, thus refuting his own theory that anything goes.

In fact, careful reading is what deconstruction is all about. A philosophical theory with wider implications, deconstruction first gained ascendency in the 1960s and 1970s as a literary theory. A deconstructive reading settles deeply into the grain of a text, sensitizing itself to its tropes and metaphors, its choice of words, the chains in which those words are caught up, and the complex and even anonymous operations of the linguistic system in which the author is working, in order to show that the text contains an unmasterable complexity – *dissemination* – that cannot be contained by the author's own intentions or conscious logic. Thus, Derrida's well-known critique of "logo-centrism." Derrida's frequent [2247] use of puns and word play is not a substitute for an argument but an exemplification of a theory about wordplay, which illustrates the unmasterable, unintended dimension of language, the semantic, graphic, and phonic chains that no intentional agent can contain. James Joyce, an early hero of Derrida's, embodies this point about language almost perfectly. This disseminative effect is not something that a clever writer or reader is doing to the text, exerting a kind of violence or mastery over it, but an auto-deconstructive operation going on within the linguistic network itself.

That this is not interpretive anarchy but responsible work, Derrida thinks, is clear to anyone who reads carefully. Anyone who reads Greek philosophy carefully knows that there is all the difference between "Plato," a shorthand for a cluster of condensed philosophical theses, summarized and passed along in prepackaged histories of philosophy, and a close, careful reading or immersion in Plato's writings, which reveals multiple voices, dramatic devices, conflicting and suggestive counter-motifs and loose threads – in short, a "text," a highly woven and interwoven complex, not a neatly argued "book" under the absolute conscious control of an "author." We might add that anyone who has studied the Jewish or Christian scriptures carefully will understand that these are "texts" in just the sense in which deconstruction describes, that is, a complex weave (or "palimpsest") of many voices, competing theological and political agendas, redactive layerings, anonymous interventions, lost stories, liturgies, and multiple extra-textual references or reinscriptions of earlier texts, texts without fixed "margins." In the same way, conservative critics charge deconstruction with being out to destroy "tradition," but Derrida would respond that he only wants to show its immense complexity and competing voices; there is no such thing as "tradition" in the singular but rather an interweaving of many traditions and counter-traditions, of dominant and recessive voices, and even of chance mutations in manuscripts. Close readings of the past – the uncovering of forgotten women, for example – opens up hitherto closed possibilities for the future. Deconstruction is very conservative, Derrida once quipped, because the only way to love and be loyal to the past is to deconstruct it.

Although Derrida's avant-garde style of writing, especially early on, lent superficial credibility to the misinterpretation of deconstruction as a form of relativism or even nihilism, no one today can mistake the sustained seriousness of the later writings, whose ethical, political, and even religious character is beyond doubt. Reading his account of the "gift without return" or "forgiving the unforgivable," more informed critics today will accuse him of a Kantian rigorism or unrealistic ethical purism, an accusation that he also rejects. From the early 1980s on, Derrida has written not only about the gift and forgiveness, but about justice and the law, hospitality, friendship, democracy, capital punishment, and international human rights. In 2003, he published *Voyous*, a book about the denunciation of "rogue states" by the western democracies. [*Editor's Note: the following passage was deleted by the editors:* Indeed it is fair to say that, after repeated declarations of the "death of deconstruction" (after it was displaced in literature departments by "cultural studies"), Derrida's work is enjoying a new life at the turn of the millennium in departments of religious studies and among continental philosophers interested in the problems of religion.]

Religious thinkers are fascinated by a distinction Derrida introduced in the 1990s between the concrete "messianisms" — the three great monotheistic religions of the book, as well as the philosophical eschatologies of G. W. F. Hegel, Karl Marx, and Martin Heidegger — and the pure "messianic" or "messianicity." The pure messianic means the formal structure of desire, expectancy or openness, the pure structure of the "to come" (*à venir*) — like the hospitality to come, the justice to come, and most famously the "democracy to come" — that is concretized in the historical messianisms. In virtue of the pure messianic, one can speak of a "religion without religion," a religious desire without confessional dogma or institutional ties. The democracy to come is not a Kantian regulative ideal, which brings a concept to ideal completion beyond its empirical limits, because, for Derrida, *democracy* is not a concept or an essence on which we are making asymptotic progress, but a moment in the open-endedness of history which makes possible an event, whose coming we cannot foresee and whose name is not known, and where nothing guarantees that it will not bring forth a monster instead of a messiah. "Secular" political theory, like philosophy generally, is always transcribing an "unavowed theologeme," like the messianic promise, thus skewing any rigorous distinction between the religious and secular, faith and reason, religion and the non-religious, prayer and social hope, theism and atheism.

This is not to say that religious thinkers were not interested in deconstruction from the very start. The early essay "*Différance*" (1967) started a discussion with negative theology that dominated the dialogue between deconstruction and theology until the late 1990s. As Derrida says, he loves the syntax, semantics, and the tropes of negative theology, which is a self-effacing discourse, a discourse that attempts to erase its own traces. Beyond matters of style, the critique of the metaphysics of presence in deconstruction (what is present is deconstructible; the undeconstructible is never present) bears a substantive analogy to the critique of idols in apophatic theology (if you comprehend it, it is not God; if it is God, you cannot comprehend it). Nonetheless, while negative theology clearly uses deconstructive techniques, deconstruction is not negative theology, because it has no commitment to a *hyperousios*, to a Godhead beyond God or a God beyond being. The exchange between Derrida and Jean-Luc Marion is the most important in this regard.

In the 1980s, deconstruction was appropriated by the theology of the "death of God," most notably in Mark C. Taylor's *Erring: An A/theology* (1984). Taylor argued that the first wave of death-of-God thinking in the nineteenth century left the old God standing under the new name of Humanity. Deconstruction is the true hermeneutics of the death of God because it has displaced any absolute center, human or divine, with the free play of signifiers. God has descended into the world without remainder, even as Scripture has descended into *écriture* without remainder, a reading that reflected the Nietzschean understanding of Derrida [2248] then dominant in American departments of literature. Since then a different appreciation of the religious dimension of deconstruction has emerged in thinkers like John D. Caputo, Kevin Hart, and Hent de Vries, for whom deconstruction is the hermeneutics not of the death but of the desire for God.

10

TEMPORAL TRANSCENDENCE: THE VERY IDEA OF "À VENIR" IN DERRIDA

[In *Transcendence and Beyond,* eds. John D. Caputo and Michael Scanlon (Bloomington: Indiana University Press, 2007), 188–203]

> "What's important in 'democracy to come' is not 'democracy' but 'to come.'"

[188] Works of Time

The word "transcendence," for all its transcendence, is a relative term. It depends upon what is being transcended or gone "beyond." It can mean transcending the subject in order to get to the object, or transcending the self in order to reach the other, or transcending beings to reach Being, or transcending inner-worldly things to reach the horizon of the world itself, or transcending the sensible world in order to attain the supersensible one, and that in turn means transcending the spatio-temporal world in order to occupy a spot outside space and time, which is the more classical meaning of transcendence.[1] There are also those who would transcend being in order to make their way to what is beyond or without being, which is I suppose about as far as one can go and constitutes the most transcendent sense of transcendence. In the past, whenever the question of time has come up in this regard, time was taken to be something to be transcended, not a way of transcending. But ever since Husserl, Heidegger and Levinas have opened up the question of time in new and more radical ways, philosophers have become more and more interested not in the transcending *of* time but in time *as* itself something transcending. In that sense we have a transcendence in reverse, where what one wants to go beyond or transcend is the classical sense [189] of transcendence (= transcending time) in order to back track *to* time now taken in a new and more radical way. The essay that follows belongs to this tradition.

Levinas is an interesting case in point in this regard. While the very subtitle of *Totality and Infinity, An Essay on Exteriority,* turns on a spatial metaphor, what Levinas had up his sleeve all along was time, which he regarded as the key to what he called metaphysics, by which he actually meant ethics. It is important to keep in mind that Levinas denounced the spatializing imagination as mythological and looked scornfully upon the fantasy, the story – Catherine Keller would say the "rumor" – of a "world behind the scenes," of which *Hinterwelt* he was as uncompromising a detractor as was Nietzsche himself. Although we are not inclined to highlight this side of Levinas, it is nonetheless the case that on a theological register, Levinasian ethics makes for a death of God theology:[2] Immortality, another world, life after death, celestial happiness, some higher supersensible being beyond sensible beings – those are all so many fantasies trapped within being, dreams of replacing this world with another, hoping to exchange a worldly kingdom for celestial one with the coin of "meritorious works," which is the celestial narcissism of Kierkegaard's ultra-eudaemonistic search for eternal happiness that Levinas dislikes. The very meaning of our being turned *to* God (*à dieu*), for Levinas, is to be deflected or turned *by* God (*à dieu*) to the neighbor. *And nothing more.* The name of God boils down without remainder into our being turned to the neighbor, *tout court*.

What then is accomplished by ethical trans(a)scendence to the other? In one very definite sense, nothing. Ethics is not for something; it is a non-profit enterprise. Ethics is all the transcendence there is. It does not buy us a ticket somewhere else. There is nowhere else to go.[3] Be good, rise up in ethical splendor (ethical transcendence), and then you die. Why? Ethical transcendence is self-validating; it raises you up above the greedy grubby sphere of self-love. The trans(a)scendence to the other is a self-transforming self-transcendence. Life is justified as an ethical phenomenon; then you die. In Levinasian transcendence, there is nowhere to *go*, no*where* to go, because for Levinas there is no *Hinterwelt*. Ethical transcendence transpires not in space but in time, not "in" time but *as* time. Ethical trans(a)scendence is the work *of* time. If the turn to the neighbor in Kierkegaard takes the form of "works of love," in Levinas it is one of the "works of time," where it provides the only true escape (*l'évasion*) from monotonous and monochromous being. But by time Levinas does not mean the subjective flow of onto-phenomenological time-consciousness, which transpires under the regime of consciousness or the understanding of the "present" – in which a future-present flows into the now/present and then is retained in the past-present. He means a more radically breached or interrupted time – one marked both by an "absolute past," a past that was never present (answering a call I never heard), and by an absolute future, one that we cannot foresee.

[190] I would be the first to agree that there is a danger in associating Derrida too closely with Levinas. There is no ontological claustrophobia, no thematics

of being "trapped in being" in Derrida, no need to "escape," no "nausea" before being. Derrida has nothing to with Levinas's grim ultra-Kantianism, the ultra-ethicism in which there is only ethics and everything else is a vanity of vanities, with the terrible neglect of nature and the animal; with the devaluation of art; with the embarrassing patriarchy and embarrassing politics. Of all of this Derrida has been discreetly, respectfully, but expressly critical. But on this precise point of transcendence as time itself, Derrida is close to Levinas. On this precise point, that there is no *Hinterwelt* beyond the temporal world, that the "beyond" that we could agree to call "transcendence" – in order to appease the organizers of this conference – is the work of time, that it *is* time, Derrida has struck a position that, for all its other differences, is close to Levinas.

Just as with Levinas, one finds in Derrida a rhetoric or a discourse, a tropics or a body of tropes, on the "beyond" – "all the movements in *hyper, ultra, au-delà, beyond, über*" – which organize for him a certain "messianic" beyond that draws us out of our (present) selves. He is often drawn to texts, such as Pseudo-Dionysius's and Plato's, which display a certain "hyperbolic" desire for something "beyond," and where "*hyperbole* names the movement of transcendence that carries or transports beyond beings or beingness, *epekeina tes ousias*." To which Derrida adds: "Its event announces what comes and makes come what will come from now on in all the movements in *hyper, ultra, au-delà, beyond, über*, which will precipitate discourse or, first all, existence. This precipitation is their passion."[4] For Derrida this passion of the "beyond," of the *hyper* or the *au-delà*, takes the form of the passion for "going where you cannot," which is, he says a "passion of, for the place,"[5] a passion for the impossible, for the impossible place of the beyond. Transcendence is a more classical term for what Derrida would call the passion for the impossible, which is also, please note, the passion for existence.

But remember that for Derrida, just as for Levinas, this hyperbolic passion for the place (the beyond) gets fired up without biting on the myth or the rumor of another world; remember that it has a *temporal* meaning and that there is no other place to go.[6] The passion for the impossible is for something that breaks up and breaks into the world that otherwise tends constantly to settle in place all around us; it means something that extends us, that draws us of ourselves beyond ourselves. This would also be the passion of existence, the spark that drives existence past itself and ignites a certain self-transforming. That for Derrida is what time is, what time does. The burden of making good on this claim falls to what Derrida calls the "event," by which he means a radical and constitutive unforseeability, a radically unprogrammable future. Our lives are pried open by the coming of the other (*l'invention de l'autre*), by something "coming" to us from beyond the horizon of foreseeability, something that destabilizes us even as it constitutes us as wounded or destabilized, as cut or circum-cut subjects.

[191] That wounding, destabilizing, circum-cutting, eye-opening yet blinding exposure to the event takes place in virtue of what Derrida calls the "to come" (*à venir*). The "event" (*événement*, from *venir*) is a function of the to-come; it occurs by reason of the very idea of the to-come. Hence the closest analogue to "transcendence" is to be found in the affirmation of the coming of the event. This is a vital affirmation, not an idle reverie about a utopic or ideal form that we never quite realize. It is not to be thought of, I hope to show, as a work of *idealization* of a definite but distant form, but rather as a work of infinite qualitative *intensification* of an immediate and pressing demand. I will argue in what follows that transcendence, if there is such a thing in Derrida, if this were ever a word we could have enticed him into using in his own name by repeatedly inviting him to the Villanova conferences, is a function of the *à venir*. In Derrida, a certain quasi-transcendence, or analogue or successor form or side-effect of transcendence, some transcendence without transcendence, unfolding under the different circumstances and transferred dynamics of deconstruction, would refer then to an infinite qualitative temporal intensification, an infinite self-transformation of our temporal lives, which we might also describe as the passion of existence.

In what follows I will track the dynamics – or the tropics – of the beyond in Derrida as a radically temporal movement or temporalizing event, as a work of time or, to give it a high spin, a qualitative intensification of temporality; I will do so by taking what Derrida calls the "democracy to come" as my point of departure.

Democracy is a Lousy Word

Let us begin by recalling the aporia of time posed by Aristotle, who said that it seems that time does not exist or that it barely exists because its parts do not exist (*Physics*, IV, 10, 218 a 1-5). That seems like a serious problem for something – to be missing its parts, like a conference at which none of the speakers show up. But the aporia that besets the "democracy to come" is quite analogous to this and it is at least as serious. The "democracy to come" is a fine idea, one of Derrida's finest, but for the fact that in virtue of the very idea of the "to come" (1) the democracy to come could hardly be expected to be or be called "democracy" and (2) it could hardly be expected to ever show up. So it seems that the very idea of the democracy to come is impossible, because its parts – both the "democracy" and the "to come" – are impossible,

To be sure, for us hardy deconstructionists, raised on the difficulty of life, who thrive on aporias, the impossible is not bad news. Indeed, the impossible is what we love, what drives our passion, and the more impossible the better. It is precisely the impossible that drives things to a fever pitch, a pitch of passion and absolute intensity, without which we would all be mediocre fellows. So instead of saying that the very idea of the democracy to come is "beset" with this aporia, as if this were an affliction to be warded off, let us say that this idea [192] is joyously and incontestably constituted by this aporia, that it is nourished by it, that what does not kill the *à venir* makes it stronger. To this end, let us pursue the impossibility of each part of this aporia and see (savor) just how impossible it is. *O quam suaviter*: taste and see how sweet is – the impossible.

If the democracy to come belongs to the sphere of the absolute future, and if the absolute future is absolutely unforeseeable, if it will come from beyond the horizon of expectation, like a thief in the night, then how do we know that the democracy to come is or will be a "democracy"? Might not what is coming turn out to be quite different or other than democracy? Let us be more bold: is it not *necessarily* the case that the democracy to come must certainly be *other than* democracy? As an "event" is not the democracy to come *tout autre*? Accordingly, is not the very idea of a wholly other democracy to come necessarily wholly other than democracy? In order to be what it is or can be or ever will be, the democracy to come cannot possibly be "democracy," not what we today call "democracy," which would not be wholly other.

"Democracy," Derrida confesses, is a "lousy" word.[7] Some of the worst and most undemocratic things are done in the name of democracy, including proposing the self-congratulatory idea that the world divides between nations that are democratic ("ours") and those that are not, the latter belonging to the "evil empire." (When George Bush was asked who was his favorite political philosopher, instead of saying "Jesus Christ" he would have done a better job of concealing the narrowness of his readings in political philosophy by saying George Lucas.) It is in the name of the basic freedoms provided for and protected by democracy – the freedom, e.g., to speak one's own mind and spend one's own money as one sees fit – that democracy is corrupted through and through; it is in the name of supporting the so called friends of democracy and opposing its enemies that the American democracy in particular has propped up the bloodiest and most undemocratic regimes. Still, even while "democracy" is a lousy word, things could be worse; the virtue of the word is that it is the least lousy, all the alternatives being even lousier.[8] Were we to say that we are dreaming of an oligarchy or a monarchy to come, or even of a dictatorship to come, that would be even lousier.[9] The best we can say is that "democracy" is the *least* bad word we have now for what is to come, for something which could be named otherwise, e.g., as a "republic" to come, as in the distinction that Hannah Arendt makes between a (constitutional) "republic" and "democracy" as mere majoritarian rule.[10] When the time comes, if it does, we may very well have another word that is not as bad or just as good, which we might signify by calling it a democracy + n.

Then what is the advantage of the word "democracy" now? Why is it not as bad as all the other words? Is it because of some "essential nature" of democracy in virtue of which there would be an essential similarity between the democracy at present and some future present democratic condition that would arise under the impulse of the democracy to come? Not if *différance* does what it says it does – not if it constitutes meaning as an effect rather than [193] expressing pre-constituted meanings. The deeply anti-essentialist drift in *différance* blocks the way to essential similarities. We might do better to say that there is what Wittgenstein calls a "family resemblance" between the two. On that model, we can say that *a* looks like *b* and *b* looks like *c*, but *a* need not look like *c*. That is a more promising avenue to the *à venir* of democracy. I am speaking of future present democracies or post-democracies that would arise "under the impulse" of the democracy to come because it belongs to the very idea of the democracy *à venir* that while it will itself never exist, as we will see below, the whole idea is to provoke a series of transformations, to set a certain seriality in motion, leading who knows where, somewhere into an open-ended future. This democracy to come may solicit, call, or provoke, or it may lure, tempt, or seduce, but it does not exist, not if it is "to come," not according to the very idea of the to-come. Thus, given what *différance* means, or rather what it does, and given what *à venir* means, then between the democracy at present and some future condition that would arise under the impulse of the democracy to come, there would not be a community of essence but only a seriality, an historical, narratival or genealogical link, not an essential continuity but only an narratival sequence. "Democracy" does not have a meaning; it has a history. Democracy is not an essence but an ongoing historical narrative; the word "democracy" is but the word we use today to mark the present slice or cut (or *epochè*) in that series.

To the extent that we do favor the word democracy it is because it would be easier to imagine a series of historical shifts or transitions, sometimes gradual, sometimes abrupt, starting out from what is today called democracy that would pass through several subsequent successor states or conditions that would come to be known as something, I know not what, some kind of democracy + *n*. Now since we cannot even be sure that what that is will be called "democracy," let us formalize this even further as "$x + n$. One could imagine that this process would go on indefinitely; in fact, I cannot imagine how it would not. That would mean that a future historian of political affairs would be able to show us how what at various times in the future is called $x + n$ could be traced back to a series of predecessor conditions that lead back to what we today call with an almost perfect blindness "democracy" (nothing is perfect). This history would have its ups and downs, so that we are not committed to saying that in this history we are approaching asymptotically some ideal or normative state. We are just coping with a shifting historical tide and trying not to get drowned. Nothing is safe or guaranteed; it's just that if we wanted to enter into that process (and how would you avoid it?) it would be better bet to start out from what is today called democracy than from any other presently available option. And then hope for the best.

But why does democracy enjoy this privilege of being the least lousy place to start out from today? Because democracy is or should be the form of life that is the most self-correcting and the least resistant to change and transition, the least closed off and homogeneous, the least given to calculating everything [194] according to a rule, the place that is most open to movement and transformation, thereby providing the setting that is most susceptible to setting off just such a seriality or narratival sequence. The very idea of a democracy ought to be that by respecting singularity it thereby cultivates polyvalence and polymorphism, anomalous and innumerable differences. The very idea is to make room for the exotic growths of singularity that spring up in the cracks of regularity, to provide just the sort of thing to allow for paradigm shifts, for unforeseeable innovations and transformations that a too-rigid and regular system precludes and excludes. So the very idea of a "democracy to come" is "openness" to the "to come." Viewed in that light, the expression "the democracy to come" enjoys a joyous and glorious tautological redundancy, its very terms fitting together like pre-fitted pieces. For if democracy means openness, and if openness means letting something come, then the very idea of the "democracy to come" means the coming of what is to come, letting what is coming come. The "democracy to come" means the "coming to come." We would get the same result if we analyzed the democracy to come as the event to come, in which case it turns out to mean the *à venir* of the *événement*, like the tautology about the *ereignen* of the *Ereignis* that makes glad the hearts of Heideggerians.

To be sure, this tautology does not relieve but only intensifies the aporia, inasmuch as the coming of the democracy to come is precisely the coming of what will *never* come, the democracy to come that is *not* going to come, so that this tautology is also very heterologous.

Some words are more promising than others and the word democracy is the most promising word we have today, which means the least bad word we have now for keeping us mindful of a certain political "promise" that is inscribed in this word. But who is promising what to whom? That is hard to say, but at least this much is clear. A promise stirs within this word even as this promise exceeds the word, since no existing or present democracy would ever meet the demands that are laid upon it by this word; no present or future present democracy could ever be absolutely loyal to this promise. The word "democracy" contains a promise that it cannot contain; the promise of the word is uncontainable. Containing what you cannot contain, by the way, which is not a bad way to describe being pregnant, is also not a bad way to describe deconstruction or an auto-deconstructive process – "in a nutshell" (one that is bound to burst).[11] On my analysis this means that there is a twofold movement at work within powerful, prestigious and promising historical words like "democracy" (there are numerous other examples of such words). The first moment I would describe as one of "*historical association*," for this word belongs to a prestigious tradition, or a complex of interwoven but heterogeneous traditions, which we have inherited, into which we have been "thrown," as Heidegger would say, but with which we also freely associate ourselves. For to have a tradition is to make certain decisions about what that tradition means and what elements within it we accentuate. To receive or inherit the word "democracy" is not a passive process but a matter of taking one's stand within, [195] and assuming a debt to, a long line or series that stretches from the Greeks to the present. Traditions thrive and survive not because they are fed from within by a deep well of essential *Wahrheit*, as Gadamer and Hegel would maintain, but because they make great promises; they live and prosper on promissory notes, on relatively empty intentions that intend the infinite but always deliver the finite, on unfulfilled pledges that we nevertheless trust and love and believe.

But having a tradition also involves a movement of "*deconstructive dissociation*," a movement of distrust and discontent – *inquietum est cor nostrum* – of recognizing and affirming the distance between the finitude of the present and the infinite promise that is embedded in the word. So to inherit or receive the word "democracy" is to be given a promise that has not been kept. We stick with this word because we fall for its unkept promise; we are suckers for its empty but good intentions; we succumb to the power of the promise and the pledge that democracy does not and cannot keep. We keep the word because of its very inadequacy, its very powerlessness, its inability to be what it says and to say what it is, which is the power of its powerlessness. The promise of the democracy to come is an open-ended intention – we do not know where it is leading us – but it is not free-floating – we have inherited it and we have some idea of where it came from. We know a little of its provenance but little of its e-venance, its eventiveness. It is heading who knows where but it does not come from nowhere. The real punch or power of the word is not the actuality it has realized but the possibility that it has not, the *peut-être* that stirs within it, the possibility that reaches out all the way to the impossible, to this necessary but impossible future, this unforeseeable possibility of needing to go where you cannot go.

Without this moment of open-ended dissociation, the word "democracy" would become an idol, that is, a finite contraction of the unfinished promise of democracy to a particular figure or construction of democracy, especially to its present form, to the one at hand, right here, wherever you are, say, the United States at the beginning of the third millennium. Without this deconstructive, dissociative moment, it would be impossible for "democracy" to function as an icon, as open-ended promise of something coming, something, I know not what. Without this moment, all the power of temporal transcendence that is harbored by the "to-come" would be blocked off.

Another way to say all this is to say, as Derrida does, that in the expression "democracy to come," and in every expression of the same form (the x to come), say, the "justice to come" or the "friendship to come" – in formulations of this same form that we cannot presently even imagine and are still to come – what is important is not the "democracy" or the "justice" but the "to come." The "to come" matters more than the "democracy," the word democracy being just a way to mark a promise, just a way of keeping the future open, the most promising foothold we can get in the present on the promise of the future.[12]

[196] It Will Never Come

But the problem is that whatever we call this something (we know not what) that is coming, whatever this unknown something may be for which we are "hoping sighing dreaming" (*à esperer soupirer rêver*),[13] the one thing we can be sure of is that it is *not* going to come. That brings us to the second part of this aporia: not only will the democracy to come not be called democracy, but also, and in virtue of the very idea of the *à venir*, it will never come. Like Aristotelian time, the expression "democracy to come" experiences distress in each of its parts.

The very idea of the to-come is the idea of what does *not* come, of what is coming but never comes. It never actually and indeed shows up, as in the old rabbinic idea mentioned by Blanchot of the Messiah who never arrives.[14] In this version of the messianic tradition, the very idea of the Messiah is to *not* arrive, his arrival always being much awaited, something "*ausstehendes*," as Heidegger said, "impending" or still outstanding,[15] which is the very structure of expectation and historical time, of hope and promise, of faith and the future. Were the Messiah ever actually to arrive, that would be like death, like the end of time and history. That is why even where it is believed that the Messiah has arrived, we are forced to ask him to please come *again*, which is – in a nutshell – the story of Christianity, the history of which is opened by *différance*, by the deferral of the coming *again*. The earliest Christians were surprised to find that they were to live on and so to have a "history." A "second" coming is necessary in virtue of the very idea of the to-come, for otherwise, if the Messiah ever showed up in the flesh, were he ever *leiblich gegeben* in some final and definitive form, that would spell death and the end of everything. The very idea of the messianic is to keep the future open, which is possible only with the deferral of his appearance. Like the alter ego in Husserl's Fifth Meditation, the very phenomenality of the Messiah depends on his *not* appearing; that is what the phenomenon of the Messiah is or means or does. For otherwise, what would there be to sigh and hope for? What would there be to dream of and desire? What would there be to pray and weep for? If the Messiah ever appeared, the curtains of time and history would draw closed. The Messiah, the messianic figure, is a figure of the very work of time.[16]

The Very Idea of *à venir*

The non-arrival of the Messiah makes clear that the "to come" is not the name of some future present moment or condition that we are eventually going to reach after the passing of a certain amount of time and trial and difficulty, if only we can last it out, but rather of our *being-toward* (*sein-zu*) the future and of the future's *being-ahead* of us, to use a little Heideggerianese. It is not a notion that requires our patience but our passion. That is, the to-come is not the name [197] of an occurrence that will transpire at some distant era in the future, which requires our patience, but rather of a structural relationship with the future that is always in place no matter what time it is, no matter what actually transpires in time, and that fires our passion. The to-come is not some happening that occurs *in* time; rather it has to do with the very structure *of* time. But what does it mean to have *being-toward* something that is *always ahead* but never comes? The answer to this question has two sides, (a) the first having to do with our being-toward (b) and the second with time itself and the structure of the being-ahead.

1. The only thing that is truly "to come" for Derrida is what we do not and cannot see coming. If one can see something coming and anticipate it – it is perfectly "possible" in this sense[17] – then to a certain extent it is already present

and it has already happened and we have compromised its coming. But the movement of what I am calling Derrida's "being-toward" is structured by the law of the *sans*, since the only way to be radically "toward" something, to "anticipate" or prepare for it on Derrida's terms, is to be radically unprepared, *sans voir, sans avoir, sans savoir, sans s'avoir*.[18] Derridean being-toward is thus the very opposite of the hermeneutic fore-structures of Heideggerian *sein-zu*, which is constituted by fore-seeing (*Vorsicht*), fore-having (*Vorhabe*), and fore-conceiving (*Vorgriff*), all of which can only lead to a "future present" as opposed to the "absolute future." But if the relationship to the future cannot be one of seeing or knowledge, then it is strictly a matter of faith and non-knowing. So true is this that "knowledge" would actually compromise being toward the to-come and weaken our faith. To the extent that we know or fore-know what we want or expect or hope for, to the extent that we are guided in advance by implicit, anticipatory clues of something vaguely and pre-ontologically fore-seen, fore-known, and fore-conceived, then our "faith" becomes just that much more assured, more determinate, more content-ful, more "credible," and so much less a "pure" faith. The oligopistologists, the ones of little faith (Mt. 6:30), are the hermeneuts who want to (fore)see and (fore)know and (fore)have what is coming. But Derrida takes the notion of faith and hope very far, even farther really than the confessional faiths, where the object of faith is relatively determinate. In that sense, the circumfessional faith of a "religion without religion" is actually more religious, more faith-filled, more filled with fear and trembling, than the confessional faiths, which enjoy the comfort of a community, of a body of canonical texts, of a tradition and common teaching, which is what Kierkegaard called the comforts of the universal, as opposed to the lonely labyrinth of singularity *coram deo*.

2. Being-toward for Derrida means preparing for something that is *always ahead*, preparing for something that will *never be*, not because we will not have enough time to get to it but because it is not something *in* time at all but the very structure *of* time, the structure of the to-come itself. What Derrida calls the "to come" is thus not merely temporal, but time itself. It is not in time; it is time. *À venir* enjoys an "infinitival" structure that can never be reduced to a [198] finite form. Looking more like *être* than an *étant*, the to-come never "is" although it would be true that *il y a de l'à venir*. We might say "it calls" but we will never say "it is." The to-come constitutes the formal structure of time in virtue of which something is always and irreducibly still outstanding, still ahead. Without the to-come, time would implode, collapse in upon itself, contract to a suffocating and unliveable now in which there would be no room to breathe, no space of time, no *Zeitspielraum*, no time at all. But the to-come is not merely

a formal mathematical function in virtue of which any time *n* would be followed by a time *n* + 1, which would constitute nothing more than a simple temporal sequence of now points. The to-come is the time of desire, of expectation and hope in a promise, the time of a prayer; it is not simply a formal, calculable, programmable or mathematical *avenir* but an incalculable messianic *à venir*. The *à venir* is the subject of a *viens*, of an invocation, a call, indeed an interplay of calls, inasmuch as the future calls to us and solicits us to come forth every bit as much as we call to the future, asking it to come to us. The future bids us come forward, provoking us, calling us – and here Derrida can use Neoplatonic tropics – "beyond being and presence" – even as we call upon it and invoke the future with tears beyond being, asking it to come. That, I would say, is why being-toward what is always ahead in Derrida is intertwined with "prayer," with what I have called the "prayers and tears" of Jacques Derrida, following Derrida who is himself describing the prayers and tears of Saint Augustine, the first born in this long line of sons of tears, of these siblings of tears beyond being.[19] That is the religious side of Derrida that I like to emphasize, to the discomfort of his secularizing admirers. But this religion has nothing to do with going to heaven. The very idea of the to-come is the very idea of life in time, of hope and expectation, of prayers and tears, of being toward a future that does not and will not arrive.

Intensification not Idealization

But if being toward what never arrives is to avoid the void, if it is to avoid falling into despair, must it not mean being toward an "ideal" or an Idea in the Kantian sense, which lifts our spirits by making the present a baseline and providing us with a goal toward which we continually approximate, slowly and asymptotically? *But that is just what it is not.* The "to come" has no determinate content, no core and invariant semantic content to be approximated, for that would only contract and narrow it to a species or an essence. The "to-come" is more open ended than any ideal, more indeterminate than any horizon of expectation, more absolutely futural than any foreseeable future present. The "to come" is not so much a core meaning as a function, not so much a semantic content as an operation that multiplies a given determinate *x* to infinity, and in so doing multiplies it to the point of impossibility, which means also to the point of non-apparition and non-phenomenality, which is why it never appears. The to-come is an infinitival infinitizing operation that [199] cannot be contracted to the finite and specific content of democracy, or friendship, or anything else.

(That raises a question: when we affirm the democracy to come, the gift to come, the justice to come, the hospitality to come, and so on, are we in the end affirming the same thing? Are these affirmations of something unconditional and unlimited "convertible" like so many medieval (quasi-)transcendentals? Are they "convertible," converging at some *focus imaginarius* "in" the future? Do the several affirmations of the to-come come together in one point? If not, how would they differ? If their content dissipates into an I-know-not-what-to-come, what would make them different? On the other hand, what would make them the same?)

[Editor's note: this *focus imaginarius* is how Caputo will later on describe "God".]

The only "content" of the to-come is the content of hope in a promise, of expectation of a coming, of faith in the future – like a prayer for the coming of the Messiah, like a movement of desire that extends any given content infinitely forward, not in the mode of making *infinite progress toward an Ideal* but in the mode of an *infinite intensification of hope*. The infinity in this infinitive *à venir* is not quantitative or progressive but qualitative or intensive. Being-toward the *à venir* is a movement of infinite intensification and not of idealization. From the point of view of the *à venir*, a Kantian Ideal is finite because what it extends to completion beyond any possible empirical confirmation is a definable and determinate concept. As an operation of idealization, this corresponds politically to imagining a utopian ideal within the finite framework defined and circumscribed by the concept of democracy. But being-toward the *à venir* does not mean idealizing a determinate empirical content, thereby bringing it to its essential fulfillment. The affirmation of the *à venir* intensifies what it affirms infinitely, and this shatters the empirical figure – of democracy, hospitality, etc. – rather than extending it to ideal completion. Idealization perfects what it idealizes rather than shattering it. If anything, being-toward the *à venir* is a *counter*-idealization, which takes the view that there is no Infinite Ideal, no *eidos*, for that would always be finite relative to the infinite intensity unleashed by the *à venir*. The to-come is not a future *eidos* up ahead toward which we are making gradual progress but an intense and merciless "white light" under which the present is made to pass. It is not a datable future time but a demand, an expectation, a hope, a desire, so much fuel for the passion for the impossible. The affirmation of the *à venir* will never be appeased by anything, not because it despairs but because it always demands and hopes for more. The infinite intensity of the "to come" means that it submits a presently available historical structure – such as any existing democracy – to an absolute demand, an infinite exaction, an impossible requirement, to be what it cannot be, to go where it cannot go. The *à venir* makes a merciless demand for mercy, an implacable insistence on justice.

"Democracy" is an historical and determinate political form, a finite empirical structure, a positive system of law aimed at providing equal rights and uniform protections to all, while the democracy *to come*, the democracy that [200] has been infinitely charged by the to-come, demands infinite respect for each and every singularity, requiring that we count every tear and take heed of every hair on the head of the least among us. Thus there is something within the positive political concept of democracy, Derrida says, that "exceeds politics,"[20] namely, an infinite demand that is demanded not by any finite political form but by the implacable demands of the to-come. If we imagine gathering the greatest minds in the history of democratic theorizing in one room and ask them, *per impossibile*, to draft the constitution of the democracy to come, to try to put it in writing, the result would be like a map that is so precise, so sensitive to the singularity of the terrain, that it would be the same size as the region of which it is the map; that is, it would be so perfect that it would be useless. Like the idea of the perfect map, the idea of the democracy to come is auto-deconstructing. That is because this idea cannot be brought to the completion of an Ideal; it is not an "idealization" of empirical democracies, nor an ideal form against which empirical democracies can be held up. It is a white light that is directed upon every historical formation – an infinite intensification of a promise that stirs within the word democracy that mercilessly exposes the defects of any given historical actuality. The democracy to come demands more, demands something different, something *au-delà*, and this because it demands the impossible, something that will not and cannot come. It is not a finite Ideal but an infinite expectation. There is no capitalized Ideal or Idealization-process, only an endless process of self-transformation and auto-deconstruction, a fragile series that is fully exposed to the risk that these transformations will not make progress but make things worse, which is not only not desired but downright dreaded. Once exposed to the harsh demands of the "to-come," the *present* in any order of representation or desire – the order, for example, of what is today called the gift, hospitality, forgiveness, democracy, justice, friendship, etc. – becomes absolutely intolerable. The present is radically relativized and opened up vis-à-vis the absolute future of that order – the gift to come, the hospitality to come, and so on, all of which might in the end be the same thing. Or different: who knows?

Je ne sais quoi

So the democracy to come does not exist because its parts do not exist; it is impossible because its parts are impossible. The democracy to come will not and could not be *democracy* and besides, it will *never come*. But it is precisely this never coming of I know not what that keeps us awake through the night, that solicits and provokes our passion, that calls to us from afar and makes us endlessly restless with what in fact has come, constituting the passion or our existence. *Inquietum est cor nostrum* – thus spoke Rabbi Augustinus Judaeus. It is the never coming of the democracy to come that makes us long and sigh for something impossible that will overtake us like a thief in the night, whenever we sigh and pray, whenever we cry out and say *"viens,"* calling [201] and weeping for the coming of something we know not what. The democracy to come is the least bad name we have for something, I know not what. For something we love with a desire beyond desire, with a hope against hope. For a time that has never been and also never arrives. The very idea of the democracy to come is not that there was or will ever be one but rather to provoke us to say and pray *"viens, oui, oui."* [21]

In another time, in another place, in another language, that might have been called a passion and a prayer – for transcendence, *s'il y en a*.

Author's Note:

The epigram is from Jacques Derrida, "Politics and Friendship," *Negotiations: Interventions and Interviews*, ed. and trans. Elizabeth Rottenberg (Stanford: Stanford University Press, 2002), 182. My reflections here on the democracy to come in this paper are stimulated by a few remarks Derrida makes in this interview. This paper first appeared in French translation as *"L'idée même de l'à venir,"* trans. Patrick Dimascio, *La démocratie à venir: autour de Jacques Derrida*, ed. Marie-Louise Mallet (Paris: Galilée, 2004), 295-306, the volume based on the 2002 Cerisy la Salle conference on Derrida's idea of the "democracy to come"; it reappears here, slightly adapted to the purpose of the present volume. Derrida kindly referred to this essay in *Rogues: Two Essays on Reason*, trans. Pascale-Anne Brault and Michael Naas (Stanford: Stanford University Press, 2005), 37.

Notes

[1] The word's most characteristic use in the high Middle Ages was in *transcendentalis*, meaning a property convertible with being (like one, true, good), where what is crossed over or transcended is the ten categories or genera of Aristotle. The word does not acquire its contemporary sense until the eighteenth and nineteenth centuries.

² See the vividness with which Levinas first poses to himself in 1935 the task of "escaping being" in *On Escape*, trans. Bettina Bergo (Stanford: Stanford University Press, 2003); and see the interesting "Annotations" by Jacques Rolland in *On Escape*, especially (no. 10), 89–90, which makes this same point about a Levinasian "death of God."

³ If Levinas says, in speaking of being, that what he seeks is not to be otherwise but otherwise than being, we might say that in contrast, in speaking of time, what he seeks is to temporalize otherwise and not otherwise than time.

⁴ Jacques Derrida, *On the Name*, ed. Thomas Dutoit (Stanford: Stanford University Press, 1995), 64.

⁵ Ibid., 59.

⁶ Spatial figures in Derrida tend to center either around *khora*, as the primal spacing or differential play "in" which all meanings are forged, or around ethico-political figures of displacement, of the homeless, the exile and the refugee, who have been driven out of their place in the name of (somebody else's) "homeland." Derrida on this account is deeply suspicious of the politics of place, of *Heimat*, and it is this above all that divides him from Heidegger.

⁷ *Negotiations*, 181.

⁸ But I do believe that I could make the case that it is worth dreaming of a "kingdom to come." If we are wary of putting our unconditional trust in any given word, [202] like "democracy," we must also be wary of unconditionally denouncing any given word. (*Lefebure* is not a bad word.) Shocking as it may seem, I could imagine speaking of a "kingdom to come," which would be not at all kingly or monarchical; indeed this kingdom might even be *an*archical, highly hier-an-archical, inasmuch as it would make the singular, the exceptional, the least among us, the *an-arche*, very sacred. So there might be contexts in which we would want to speak of a kingdom to come, in which we would pray let the kingdom come, for that would be a kingdom *ironice*, a kingdom tongue in cheek, a kingdom of the unkingly, without a purple robe in sight, a kingdom of the unroyal and the powerless, that makes a mockery of what is called a kingdom in politics. That, if I may be permitted a shameless reference, is the point of my *The Weakness of God: A Theology of the Event* (Bloomington: Indiana University Press, 2006).

⁹ Hannah Arendt, *On Revolution* (New York: Penguin Press, Viking Books, 1963), 164–66.

¹⁰ Derrida, *Negotiations*, 180.

¹¹ I have made several attempts to find such nutshells in *Deconstruction in a Nutshell: A Conversation with Jacques Derrida*, edited with a commentary (New York: Fordham University Press, 1997).

¹² All of this means that what we call "democracy" today is an "interim" solution, an interim politics. Democracy is always to come, but in the meantime, we need democracy now, today. Democracy is a politics for the time being that is held together by a lick and a promise, a provisional arrangement that has been hastily erected for the moment, thrown together for the time between now and the *eschaton*, the time of the to-come, something with which we just have to make do in the meantime. The thing is, it is *always* the meantime. The very idea of the *à venir* is that the time to come is never going to turn up; it will never arrive, so there is only ever the meantime, being-toward in the meantime. It is always the time between now and what is to come. We live our lives in the interim, constructing an interim ethics, an interim politics, an interim democracy, one that will see us through the day and, if we are lucky, that will last us through the week, and maybe until the democracy to come arrives. Which will never happen. We are always to do with interim democracies and transitional regimes. Democracy cannot wait. That means (1) democracy cannot wait to get here, it is eager to make its appearance, if only it can, if only it is permitted to arrive; (2) we cannot wait for democracy, we must have democracy now, in the meantime, even before it comes. It must come before it comes because we cannot wait for it to

come. It is impossible but it is needed immediately and urgently. The democracy to come must already be here, today, otherwise we would not know what we are waiting for, even as the democracy to come cannot possibly be here, otherwise we would not be waiting.

[13] Jacques Derrida, *"Circonfession: cinquante-neuf périodes et périphrases,"* in Geoffrey Bennington and Jacques Derrida, *Jacques Derrida* (Paris: Éditions du Seuil, 1991), 290; "Circumfession: Fifty-nine Periods and Periphrases" in Geoffrey Bennington and Jacques Derrida, *Jacques Derrida* (Chicago: University of Chicago Press, 1993), 314.

[14] Cited in Jacques Derrida, *Politiques de l'amitié* (Paris: Galilée, 1995), 55; *Politics of Friendship*, trans. George Collins (London & New York: Verso, 1997), 46, n. 14.

[15] *Ausstehehen* also suggests something dreaded, which is likewise a part of messianic expectation.

[16] The Messiah is an inherited and historical concretization of very idea of the to-come which clothes the to-come in the determinate historical garments of a particular [203] (biblical) tradition – rather the way Johannes Climacus clothed his account of the "condition," the "paradox," and the "god" in the *Philosophical Fragments* with the historical name of "Christianity" in the *Postscript*. The other way to look at it – there being no way to decide between these formulations – is to say that the very idea of the to-come is the "formalization" of the concrete idea of the Messiah that we have inherited from the biblical tradition.

[17] Derrida, *On the Name*, 59.

[18] Jacques Derrida, *Parages* (Paris: Galilée, 1986), 25. I have added *s'avoir* to Derrida's string in *Parages*.

[19] John D. Caputo, *The Prayers and Tears of Jacques Derrida: Religion without Religion* (Bloomington: Indiana University Press, 1997).

[20] Derrida, *Negotiations*, 181.

[21] Derrida, *Parages*, 116.

11

OF HYPER-REALITY

["Foreword" to Ewan Ferne, *Spiritual Shakespeares* (New York and London: Routledge, 2005), xvii–xix]

FOREWORD

[xvi] The essays that follow are meant to open up links between the world of Shakespeare and that surprising twist in postmodernism sometimes called its "religious turn." They proceed from the premise that literature does not illustrate pre-established philosophical principles but can instruct philosophy about matters too concrete and singular for philosophy's purview. So if, as Peter Brook says, theater is "life in a more concentrate form," an intense distillation of life, condensing a lifetime into a few hours on the stage (cited in Janik 2003), then who better than Shakespeare can instruct philosophy about the texture of concrete existence? Who better than Hamlet, to take a famous example, can teach us about the dynamics of decisions made in the midst of life's uncertainties? To this exciting venture I wish to add my modest oar. I suggest that these essays should be read as operating within a uniquely postmodern horizon that I will call "hyper-reality" (Caputo 2001).

The nineteenth century's prophets gave us every assurance that God is dead. According to Marx and Feuerbach, the absolute has renounced its transcendent foothold in the sky and come down to earth, annulling the alienation of its absolute alterity for a life of immanence in the sublunary world. The positivists said that the mysteries that were once the province of myth and philosophy have found a demystified resting place in modern science. But in 1967, Jacques Derrida remarked, "what is dead wields a very specific power" (Derrida 1972: 6). There are signs of advanced secularization, like the decline in regular church attendance among the larger confessions or the virtual collapse of vocations to the Catholic priesthood in the Western countries. But non-traditional forms of spirituality flourish. Above all, the [xvii] entire world, west and east, north and south, has been swept by surging tides of Christian evangelicalism and Islamic fundamentalism. These are contemporary realities with which academic skepticism is totally out of touch.

"Modernity" is more complicated than previously imagined. The very idea of the death of God in Nietzsche constituted a denial that there is some such Overarching Truth, be it scientific or theological. There are only as many little pragmatic truths (Nietzsche called them "fictions") as are required for the complexities of life. Secularism's monopoly is as dead as God's, allowing many flowers to bloom.

The ancients invested a considerable effort trying to convince us that the supersensible sphere is "really real," while the nineteenth century proclaimed that realm to be an "un-real" fantasy and asked us to content ourselves with the sensible reality below. But in this post-modern age it is the "hyper-real" that holds sway. In a world of interplanetary space probes the very pre-Copernican distinction between an upper world and a lower one had lost all sense, even as totalizing omni-explanations have lost their cachet. Our world is what James Joyce called a "chaosmos" (See Eco 1989), neither *simple* cosmos nor *simple* chaos, but a complex loosely joined and supple configuration given to chance and the unexpected, open-ended and reconfigurable. We live no longer by the simple distinction between presence and absence. Our lives are suffused and haunted by shades and specters, quasi- and virtual realities. Within the ultra-horizon of the "hyper-real" diverse patterns of what this book calls "spirituality" unfold.

In speaking of the "hyper-real," I am first of all commending to the reader Baudrillard's analysis of an electronic replication of reality in a "virtual" world so uncanny as to blur the distinction between the real and the unreal (to what extent was the "Gulf War" real and to what extent was it a media event?) Baudrillard's point, whose importance cannot be overestimated, goes to the heart of one of the senses of postmodernism that has been artfully explored in the works of Mark C. Taylor (See Taylor 2003 and 2004). In such a world, the insubstantiality of what the materialists call matter is visited upon us with a fury. We lead lives in which the lines between nature and *techne*, bodily organs and artificial [xix] transplants are so complex that the very meanings of "mother," "birth" and "nature" have been made to tremble. In such a world materialistic reductionism or "naturalism" is a naive nineteenth century anachronism, an antiquated paradigm, while Elizabethan ghosts and angels have become interestingly timely.

But I use "hyper-real" in a second and distinctly ethico-religious sense which bears quite directly on the present volume. For if it is true that contemporary theorists are critics of realism and essentialism, as they certainly are, still it brushes against the grain to call them (simply) "anti-realists." For the truth is that by and large contemporary theory is turned toward the affirmation of the

"Other. This is the very opposite of selfishness or fantasy. Derrida's discontent with realism arises not from anti-realist motives but from hyper-realist ones, from a love and a desire for the real beyond what today passes for real, which springs from a desire beyond desire for a justice or a democracy to come!

And yet the point here, let us recall, is not to fit Shakespeare into any preestablished theory but to shush the philosophers and make them listen to the play because the play's the thing, *die Sache selbst*, in which the whole of life is concentrated.

Shakespeare knows that our lives are haunted by shades and shadows of the dead who remind us of what they expect, that they are uplifted by the voice of a "divinity" who "shapes our ends," and that they are disturbed by the demonic distortions of evil. He knows that we are called to respond in the present even as we are solicited by the promise of things to come.

There are more things in heaven and earth, Horatio, than are dreamt of in secular materialism, theology, or contemporary theory. That at least is what the present collection sets out so suggestively to explore.

References

Caputo, John D. (2000) "For the Love of the Things Themselves: Derrida's Phenomenology of the Hyper-Real," *Journal of Cultural and Religious Theory*, 1.3 (July), www.jcrt.org.

Derrida, Jacques (1972) *Positions*, trans. Alan Bass (Chicago: University of Chicago Press).

_____. 1994. *Specters of Marx: The State of the Debt, the Work of Mourning, and the New International*, trans. Peggy Kamuf (New York, Routledge).

Eco, Umberto (1989) *The Aesthetics of Chaosmos: The Middle Ages of James Joyce*, trans. E. Esrock, Cambridge, MA: Harvard University Press.

Janik, Allan A. (2003) "Allan Janik Talks to Knut Olav Amas," https://www.eurozine.com/weiningers-vienna/

* * *

Editor's Note: Because the published version of this piece was extensively edited, we are publishing below the full unedited version.

OF HYPER-REALITY

The essays that follow are meant to open up links between the world of Shakespeare and that surprising twist in postmodernism sometimes called its "religious turn." They proceed from the premise that literature does not illustrate preestablished philosophical principles but can instruct philosophy about matters too concrete and singular for philosophy's purview. So if, as Peter Brook says, theater is "life in a more concentrated form," an intense distillation of life, condensing a lifetime into a few hours on the stage (cited in Janik 2003), then who better than Shakespeare can instruct philosophy about the texture of concrete existence? Who better than Hamlet, to take a famous example, can teach us about the dynamics of decisions made in the midst of life's uncertainties? To this exciting venture I wish to add my modest oar, which takes the form of a framing hypothesis, that these essays should be read as operating within a uniquely postmodern horizon that I will call "hyper-reality." (Caputo 2001)

The nineteenth century's prophets gave us every assurance that God is dead or, at the very least, that the Ancient of Days is on his last legs and is hardly expected to live out the week. Marx and Feuerbach explained that the absolute had renounced its transcendent foothold in the sky and come down to earth, annulling the alienation of its absolute alterity for a life of immanence in the sublunary world. The positivists said that the mysteries that were once the province of myth and philosophy had now found a demystified resting place in modern science, which will do all the explaining from here on in, thank you very much. Nietzsche's Zarathustra summed it all up in the famous prophecy that "God is dead." The Grand Old Man was slipping fast; the divine demise was in sight, and all one could hope for was a worthy send off.

A century later, in 1967, Jacques Derrida somewhat more circumspectly remarked, "I do not at all believe in what today is so easily called the death of philosophy (nor, moreover, in the simple death of whatever – the book, man or god, especially since, as we all know, what is dead wields a very specific power)" (Derrida 1972: 6). The dead for Derrida have a curious way of living on, like the ghosts in *Hamlet* and *Macbeth*, of revisiting us from their spectral haunts, so that in their death they are as much a force, or even more a force, than ever they were in life. Nothing is simple, certainly not death. That became the basis of the famous "spectral" effect in *Hamlet* and *Macbeth* that Derrida later on deployed in *Specters of Marx* (1993), in which he found it necessary to hasten to the rescue of Marx himself, whose own death was now being widely proclaimed by the right-wing prophets of the "New World Order."

At about the same time Derrida was giving that interview American sociologists were formulating what they called "secularization theory," the Enlightenment idea that modernization leads to secularization and the decline of religion. But as Peter L. Berger said, on the whole the thesis proved to be "false," "essentially mistaken," and the world is "as furiously religious as it ever was, and in some places more so than ever" (Berger 1999: 2). There are clear signs of secularization, like the decline in regular church attendance among the larger confessions or the virtual collapse of vocations to the Catholic priesthood in the Western countries. But even as public structures have tended to secularize, private life has become increasingly religious. As institutional religion declines, non-traditional, even non-western, forms of spirituality flourish. Above all, the entire world, west and east, north and south, has been swept by surging tides of Christian evangelicalism and Islamic fundamentalism. Counter-secularization, the direct reaction against the forces of secularization, has swamped secularization, which tends to prosper best among academics in faculty clubs in North America and western Europe while much of the world around them is, well, "furiously religious." As Berger says, "to say the least, the relation between religion and modernity is rather complicated" (Berger, 1999: 3). As Derrida could have told him, do not count on the simple death of anything! Nothing is simple (deconstruction in a nutshell!)

To recognize that "modernity" is far more complicated than anyone ever imagined is to have begun the transition to the post-modern, which I view as the continuation of modernity by another means. For the postmodern is not anti-modern – it is no less committed than modernity to an egalitarian emancipation from authoritarianism and to Enlightenment freedom of inquiry – but it has a finer eye for complexity. The big mistake made by modernity was an excessive concern with tidy distinctions like fact/value, objective/subjective, reason/faith, and public/private, which betrayed an intolerance for the messiness of life. Kant, most famously, made a career out of drawing critical boundaries whose borders he then patrolled in three famous "critiques." Modernity was moreover hoodwinked by the desire to reduce everything to One Big Principle, like "Reason" or "Spirit." But the very idea of the death of God in Nietzsche constituted a denial that there is some such Overarching Truth (what Nietzsche called the "ascetic ideal") – be it scientific or theological – in reference to which all lesser debates are adjudicated. There are only as many little pragmatic truths (Nietzsche called them "fictions") as are required for the complexities of life. So if God is dead, a funny thing happened on the way to the funeral. The very declamation of God's death spells the death of "reductionism" itself (*mors mortis!* the death of the death of God), thus allowing many flowers to bloom. Contemporary theory has caught up to contemporary life; postmodern means post-secular. Berger's quip, meant to illustrate the uncertainty of sociological prediction, "Who knows – perhaps the next religious upsurge in America will occur among disenchanted post-modernist academics!" (Berger 1999: 13), is not far from true! For what has proven to be moribund is the very movement of materialistic reductionism, the very idea of saying that x is "nothing more than" y – for example, that religious faith is nothing more than a displaced desire for our mommy. Nothing is that simple.

By the postmodern I mean an affirmation of non-totalizable complexity (like the internet), non-formalizable ambiguity (of the "natural," e.g.) and irreducible multiplicity ("pluralism"). Experience cannot be reduced to a monochrome, either of economics or ethics, body or soul, crass materialism or exalted idealism. The ultimate horizon of postmodernity is that there is no ultimate horizon. There is no way to drive off the ghosts, the specters and the spirits that haunt our lives, which are as truly given to us as enzymes, electrons and economic cycles. The ancients invested a considerable effort trying to convince us that the supersensible sphere is "really real," while the nineteenth century proclaimed that realm to be an "un-real" fantasy and asked us to content ourselves with the sensible reality below. But in this post-modern age it is the "hyper-real" that holds sway. In a world of interplanetary space probes the very pre-Copernican distinction between an upper world and a lower one had lost all sense, even as totalizing omni-explanations have lost their cachet. The world had become what James Joyce called a "chaosmos," neither *simple* cosmos nor *simple* chaos, but a complex loosely joined and supple configuration given to chance and the unexpected, open-ended, and reconfigurable. The world is not a simple presence/absence system. It consists of all sorts of shades in between, of realities and quasi-realities and virtual realities, of living bodies and spectral shades, of what cannot easily be reduced to matter or sublimated into spirit. Such a world provides an opening for the religious, or what are called in these essays the diverse patterns of "spirituality," to blossom in the ultra-horizon of the hyper-real.

In speaking of the "hyper-real," I am first of all commending to the reader Baudrillard's analysis of an electronic replication of reality in a "virtual" world so uncanny as to blur the distinction between the real and the unreal (to what extent was the "Gulf War" real and to what extent was it a media event?) Baudrillard's point, whose importance cannot be overestimated, goes to the heart of one of the senses of postmodernism that has been artfully explored in the works of Mark C. Taylor. In such a world – the *Matrix* movies popularize this point, which was first made by Bishop Berkeley's famous axiom, *esse est percipi* – the insubstantiality of what the materialists call matter is visited upon us with a fury. We lead lives in which the lines between nature and *techne*, bodily organs and artificial transplants – talk about the logic of the supplement! – are so complex that the very meanings of "mother," "birth" and "nature" (*natus ÷ natura!*), have been made to tremble. In such a world materialistic reductionism or "naturalism" is a naive nineteenth century anachronism, an antiquated paradigm, while Elizabethan ghosts and angels have become interestingly timely. (The title of one of Berger's books is *A Rumor of Angels!*)

But I use "hyper-real" in a second and distinctly ethico-religious sense which bears quite directly on the present volume. For if it is true that post-structural theorists are critics of realism and essentialism, as they certainly are, still it brushes against the grain to call them (simply) "anti-realists." For the truth is that by and large contemporary theory is turned toward the affirmation of the "other," outside and beyond language. Deconstruction, to take my favorite example, is well defined as the *viens oui, oui* of hospitality, as the welcoming of what Levinas calls the "wholly other;" hence it is the very opposite of some sort of vicious subjectivism. Derrida's discontent with realism arises not from *anti*-realist motives but from *hyper*-realist ones, from a love and a desire for the real beyond what today passes for real, which springs from a desire beyond desire for a justice or a democracy to come! That hyper-realism is what he calls the "messianic," a notion explored in several of these essays, by which he means the porous open-endedness of the present to the future (as also a paradoxical Benjaminian "messianic remembrance" of the dead), in which it would be a kind of idolatry to allow the present – like what currently passes for justice or democracy – to assume the form of final presence. In his "critique of the metaphysics of presence" – like a certain a/theological counterpart to the biblical critique of idols – the present is never enclosed in presence, the materialities of existence are never held captive by materialism, even as the spiritual is never relegated to a far off super-sensible sphere.

But if the messianic motif in Derrida has been contested by Slavoj Žižek and Alain Badiou on the grounds that it indefinitely defers decision, we are asked to consider in the present volume whether it might not also be contested by Shakespeare himself, in the final act of *Hamlet*, when the knot of all the prince's doubts is cut by deadly and decisive action. Is this a point on which contemporary theory is itself instructed by the Bard? The point here, let us recall, is not to fit *Hamlet* into a preestablished theory – Derrida's or Žižek's – but to shush the philosophers and make them listen to the play because the play's the thing, *die Sache selbst*, in which a whole lifetime has been concentrated.

The real does not form a hard and impermeable block of presence, a closed sphere in which being clings fast to being, but it is made porous by the tensions of the hyper-real. To see that our lives are haunted by shades and shadows of the dead who remind us of what they expect of us, uplifted by the voices of the angels who summon us to action, disturbed by the demonic distortions of evil, to understand that we are called to respond in the present even as we are solicited by the promise of things far off and undreamt of, pursued down labyrinthine paths by spirits of some unknown and insubstantial quality – is that not a common wisdom in the world of Shakespeare to which we today are trying to gain access under the name of the postmodern?

There are more things in heaven and earth, Horatio, than are dreamt of in secular materialism, onto- theology – and contemporary theory.

That at least is what the present collection sets out so suggestively to explore.

References

Berger, Peter L. (2000). Editor. *The Desecularization of the World: Resurgent Religion and World* Politics (Grand Rapids: Eerdmans).

_____. *A Rumor of Angels: Modern Society and the Rediscovery of the Supernatural.* New York: Doubleday Anchor Books, 1970

Brook, Peter (1994). *The Shifting Point: Theatre, Film, Opera 1946-1987* (New York: Theatre Communications Group).

Caputo, John D. (2000). "For the Love of the Things Themselves: Derrida's Phenomenology of the Hyper-Real," *Journal of Cultural and Religious Theory*, 1.3 (July), www.jcrt.org.

Derrida, Jacques (1972). *Positions*, trans. Alan Bass (Chicago: University of Chicago Press).

_____. 1994. *Specters of Marx: The State of the Debt, the Work of Mourning, and the New International*, trans. Peggy Kamuf (New York, Routledge).

Janik, Allan A. (2003). "Allan Janik Talks to Knut Olav Amas," https://www.eurozine.com/weiningers-vienna/

12

IN PRAISE OF AMBIGUITY

[In *Ambiguity in the Western Mind*, eds. Craig J. N. De Paulo, Patrick Messina, Marc Stier (New York: Lang Pub. Co., 2005), 15–34]

[15] What could be clearer than that our lives are ambiguous – deeply, provocatively, dangerously, beautifully ambiguous? I am not complaining, for ambiguity is a gift that gives life its interest, its mystery, its passion. Ambiguity lures and entices us, drawing us into the mystery of things, the mystery of one another, the mystery of God. Ambiguity raises the stakes of life; it makes life risky and is liable to lead us astray; that makes life a prize worth winning. Ambiguity leaves us restless, uncertain, questing and questioning, searching and researching; that makes life a treasure worth finding. *Factus sum mihi terra difficultatis*, Augustine said, "I have become a land of difficulty for myself," but it is the very difficulty of life that gives life substance and texture.[1] Whatever is important, valuable, significant is ambiguous – love and death, God and suffering, right and wrong, the past and the future. Just so, if something is unambiguously clear, transparently simple, is that not because its substance is spent, its future is over? Ambiguity is like the blackness of the night sky, which makes the stars glow more brilliantly and leaves us wondering what else stirs in those dark depths from which they shine forth.

Ambiguity is a gift: that is the hypothesis that I will pursue here – in praise of ambiguity, but with all due clarity.

The Principle of Ambiguity: Both/And

Let us begin *in principio,* in the beginning, with a principle of great clarity, for which I turn to Kierkegaard, who launched his career, or rather that of his pseudonyms, with a book entitled *Either/Or*, to which I would like to pay a tribute, or a counter-contribute, entitled "Both/And." I do not in this way mean to defy Kierkegaard but rather to reinforce his position and make it stronger. In my view "both/and" is the other side of "either/or," its complement, the silent partner in the firm of Johannes de Silentio and Victor Eremitus, et al. Were I myself bold enough to write in the fanciful manner of the pseudonyms,

I would say that my little eulogy to ambiguity today could be called "Both 'Both/And' and 'Either/Or'."

As it happens, that mind bending expression is in fact also a good description of what is called "undecidability" by Jacques Derrida, whose peculiar proximity to Kierkegaard I am constantly insisting upon, instigating, or otherwise insinuating. Undecidability should not be viewed as the sworn enemy of decision, as Derrida's unfriendly critics persist in doing, but rather as its condition of possibility. There is only something to decide when we do not know what to do, whereas when what is to be done is obvious from the start, so that there is little wavering and even less deliberation, then there is very little to decide. However much deliberation is in order, however long deliberation may go on, the actual moment of decision is a leap. Otherwise, deciding is just a question of going through the motions, running the program, connecting the dots. But really to decide something – the root of this word means to *cut*, so that every de-cision is also an in-cision – means to feel oneself pulled in several directions at once, to see the merits of this and the merits of that, of *both* this *and* that, to see that *both* alternatives are right, or perhaps *both* are wrong, or even perhaps that both are right and both are wrong, and to know that nonetheless something, some *one* thing, has to be done. We just can't stand there and deliberate while the city burns. The real decision is urgent; the decisive cut has to be made. So what gives the either/or its passion, its real cutting edge is both/and.

[17] Furthermore, "both 'both/and' and 'either/or,'" which fairly describes what Derrida calls "undecidability," is no less fair a description of *ambiguity*, which comes from the Latin prefix *ambi*, meaning "both," and *agere*, to act or to do. Ambiguity describes a situation in which there is something that must be done but we are of two minds about what to do. Had our linguistic history taken another turn or two, we might have words like ambi-active, ambi-action, or ambi-agile. The German word for ambiguity describes the duality, *Zweideutigkeit*, having two meanings or interpretations, but it does not pick up the *agere*. Things get ambiguous precisely when the case for one alternative is as pressing as the case for the other, and we are forced to choose the greater good and sacrifice the lesser; or, alternately, when the case *against* one alternative is as pressing as the case against the other and we are forced to choose the lesser evil and avoid the greater one. Both are right and/or both are wrong, so what is to be done? I hasten to add that I am not complaining about this situation. On the contrary, I, who am a great lover of what the young Heidegger called the difficulty of factical life, intend here to praise ambiguity, to praise "both/and," to praise everything that is ambi-this or ambi-that – ambidextrous or ambi-

sextrous or ambivalent – and I look approvingly upon all ambi-tendencies, and this on the general grounds of their wider ambit and more delightful ambiance.

So, with a fear and trembling that befits my humble condition, I stand here, *ich kann nicht anders,* in open defiance of a long and venerable line of thinkers who have preceded me, ready to defend a little thesis or counter-thesis or unconventional hypothesis that ambiguity is a gift, that everything deep and provocative, everything beautiful and mysterious, everything decisive and meaningful, is ambiguous. Ambiguity is not an acid dropped on life's clarity but the veil in which life's *mystery* is kept safe, by which it is protected from the harsh and destructive light of univocity and programmability. My task here is to show that things really have a cutting edge, a meaning that it is worth taking note of, that things are really meaningful, when they are awash in ambiguity, while clear cut and unambiguous matters mostly merit a yawn. Something is really happening when there is ambiguity [18] afoot (with *both* feet, of course). Ambiguity is what makes the great books great, what gives decisions their decisiveness, what gives life its passion, its force, its grip on us. In the classical language of transcendental philosophy, one might formulate my hypothesis by saying that ambiguity is the condition of possibility of everything worthy and important. But if we remember our principle of great clarity, both/and, we would have to refine this into a more ambiguous quasi-transcendental principle: ambiguity is the condition *both* of the possibility *and* of the impossibility of everything meaningful. That means that ambiguity makes our beliefs and practices possible by also making them impossible, that is, ambiguity sees to it that our beliefs and practices are made possible by simultaneously threatening action and menacing meaning, by making them hover over the abyss. Ambiguity is a gift but remember *die Gift vergiftet* and can very well poison us.

Philosophers Against Ambiguity

The case against my hypothesis about the gift of ambiguity among the philosophers – who have long preferred unity to multiplicity, simplicity to complexity, univocity to plurivocity, the one to the many – is formidable and long standing. Ambiguity has been in trouble with the philosophers right from the start, when ambiguity first fell afoul of father Parmenides' passion for monothetic univocity. Parmenides singled out for derision in his poem those "two-headed" (*dikranoi*) types,[2] those deplorable both/and people who wander about saying both "it is" and "it is not," who dwell in the land of *doxa*, which is the sphere of mere opinion and appearance. These woeful ones Parmenides opposed to the clear-headed – by which, of course, he certainly meant the one-headed – followers of the way of being, who stick single-mindedly to the "it is," which is the way of "truth" shown by the goddess. But on my heretical account, two heads are better than one, and the dicranial is better than those monocranial, monomaniac, monotonous, Parmenidean types. Is it not written (somewhere) that two heads are better than one? Having two heads, or being of two minds, is just the sort of thing that is [19] needed in order to see both sides of the story and to understand the difficulty of a complex situation. In just the way that Kierkegaard tried to write with both hands, to write the signed "edifying" or "upbuilding" works with his right hand, while writing indirect more seductive and sinistral and pseudonymous works with his left hand, so it is better to be thinking with two heads rather than one, especially when they are combined in one skull. In general, I prefer plurality, plurivocity and pluralism to all this Parmenidean unity, identity and univocity, where being is a well-rounded, self-identical, and solid sphere, which seems to me uninterrupted, undivided boredom.[3]

In modernity, Descartes made his reputation explaining to us how to clarify our ideas, how to think with methodic precision, how to avoid the abyss of ambiguity in which all our "clear and distinct ideas" are lost like a ship in a fog or a diver in a bottomless sea. Even Heidegger, the great critic of Descartes and the thinker of Being's concealment, denounced *Zweideutigkeit* in *Being and Time* as the refuge of the inauthentic, as the sounding cymbal of those who say they understand something, like the fact of their mortality, precisely when they do not.[4]

Ambiguity is, alas, the Mary Magdalene of philosophical concepts, a woman whose reputation has been unjustly tarnished by the boys just when she may have been the Beloved Disciple herself. Ambiguity is a good woman whose name has been smeared by phallocentric philosophers too much in love with pure Forms, solid substances, clear and distinct ideas, transcendental consciousness, authentic being-unto-death, and other fantasies of an excessively purifying or unifying and very virile frame of mind that has more or less constituted philosophy right from the start. Indeed, philosophy's aversion to ambiguity goes hand in hand with a very virile love of power, of top-down systems with clear directions coming from on high.

Indeed, what is arguably the opening scene of philosophy in the west has Socrates prowling the agora in search of clear definitions of things that most people thought they understood just fine but found they could not define when they came under the fire of Socratic inquisition. Philosophy got off the ground with that kind of passion for purity, pressing for definitions. [20] Philosophy first opened its doors for business by announcing that it could sort out the clarity of "truth" from the ambiguity of rhetoric, for the only rhetorical skill one needed was the skill to tell the truth (*Apology*). The first act of philosophy ends with a death scene, with Socrates on stage dying for the right to ask his questions.

Nietzsche was the first one to dare criticize Socrates, the first to regard him not as a martyr but a monster, who instead of having an overgrown ear or nose had a grossly overgrown cerebellum. Socrates pressed for well-defined conceptual clarity, Nietzsche complained, just where none was needed or even in order, even as he devalued the importance of the implicit, preconceptual, instinctive capacity to do things, which characterizes everyone who really manages to *do* something. Socrates grossly exaggerating the importance of explicit conceptual definition and precision, precisely the sort of thing prized by professors who are sometimes better at *talking* about things than actually *doing* them.[5]

To that end, and having my own spine stiffened by Nietzsche's audacious critique of Socrates, philosophy's patron saint, I will stick by my perverse philosophical thesis, which is a kind of counter-philosophical thesis or counter-thesis, a hyperbolic hypothesis that will no doubt incite the philosophers against me because it flies in the face of one of philosophy's most fundamental articles of faith. On the view that I am taking ambiguity is a gift in spite of the fact that, or rather precisely because, ambiguity is a menace that threatens to undermine meaning. Ambiguity is for me the condition that makes meaning possible by making pure and unambiguous meaning impossible. In such a view pure and perfect clarity is an auto-deconstructing event. For if you are completely clear and certain about what you think or what you feel you must do, that is because the life of meaning has gone dead for you, because meaning has stagnated into a settled dull affair. On the other hand, the more you are stuck and quite bewildered about what the next step is and the more up against a stone wall you are driven, the more you are really on the move.

[21] The Auto-deconstruction of Univocity

To advance my unpopular cause, let us consider the deadening effects of clarity and univocity, as opposed to the open-ended ambiance of ambiguity. To that end, I take up the opposition, or the "transcendental parallel,"[6] as he calls it, that Derrida stages between Edmund Husserl, the German philosopher who first formulated the method of phenomenology, and as sober a judge as philosophy has ever produced, and James Joyce, the Irish writer whom even the Irish could not tolerate, who raised passions everywhere with his ribald, bawdy and almost unreadably playful prose. Husserl is writing about the history of geometry (a topic about which James Joyce had little to say), and he is insisting that our use of language be unambiguously clear, that no science, geometric or any other, can move forward unless its meanings are formulated in unambiguous expressions that can be passed on from generation to generation, that retain an "ideal identity" that "allows communication among generations of investigators" across the ages. Otherwise, we will be plunged into the night of equivocity. But consider the paradoxical consequence of this notion that Derrida points out, which on the face of it seems otherwise perfectly obvious. History and historical transmission would be possible, on Husserl's account, just on the condition that every trace of historical alteration and deviation is extinguished. The result of this Husserlian demand, Derrida writes, would thus be "to sterilize or paralyze history in the indigence of an indefinite iteration," a repetition of the same that makes for no movement forward, that is, no real movement, no room for movement, no ambiance.

The other alternative is Joyce's, "to repeat and take responsibility for all equivocation itself, utilizing a language that could equalize the greatest possible synchrony with the greatest potential for buried, accumulated, and interwoven intentions within each linguistic atom, each vocable, each word, each simple proposition," a language that instead of trying to translate the common semantic content from one language to another, "circulates throughout all languages at once, accumulates their energies, actualizes their most secret consonances...cultivates their [22] associative syntheses instead of avoiding them," a language that does not avoid complexity but settles within its "labyrinthian field." Nonetheless, without some unity, without some univocity, "the very text of its repetition would have been unintelligible."

In short, historical movement is equally impossible for both Husserl and Joyce, albeit for opposing reasons. Husserl tries to account for history with a power of transmission that is so univocal as to cut off something *new* from happening; nothing different is allowed to be introduced; pure univocity is pure paralysis. But Joyce tries to dominate history from another direction, by exploiting every equivocation, every novelty, so that there is no novelty left that would not be an empty repetition of what Joyce has already deployed. Joyce's pure equivocation makes historical transmission not only unintelligible but unnecessary. What makes history move, what makes movement possible, what makes for historical ambiance, is what Derrida calls "repetition" or "iteration," by which he means the repetition – and the production by repetition – of the different, the mobility of ambiguous transmission, passing along a multiplicity of meanings, multiple associations, more or less loose links, trembling and loose transmissions which are not simply garbled but polyvalent, not confused but polymorphic, not chaotic but astir with a multiplicity of meaning that opens up the future, disclosing possibilities, even as they demand decision and resolution.

Perfect univocity is auto-deconstructing. If a word is unambiguously clear, it has lost its suggestiveness and become a technical term. If a character in a fiction is unambiguously clear, the novel is a bore. If a text is completely readable, completely unambiguous, it would not be worth reading or it would soon lose its interest. Unreadability is the condition of possibility of genuine readability. Progress is made when otherwise smoothly running systems run into an anomaly which forces the system to reconfigure on a higher level. In the sphere of action, of the ethico-political, if someone is unambiguously male or female, white or black, American or anti-American, Christian or Islamic, Republican or Democrat, then God help them and, more importantly, God help the rest of us. If one is faced with a [23] devilishly difficult decision, the only fellow whose advice I would trust is the fellow who does not know what to do, who is absolutely stuck, who sees both sides of the story and is sympathetic with both and is completely paralyzed by the difficulty of the situation. That is a man whom I admire, someone who is thinking clearly, who is using his head, who is using both his heads, that is, thinking with a clear sense of the ambient ambiguity of the situation.

The Limits of Ambiguity

I hasten to add – before the police of philosophy arrive to cart me off for my civil disobedience – that ambiguity is not imprecision and that I am not simply against precision, clarity, and method. Ambiguity is an excess of meaning, a multiplication of too many meanings, so that we find ourselves drawn in several directions are once. Imprecision is not an excess but a lack, viz., a lack of precision where precision is required. Let me be clear that I am unambiguously opposed to imprecision. The most general theory I hold is not about clarity or ambiguity, but about contextuality, according to which everything has a context, and nothing happens outside a context, so that the sense and value of our beliefs and practices are ultimately a function of the context in which they are found. There are clearly contexts in which univocal precision and exactitude are exactly what is in order – when I look at my watch on the way to the airport, balance my checking account, turn the ignition of my car on a dark and freezing cold night far away from home, turn on my computer, or have an MRI or an X-ray of a medical condition that needs treatment. Then I want precision.

So in any discussion of ambiguity, it is necessary to be clear and to make clear distinctions. There are technical instruments and formal systems where unambiguous exactness and precision are a virtue. The lack of virtue is to think that such univocity applies everywhere and to everything, to think that univocity applies univocally to everything. The mistake is to think that such univocity applies to the humanities and the social sciences – although of course even there computer searches not only of [24] bibliographies but of the occurrence of words, expressions, etc. are very much in order. It would also be a mistake to think that it applies to the mathematics and the natural sciences at their cutting edge, where theoreticians are breaking new ground when they find themselves faced with paradoxes and aporias that are best met not by method but by imagination. What else is Kuhn's famous account of a scientific crisis if not an account of scientific ambiguity, and what else is a crisis than an opportunity for a revolutionary advance? So the relevant distinction for me is between the formalizable and the non-formalizable. There are things that can be gotten down cold, mastered, reduced to a "method" or "program," so that they can be run with the flick of a switch. There are things that we can calculate, formalize, axiomatize, submit to a methodic procedure that works every time, and there is surely a place for that. When Johannes Climacus distinguished subjective from objective truth, he was not proposing the abolition of the latter, but only that Christianity not be confused with objective truth.

In a similar manner, to the sphere of programmable things I oppose the – in the end – more interesting sphere of things that we cannot formalize or program, master or axiomatize, regularize or normalize, or reduce to a method. It is the latter that concerns me here, for it is the latter, I would say, that belongs to the avant-garde of our beliefs and practices, to the cutting edge of the things to be made or done or known. It is only with the latter more ambiguous things that we reach the point where the gears of our minds are fully engaged. When we hit the point of the unprecedented, the point where we have no guides or guard rails to make safe the way, then we are on our own and must fall back upon the raw resources of raw intelligence. But by the time our beliefs and practices have become crystal clear and precedents point the way, they are more or less spent, worn out, tired, exhausted, on the downward trend in their life cycle. The things that have a future are ambiguous just because we haven't figured them out yet, and their competing possibilities keep the future open. They are ambiguous because they are replete with possibility, tossed and turned about by multiple potentialities, [25] capable of going in many directions at once. When I have to make a first cut into something that I have not encountered before, when I have to think something I have never thought before, or say something I have never said before, or do something that I have never done before, then I am thinking, speaking and acting in a manner worthy of those very worthy names. Otherwise, I am cruising on automatic pilot, half-asleep at the wheel.

On my accounting, clarity and ambiguity should not be viewed as simple logical opposites on a timeless spectrum but different stages in the process of making meaning, of producing meaning as an effect. Clarity is a late product, something that emerges at dusk, at the end of the process, when a belief or practice has more or less run its course, and has acquired a kind of distilled, stable, settled, literal sense. Then we can write its history, analyze it, formalize it. The ancients said, call no man happy until he is dead; I would say, call no idea clear until it is dead. It has been passed along so long and so easily, is so readily reduced to a formula, that it has been rubbed thin and lost its future. Ambiguity on the other hand belongs to an earlier matinal stage, to a deeper stratum of meaning, where meaning is sending up its first shoots, where things have an irreducible richness that cannot be definitively laid out or decisively nailed down, finally settled or straightened out. Ambiguity is ambi-valent, that is, bristling with multiple values, indeed poly-valent, alive with possibilities that cannot be neatly ordered or contained.

The Ambit of Ambiguity

As a final effort in my uphill battle to make a case for ambiguity, I wish to explore something of the ambit of ambiguity, to investigate something of the varieties of ambiguous experience. To this end, I will take up four revealing cases – the work of translation, the case of avant-garde art, the act of ethical judgment, and the movement of religious faith. Each of these examples reveals a different kind of ambiguity which I hope here to tabulate and elaborate: the ambiguity of the text, the ambiguity of the first [26] or innovative, the ambiguity of the concrete and finally what I will call essential ambiguity.

(1) *Translation and the Ambiguity of the Text*. The late German philosopher Hans-Georg Gadamer, the author of the twentieth century's most important theory of "hermeneutics," says of the process of translation in his magnum opus *Truth and Method* that one of the most important differences between a text in the original language and a translation is that the translation "is at once clearer and flatter than the original" while the original is richer but more ambiguous than the translation.[7] That is because the translator has been forced to decide, to narrow down and determine, to resolve the ambiguity of the original, to translate a word that is astir with multiple associations and connotations with a word that chooses but one association. The translator inevitably emphasizes something that is important to him or herself and downplays other things. The translator must "show his colors" and state clearly how he or she understands

something that in the original can be understood in several ways. The translation has thinned out the original and produced a leaner, cleaner, clearer text, while the original retains a dark depth of suggestiveness that inspires multiple translations. That is why texts that Gadamer calls "classics," texts that are great enough, deep enough, *rich* enough to outlive their original context and find a new life in ever changing times, have to be translated again and again. Classic texts are constituted not by their utter tranquility and harmony, but by their polyphony, by their tensions, equivocations, and inconsistencies, by the overrich and overflowing lines of force that compete with each other and keep the text in motion over the ages. We never get to the bottom of what the classics mean, even as they never exhaust what they mean in any one context. That is the gift of tradition, which means to give over (*trans-dare*).

Now it is important to see that for Gadamer translation is not an isolated exercise but illustrative of the general structure of hermeneutics itself, that is, of the structure of reading and consequently of hermeneutic understanding generally, which always means bringing something within the horizon of the reader. To read is to interpret, to interpret is to apply, and to apply [27] is to translate something into the situation of the reader, to appropriate a text and bring it within the horizon of the reader's understanding. What then is a "text?" The text for Gadamer is not a fixed and determinate actuality but a "potentiality," something that is astir with possibilities that are "actualized" only on the occasion of the reading. The best example of a "text" in this sense is a musical score, which is a potentiality that is actualized only in the performance. To read is perform, to actualize, to translate a text that is multivocal, able to be given reality in several ways. As such, as a potentiality, the text is marked by a creative ambiguity, by polyvalent possibilities, which is why a classic text always has a future, and why a text does not so much have a fixed meaning as it has an unfolding history.[8]

(2) *Avant-garde Art and the Ambiguity of the First*. Let us turn now to Lyotard's account of the case of avant-garde art. What makes such art "avant-garde" is precisely what we object to in it, viz., the perplexity – the ambiguity – that it produces, which is such that it leaves the observer wondering whether such a thing is art at all. For Lyotard, the defining and paradigmatic reaction to avant-garde art is that the observer is brought to the point where one is forced to ask, "but is it art?" That is not an objection against avant-garde art or rather that objection is the very thing that constitutes avant-garde art. If anything less happens, if we are not led to object, then it is not avant-garde, but part of the rank and file, that is, part of an already constituted style or genre to which we have no objections. The reason for this is that the work is of such novelty that

standards of interpretation have not yet been formed. There are no criteria to recognize it either as such and such a kind, or to judge it as a good or bad specimen of its kind. None of that has been produced yet. When once it has, which means, when once a community of judgment has been formed, then artistic judgment becomes a matter of the more or less skillful application of these standards – is this is a good example of expressionism, of a dramatic dénouement, of a classical tragedy, of a modern musical comedy? If a new and hitherto unknown libretto of a Gilbert and Sullivan operetta were discovered, the question would be whether this is a good specimen of the kind, because the kind is well established; that would require a [28] judgment by those whose taste has been formed by experience with the form. The question provoked by avant-garde art is, as Lyotard puts it, whether a given work of art represents a new move in an old game or the invention of a new game altogether.[9]

Now what is instructive and illustrative to us about this example is that it goes without saying that there is no way to decide in advance whether the piece before us represents a bizarre oddity with no future or a breakthrough to a new level and kind of artistic expression, one that will be imitated and, by being imitated, established as a new style. There are no established rules or criteria to decide that because rules and criteria are things that are applied within paradigms or genres, whereas the creation of new paradigms or new genres is unformalizable. If the new work is successful, the piece in question is going to establish the rules by which things of its sort are to be judged, but there are no rules to determine what sorts of works will create new paradigms and allow communities of judgment to be formed. But that is not to be taken as a fault or a lack. The ambiguity of the first appearance of the work goes to the essence of *the ambiguity of the first*. Let us say more generally, the ambiguity of the innovation, of what is "first" or "new" or novel, constitutes the first in a positive way; it is an essential feature of the very idea of a breakthrough to something new, not an accidental defect to be removed in a better world. This undeterminability or unregulability – that is, this ambiguity – is so much a defining feature of the first, so much the mark of everything original, innovative, or novel, that were we to remove all ambiguity, we would destroy the possibility of original creation.

(3) *Ethics and the Ambiguity of the Concrete*. By the same token, ambiguity goes to the heart of ethical judgment. That is so true that the title of Simone de Beauvoir's book *An Ethics of Ambiguity* from years ago seems to me to pose not a paradox or aporia but a paradigm of good ethical sense, almost a truism. Aristotle recognized this long ago. On the opening pages of the first and, in my opinion, greatest of all the ethics books that have ever been written, Aristotle

cautioned us not to look for too much certainty; if it is certainty we are in search of, we should take up mathematics instead, not ethics. That is because ethical judgments [29] are made in the concrete and the concrete ethical situation is always slightly unprecedented, and often times not just slightly. In ethics, Aristotle said, we can offer the reader only general "schemata," more or less loose-fitting paradigms that must be kept essentially vague in order to preserve their flexibility. Ethics can only tell us in a general way about courage, e.g., that in general courage lies in a middle state between cowardliness and rashness. Courage does not consist either in running away from dangers that we should stand and face, or in rushing headlong into hopelessly dangerous situations in which there is no chance that we will achieve our goals and every likelihood that we will be destroyed. Yes, yes, we reply impatiently to Aristotle, but precisely what is that middle state? For that, the Philosopher patiently replies, you need a practiced eye, one that has been schooled in sizing up the complexities of the concrete situation and has learned how to make a concrete judgment. But you are being very ambiguous, we complain to the Philosopher. Precisely, the Philosopher would reply. He is being precisely ambiguous or ambiguously precise, for the precision is introduced in the practical application. The virtue of making such practiced practical judgments is what Aristotle called *phronesis* by which he meant, for our present purposes, the power to cope with the shifting sands of practical circumstances, the power to deal with the ambiguity of the concrete.

Aristotle was a superbly sensible philosopher who had the remarkably good sense to see that there was a place for everything, to sort out both a place for *theoria* or *episteme* when it came to unchanging and necessary things, and a place for practical know-how when it came to changing and variable things, things that could be otherwise, which is what we mean by the concrete situation. Aristotle had a sharp eye for the hermeneutics of singularity, for the hermeneutics of the concrete, and he had the good sense to know that the concrete situation is always slightly different and a not a little ambiguous.

What we call "postmodernism," if it means anything anymore (which is not certain), means among many other things an irreducible pluralism, a kind of endless contest of competing paradigms, world views, and "incommensurable" differences. [30] Understood in that way, postmodernism would represent a kind of intensification or radicalization of this Aristotelian point about the concrete or what we today call "singularity." What is "classical" about Aristotle and not post-modern, is that he thought the general schema or paradigm was settled and in place, that we don't choose it but it chooses us, that we are born into it by being born in a particular *polis*, and so the trick to growing up in your culture, in your *polis,* is to get practiced in its vagaries and variable applications. But the more postmodern view, which is more cosmo-politan and multi-politan, would insist not only on the ambiguous *applicability* of the paradigm but on the ambiguity that besets the paradigm *itself.* Aristotle thought there was a more or less identifiable *phronimos,* a prudent man, and that the difficulty lies in learning to imitate him. But the postmoderns locate the difficulty back a step, in coping with irreducible plurality of competing and incommensurable paradigms. For there are a lot of different prudent men, and quite a few prudent women, too, and more than one *polis* to consider which we meet every day in the media or over the internet, and so we need a kind of "meta-phronesis" about just what to take as paradigmatic, if indeed there is one at all.[10]

I might add that this idea of postmodern polyvalence would be grossly misused if it were used to stoke the fires of violence by allowing us to dig in and balkanize our differences – which is what its critics charge it does. For the whole idea is to provide the key to non-violence. Here is where the idea of ambiguity plays a vital role. We are witness today, and to our regret, to an ancient but it seems almost unlearnable lesson: that ethical and political action is never more dangerous – to oneself no less than to others – than when it is carried out *without* ambiguity. By this I mean, an ethics without a sense of self-questioning, without a sense of the multiplicity of ethical perspectives, without a sense that right and wrong, good and evil, are not univocal terms. If we maintain a heightened and salutary sense of ambiguity, we will not dig in about our differences and make them the basis of war but concede the ambiguity of our respective situations. For ambiguity instructs us that there are many ways to lead the good life, which should make us wary of enforcing our own ideas, which is after [31] all just one idea. The ethics of ambiguity thereby takes an interesting turn and so takes on an additional sense: from the ambiguity of the ethical situation to the ethics of ambiguity. That is, not only is there something irreducibly ambiguous about ethical judgments – they vary with the variable – but there is an ethical quality in ambiguity, something irreducibly ethical about respecting ambiguity, which respects variation.

(4) *Religious Faith and Essential Ambiguity.* That brings me to my last and final example of ambiguity, the movement of religious faith and what I will call the essential ambiguity of the human situation. In the view that I am defending here, someone who confesses or professes a religious faith is also at the same time confessing to the essential enigma of the human condition; one has faith just because one does not know. To say *credo,* I believe, to confess one's faith, is at the same time to confess to the multiplicity of voices within what we call, by a kind of shorthand, the "self." On this view, the self is made up of multiple

selves, of several voices within the same self, at least one of whom — in the case of religious belief — is a firm believer and the other is an ornery disbeliever. What we call the self is like the chairperson of a committee who gets to write up and put his own slant on the committee report thereby concealing how much dissension there is back on the committee. When I confess, when I say "I believe," I am not quite confessing the whole truth, not quite acknowledging that the "I" is a just a bit of a fiction, a kind of cover for an unruly committee, a condensation of a multiplicity of voices, so that the voice of belief is inwardly disturbed by multiple voices of unbelief that also stir within me and want to make themselves heard. In the end, "univocity" is a fiction, the acoustical illusion of having only one voice; it pretends to speak with one voice, *una voce*, while in fact a keen listener can pick up muffled voices in the background.

To be sure, the multivocity to which I expect the believer to confess is no less a problem for the unbeliever. I think that a truly honest and non-dogmatic expression of disbelief in God would always need to confess that it is haunted from within by competing voices, by an inextinguishable anxiety that one is closing oneself off to another voice, to something deep and important. If [32] the truth be told, one does not know and cannot say if one *is* a believer or a non-believer. That is why Derrida says of himself, "I quite rightly pass for an atheist," instead of simply saying, "I *am* an atheist."[11] Derrida understands the multiplicity within the subject which makes the subject a kind of corporation or committee or debating society. But as we have seen when Derrida speaks of "undecidability," he does not mean indecision, which makes life easy by sparing us the onerous task of deciding. Undecidability describes the conditions in which the difficulty of a true decision is made and has to be continually remade by being continually exposed to its opposite. In undecidability, the passion of our lives is forged. That is also why Johannes Climacus would never lay claim to *be* a Christian, but to be at most on the way to *becoming* one, which means that he would always confess to a kind of ambiguity about whether or not he is a Christian. "Rightly passing" for this or that is it seems to me the most one can ask for in this ambiguous life of ours.

Once again, this same law of reversibility that sets in when we considered the ethical — that the ambiguity of ethics reveals the ethical quality of ambiguity — is repeated here. For not only must we attach an irreducibly ambiguous character to any religious belief, in order to preserve the diversity and variability of the expression of religious life, the multiplicity of religious paths, the plurivocity of being-religious, but we should also see the essentially religious quality of ambiguity itself, and it is on that point that I wish to conclude. For as Jacques Derrida likes to say, with a devilish gleam in his eye, we do not know the secret. By the secret he does not mean the relative secrets that lawyers learn from their clients, or physicians from their patients, or that priests learn in the confessional, or that the government keeps as classified information, all of which could in principle be revealed under the proper circumstances. We have laws to protect such secrets just because it is entirely possible to reveal them. What Derrida means has to do with what he calls the "absolute secret" that no one could reveal to anyone because it is not known by anyone.[12] He means that we do not know who we are, that our lives are caught up in an irreducible unknowability, and that this unknowability goes to the heart of our human condition.

[33] Derrida is touching upon the deepest ambiguity of all, what I am calling here "essential ambiguity," by which I mean the ambiguity that goes to the heart of the human condition, that envelops what theologian Paul Tillich liked to call matters of ultimate concern, which are also matters of ultimate passion. When St. Augustine asked in his *Confessions, quid ergo amo cum deum meum amo?*, "what do I love when I love my God?" (*Confessions*, X, 6–7), that is a question that we lovers of ambiguity take to heart. If by God, we mean the profoundly ambiguous object of our desire, the indeterminable object of our *cor inquietum*, that which provokes the essential restlessness of the human condition, then that is a question that we all can and should ask ourselves all the time. If the truth be told, our lives are shrouded by this most essential and irreducible ambiguity, the essential secret that there is no secret truth, no truth of truth that will show us the way or lift us like a hook out of the flux.

The essential ambiguity of the secret is disquieting and disconcerting, provoking and provocative, but it is a productive unrest and a positive provocation. For the secret is what impassions us, provoking our interpretations, multiplying our translations, our readings, our narratives, our stories. This essential secret is not simply one more ambiguity in the list of four ambiguities that we have been enumerating, but the one that underlies and in part explains the endless translatability of the text, the restlessness of avant-garde art, and the shifting sands of ethical situations. Rightly understood, the secret by which we are all held captive should fill us with compassion for one another, with a sense that we are all fellow travelers in this darkness, siblings of the same dark night. It is this essential secret that injects an irreducible ambiguity into things, into our relationships with one another, into our relationship with God. It is this essential secret that makes it impossible to resolve things into clear and simple essences, as if there were or could be maps or guard rails when it comes to matters of ultimate concern.

Ambiguity is a gift. It is not a fog that settles over things and blurs our vision but a veil that preserves the essential mystery of our existence, that ensures that life will not wither under the harsh [34] light of the program or the rule, insuring that life will be an endless provocation, an infinite passion.

Our lives are deeply, disquietingly, dangerously ambiguous, which is why life is what Levinas calls a "beautiful risk" (*beau risque*).[13] Ambiguity is a gift that gives our lives ambit and ambiance, open-endedness and possibility, danger and riskiness, passion, and compassion. The woods of ambiguity are lovely, dark and deep, and we have promises to keep – to the substance of the earth, to the flesh of one another, to the body of God – and who knows when we will ever get to sleep.

Notes

[1] Augustine, *Confessions*, Book X, chapter 33. This text is also famously cited by Martin Heidegger, *Being and Time*, trans. J. Macquarrie and E. Robinson (New York: Harper & Row, 1962), §9, page 69, and was a touchstone for the "existential analytic."

[2] G.S. Kirk and J.E. Raven, *The Presocratic Philosophers* (Cambridge: Cambridge University Press, 1962), 271 (Parmenides, Fr. 345).

[3] As a purely formal matter, Aristotle, who will ultimately be a defender of ambiguity in the sense which I want to champion, complained that ambiguity represents an error in reasoning. In the Middle Ages, Thomas Aquinas wisely conceded that we cannot say a thing about God if we insist upon speaking about God in absolutely univocal terms, but that was no license for ambiguity, Thomas warned. While we must be prepared to admit a certain analogical quality into our language about God, nonetheless *analogia* must never be allowed to degenerate into *aequivocatio*, a wily equivocation.

[4] Heidegger, *Being and Time*, §37, page 217.

[5] Friedrich Nietzsche, *The Birth of Tragedy*, chapter 13, in *The Birth of Tragedy and Other Writings*, ed. R. Geuss and R. Speers (Cambridge: Cambridge University Press, 1999).

[6] Jacques Derrida, *Edmund Husserl's "Origin of Geometry"*, trans. John Leavey (Boulder: John Hays Co., 1978), 101–103.

[7] Hans Georg Gadamer, *Truth and Method*, 2nd rev. ed., trans. Joel Weinsheimer and Don Marshall (New York: Crossroad, 1989), 386.

[8] Occasionally, to be sure, a translation can itself become a classic, which occurs when its own deployment of the resources of the target language becomes an event in its own right. So even though modern readers will always need modern translations – the New Revised Standard Version – we will forever treasure the flavor and suggestiveness of the King James Bible. That means that a good translation can enrich the original, adds to its history, extends its suggestiveness, multiplies its valence in such a way that the original is not distorted but enriched and made more complex. The original and the translation are, in that case, related then, not as model and copy, but as root and branch, parent and child, forming together a greater whole in which the original has acquired an enlarged life.

[218] [9] Jean-François Lyotard and Jean-Loup Thébaud, *Just Gaming*, trans. Wlad Godzich (Minneapolis: University of Minnesota Press, 1985), 10.

[10] On the idea of "metaphronesis," see John D. Caputo, *Radical Hermeneutics* (Bloomington: Indiana University Press, 1987), 261–62.

[11] Jacques Derrida, "Circumfession: Fifty-nine Periods and Periphrases," in Geoffrey Bennington and Jacques Derrida, *Jacques Derrida* (Chicago: University of Chicago Press, 1993), 155.

[12] For Derrida on the secret, see Jacques Derrida, *On the Name*, ed. Thomas Dutoit (Stanford: Stanford University Press, 1995), 27–31.

[13] Emmanuel Levinas, *Otherwise than Being or Beyond Essence,* trans. Alphonso Lingis (The Hague: Martinus Nijhoff Publishers, 1981), 20, 94, 167.

DIALOGUES AND CONTROVERSIES

13

BEYOND THE DEATH OF GOD: A DEBATE WITH T. J. J. ALTIZER

[Unpublished, first given September 23, 2004, Lebanon Valley College (PA); revised 2005]

The premise from which I start is that the name of God is the name of what I desire, the name of a desire beyond desire. Viewed thus, the death of God in any simple or absolute way would mean the death of our desire. While it would always be proper to assert the death of this or that idea of God, so as not to trap God within the endless idols we invent, the death of God *simpliciter* would spell the death of what we love with a love that surpasses understanding. In what follows I will explain why, as regards the name of God, I prefer the figure of desire to the figure of death and why I am more interested in a certain rebirth of religion than in the death of God. To be sure, the relationship between the two is more complicated than the simple binarity of life and death, since the dead have a special way of living on, or of death and desire, since death is included among the things that we have been known to desire.

The Desire of God

So let us begin again, and to do so let us return to the structure of desire. The name of God is the name of what I desire, where desire, as Levinas says, springs not from a lack but from an affirmation, not from a negation but from saying *yes* to what I desire. So by desire I do not mean garden variety desire, which is the desire to have, but what I will call, following Derrida, a desire beyond desire, which is the desire to affirm. To be desirable on this accounting is not to be possessable but to be affirmable. In garden variety desire, the object desired is negated by being made my own; desire is the negation of the alterity of the desirable in which I desire to appropriate the other for my own. It is a will to possess what is missing or to fill up a gap, of which eating is a paradigmatic case. But the distinctive feature of a desire beyond desire is to affirm the alterity of the other in its irreducible alterity, to wish the other well and affirm its flourishing without attempting to consume it – and of this love is the paradigmatic case. (And of course, that this is not a clean distinction is seen in the expression that we "love to eat.") The general line I am pursuing in these remarks is that, of all the names that we are visited by in the tradition, the name of God – this is, at least, one of its most famous effects – elicits our desire beyond desire, our unconditional affirmation – as in Angelus Silesius's mystical quip "*Ja*-weh" – for by God we mean the excess of desirability and affirmability. The name of God is the name of that than which nothing greater can be conceived – or desired or affirmed. That means that, as regards the name of God, the figure of desire is more suitable than that of death. The logic of finality that surround the figure of death, as well the grammar and the rhetoric of what is moribund, are all wrong as regards God. The death of God makes sense only as a regional declaration, as the death of this or that idolatrous image of God. But as regards the name of God itself, *simpliciter*, the "desire" of God is vastly to be preferred, as affirmation is preferred to negation, life to death, the gift to sacrifice, and peace to violence.

As a little addendum meant for the present dialogue with the gospel of the death of God, I would also add that the desire for God is to be preferred to the death of God just because the postmodern is a more nuanced frame of mind than the modern, the post-secular is a more sensitive rendering of the historical situation of the times than the secular, because the event is a more suitable figure for thinking about history than is dialectical movement, and because undecidability is a more epistemologically responsible and appropriate way to use this name than self-certain dialectical necessity.

So then we ask, "What do I love when I love my God?" – which is the question that Augustine asks in the *Confessions* and which Derrida has famously repeated in "Circumfession." What is interesting about the question is that it does not turn on a "whether" but a "what;" it does not ask whether there is a God, or whether one loves God, or whether God should be loved, but what one loves when one loves God. It proceeds from the idea that love is something deeply worthy in itself and that God is above all what one loves if one loves anything at all. Everything turns on the question of *what* it is that one loves when one loves God, what is going on when I love my God. What I love about this question – something that Derrida has forced out of it – is the open-endedness of "God," so that what the name of God "means," what God is, God's "what-ness" or "quiddity," as the medieval philosophers say, is what is questionable, and only the fool would say in his heart that the love of God is dead.

To take but one obvious example, the Gospel of John tells us that God is love so that to love God is to love the God of love, to be in love with love. But when I say that "God is love," am I saying that "love" is the very highest name of God or that "God" is the best name I have for love, that love is divine, a godlike, godly thing, a certain god. Viewed thus the question is not whether God is dead – for that would mean, God forbid, that love is dead – but rather what is going on when we love our God. Or, to take another famous example from the Jewish Scriptures, when the prophets says that God is justice, do they mean that God above is just through and through or that justice is something divine and godlike? Do those who battle mightily all their lives for justice for the least among us and in the end give their lives for that cause "love God," whatever theological assertions they do or do not affirm? What is interesting about names like God, love, justice, goodness, and beauty is the *mis en abyme* to which they are subject, the mirror play in which each throws back the image of the other, which was stabilized in the middle ages by saying that they are "convertible" with one another inasmuch as they are all convertible with being (*ens*), which is of course a decision the scholastics made to bring this play to a halt.

But for me, the point is the endlessness of this convertibility by which I mean that they are subject to an endless translatability, and we are forced to confess that we do not know which is a case of which, which is an example of which, which we might also call the problem of exemplarity. Both this endless translatability of names like love and God, and the problem of exemplarity to which they are exposed, fall under what Derrida calls the general condition of "undecidability." To no one's surprise, the richer and more important a name is to us, the more beset it is by undecidability. That is also why these names are subject not only to convertibility but also reversibility, why they can so easily pass into their opposite, with the result that hatred wears the mask of love and violence wears the mask of justice.

Name and Event

Augustine's question presses us to ask: what is *going on* when I love my God? What is *happening* under the names of "God" and of "love"? To deal with this question, I propose that we distinguish between a name and the "event" that this name contains. Names are limited and historically contingent because they belong to what we call the "natural languages," so that if you do not have the language, you do not have the name; you only have the names given to you by the languages you have. (By "natural," by the way, we actually mean "historical," or "natural" as opposed to formal or artificial, like the "0, 1" language of a computer programmer). Names contain events but they cannot contain them, that is to say, names contain uncontainable events. Something is happening or going on in or under that name – something that is promised – that the name itself cannot limit or define, cannot police or predict, cannot inhibit or prohibit.

An event is the pent up potency of a name, something stirring and restless that is going on under the prompting of the name, something promised by the name. Of course, we should not underestimate the actual power – the real force – a name can exercise over the event it harbors. Names acquire institutional authority and historical prestige; they can pack all the accumulated power, punch and prestige of venerable "traditions" which have the effect of violently containing the event they harbor. Names even have armies while events do not bear arms. Armies march in the name of the name, of this name or that, of one name or another, above all, very famously or infamously, in the name of God. A religious war – which is a great embarrassment to religion, not to mention to the name of God – is a war waged in the name of God, in which competing armies each fight in the name of God, God against God, the God of Love against the God of Love, which means of course that they are wars of men against men, having more to do with idols than with God, and more with hate than with love. But religious wars are undeniably part of what is going on under the name of God, which is another part of the undecidability of that very powerful name. Religious wars and warring parties that make use of religion make the question, what do I love when I love my God, all the more pressing.

With this distinction between name and event in mind, we can ask, what is going on, what is happening, what event transpires when we speak of the desire of God? What do we desire when we desire God? What desires or is doing the desiring? What is being desired? Desire on my accounting is inextinguishable, so that if we come across someone without desire it is because he has just been buried. And even then, what the dead desire of us cannot be buried, which is why, if we buried God, God would look back at us from the grave and make demand upon us, like the eye of Abel. Desire is open-ended, on-going, outreaching, overreaching, expansive, futural, in a word, a word that is very apropos in this context – desire is "deathless." The death of desire is death pure and simple, so that wherever there is life, there is desire. The opposite of desire is despair, which is the death of deathless desire, which Kierkegaard therefore very appropriately called the "sickness unto death." In a certain way I am arguing for the deathlessness of desire even though and especially because we ourselves who desire certainly die and even though and especially because there is an undeniable mortality attached to what we desire. That deathlessness of desire and of the desirable is what Derrida calls the "undeconstructible," a notion that, on my accounting, flies in the face of Mark C. Taylor's famous declaration that deconstruction is the hermeneutics of the death of God. I would rather say that deconstruction is the (radical) hermeneutics of the deathlessness of God and of the deathlessness of our desire for God.

That little aporia – about the deathlessness of desire in the midst of our mortality – may be explained as follows. However deathless a being's desire may be, it is always something concretely situated and factual, always located in some particular datable time and locatable place. Desire is the desire for something that bears an historical name, sometimes a proper name like the name of a person to whom we are unconditionally devoted, or the name of a cause, like freedom or democracy. Or, paradigmatically, God. Desire always has a fixed point of departure in the concrete setting in which we find ourselves, in the names that we inherit, that name what we are taught to desire, the desire of which goes to make up who or what we are, which is constitutive of us. What else can we desire except what it has been given us to desire, what has been handed down to us as worthy of desire? We love and desire what is nearest and dearest to us, friends and family, say, where love first loves what is familiar and like itself, like children clinging to their mother, and then, as our minds and hearts expand, we learn to love, we become life-long apprentices in loving what is farther off and strange, distant and unlike ourselves, but always in the name or under the name of one inherited or given name or other (like the name of "love" itself). We associate ourselves with or attach ourselves to inherited or given names. That at least is the first and more finite moment of desire, let us say, its point of departure, which is a finite and "factical" *terminus a quo.*

But there is a second and more radical movement to desire, which is the more proper movement of a "desire beyond desire." To see what this is let us take up the case of what Derrida calls our affirmation or desire of the "democracy to come." The affirmation of democracy is unconditional even if democracy itself, what at present goes under the name of democracy, is a highly conditioned and historically contingent thing. What we aspire to when we breathe the name of democracy is not realized in any existing democracy. But we do not know or have a better name than democracy – we do not, for example, sigh and long for a "monarchy to come" or an "oligarchy to come" or a "National Socialism to come," even if we are threatened by such a thing. So what we call democracy, with all its warts and scars, is the least bad name we have for something that we desire in and under the name of democracy.

In the language we have been using here, we desire what is happening in the name of democracy, some event that transpires under that name, an event that name contains without being able to contain, something uncontainable that the name harbors, something, let us say, interminable in what is termed (marked and limited) "democracy." If the point of departure – existing democracies – is determinable and finite and deconstructible (and how!) – the *terminus ad quem*, the telos without telos, the "democracy to come" – is interminable and infinite and undeconstructible. Democracy is the name that we have been given, a name that is handed down or inherited, to which we attach ourselves with an unconditional desire. But at the same time we understand that democracy is not here, is not present, that anything that currently passes itself off as democracy is an imposter, for no existing democracy is truly democratic, and for that reason we are able to detach ourselves from that name in virtue of the event it harbors. Democracy is the object of an infinite, interminable, undeconstructible desire, a desire beyond desire, for the event that this name contains.

Derrida's position on the democracy to come should not be mistaken as another case of utopian idealizing, where "democracy" has become an Ideal Essence, an Idea in the Kantian sense, to which empirical or existing democracies can only asymptotically approach. Remember that Derrida, in virtue of his notion of *différance*, rightly passes for an anti-essentialist; he thinks of names as contingent unities of meaning, linguistic "effects" that are never identical with themselves and are subject to endless and undecidable fluctuation. Democracy is not an "ideal essence," which is a paradigmatic form of "presence," just as much as, even more so than, empirical or perceptual presence, and one that his entire critique of Husserl set out to dispel. (Derrida was more interested in the deconstruction of Husserl than of Merleau-Ponty, of ideal essences than of perception.) "Democracy" is rather more a place holder, a *nomen*, for something that is happening in that name, something unforeseeable, something that we desire with a desire beyond desire. Such a desire we can now plainly see means a "transcendent" desire, which means:

(1) a desire that transcends garden variety desire, which is always a desire to possess;

(2) a desire that transcends any determinate, determinable thing, anything held captive by its name (like existing "democracies");

(3) a desire that transcends anything we know, for something we know not what that is transpiring in the desire, something that is going on in the name of what we desire.

We can see that it goes to the heart of what Derrida means by the "democracy to come" that we cannot foresee what this will be. It will take the form of an "event," something that shatters the present horizon of foreseeability, which he also calls, still drawing upon the resources of the Latin root *venire*, the "invention" in the literal sense of *in-venire*, the in-coming, the coming-in, the come-over, the coming-upon us of something unforeseeable. An event belongs to the future, *l'avenir*, *l'à venir*, to what is coming. But in that case we must distinguish between the relatively foreseeable future, which is a relative future, the future present, which to the extent it is foreseeable is more present than future, and what he calls the "absolute" future, by which he means the unforeseeable future, the future which comes over us like a thief in the night, an absolute surprise, the future which is kept secret from us, which is the secret to the future, the secret to what "future" really means.

Now given the absolute unforeseeability of the absolute future, we must confess that we have no way to know and no assurance that what is coming will be or will be properly called "democracy." In the expression the "democracy to come," the "to come" is more important than the "democracy," with the result that we only know that what is today called democracy is some sort of predecessor state or antecedent, the best one we have available, of something coming. That is to say, the name of what we today call "democracy" is interminably restless with an undeterminable infinite future, for there is something transpiring in the name of democracy, something that this name contains without being able to contain, something interminable in this term, something we desire with a desire beyond desire, something that we long for, something for which we pray and weep.

At just this point, faced with that absolute future, Derrida has recourse to religious discourse, to what he calls the messianic, which is the object of an unconditional hope and expectation, of undeconstructible desire. So if, in its first moment, desire is rooted in and initially launched by the names we have inherited, the names by which we have been nurtured, and to which we attach ourselves unconditionally, then there is a second moment, in which we desire with a desire beyond desire. Then we are able to detach ourselves from the names to which we are attached, and this just in virtue of our unconditional attachment to the event that is transpiring within them. For in affirming these names, we desire what they promise, with the structure of a messianic promise. A name is or contains a promise of something coming, promises on which the name cannot presently deliver, a promise of an event, of what is coming, which fills our heart with hope and expectation. That is what I have called Derrida's "religion," his "religion without religion," in which, it seems to me, a religious paradigm – and specifically the religious desire of God – is unmistakably at work. At that point, deconstruction is as far can be from a "hermeneutics of the death of God."

That is because what we have said about "democracy," which is a venerable (and treacherous) name, holds *a fortiori* for the name of God, which is an even more venerable (and so even more treacherous) name, more widespread, more deeply imbedded in our unconscious, more liable to leap to our lips in moments of crisis, of deepest sorrows or greatest joy. (In virtue of the undecidability of names, what is venerable is also treacherous, in the same way that every promise is a threat.) Indeed, if any objection can be made to the preceding analysis, it might be that the name "democracy" cannot bear that much weight; perhaps we should speak of "justice" rather than "democracy." But the name of "God" is above all the name of what we desire, of what we love with a love that is stronger than death, with a desire that is deathless, with a desire beyond desire. The name of God is the most undecidable, the most difficult to discern, the most open-ended and interminable *terminus ad quem*, that than which nothing greater can be conceived (*id quo majus cogitari nequit*).

The name of God is an auto-deconstructing excess — and this supplies the point of contact between apophatic theology and Derrida's religion without religion — a name that un-names itself (that de-nominates, as Jean-Luc Marion says). We know in advance that whatever we say God *is*, that is just what God is *not*, not because God is less but because God is more, not because God does not get as far as that name but because that name does not get as far as God. God is the very structure of excess, of going beyond, of transcendence, and the most proper object of that desire beyond desire which is deathless or undeconstructible. That is why the very notion of the death of God, which I do not dismiss out of hand, can only have a relative significance, for the death of God *simpliciter* would mean the death of what is deathless, not in the Christian Neo-Platonic sense of an eternal supersensible being, but in Derrida's sense of the deathlessness and undeconstructibility of desire, which is an inextinguishable desire for something coming, for something stirring in words of elemental power, words like democracy and justice, love and God, words which are infinitely restless with an open-ended future.

The Danger

Now we reach a delicate point in our reflections, a point where we are forced to face the "danger" in what we have been saying. I single out two dangers.

We must, in the first place, concede that in giving up the iron laws of assurance supplied by dialectical metaphysics, that necessity in virtue of which deep and radical negations will inevitably become affirmations, we have exposed ourselves to the hazards of history, allowing the nose of chance to insinuate itself under the tent of our desires and affirmations. For if the truth be told, where truth is something you have to be tough enough to endure so that it will not kill you, as Nietzsche liked to say, the coming of this future is a large roll of the dice. We have no assurance that the Messiah will show up and no guarantees that what will appear will not be an Anti-Messiah (anti-Christ). In speaking of the unforeseeability of the future, we concede we have no idea what is coming. The "absolute *novum*" of which Altizer speaks might turn out to be an absolute nightmare. Or it might turn out that nothing very good or very evil at all will eventuate. We lack dialectical-metaphysical assurances about whether the promise of democracy, or of justice, or the promise that is harbored by the name of God, will be delivered, or whether this promise will turn out to have been a dangerous threat.

What will be revealed in the apocalyptic unveiling, the *monstratio*, might be a monster, not the Messiah or the democracy to come. After all, it is not hard to imagine – it is happening all around us – that the struggle for democracy will be conducted in an imperial manner that will result not in democracy but in the domination of the world by a global capitalism that will undermine local values and traditions and turn everyone over to the unrestrained will to consume. Nor is it hard to imagine that the desire of God, the recovery of the religious in these post-secular times, will eventuate in the triumph of fundamentalist and reactionary religion in endless strife with democratic culture and in a new wave of religious wars. That is not very hard to imagine either. The future is not the issue of some simple dialectical law, some assured swing from one opposite to another, but of the play of the "event," where chance is irreducible, where the world is what James Joyce called a "chaosmos," neither simple law, order and necessity (cosmos), nor simple chaos, but an open-ended, non-formalizable quasi-system in which we do everything we can to keep the chance of the "event" alive. At that point, we do not rely upon the laws of dialectical metaphysics, but upon something more classically religious, like faith and hope and love, which are the virtues of "the impossible." For when are we more in need of faith than when what we believe begins to look incredible, and when is hope more truly hope than when things look hopeless and we must hope against hope, and when is love more necessary than when we are up against what is unlovable? Then we look not for a massive dialectical swing in the opposite direction but the chance of an event, of an intervention, that will open the possibility of something new.

Secondly, we must concede that when we make the distinction between the name of God and the event that is astir in that name we expose that name to danger. We must concede that, like the word "democracy," the name of God contains something that it cannot contain, something uncontainable, that may very well burst the seams of the name, leaving the name of God behind. But if we would give the name of God up to the unforeseeable future, would we not give it up to death, and at that point would not the tips of our fingers touch the tips of the gospel of the death of God? To be sure, at this point, our two ships pass close to each other in the night. But there is all the difference between the dialectical-historical claim that the transcendence of the Absolute has died away in favor of a life of absolute immanence, which is a claim belonging to an unbelievable metaphysic of history, on the one hand, and the deconstructibility of the name of God, which is a structural and analytic claim. The name of God is deconstructible just because it has been historically constructed to begin with, but that does not say anything about its demise. On the contrary, it is just because the name of God is such a living force that it is so important for deconstruction.

The Deconstruction of the Name of God

Rather than a decidable, dogmatic dialectical logic of "death" I have recourse to an undecidable deconstructive logic of the "without," *la logique du sans*. Rather than a gospel of the "death of God" I speak instead of a religion without religion, a religion that turns on the movement of the "without" (*sans*), in which something is crossed over without being altogether extinguished or killed off, living on, *sur-vivre*, sometimes like a ghost. For the name of God is deconstructible just in virtue of the undeconstructibility – and hence of the deathlessness – of the desire for the *event* that is alive and well and much astir in the name of God. I speak not of the gospel of the death of God but of the good news of a religion without religion, which turns on an open-ended messianic impulse which cannot be contracted to a concrete messianism, on an event that cannot be trapped inside a name. I speak not of the death of God but of the desire that is astir in the name of God for a God – without God. The figure of God without God is itself a classical one in mystical theology, most famously in Meister Eckhart who wrote the perfect deconstructionist prayer, "I pray God to rid me of God" and whose sermons deployed a logic of the *sine* (Latin) or *ohne* (German), most famously in his claim that love is "without why." I pray God to rid me of attachment to the *name* of God in order to free me for the unconditional affirmation of the *event* that is astir in the name of God, of the deathlessness of an event that is alive and inextingusihable.

That means that in the expression, the desire of God, the word desire is more important than the word God, for the name "God" is an historical name that is directed at something identifiable and determinable whereas the word "desire" is directed at the undeconstructible event that stirs restlessly within that name.[1] What is important about the name of God is that it is preeminently auto-deconstructing, that it un-names everything that it names, which is why, as far as I am concerned, Meister Eckhart's expression can hardly be improved upon. I pray God, in the name of the event that is astir in the name of God, not to allow that name to prevent that event, which it too often does. So if it is true that the name of God is deconstructible, that is not because it is dead or dying or on its last legs – who would know so much as to know that? The deconstructibility of the name of God is neither a metaphysical a priori nor an historical prediction about its historical fate. Historical predictions are notoriously unreliable, at least as unreliable as the apocalyptic announcement in the 1960s about the death of God, which was followed by massive *de*-secularization in the United States and massive evangelical and fundamentalist movements that have overrun the world north, south, east and west. The name of God may live forever, something we are happy to concede just in virtue of the unforeseeability of the future. I myself cannot imagine a future without it, but then again what I cannot imagine is just what the radical or absolute future means! The name of God may well be quite indispensable and we will never be visited by a better one. I have no inside information to relay on that point. But I can say that the name of God is – structurally – deconstructible just because it has been historically constructed. Still, it is not just any name, but an historical name that has accumulated a huge history and an enormous potency so that it harbors – shelters, protects and conceals – an infinite, interminable, indeterminable future within itself, for better *and* for worse.

Deconstruction as I conceive it has a special place in its heart for the name of God because deconstruction turns on the undeconstructible. That is because, perhaps more than any other name, the name of God is a self-effacing trace, a trace that once deployed tries to erase its very trace, and this not because it is a virus we are trying to kill off but because of what the name is trying to name. The name of God is everything save (*sauf*) the limits that are imposed upon by that name, which is why we want to keep that name safe (*sauf*). Every name, including the name of God, is deconstructible, but deconstruction is always undertaken in the name of what is undeconstructible, which is the object of an unconditional affirmation, which is what we mean by desire, or by a desire beyond desire. Every name, including the name of God, is deconstructible, but the name of God tries to pick up the trace of undeconstructibility and to inscribe it in itself. For the name of God is the name of what we desire with a desire beyond desire so that as soon as you name your desire you must strike it out, for desire is a desire beyond desire for the undeconstructible. If you comprehend it, that is not it, St. Augustine said about God. If you know what you desire, we can add, that is not what you desire. *The* name of what we desire, the one final and undeconstructible name of that desire, is lacking and always will be lacking, so long as we are creatures of time and tide. That lack is not a fault to be fixed with an influx of total presence but precisely what nourishes desire; it is not a gap to be filled but the open-endedness of desire itself which is fed by the affirmation of the irreducibly other.

The radical undecidability of the name of God that emerges under a deconstructive analysis seems to be truer to what we call today a post-secular situation, which functions for me on an analogy with the expression post-critical, that is, having passed through a movement of secularization or critique, through modernity, which is the main thing that the word postmodern should mean, had it any meaning at all. The worst side of modernity was its reductionism, its desire to explain things in terms of a single overarching principle, and its insensitivity to irreducible plurality. But what is wrong with the word "post-modernity" is that it conceals the way in which what we call post-modern is really a continuation and a further intensification of the already intensely critical point of view of modernity. Modernity's failure was to think that critique requires a single point of critical leverage, an Archimedean point external to the system, in virtue of which all critical operations could be launched. Postmodern "critique" is critique but one that is critical of just such a leverage point, and so it is a post-critical critique. That is the opening that is provided for religion. We suspect religion – that is what Husserl called an infinite task – but we also infinitely suspect all the suspicion that has been cast upon religion, because we do not think that "religion" is a single thing, just one phenomenon, or a collection of phenomena that can be *reduced* to just one thing, as if all these phenomena were symptoms or manifestations or versions of some Super-X which some Super-Critique has discovered and announced to us – like religion is reducible to an opiate of the masses, or to the resentment of the strong by the weak. The assertion that God is dead belongs to a modernist and reductionist discourse.

But postmodernism is not simply critique, even as modernity was not simply the Enlightenment, but contained within itself a critique of Enlightenment called "Romanticism," which shows up in Hegel's critique of the abstract ahistorical onesided-ness of what he called the "understanding" as opposed to concrete historicality of "reason." That point is true as far as it goes, but Hegel went too far by taking "reason" to be "history" conceived as a systematic all-encompassing unfolding of the absolute spirit, instead of a radically unsystematic often highly unreasonable eventful happening.

Conclusion

In the end, it is not a matter of closing down the undecidability of the name of God and deciding whether God is dead or dying fast or still alive and well, or whether what is transcendent has become immanent. In the end what is objectionable about speaking of the "death" of God is the deadly dogmatic dialectical decisiveness and finality, the totalizing force, of the figure of "death." As Derrida said, "I do not at all believe in what today is so easily called the death of philosophy (nor, moreover, in the simple death of whatever – the book, man or god, especially since, as we all know, what is dead wields a very specific power)."[2] In the place of the decisive swings to and fro' of the great dialectical machine, in the place of a dogmatic dialectical opposition between darkest death and the parousia of total presence, I put the figure of undecidability of the name of God. In the place of historical dialectical gnosis I put a non-knowing openness to the future, in which everything depends upon keeping open the gap between the name of God and the event this name harbors, which means keeping the future open.

In that gap there opens up, in the end – and this is a matter I can only adumbrate here by way of a conclusion – the freedom that frees us from the search for the name, for what matters is not the name but the event. Life is not a riddle in which the winner is the one who guesses the secret word or secret name, or who chooses rightly whether God is hiding under the shell of the transcendent or the shell of the immanent. Life unfolds in the concrete where, as Kierkegaard says, the name of God is not a *nomen* but a *deed*, a point that is made perfectly in the Scriptures when the servant asks the master, "Lord, when did we see you hungry and give you to eat?"

The truth of the event is not a proposition but a deed, which is what St. Augustine meant when he spoke of *facere veritatem*, making the truth happen, doing the truth. If God is love, then that is to be taken neither as a constative nor a performative utterance, indeed not as an utterance at all, but as an event that is something to be done. At that point, in the end, it does not matter under what name that event goes. We might not ever know the name.

Lord, when did we see you hungry and give you something to eat?

Lord, is that you?

Notes

[1] To be sure, the name desire is also an historical name, so that the question is, what event transpires under that name, what is going on when someone "desires" something. What is being desired by desiring? That question is not only a psychoanalytic one.

[2] Jacques Derrida, *Positions*, trans. Alan Bass (Chicago: University of Chicago Press, 1972), 6.

14

ON BEING DONE WITH GOD: IN DIALOGUE WITH MARK TAYLOR

[Unpublished, paper presented to the Religious Theory Group, American Academy of Religion, November 22, 2003; revised in 2005]

"I thought I was done with God – or that God was done with me. But I suppose I am not, at least not yet. And I am beginning to fear not ever. *Erring* was to have ended it all but it has not." My remarks today are a brief reflection on this remarkable and provocative formulation of Mark Taylor from his *About Religion*.[1]

Living On by Dying

The very idea of God, *s'il y en a,* requires that God die. Above all if by God we meant what Aristotle meant, a pure, separate, and supreme form unmixed with matter, knowing himself and only himself, while sublimely unaware of us sublunary beings down below. Nothing is more in order, nothing more necessary, than for such a being to suffer a mortal blow, to surrender such a separate celestial life and perfect actuality and to spend some time with us mortals mixed with potency down here below. It is high time that such a *theos*, which has been more or less behind every "onto-theology," come down to earth and dwell among us, lest he be of no earthly use. Why in heaven's name would we bother about him who does not bother himself a whit about us? Let him go his heavenly way; let pure acts bury pure acts. We here on earth have no time for such idle circling in the sky. If that is pure act, we prefer potency, which is much more dynamic. As Schelling argues, God's fall into the world is a gain, in which the lifeless eternity of "pure act" acquires temporal life and activity. It was in this same spirit that Meister Eckhart asked, what good does it do me if God passes all his time (so to speak) generating the Son in eternity if he does not also give birth to the Son in my soul? The eternal spiration of the Trinity is not very inspiring if this is not a process that also comes to pass in my soul. When Angelus Silesius put Eckhart's sentiment to verse, he said that God needs us as much as we need God. What spirit is there in all that spiration if it does not inspire me? O thou great sun, Zarathustra said, what would you be if you did not have us to shine upon?

The very idea of God thus involves dying in order to live, living by dying, what Irigaray calls our "becoming divine." "I am the bread of life." God lives on by dying, the way the bread we consume is broken down and gives up its living substance in order to pass over into ours. If the divine death is built right into the idea of God, the question shifts away from whether God has died to what is being born from God. To what extent and in what way does God's death give birth? What is the gift God's death has brought forth?

My hypothesis in these remarks is that if the very idea of God is excess or infinity, then it seems there can be no end to his living on by dying, to his and our becoming, in space or time, in quantity or quality or modality.

And God lit up the Strip

Mark Taylor has been meditating upon the idea of the gift of God's death right from the start and what he has been "pondering for many years" is whether this death, this "inevitable loss can be embraced in a way that leads to creative engagement rather than the endless melancholy of interminable mourning" (AR, 6). The death of God is not God's final discrediting because "God *lives* by dying." For Taylor, the pivotal figure in this movement is Hegel, in whose speculative system the transcendent God of the west descended into space and time and unfolded his life in nature and history, in a kind of parousia of the metaphysics of total presence (AR, 33). In his work on religion Taylor has argued, figured, enacted, mimed, and audaciously mimicked this Hegelian scheme. He began with Kierkegaard, who wanted to solicit the Hegelian totalization, to mock it with his acidic irony and wit, to speak on behalf of the fragments and remainders that the System omitted (AR, 37). Today, Taylor's work represents the continuation of Hegel by another and very post-modern means, in which the "System" is not mocked and ironized, as in Kierkegaard, in the name of a renewed sense of transcendence, but redescribed and reinscribed in virtual culture. Thus the infinite substance of God resurfaces in the infinite, decentered, lateral links of the internet; the *hyperousios* is realized by way of hyper-links; and the absolute *Geist* is reinscribed as "virtual reality," a timely illustration of which is the "Matrix" trilogy.

The result is not God become the *Geist* of the Absolute System but God become the electronic circuits of post-modern culture, circulating through the literature, economics, art, and high-tech world of the information technologies, all of which bear the marks of a forgotten or repressed theology. The Hegelian Spirit is thus turned on its head, not by way of its transformation into Altizer's "total presence," or by a dialectical opposition between Hegel and Kierkegaard, or Altizer and Barth, but rather by a non-dialectical a/theology (AR,3), which "rethinks the death of God as the "the impossibility of the realization of the Parousia." A/theology is not atheism, which is Godless, but a meditation upon the "sacred" (AR, 31), which is not God, but the trace that God leaves in the world. The sacred is not God but what has become of God after God's death, the way God survives, lives/on in and through and after his death. The sacred is not the negation of God, nor the simple negation of this negation, the death of the death of God, but rather its un-negation, a negation without negation that does not achieve the full force of negation, but allows God to live on *sous rature*, under the sign of the without; the sacred is the scene that God "haunts" (AR, 46). So one cannot be *simply* done with God, which would be "every bit as reassuring as the belief in God's abiding presence" (AR, 46-47). The sacred is the play of the presence and absence of God.

Mark works this out in the concrete through a series of studies that follow the trace of God in the neon lights of popular culture. The *Herrlichkeit* of the Lord has died and been reborn in the Magic Kingdom. Las Vegas is "the realization of the Kingdom of God on earth" (5), the scene in which the death of God is staged as the kingdom of God on earth (170). And the light came into the world and lit up the Strip and the darkness did not overcome it (John 1:5). God dies for Taylor by being realized in the virtual world (22), by abandoning his heavenly vault and pitching his tent among us on the internet. Religion shows up not where it is (the churches), but where it (often) is not, in secular culture, the seemingly secular culture, which is the continuation of religion by another means. Religious faith is transubstantiated into economic credit, even as the substance of the material world is transformed into the immaterial virtual world. When the gold standard is removed, the dollar is only worth the paper it is written on and the "faith" of the United States Government, but even the paper can be removed, so that money becomes the invisible stuff of an electronic exchange, virtually immaterial, like God (158). God's trace or sacred effect is likewise found in the work of art, and religion is displaced by art, even as the kingdom of God is realized by an aesthetic utopia (175).

Ethics, Politics, and Desire

I am, as are we all, deeply grateful to Taylor's re-Mark-able achievement, before and after *Erring*, from which we have all learned so much and for so long, to which I would like to pay tribute with the gratitude of questioning. My questions are concerned with the excess of God and therefore with heading off a precipitous constriction of the way God lives by dying in an unnecessarily narrow way. There is more to Kantian *Kritik* than the *Critique of Judgment*, more to a postmodern version of post-Kantianism and post-Hegelianism than a postmodern aesthetics, and more to God than light and glory. Without dismissing for a moment the transforming character of the revolution in information technologies and the emergence of virtual culture, without doubting for a moment the insight and acumen that Mark has displayed in mapping out this transformation, it needs to be said that there are other dimensions to the death of God that are at least as important, and for those who suffer through it, more important, than the aestheticization of the death of God that Mark has been thematizing. God, who is infinite excess, is capable of multiple and innumerable life/deaths, is capable of living on by dying in more ways than we can count, so that his life/death can never be exhaustively accounted. I will single out three such neglected possibilities here, under the names of ethics, politics, and the desire for God, which I will emblematize with the proper names of Levinas, Derrida and Augustine.

(1) *Ethics*. It is perhaps not widely noticed that Levinas is also a philosopher of the death of God. Levinas is no less convinced than Nietzsche of the death of the God behind the scenes, the death of the two worlds theory inherited from the Greeks and perpetuated in Christian Neoplatonism. Levinas is no less persuaded that philosophy cannot be directly a theology, a direct discourse on God, but only a kind of a/theology which follows the traces that God has left behind in withdrawing from the world. His thought also represents a displacement of religion in the classical sense not however by art but *by ethics*. The kingdom of God is to be realized not in the Magic Kingdom but by an ethical or moral kingdom of ends. So cast in Levinasian terms, Taylor has been content to find the trace that God's death has left in the world in the *sacred* but he has failed to look for it in the *holy*. Mark has confined the death of God by consigning God to live on only in a show of lights, a display of visibility, like the laser beam show at the end of every day at the Epcot Center, the neon strip of Vegas, the luxury of the Luxor Hotel, or in the aesthetic glow of contemporary art.

It is as if the theology of culture must always be keyed entirely to a theology of glory, not a theology of the cross, as if there is no other kind of theology and no other kind of God and no other kind of death of God than an aesthetic one. It is as if the death of God can only be justified as an aesthetic phenomenon. But for Levinas the trace that God leaves behind is invisible, not visible; and this invisibility is not the invisibility of an electronic or virtual world but the moral invisibility of the face that commands. The trace is found not in the visible work of art but in an invisible imperative. To apply this Levinasian point to Mark Taylor, what is as least as important about money today is not only that it turns on faith in invisible electronic exchanges but also that the electronic revolution enables capitalism to globalize with the speed of light and to exacerbate poverty and widen the economic divide. The kingdom of God on earth is found not only or even primarily in Las Vegas, but it is inscribed on the faces of the paupers who will never get invited to the banquet of God's luxurious incarnation in the Luxor.

For Levinas religious discourse is not discourse *about* God or *about* religion. To speak *about* something is to stand outside it and represent or objectify it (*le dit*). We will not get very far with language, Heidegger said, if we speak "about" language, instead of trying to settle ourselves inside what is happening in language and trying to speak *from* there, from *out of* what language puts us through (*aus der Erfahrung*). To speak about religion or about what religion is about, is not to touch the nerve of religious discourse. When I say *adieu* to someone I love, I commend you to God, God be with you, I am not speaking about God, but to God, *à Dieu*, to God for you, to you and God. But the name of God is barely overheard in "*adieu*." Indeed, the name of God is sometimes most alive when it is not on our lips at all – which is a case of finding religion just where it is not being mentioned that Mark does not consider. Whether I serve the neighbor in the name of God, Levinas says, or whether I serve the neighbor *tout court*, it is all the same. The name of God, Levinas said, is a not a great semantic event, a semantic explosion that sends shock waves up and down the lines of our vocabularies; rather it is inaudibly at work in a quiet and humble act of saying "*après vous*."[2]

(2) *Politics*. By the same token, the death of God is also enacted in the political sphere. For Derrida, politics today cannot be properly analyzed unless we see the extent to which it operates under the influence of a hidden theological motives, secularized extensions of theology. However secular modern democracies think they are or have become, the truth is that secularization always presupposes a theology to secularize, so that, for better or for worse, secularism is the continuation of theology by another means. There is always what Derrida calls in a recent book entitled *Voyous* "some unavowed theologeme,"[3] a certain bit of undigested theology lodged in the throat of even the most secular societies. That is above all true of the idea of national sovereignty, which is, he says, the "heritage of a barely secularized theology."[4] Any effort to radicalize democracy, to carry the democratic revolution one step further, would involve extricating democracy from the politics of sovereignty altogether. That means that the coming of the democracy to come must be

accompanied by a new theology. A radical democratic revolution would not mean jettisoning theology once and for all and a final accomplishment of secularization – for God lives by dying – but rather a parallel radicalization of theology.

But what would be it like to rid ourselves of the theology, the politics, and the anthropology of sovereignty? What would it be like to refashion theology around a God without sovereignty, to refashion a politics without sovereign nation states, and to refashion our self-understanding in terms of a self without sovereign ipseity? Can we imagineا God without sovereignty, imagine the coming of such a God? To thus imagine God would be as difficult – as impossible – as trying to think of the coming of a self without the ipseity of the self, the *per se* or *a se* subsistence of one who is the lord of one's own domain. What is called for is to imagine God otherwise, to turn our thinking about God around, almost upside down or inside out:[5]

> In speaking of an onto-theology of sovereignty, I refer, under the name of God, of One God, to the determination of a sovereign and hence indivisible omnipotence. But when the name of God would give us something else to think, for example a vulnerable non-sovereignty, suffering and divisible, mortal even, capable of contradicting himself, of regret (a thought which is neither impossible nor without example), that would be a wholly other story and perhaps that of a god who would be deconstructed even in his ipseity.

In Derrida, the death of God unfolds in the democracy to come, in a new political paradigm without sovereignty, modelled after a God without power or ontological prestige, vulnerable and mortal, who has not the wherewithal to lay down his head, whose only power is the power of a powerless but unconditional appeal. God dies by living on in the democracy to come.

(3) *The Desire for God.* Thirdly, and this concern goes under the name of Augustine, I wonder about the extent to which Taylor's a/theology is truly and open-endedly a/theological in keeping with the open-ended excess of God. I am touched by the sentiment from *AR* that serves as the epithet to these remarks, which seems to signal a change of heart about God on Mark's part – is that true? – but I wonder about how true Mark is to his notion of denegation, which is meant to allow God "to haunt from a distance that grows ever more proximate" (AR, 46), which allows for the indecisiveness with which one could never be done with God, as he says so beautifully. The simple denial of God, as Mark very pertinently points out, "would be a solution every bit as reassuring as the belief in God's abiding presence" (AR, 46-47). I wonder to what extent

he sticks to the terms of undecidability or instead allows God to dissolve *without remainder* into the world, thus dissolving God's infinite excess. That also amounts to worrying over the extent to which Mark remains within an early reading of Derrida common in the 1970s about the simple dissipation of the transcendental signified into the free play of signifiers, a reading that has not been abandoned but simply transposed to or reinscribed in the play of electronic signifiers.

A/theology is a function of the undecidability that settles over us, and over theology. Undecidability is archaic; it goes all the way down. Undecidability is first, last, and constant, the alpha and omega, the letter itself of iterability, in virtue of which whatever is said or inscribed can be reinscribed. There is no way to arrest the play of undecidability that settles over the name of God, in virtue of which the name of God, and hence the death of God, is endlessly translatable into other names. We can never quite answer Augustine's question, "what do I love when I love my God?" for the constancy of the name of God in my life goes under many names. When I say "my God" I cannot say what I said. In negative theology, that confession of unsayability is of course a way to pay God the highest of praise. But outside negative theology it is a confession of a less sublime sort, a confession of sliding, slippage, and ambiguity, so that I am at a loss to say what the name of God is about.

For the present purpose, I would gloss this notion of undecidability by invoking what the late Charlie Winquist called a "desiring theology." Winquist thinks that only theology has the massive interrogatory power to awaken questioning, that only the unbearable "pressure" of theological interrogation awakens thought. If that is so, I think it is because the name of God is uniquely inscribed in *theo*logy, because theology bears God's own name, because theology was named after God and is God's namesake, God's word or logos. Only the name of God arises from such bottomless and dark depths and only it can cause such an enormous provocation. "I thought I was done with God – or that God was done with me," Mark writes, which he fears can never be (AR, 29). The desire for God is inscribed so deep in our unconscious, is given to us with our mother's milk, is the name that leaps to our lips at times of birth and death, of desperation and separation. What do the philosophers have to compete with such a name? What do they offer as an opposing candidate? "Being"? "Consciousness"? "Substance"? Are they serious? The last cloudy streak of evaporating reality, mummifications, conceptual embalmings, Nietzsche said, as he pointed at such names in ridicule, holding his sides, collapsing with laughter, wiping the tears from his eyes.

The upshot of undecidability is that theology is every bit as much and undecidably a hermeneutics of the *desire* for God who lives by dying as a hermeneutics of the *death* of God who dies by living on. For by dying, God lives on otherwise and awakens our desire. By dying, God comes down to earth and stirs anew the waters of desire and discontent. The death of God *simpliciter* would be the death of desire. By the death of God *simpliciter* I mean a positive and final declaration of death, a closure, and a totalization, which belongs to a neo-Feuerbachian presence absence system. Derrida says he does not believe in what can be so easily called the *death* of anything, of philosophy, of the book or of God, for "as we all know, what is dead wields a very specific power."[6] Death, which is never simple, is always a life/death, living on, *sur-vivre*. So we must guard against the reassuring conviction that God dies in such a way that his life *simply* passes over into culture, language, or the world, into aesthetic, ethics, or politics, *without remainder,* a total death in which God becomes *exhaustively incarnate* in a new system, material or virtual. If we think about theology as a hermeneutics of the name of God, then the hermeneutics of the death of God is just as much a hermeneutics of the desire of God, of the anarchic and atelic desire that is inscribed in this name. For the name of God is the name of what we love, and this above all when we do not know what we desire, when we do not know what we love when we love our God.

The groundless ground of theology is a hermeneutics of undecidability, of what we might call the indiscernability of our ultimate concern. The death of God *simpliciter* would arrest the play, still the unrest, resolve in some final way, dissolve in a decisive and deadly terminal way the ambiguous play of desire by circumscribing what we desire within a single domain – be it aesthetic, ethical, or political, sacred or holy – and hence inflict a mortal wound on desire. The death of God *simpliciter*, which would contain the way God lives on by dying, would constitute the death of what we love and desire with a desire beyond desire. The death of God *simpliciter*, being simply done with God, would be the death of everything that exerts pressure on our beliefs and practices, the death of everything that causes our beliefs to tremble, forcing them to open up like an abyss when they come in contact with the name of God, with something, I know not what, that is named with that name. The death of God *simpliciter* would abandon us to wandering the shopping malls in search of what we desire and relegate us to reality TV to search for what is real. It would consign us to the sickness unto death of the streets of Las Vegas, abandoned to the despair that does not even know it is in despair.

Notes

[1] Mark C. Taylor, *After Religion: Economies of Faith in Virtual Culture* (Chicago: University of Chicago Press, 1990), 29. Hereafter "AR".

[2] The name of God, Johannes Climacus says in a similar vein, is not an objective matter, which is his way of saying that it is not a semantic event at all, but a *deed*; it not something that is said but something that is done or enacted, something that transfixes subjective existence. The name of God is the name of justice, the prophets stormed. Yahweh is *tequadah*, Amos said, so do not let me hear that name on your lips if you are oppressing the poor. I do not want your liturgies or your sacrifices – and let us add your theologies or your "religious studies," the God of Amos said, but to let justice flow like water over the land.

[3] Jacques Derrida, *Rogues: Two Essays on Reason*, trans. Pascale-Anne Brault and Michael Naas (Stanford: Stanford University Press, 2005), 110.

[4] Jacques Derrida, *Without Alibi*, ed. and trans. *Peggy Kamuf* (Stanford: Stanford University Press, 2002), 207.

[5] Derrida, *Rogues*, 157.

[6] Jacques Derrida, *Positions,* trans. Alan Bass (Chicago: University of Chicago Press, 1972). 6.

15

LAUGHING, PRAYING, WEEPING BEFORE GOD: A RESPONSE

[In *Styles of Piety: Practicing Philosophy after the Death of God*, eds. S. Clark Buckler and Matthew Statler (New York: Fordham University Press, 2006), 253–69]

[253] I work my way through things by writing. So whenever I read what others have written about my work, whenever what I have written is read back to me by others – never, of course, without a gloss – it is as if the inert pages of books and journals have come to life and begun to talk back to me (and sometimes even to bite back). It is as if something that is structurally private, written in solitude, my most secret thoughts, meant only for me and God – like Augustine confessing to God in writing, *cur confitemur deo scienti?* (Why do I know anything at all? Why do I confess to God, who knows all?), to God who knows everything already – have now to my surprise become a public matter, flushed out in the open for everyone to see. I am honored by the attention paid to my work by Frank Ambrosio, David Wood, and Edith Wyschogrod, and embarrassed by their generosity. If what they say of my work is not true, it is at least an illusion that I would like to entertain – until the next departmental meeting I attend where all such illusions are dispelled.

Let me begin by saying that by piety I mean to stand before God, *coram deo*, like Augustine in the *Confessions*, making myself a question unto myself in front of God Who has counted every tear in my eyes, every hair on my head. The question that I am made unto myself (*quaestio mihi factus sum*) – rather than one that I abstractly "pose" – is what do I love when I love you, my God? In general, I think that what goes on in our lives is more like faith, faith without [254] truth, than the disputatiousness of reason; more like hope, hope against hope, than the scurrying about of programming and long-term planning; more like love, love without why, than developing interpersonal skills. At one point in her paper, Edith Wyschogrod wonders what I would do with the "name of God." Where would the name of God be inserted into this religion without religion? Would this be a religion without God? The question of the name of God is the right question, the *religious* question, the question I am. But I do not take this to be a question of *whether* we believe in God or not, or even of whether *what* we believe in is God or not. I assume the "name of God," always and from the start. Rather, the question is Saint Augustine's question, "What do I love when I love (my) God?" (*quid ergo amo, cum deum [meum] amo*). Who would be so hard of heart, so cold and unfeeling, so incredulous and unbelieving, as not to love God? Who would deprive themselves of the love of God, of the name of God? The difficulty is rather to find what it is that we love when we love God. "My God" is the secret that is first, last, and constant; "my God" is what keeps me up at night, pacing the floors. Can I do anything, as Derrida asks, than repeat that question day and night?[1]

I have arranged my responses in an order that will best allow me to keep my eye on that question.

Deconstruction's Diamond Cut

I am very grateful indeed to David Wood for his discussion, which, as always, is clear, incisive and probing. David makes two excellent points in his commentary. With the first, which has to do with the nature of autobiographical texts like "Circumfession," I entirely agree. One of things that people like Augustine, Rousseau, and Kierkegaard – and more lately, Derrida, although he would blush to be added to this list – must be thinking when they write their various and very personal confessions is that their confession is in some ways everybody's confession, that their story is everybody's story. The fact that these books are read again and again proves that they are more or less right about that, whatever the explanatory "logic" behind it. If for a flat-footed formal logician, autobiography commits the fallacy of a hasty generalization, then so much the worse for flat-footedness. To use David's superb image, to which I will have occasion to return, "if one cuts the diamond of subjectivity at just the right plane," one [255] can simultaneously light up what is most uniquely personal and also sweepingly universal with one blow.

But what is Derrida (like Kierkegaard and Augustine) confessing or circumfessing from his secret heart of hearts? That he has all along had a religion about which no one knows anything, not even his mother, that he prays all the time, that he is like Augustine a man of prayers and tears. That brings us to David's second point about religiosity, which is the point that makes him squirm. As indeed it should; it is supposed to make him (and "Geoff" up above), and every careful reader of Derrida squirm. Squirming is what deconstruction is supposed to do to you; it is not supposed to make you sit back, relax, put your feet up, light up a cigar and feel affirmed and confirmed that your most cherished assumptions are rock solid, like money in the bank. Garden variety deconstructors take an inordinate delight in making everyone *else* squirm. They delight in tormenting the orthodox of all sorts – in disturbing orthodox physicists and metaphysicists and religionists, unsettling all those who think there is something definitively centered and settled out there if only we can measure it or let it take our measure, or if only we can get out of the way and let it speak for itself, from itself, as it is in itself. Deconstructionists delight in cutting right-thinking phallo-philosophers down to size, watching them squirm when they are shown that they are up to their ears in literature, held firm by the force of the letter, that phallo-philosophical reason is not quite what it cracks itself up to be.

Fair enough. Great fun.

But suppose some prankster comes along and shows these same intrepid deconstructors that they too are not quite what they are cracked up to be, not quite the demystifying demythologizers they make themselves out to be? Suppose this rogue says that there is a widespread rumor in circulation that they are known to pray, that there are reports from the most reliable of witnesses that they have been seen with a tear in their eye looking wistfully towards heaven? And even – don't ask me how this got out – that the men among them have been circumcised? That makes them squirm. But why should they squirm? Why worry when a text like Derrida's is translated and recontextualized and reinscribed within another context, when it is shown to have hitherto unsuspected or only vaguely suspected interweavings with other discourses? Why not think that this interweaving will be productive, not only for deconstruction, but for the "target" text, that it will loosen and reanimate the texts with which it comes in contact? Why worry if Derrida's discourse is contaminated [256] by other discourses, like those of religion and faith? Does not Derrida's argument about the irreducibility of the letter and the differential play mean that the borders between philosophy and literature, or other discourses, are porous, that only institutional police can prevent border crossings? Is not contamination one of the things deconstruction loves and does? Or does that only go for literature? Is this only permissible for literature? Do deconstructors not mind being contaminated just so long as this is confined to literature and poetry? Are they comfortable with only one kind of contamination? Then is it just by *religion* that they do not want to be contaminated? Is that what makes them squirm? Are they being very fastidious about the things by which they will allow themselves to be contaminated?

Let us get down to business. David argues that religion arises as an artifact of philosophy, a residue of the failure of the classical philosophical project. Traditional philosophy turns on a mistaken belief in the autonomy of the subject, and religion arises as a way to counter and undermine the autonomous subject. But once the philosophical misconception of the autonomy of the subject is undone or deconstructed, we are relieved of the need to counter it with religion, and something like Nietzsche will do very well. So, if Derrida has taken a religious turn, then he has aborted his own project, which is or includes the deconstruction of the autonomous subject, the successful completion of which would obviate the need to restore religion as a counterforce, there being nothing left to counter. Derrida would only be making use of "religious" structures like faith and the messianic because he retains an idea of reason and philosophy that he himself has undermined, the former feeding parasitically upon the latter.

To respond to that very probing point, for which I am very grateful, allow me first to back up a little bit. Viewed from one side, deconstruction is delimitation and displacement, an endless work of showing how there is no transcendental signified, no center, no stable resting point outside the text, a work of exhibiting the bottomless deconstructibility of things. But viewed from another side, deconstruction is affirmation, the affirmation of the "undeconstructible" (which is a remarkable enough expression, if you let yourself think about it), the affirmation of the experience of "the impossible," of the coming, or in-coming of the other (*l'invention de l'autre*), a longing or desire for a Messiah who will always be to come. Viewed from the first side, deconstruction looks a lot like Nietzsche and establishes friendly relations with literature; viewed from the latter side, it looks a lot like religion. Since the first view has been nearly worked to death [257] in the literature and is just about the only thing anybody ever hears about deconstruction, in *Prayers and Tears*, I thought I could put my sabbatical to better use if I viewed things from the second side. Mark Taylor made the first approach to Derrida in terms of religion, but his Derrida and his religion still looked like Nietzsche.[2] So my idea was to set out the religion in Derrida so that it actually looked like religion, not like Nietzsche, but then not exactly religion, but a religion without religion, which meant not only without "institutional" religion, which David mentions, but without any determinate doctrinal content. Clearly this is not likely to give the local rabbi or pastor much comfort that religion was making a comeback and that his pews would soon be swelling with worshipers, which would soon occasion an inevitable uptick in overflowing collection plates. After all, I would be the first to insist that Derrida rightly passes for an atheist. Still, looking like religion at all would be enough to make sharp witted deconstructors like David Wood squirm, enough to reduce them to tears and hope that Caputo was wrong, which would satisfy me that I had used my sabbatical well. *Nunc dimittis servum tuum*.

So when David says that "religion" (let us all agree in passing that any one thing called "religion" is a fiction) arises from the delimitation of the autonomous subject, that is half true, the Nietzschean half. The other half is that it arises in an affirmative way from a movement of hope and expectation for a messianic age, which also include a movement of mourning that these dead will not have died in vain. That gives deconstruction an ethico-politico-messianico-religious edge, with generous borrowings from Benjamin and Levinas, which is the tone I think that Derrida lately tries to strike and that I was certainly trying to strike for him. The delimitation of the autonomous subject is only half the job; the other half is the constitution of the responsible subject, the heteronomous subject of the claim of the other – not the nominative "I" subject but the subject in the accusative "me," the subject as the hearer of the call of the coming of the other. It is perfectly true that you can displace the autonomous subject in some other way, in the Nietzschean way described by David, where the "gift" means that forces inwardly build up and accumulate to the point that they can no longer be contained but spill over and explode in an excess of giving without return. That's one way to go, let us say the ejaculatory, orgasmic or phallic way.

A second way is to give, not what you can no longer contain within yourself, but what you need for yourself, in response to the approach of the other – to give what you do not have and cannot afford to give. [258] The first way, the more phallic way, displaces autonomous subjectivity but it does so very imperfectly and can do only limited service in this regard. That is because it does not have a true "other," nothing radically heteronomous that interrupts the inward accumulation of forces and elicits a "response" from them, for, on Nietzschean terms, every response is seen to arise from a bent, tormented "reactive" force. The second way is not ejaculatory but responsive, "religious" in the sense I am developing in *Prayers and Tears*, less phallic and more circumcisional, less explosive and more cut down to size by the coming of the other. Nobody says you have to be religio-responsive. To each his own. And I am not against orgasms. I have spoken "against ethics" but far be it from me to come out against orgasms. But it seems to me that you get more work done in overcoming autonomous subjectivity, if that is what you really want, by the affirmation of the coming of something radically other than by an orgasmic discharge, which seems to me still a tad too auto- and phallo-centric. Would it be too impudent, too impious, to say you get further in the direction of overcoming subjectivity by the coming of the other than by the coming of the same?

Wood is quite right to say, and with this I am quite in agreement with him, that once you have recognized the proximity of religion and deconstruction religion will never be the same. *Oui, oui.* That indeed is my point, one of them, at least, in *Prayers and Tears*. Religion, too, comes unstuck, is also forced to squirm, is made to see the contingency of its constructions, the relative determinacy, constructedness, and deconstructibility of what it loves when it loves its God, of what I love when I love my God, remembering what Wood has told us about the universal force of the word "I" if it is cut at the right angle.

Derrida makes his cut on the fault line between the concrete or determinate religious messianisms or Abrahamic religions and a more general, formal messianic structure or messianicity, which has the effect, in my view, of describing deconstruction as having the structure of a religion, the structure of messianicity, but not the determinate content. The opposite, or one opposite, and on my hypothesis the best opposite, of an autonomous subject is a prayerful praying circumcisional circumfessional subject who utters what Jean-Louis Chrétien calls a "wounded word."[3] If I am right about Derrida in *Prayers and Tears*, then the difference between Derrida and a very religious writer like Augustine is not to be found in the fact that Augustine prays and weeps while Derrida does not (which I think is what Wood hopes and prays is the difference), since Derrida tells us [259] he is a man of prayer (which makes Wood squirm). The difference lies in the relative determinacy of the terms in which Augustine gives voice to his prayers and tears, or to his wounded words. It lies in the proper names, the specific texts, the determinate historical tradition and community in union and communion with which Augustine prays his prayer. For Augustine confesses his faith in the name of Jesus, which is a proper name above every name, at the sound of which every knee should bend on earth and in heaven. And Augustine says, "*Our* father," the father of this community of faith, the father of us who have been praying here together from Abraham to the present.

But Derrida's prayer is conducted in the desert, in a desert *chora*, so that there is no such proper name known to him, no name that cannot be translated into or replaced by some other name, so that in some deep and deadly serious sense he does not know what he is praying for. "Democracy" or "hospitality" or "justice" are only the least bad names we have now for something that to come, something so unforeseeably to come, that in the expression the "democracy to come," the "to come" is more important than the "democracy," for we do not know if what is coming will be or should be called democracy. The *structure* of prayer, the gesture of hope and aspiration (and of mourning), simultaneously borrows upon religion and makes religion tremble. It borrows and reinscribes the confessional and circum-fessional character of Augustinian prayer. In a sense it represents an even *purer* prayer than Augustine's. For Augustine has the content and the comfort of praying the prayers of an ancient community which, to a certain extent, compromises its faith-fulness and gives it a certain assurance. So, too, the Augustinian "God" and the "subjectivity" that is correlate to it – which David rightly says (and I agree with him on this point) should be made to tremble – belongs to the relatively determinate God and subjectivity on the Augustinian side of the comparison, and constitute a sphere of only "relative" secrecy. But Derrida's call, his *"viens, oui, oui,"* both as regards the one who calls, if there is one, and what he is calling for, trembles in a *chora* space and gives testimony to an "absolute" secret. Derrida does not know who he is, or if he is one, or what is what, and he is only being quasi-Augustinian, Augustine's *Confessions* providing him with a lush and auto-biographically suggestive point of departure for making a different point about an absolute secret.

[260] Thus, if we did "finish" deconstructing this Pauline-Augustinian-Kierkegaardian tradition of subjectivity-and-God, as Wood desires, the issue would not be what Wood hopes for, no religion at all, but rather what Derrida calls a "religion without religion." If we dissociated Derrida from the determinate features of the Augustinian tradition with which he is rhetorically associating himself in "Circumfession", we would not be left with "reason" and "knowledge," updated and redefined, *sans* faith, *sans* passion, *sans* religion. Rather, we would be left with something that is neither religion nor philosophy, neither faith nor reason, but rather a faith without faith and a reason without reason, a more radical and *chora* faith and hope in something undeconstructible, which has the structure of a religion without religion. That undeconstructible I know not what to come is the point, the stylus tip and goad, of deconstruction, that unnameable in the name of which deconstruction is undertaken, which holds the white light of the undeconstructible against the deconstructibility of the present, which makes the present tremble in the name of what is to come, *s'il y en a.*

My hypothesis in *Prayers and Tears* is that it is just because he is marking off the structure of a religion without religion, repeating religion precisely without the doctrinal contents of the determinate and determinable faiths, that Derrida's story in *Circumfession* is indeed everybody's story, whether they rightly pass for theists or atheists, Jews or Christians, or whatever they rightly pass for. To return to David's felicitous phrase, for which I thank him very heartily, to my mind Derrida has cut "the diamond of hope and aspiration at just the right plane."

Those Seeing Tears

Edith Wyschogrod's paper is very much a meditation on my work by which I myself have been instructed, in which I have learned a great deal in particular about *Against Ethics*. In her comments, this book has been read back to me by someone who has thought long and hard about these matters and shown the rest of us the way to write about them. By relating it to Deleuze on the "theophanic plane of immanence," she has put what is going on *Against Ethics* in a new light, one that I did not myself quite appreciate. She has extended the reach of this book, deepened its grasp of things, made it look good, better than it is, made it look respectable, despite its insouciant, disreputable discourse. My idea in writing *Against Ethics* was to [261] delimit "ethics" in order to make "obligation" possible. I have found it necessary to deny ethics, to paraphrase Kant, in order to make room for obligation. "Ethics," after all, is a very philosophical idea – the Christian right will be saddened to hear that the word is not to be found in the New Testament, for example (at least I can't find it!) – while "obligation" has to do with the singularity of the situation in which what we call "ethical" events continually transpire. When Wyschogrod says that when it comes to writing an ethics, the way to write is to "write without writing," she displays her usual perfect pitch for hearing what is going in my texts. For according to the marvelous logic of the *sans*, the "without" does not obliterate but liberates, breaking down the shell in order to let the life break out.

I feel a wonderful kinship with Wyschogrod's work, and I follow her lead as best and as well as I can. No one who has read both *Saints and Postmodernism* and *Against Ethics* – and of course we both hope that your number is as great as the stars in the heaven and the sands on the seashore – can miss their inner affinity, despite their different styles. I would like to think – and this would be a high honor for *Against Ethics* – that these books will be seen as cousins, even siblings, sister and brother, under the same Abrahamic tent. This is true, above all, in the symmetry between her analysis in *Saints and Postmodernism* of a "fault line" between philosophers of difference (Levinas, Blanchot, Derrida) and philosophers of the plenum (Deleuze, Guattari, Genet) and my distinction between heteromorphism and heteronomism in *Against Ethics*.[4]

By heteromorphism I mean a more Nietzschean affirmation of *diversitas*, the polymorphic variety of the forms of life that we can celebrate and affirm, while by "heteronomism" I mean a more Kierkegaardian and Levinasian affirmation of alterity, from *alter*, the "other one," what is (almost) "wholly other," which breaks in upon the centripetal forces swirling within the same and compels them outward, turning the same toward the coming of the other. I am thus distinguishing between the "invention of the other" in the sense of the production and multiplication of diverse forms of life, "dreaming of the innumerable," as Derrida says, and the "invention of the other" in the sense of the *in-veniens*, the incoming of the other who breaks in upon the same. But the distinction is not a simple binarity – nothing is simple – and it is not a matter of choosing between them, as my impudent image of a Dionysian rabbi illustrates, but a matter of moving about in the space between them. Now if I am not mistaken, this [262] distinction organizes the space in which Wyschogrod and I move about.

This is a distinction that is pertinent to the discussion we have just conducted with David Wood, in which I maintain that Wood is advocating a more heteromorphic way of displacing autonomous subjectivity, which is all well and good, and I am not against polymorphism, but that the heteronomous responsible subject constitutes a more radical way to displace autonomy, while also adding that it is not a question of choosing between the two.

In entitling her commentary "Those Weeping Eyes, Those Seeing Tears," Wyschogrod has captured an image that ties her work to mine, and Derrida's work to Levinas, and all of us to St. Augustine, who is surely the weepiest philosopher the West has known. "See in what a state I am, see what a mess I am [*ecce ubi sum*]," Augustine writes. "Weep with me and weep for me [*flete mecum et pro me flete*]." "But do thou O Lord my God hear me and look upon me and see me and have mercy on me and heal me" [*Tu autem, domine deus meus, exaudi et respice et vide et miserere et sana me*] in whose eyes I have become a question to myself [*in cujus oculis mihi quaestio factus sum*], and that is my infirmity [*et ipse est languor meus*]."[5] I do love that, and like Augustine I wonder why tears can give us joy.

It should not go unnoticed that both Heidegger and Derrida have commented on Augustine's *Confessions*, and both have singled out Book X for special attention. Heidegger's analysis, very brilliant and groundbreaking, seizes upon the *quaestio mihi* motif, the *terra difficultatis*, what I called in *Radical Hermeneutics* the "difficulty of life." The Augustinianism that emerges from Heidegger's lectures is the philosophy of *cura* that turns on a being struggling for all its worth with the trials and tribulations of *temptatio*, with the trials of life, the life of trial. From these lectures the outline of resolute Dasein emerges in full clarity from the Christian soldierism he finds in the *Confessions*. Heidegger loved the Pauline image of the church militant armed with the breastplate of faith and the helmet of hope. But the Augustine who emerges from Derrida –

to whom Wyschogrod and I are both drawn – is a man of tears, pleading for mercy and help, not authentic Dasein but weeping flesh. His eyes are blinded by tears and, in that blindness, he sees with the eyes of faith, and in that weeping he has such healing as is to be had. Our Augustine is more Derridean than Heideggerian, more in need of healing (*cura*), than a man (sic!) of care-and-struggle (*cura*).[6]

[263] Edith Wyschogrod has not confronted or interrogated *Against Ethics* so much as she has grafted certain new lines upon its surface, wired it up in a more complicated way, for which I am very grateful. But in the course of underlining the salience of four critical motifs in *Against Ethics*, she has also raised certain questions.

1. Wyschogrod has adeptly conceptualized this book as an effort to write without writing, to write ethically without writing an ethics, to write against the grain of the desire of ethics to command and spell out duties, to write a counterethics, an ethics without or against ethics, where writing is meant to preserve and cultivate the fragile shoot of obligation while renouncing the towering grandeur of ethical conceptuality. Here obligation has the structure of the secret. The secret must be kept, for ethics cannot prescribe what is to transpire in those secret transactions between flesh and flesh, even as the secret must be divulged as a secret, revealing that something, let us say, obligation, is at work there, something that brings us up short. Obligation takes place in a non-place, a secret place of incommensurables. The dilemma of such writing without writing about ethics is as old as Aristotle, who warned us, at the beginning of a very fine book about ethics, that you can write a book about mathematics but not about ethics, not strictly speaking. That is because ethics – which treats of what I am calling obligation – deals with the τόδε τι, in the *hoc aliquid* (this particular thing), which is where life breaks in and the book leaves off, where singularity erupts and the cool winds of concepts are stilled. The transactions of obligation take place beneath the radar of philosophical concepts. A similar dilemma was experienced by Johannes Climacus, who wanted to write about poor existing individuals.

What then of the "professionalize[d] expressions of generosity and self-giving," Wyschogrod asks – trained relief workers and HMOs, for example – in which singularity is assigned to institutions, which have rules and regulations? I would say that rather than simply pronouncing a Jeremiad upon these institutions, we should remind them and ourselves of the gift. I would argue, again in keeping with Derrida's logic of the gift, that the gift does not stand outside in simple or pure exteriority to the circle of exchange (economy, institution). Instead, it sets the circle in motion, preventing teaching, healthcare, or social work from being degraded into a pure contract, producing what she calls "holistic" rather than "totalizing" institutions. Institutional structures are the only way things get done, but they must be kept continually off guard, off balance, [264] porous and punctuated by the gift. In this model, the contract *turns* on the gift – for if it does not turn, it grinds to a halt – even as the gift is inevitably turned into a contract. As the title of a recent collection of interviews with Derrida bears out, deconstruction is always a matter of "negotiating" differences – between the gift and economy, between hospitality and protecting one's home, between Levinas and Nietzsche, between the prophets and the philosophers, between "Jew and Greek." As Derrida said a long time ago in "Violence and Metaphysics," we live in the difference between these two, between these twosomes, let us say, a difference that is called "history."

2. That is also why it is important to attend to what I called, somewhat impishly, the "shuttle" that is run between Abraham and Dionysus, the undecidability, the fluctuation between Dionysus and Abraham, between Nietzsche and Levinas, because as I would say to David Wood, these two are not simply exterior to each other and there is no need to choose between them. Wyschogrod has seized upon this point, again with perfect pitch, for which I am very grateful. For without it the whole book, whose style invites misunderstanding, is misunderstood. Critics of this book have tended to let one of the two terms dominate over the other: so my excessively conservative, sometimes Catholic friends have found the book to be a despairing nihilism which has succumbed to an extravaganza of relativism and anarchism. Others, like Charles Scott, have found it weighed down by the heavy burden of the ascetic ideal.[7] Too frivolous and light and lacking in *gravitas*? Too weighed down by the spirit of gravity? But Wyschogrod has perfectly preserved the tension in the finite event of obligation, which I meant to depict in the image of Abraham of Paris, a Dionysus with a beard and tallith. She is sensitive to the structure and the danger of a finite event, which she figures in the image of a monorail that screeches to a halt and sways over the chasm, which beautifully extends my image in a way I did not originally have in mind. Obligation flares up momentarily against an endless night, like a falling star; it happens in the finitude of a transaction between flesh and flesh, in which flesh calls out to flesh. Obligation happens in the non-space *between* Dionysus and the rabbi, between the *tohu wa bohu* and the God of Genesis, between the play of forces and the face, between *apeiron* and *l'infini*, between the *il y a*, which is a great cosmic stupidity, and responsibility to the other. That is why I am happy to accept her reminder of the irreducibility of the aesthetic, of the work of art, [265] because, as Lyotard says of Levinas, the ethical is not the only language game.

What becomes of Abraham in this analysis, Wyschogrod asks? Does this not make Abraham look different, in danger of being "sucked in" by *il y a*, as Wyschogrod says, like a pagan worshiping the elements? On this view, Abraham is not so much being asked to "suspend the ethical" for the purposes of the "religious," which is the way Kierkegaardian stages this scene, as he finds himself faced with a conflict with the voice of God and the facelessness of being, of *il y a*, of the creator God or the *tohu wa bohu*, of which *il y a* is a transcription, so that he does not know who or what calls him. For how does he know who or what this voice is that calls to him from the abyss and to which he says *me voici*, in his best French? Is it God or the anonymous abyss, which is of course the binarity with which Genesis opens up? Thus conceived, Wyschogrod argues, Abraham's dilemma does not reflect a battle between ethics and religion, as in Kierkegaard, but a struggle between competing religions, competing Mesopotamian myths about the origin of things. That is a suggestive point. The reinstatement and rehabilitation of the *tohu wa bohu*, the formless void that God forms in Genesis, which has disappeared from view in the later metaphysical accounts of *creatio ex nihilo*, is something that interests me greatly these days. Apart from its Scriptural credentials, for it belongs to the letter of Genesis, it has received powerful phenomenological support from Levinas's striking analysis of its "anonymous rumbling." And apart from both of those considerations, the *tohu wa bohu* gives us a sense of a God who has to dominate something truly other than God, which gives the created world a more resistant sense of reality and alterity. If we hold on to the *tohu wa bohu*, the result is that the world is not a place in which God always gets his way. The face of the other is a trace left behind by God who withdraws from the world, leaving an unstable mark on the chaos. From the face there issues a command that is easily lost or ignored, whose faint call is easily drowned out by the anonymous rumble. For the face arises in a world formed from a formless void which ceaselessly stirs beneath the surface of form.

3. Wyschogrod has also identified the genealogy of this phenomenology beyond phenomenology, of this anti-phenomenology of what she calls the "cut, bleeding, festering malodorous" body, in classical phenomenology itself, of which it is the impudent, ungrateful heir, a kind of heretical variation. I do not know how to describe what I do [266] as phenomenology, if phenomenology retains its classical protocols of intuition and givenness, but since I do not know how to philosophize except phenomenologically, I must insist that what I do is a kind of dissident and heretical phenomenology. I think the same thing is true of Derrida. How else can we describe his descriptions of the gift, forgiveness, hospitality, and so on? To this point, Wyschogrod has added the welcome

insight that such an (anti-)phenomenology makes an ethical cut across the opposition of the lived body and the body reduced to genetic information and brain processes, which is something I simply was not considering but which I gladly embrace.

4. Finally, Wyschogrod has identified my preoccupation with the texture of ordinary life, with the broken narratives, the interrupted stories that keep starting all over again, the web of little things, the *minima moralia* of everyday life that are stitched together in those of us who manage to get through the day even as they are torn asunder, in those of us whose prayers and tears call out for help. What then of the lives of the saints, which she has thematized in *Saints and Postmodernism*? This puts them in a slightly different light, as stylized, highly edited fictions that are sustained by the willful suspension of disbelief, *petits récits* that must be reinserted into the torn fabric of everyday life. We should understand that saints are people, no less ill-tempered and self-willed than the rest of us, maybe more, but a little less narcissistic, advocates of a more open, hospitable narcissism, which makes them stand out against the rest of us like stars against the night sky.

Pilgrims of Piety

We can all be grateful to Francis J. Ambrosio for making an unexpected connection between Derrida and Dante. For Ambrosio, these two unlikely fellow travelers are feeling their way in the dark toward a mystery, each pilgrims of piety – to the point that Ambrosio stages a fanciful meeting between the two men on the road to Canterbury. Ambrosio's work is an index of a line of inquiry that I applaud, of a possibility that is opened up once one overcomes the mistake of treating Derrida as the sworn enemy and reckless destroyer of the classics – in particular of religious classics. That is a prejudice against Derrida that is based, I might add, upon an almost perfect ignorance of his texts (nothing is perfect).

One does not need to say that Derrida deserves to stand alongside Augustine or Dante, to take his place among the immortals of the [267] ages; he would certainly blush to hear that said about himself. None of us knows whether, once the hourglass of history is turned once again and things reconfigure still one more time, his texts will have that kind of endurance. We do not know, not yet, whether Derrida's story really is everybody's story. But, in *Prayers and Tears*, I have been arguing that he is at the least something of *our* Augustine, an Augustine for us turn of the century post-secular post-metaphysical Jewgreek confessors who do not know what we love and confess when we confess and love our God. My wager, bet on top of the wager between

Derrida and Bennington, is that Derrida reproduces the journey of Augustine, or at least of a certain idiosyncratic version of Augustine, for an age in which the structures both of institutional religion in general and of the specifically Christian imagination have lost their grip, at least for the intellectuals (since religion shows no signs at all of abating in the popular culture, at least in the United States). My wager is that Derrida evokes a response from whatever is still religious in us, whatever is still religious in a post-religious post-secular age, where by "religion" I mean something that is detachable from the positive doctrinal content of Judaism, Islam or Christianity (to stick to the children of Abraham), which is what Derrida calls religion without religion. Whether that will last for a thousand years is not my concern or my responsibility; it is enough that Derrida has tapped into something and draws nourishment from something of classical importance.

Ambrosio's wager is that Derrida is our Dante, at least, an avant-garde and impudent repetition of Dante, who can be viewed as revisiting the site from which Dante's poetry issues. Ambrosio is trying to take us by surprise rather in the way that Jackie tries to outflank Geoff. Am I surprised? Yes and no. I am indeed surprised that Dante and Derrida are alike pious pilgrims, but then again I am not surprised that I am surprised, at least, I cannot say I am lost for words (never fear). I should have predicted that something as unpredictable as this would happen. That is, *if* I am right in *Prayers and Tears*, then one ought in principle to be able to undertake this sort of comparison; it ought in principle to be possible to relate Derrida's texts in a sustained and serious way with the likes of a classic like the *Divine Comedy*. If I am right, then we should be prepared to be overtaken by something for which we cannot be prepared, like the daring venture that Ambrosio undertakes. For he dares, at once, to scandalize many if not most deconstructionists, who will bridle at the association of Derrida with Dante's religious imagination, and to [268] scandalize as well the world of Dante scholarship, which will bridle at the very mention of the name of Derrida in their sober scholarly midst. He pursues a dangerous strategy that is calculated to please no one. I can only wish him well on his wager and hope that he is right, that someone who knows the texts of Dante better than I do will find themselves thinking better of Derrida and thinking differently about Dante.

When I write my own *confessiones* or *retractiones* one of the things I will be forced to confess, one of the most acute sources of tears of contrition for me, is that in the course of three generations, from Napoli to Philadelphia, the Italian language was allowed to disappear from my family, which deprives me of the ability to read Dante's Italian. But, beyond that scandal, I must also confess my perfect, well, almost perfect, incompetence to discuss Dante even in translation, and hence to comment upon Frank's analysis of Dante, except to express my admiration and gratitude to him for it and to say that I found it both fascinating and surprising. He has delineated an impressive series of analogies and correspondences between texts that are tremendously different, yet strangely interconnected. By extending the analogy between Jacques/Georgette and Augustine/Monica to include Dante/Beatrice, he widens the scope of the analogy of the son of these tears and what Mark Taylor calls the (m)other, the woman who also bears the image of God, and thus ushers the Virgin Mary into this already strange and crowded stage. With almost systematic rigor, he identifies analogous structures of promise, questioning, conversion, hope, tears of repentance, forgiveness and blindness. What are we to make of this astonishing parallelism? My limited skills permit me to comment upon this matter only one-sidedly, from the side of Derrida, to see what light it throws upon the attempt I made in *Prayers and Tears* to resituate Derrida's work within a religious context.

Let me raise only one point, concerning blindness, which is symptomatic of a general question that I have about the relationship that Francis Ambrosio is unfolding for us. In general, whenever Derrida's texts are entered into association, *mutatis mutandis*, with classical religious texts one must remain alert to a general and massive mutation. By this I mean that Derrida is a pilgrim who in a very serious sense is lost, errant, who does not know where he is going, for whom there is no unique name – "God," for example – that cannot be translated into or reduced to some other name. If he were to be found among the pilgrims on the way to Canterbury he would be like a pilgrim who never heard of Canterbury and is not convinced that Canterbury is the place he needs to go. Thus, while Plato talks about [269] the Good beyond being, Derrida likes to say that he is interested in the *chora* beneath being. If Derrida is a pilgrim, he is a blind pilgrim who needs a walking stick. Now the question I have is whether the blindness that Ambrosio finds in Dante is the blindness of the beyond being, a river of light, a celestial blindness that comes of being blinded by a sun of unbearable brightness, as in Marion's saturated phenomenon, and hence a certain beatific vision of Beatrice, and whether this is not different from the blindness Derrida is speaking of, his *chora* blindness where there is no light or sun, where one is blinded not by the splendor of the secret, but by its darkness, by the secret that there is no secret? I suspect that it is. And if this difference is symptomatic of what divides Derrida and Dante, then I would want to know what difference this difference makes for Ambrosio's analysis, how this difference affects the other correspondences he has unearthed.

Conclusion

How else to conclude than with a question, we who are a question to ourselves, where piety means to make ourselves a question before God?
Of what do I dream when I dream of my God?
What do I desire when I desire my God?
For what am I praying?
Over what am I weeping?

Notes

¹ See John D. Caputo, *On Religion* (New York and London: Routledge: 2001) for an extended meditation on this question.

² See my review of Mark Taylor's *Erring: A Postmodern A/theology* (Chicago: University of Chicago Press, 1984) in *Research in Phenomenology*, 212 (1988): 107–14 [reprinted in John D. Caputo, *The Collected Philosophical and Theological Papers, Volume 2, 1986-1996: Hermeneutics and Deconstruction*, ed. Eric Weislogel (John D. Caputo Archives, 2022), 397–404], and in *The Prayers and Tears of Jacques Derrida: Religion without Religion* (Bloomington: Indiana University Press, 1997), 16.

³ Jean-Luis Chrétien, "La parole blessée: Phénoménologie de la prière," in *Phénoménologie et théologie* (Paris: Criterion, 1992), 41–78; "The Wounded Word: The Phenomenology of Prayer," trans. Jeff Kosky in *Phenomenology and the "Theological Turn:" The French Debate* (New York: Fordham University Press, 2001), 147–75.

⁴ *Saints and Postmodernism: Revisioning Ethics* (Chicago: University of Chicago Press, 1990); see *Against Ethics* (Bloomington: Indiana University Press, 1993), chapter 3, pages 42–68, 263 n63.

⁵ *Confessions*, X, 33.

⁶ See John D. Caputo, "Toward a Postmodern Theology of the Cross: Heidegger, Augustine, Derrida," in *Postmodern Philosophy and Christian Thought*, ed. Merold Westphal. (Bloomington: Indiana University Press, 1999), 202–225.

⁷ See John D. Caputo, "Infestations: The Religion of the Death of God and Scott's Ascetic Ideal," *Research in Phenomenology*, 25 (1995): 261–68 [reprinted in John D. Caputo, *The Collected Philosophical and Theological Papers, Volume 2, 1986-1996: Hermeneutics and Deconstruction*, ed. Eric Weislogel (John D. Caputo Archives, 2022), 379–386].

16

TOWARDS AN IDEA OF DANISH DECONSTRUCTION: IN THE WAKE OF LOUIS MACKEY

[Unpublished paper, Memorial Symposium for Louis H. Mackey, University of Texas, Austin, Sept 30–Oct 1, 2005]

Living Presence

Most of you have the advantage over me of having known Louis Mackey better than I did, and more in the flesh than at a distance. Louis and I met only a couple of times, once at an American Philosophical Association panel on Derrida and theology with Mark C. Taylor. For the most part, we were pen pals in the days before email and something of intellectual soul mates, having shared a common constellation of interests, which amounted to an uncommon combination of interests – in medieval philosophy, Kierkegaard, and deconstruction (to list them in both historical order and my own biographical order). But I suppose that for a couple of deconstructionists like us, it was fitting that our relationship should transpire in the mode of distance and mediated by writing, rather than of living presence, of whose complications we had both, following Derrida, tried to make ourselves acutely aware.

I remember, in particular, his letter to me in 1998, when I was planning the second of four "Religion and Postmodernism" conferences at Villanova, which brought Jacques Derrida into dialogue with a series of major philosophers and theologians. Mackey was one of the people I was particularly eager for Derrida to meet. He was one of the first philosophers who picked up the scent of "Derrida and theology," one of the first to see that it importantly involved Kierkegaard, and he was certainly the most clear-headed of these writers, a veritable sober man among intoxicated revelers in that new brew. What Mackey said was not buried under an avalanche of deconstructive strategies that provoked the impression, however unjustified, of frivolity. Unlike Mark Taylor, Mackey saw in deconstruction a genuinely and recognizably *religious* import. Mackey did not see in deconstruction the dissolution or the death of religion into the free play of signifiers but rather a penetrating account of the difficulties and complexities under which religious beliefs and practices labor. This is not a difficulty to be removed, but a constitutive difficulty, the one that makes faith a matter of seeing in part, through a glass darkly, which is the very difficulty that makes faith *faith* and prevents the dangerous slide of faith into (purported) knowledge.

I would dearly have loved to have had Mackey present at that conference. He was in many ways the reason it was taking place, just as he was an invisible presence in Toronto in 2002, when Derrida addressed a plenary session of the AAR of some 1500 plus people. His letter to me declining the invitation was not the usual expression of regret. It was a lot more an expression of heartbroken disappointment. "I am greatly honored, not to say extravagantly praised, by your generous invitation," he began, and after explaining that he was suffering from emphysema – "honestly acquired by 50 years of serious smoking" (to which he would succumb six years later) – he concluded, "So I decline what is perhaps the most generous and ingratiating invitation I have ever been tendered, with what is perhaps the greatest quantum of regret that I have ever borne. I *do* thank you." I was almost as disappointed as he was.

Danish Deconstruction

Some wag somewhere has written that originality is forgetting where you first read it. I was reminded of that humbling little maxim when I recently reread his "Slouching Toward Bethlehem: Deconstructive Strategies in Theology,"[1] an essay that I have often had in the back of my head ever since it first appeared in 1983 (it was written in 1981). This article either gave me my original bearings on the question of Derrida and theology, or it gave me the support and encouragement I required that I was headed in the right direction on this question. I do not remember which is the case, and I am afraid to press the case, lest the wag I mentioned be proved all too right. Be that as it may, it is no exaggeration to say that there is a straight line from "Slouching Toward Bethlehem" to *The Prayers and Tears of Jacques Derrida* (1997). There it appears in the bibliography, ever so innocently and inconspicuously, as if it were just one more article on the subject, instead of a crucial, formative, ground-breaking and indispensable contribution to the literature, which should be required reading for everyone who takes up this question.

In this article, Mackey provides a perfectly clear and eminently sensible account of deconstruction which clears away the brush and bramble of the charges of atheism and nihilism, the mistaken idea that deconstruction is a "demolition device" or a "counsel of despair" (255). Deconstruction is rather an analysis of the use of signs that insists relentlessly on the two-edged sword of the substitute or stand-in. A sign is by its very meaning to double business bound, its strong point and weak point, both in one, lying in its capacity to function in the absence of what is signified. Without the substitute, the signifier, the stand-in, the representation, the mediation – I am not suggesting that these are all identical or that they do not call for finer discriminations – we have no access to what we like to call the things themselves. Without the substitute, we would be bound to what is before our nose like a horse tied to a hitching post, unable to represent, remember, imagine, to write or to speak of what is not present, since this point is made at a level that cuts across the distinction between what is commonly called "speech" and "writing." But by the very same token (or signifier), this very means of access also defers the presence of what it signifies. We are never delivered immediately into the bosom of being, presence or the things themselves. Rather we must make use of such means as are available to us to gain access to them, to rely upon the constellation of signifying systems that are available to us – for our use, conscious of the extent to which we are used by them.

What language does with the writer, Mackey says, "is at least as important as what he does with his language" (263). That this is not exactly, or not only, or not primarily a limitation or restriction is easily confirmed by new parents (or new grandparents!) who boast profusely and shamelessly of the extent of their new child's vocabulary. It *never* occurs to these insufferable braggarts that having fewer rather than more signifiers at their disposal would put the little ones more closely in touch with the things themselves! The upshot of deconstruction, on Mackey's analysis, is not to throw us to the winds of nihilism or atheism, but to remind us of both the majesty and the misery of our situation, of the uniquely human and finite condition, which I like to call the radical hermeneutic situation. We must make our way by means of systems of signification that are indispensable but fallible instruments, necessary but tricky means of commerce, conceding that nothing has dropped from the sky, without need of interpretation, of parsing, analysis, criticism, and discussion. There are no uninterpreted facts of the matter; the need for reading, for interpretation, even for fine and close micro-analysis, goes all the way down.

In the second part of his essay, Mackey argues that none of this should be surprising or disconcerting to Christian theologians; it is indeed part and parcel of the good news. For Christianity is after all a religion built upon the very idea of mediation, that Jesus is the *icon* of the living God. Now an icon is not an idol, as Marion would say, not something in which we behold our own image, but a sign that carries us off into a distance that we can never cross, in which our vision fails us. In Jesus, God is brought near to us just because God is at an irreducible distance. Christianity, Mackey shows with unflappable aplomb, turns on the structure of *différance*, of spatial and temporal difference. Christianity is premised, first, on the irreducibility of a (spatially) deferred presence, of a presence that is never given immediately but always through a Mediator who bears the trace of God; and secondly – here I am taking up Mackey's allusion to the second coming in his title[2] – "Christianity" opens its doors for business, that is, it begins to write things down and get organized institutionally – with a temporally deferred coming, with the gradual realization that the expected second coming is being indefinitely deferred. Christianity presupposes and negotiates the differing-deferred effects of *différance* and makes no sense without it. It is not a religion of absolutely timeless, spaceless, wordless, worldless, body-less, history-less unity with the absolute Godhead, and when Christian mystics start to talk like that, they arouse suspicion and are, as Mackey says, on the most generous accounts, said to be the recipients of an "exceptional grace" (267).

Christianity is a religion of the Book, of a sacred Scripture, which is the irreducible "source" of the Christian faith. But a source does not constitute an absolute origin. The Scripture is, to use the language of a later Derrida, not exactly and precisely an *arche* but an *archive*, a record of what Jesus said and did, based on memories and stories and liturgies, not eye-witness accounts; it is a text, and as such it is subject to all the rules of textuality. *Écriture sainte* is still *écriture*, in which the memory of Jesus is both delivered and deferred. The memory of Jesus is conveyed by means of a manuscript tradition and all that implies – the historical critique of sources, the examination of the multiple layers of authorship, the multiple and competing theologies crafted with different churches, or communities of readership, in mind, the Jewish background of the text, the Greek cultural context, the Greek language itself. One of the many lumps in the New Testament that the Bible thumpers cannot pound out is that this primordial archive of Christian faith and life is already a *translation*, that the "Word of God," or the *ipsissima verba*, is a rendering in Greek of something that took place in Aramaic, at least one step removed from the things themselves. That is to say, the Mediator is himself mediated.

I have chosen to speak of "Danish deconstruction," that is, of Mackey's and my common predilection for Kierkegaard with Derrida, for it is Kierkegaard who intervenes at a crucial point in this essay. Suppose, Mackey says – recalling the *Philosophical Fragments* – we imagine by an impossible feat of time travel (265), that we could make ourselves contemporaries of Jesus, standing in his living presence, hear his marvelous words and see his marvelous deeds. Even then we would have no advantage. For what we would see with our bodily eyes is not see a divine man walking about the dusty roads of ancient Galilee performing visible wonders that would have absolutely resolved any doubt about his invisible being. That is immediacy, and immediacy in matters religious is paganism. As Climacus says, if God were of a mind to make Godself palpably present, God could have appeared as a large green bird, which would have gotten everyone's attention, but at a considerable cost to faith. Were we contemporaneous with Jesus, we would have seen with our bodily eyes a man about whom everyone was curious; we would have encountered not an answer but another question: Who do men say I am, he asked. By such a magical feat of time travel, then, we would have succeeded not in crossing over the abyss of undecidability but only relocating the undecidability: from now, two thousand years later, where it is filtered through all the accumulated layers of the history of the church and theology, of the history of interpretation, to then, when the man from Galilee would have been as much a mystery as ever.

Kierkegaard's project was to make us contemporary with Jesus, not because he held to a notion of immediate presence but because he did *not*, because he in fact had a crucially important notion of undecidability – and faith. Kierkegaard wanted to situate us in the shoes of Abraham before the Voice, which was a prefiguring of what he was really interested in, in situating us in the shoes of the fishermen, of the contemporaries of Jesus who were faced with the provocation of a man who was just like other men but also greatly unlike them, who was both in our likeness and in God's, who was neither simply our likeness nor simply God's, a man whose phenomenality was constituted by a memorable undecidability. Kierkegaard wanted to settle us into the shoes of that undecidability and to cut off, to undo or disabuse us of – let us say to deconstruct – every means of escape that we have devised for ourselves, both the illusion that the contemporaries would have seen a divine miracle man and the illusion we later ones weave, that there is some solace from the intervening two thousand years, from the theologies and the institutions in which the provocation has been given time to be assimilated. Kierkegaard wanted to make palpable not the divinity but the undecidability.

To do this, Mackey shows, Kierkegaard had recourse to the resources, the strategies, the tropes, the figures, the repertoire not of mystical theology or the fine points of scriptural theology, but of deconstruction *avant la lettre*! To do this, Kierkegaard required an implicit concept of a "text," not as a systematic delivery of the goods in clear and unambiguous terms – let us say, a "direct" communication, *s'il y en a* – but as a bit of woven goods, composed of many threads or textual tendencies, which often enough come together and reenforce one another, but often enough pull against each other, leaving us to wonder what is being said, and to whom, and finally – and this was a special interest of

Kierkegaard's – *by* whom, all of which he summarized by saying that he has redirected his attention from the what to the how.

Kierkegaard wrote with an acute appreciation of the situation of the *reader* – whom he wanted, like Socrates, to throw into a certain holy confusion in order to maximize the reader's responsibility – and therefore with an acute appreciation of the situation of the *writer*, from whom he wished to withdraw all authority. He wrote as an author without authority for someone he called my reader, the single one, who was a reader without assurances, one who was thrown into undecidability about what she was reading, thereby intensifying her responsibility. He knew that texts were tricky business and he wanted to make use of every trick in the book, every trick of the book, to write tricky books which sprung upon the reader the surprise of existence, that delivered to the reader the shock of existing, of choosing, nay, of choosing to choose, and not of having choices prepackaged and ready for consumption. Ay, there's the rub. How to do that! How to write a book that does not make the reader's choices for themselves. How to write a book that provokes, evokes, solicits, entices the reader into the choice. Kierkegaard's own task as an author lay in being an author without authority, who composed books as if he had not composed them, whose issued books were accompanied not by an *imprimatur* which assured the reader of their authoritative status, but by a revocation that withdrew from them whatever authority the reader might be inclined to attribute them in view of their having been published.

Divine Seduction with Constant Reference to Deconstruction

Mackey was on the trail of this deconstructive twist in Kierkegaard as early as 1971 when he described Kierkegaard in Kierkegaard's own words as a "kind of poet," that is, as a "writer" the *literary* character of whose work must be taken seriously. When in a second book he pluralized the title of Kierkegaard's apparently authoritative self-interpretation, not *The Point of View* but *Points of View: Readings of Kierkegaard*, Mackey was much more explicit in alerting us to this uniquely deconstructive state of affairs.

Consider the delicacy of the task. How do you write a book whose main thesis is that you, my dear reader, are on your own, you must assume responsibility for yourself? For there is every likelihood that the reader will brush aside this excellent advice and regard it as one more exercise of tiresome didacticism. On the other hand, suppose the reader believes the author, takes what the author says as well-put and definitively argued, and decides to act on the author's advice? Then the reader is not assuming responsibility for himself but doing exactly what he is told by another, viz., the author of this book. The reader is not thinking for himself but thinking just what he has been told to think by the author. How, in short, can one possibly urge someone to choose for themselves! If they do, they are choosing what you have urged them to choose, and so they do not choose for themselves; and if they do not, well, then they do not. Either way, they do not choose for themselves.

Suppose furthermore that what you want to do as an author is to address the "single individual," the unique and irreplaceable one whom we describe by the postmodern category of "singularity," which is a category unknown to Greek philosophy that emerges with clarity for the first time in Kierkegaard. How else can you do this than by means of the universal categories of language? Thus when you address yourself to the "single individual," you use a term with such sweeping universality that it applies to anyone at all, not just to that single individual.

Again, suppose your task as an author is to write a book that is addressed to the situation of the individual who stands alone before God? How can you do that without interfering with the very God-relationship you are describing, without intruding yourself as an unwanted third party into the intimate and absolutely private relationship of the single individual before God, the individual's absolute relationship with the absolute?

Suppose further that what you want to talk about is what Kierkegaard called "inwardness," a deeply private sphere in which the reader must make her own decisions and Kierkegaard, or any other religious author, is the third man out. How to talk about inwardness in such a way as not to insinuate yourself as an unwelcome outsider into this very private sphere?

So Kierkegaard spent a great deal of time mulling over the conundrum of the *how*, of how to move his readers to do something in such a way that they have done it on their own and he had not done it for them and they have not done it thanks to him. Kierkegaard had to write in such a way as to be profoundly respectful and circumspect about the freedom of his readers given the special delicacy of his subject matter. His subject matter is the secret one-to-one relationship between the individual and God where everything depends upon the individual's acting on his own, and upon God, of course, but not upon Kierkegaard. His aim must be somehow gently to stimulate or motivate or agitate his readers' freedom, somehow to move them to exercise their freedom, but to do so freely, on their own, not because they read it in one of their favorite authors.

In his *On My Work As an Author*, Kierkegaard described this as a matter of "deceiving" (or seducing) someone into the truth, a figure that evokes a comparison to the *Diary of the Seducer*.[3] It is a disturbing image insofar as a deception usually means getting someone to do the wrong thing not the right, and to proceed by misrepresentation, so this striking analogy bears witness to the violence Kierkegaard is seeking to avoid. He meant that when it comes to Christianity the usual "introductions," preoccupied as they are with the what and not the how, fall on their face, and that what is required instead is not to introduce one's readers but to induce or seduce them into embracing Christianity on their own. As John Updike shows, Kierkegaard wrote a very famous and for its day quite shocking "Diary of a Seducer," the story of a diabolically clever fellow named Johannes who went to great lengths to deceive a girl into doing exactly what he wanted her to do while getting her to believe that it is was all her idea in the first place.[4] To effect an action of that sort is the very stuff of seduction.

It is not my task here to reconstitute the "Diary of the Seducer," but if you have a taste for Kierkegaard, for being drawn out over the 70,000 fathoms, you are of course perfectly free to take a look at this famous story on your own, just so long as you are not doing it because John Updike said so. But if you do, remember that it is an allegory, a dark counterpart, written in what Kierkegaard would call the "aesthetic" mode (which we might for the moment take to mean "for one's amusement"), for what really concerned Kierkegaard. Kierkegaard was writing about a kind of divine seduction, whereby God draws the individual to himself down labyrinthine ways, as the poet says. Here Kierkegaard occupies the infinitely delicate position, really the almost impossible situation, of the "religious author," that is, of a man who runs the solemn risk of interfering with the God relationship of the reader, of inserting himself in between God and the reader and thereby doing more harm than good, namely, of producing not a God relationship in the reader but, let's say, if the religious author is named Kierkegaard, a Kierkegaard relationship. For if Kierkegaard could write with the tongues of angels (as it seems he sometimes does), then the reader might well come under the spell of Kierkegaard, not of God. That is his problem as an author, a problem he once described as the problem of how to write a book in such a way as not to have written a book.[5]

He called this the problem of the "double reflection," the problem of reflecting not merely on the *what* but the *how*, of taking into account not only a certain content, but how this content will be received by the reader. The problem is to prod someone into realizing that they are *not* who they think they are and that the task that lies before them is to *become* what they believe they already are, and furthermore to do so completely on their *own*, not because you have prodded them into doing it.

You might say that this is all very odd, that St. Paul sailed around the known world shouting what Kierkegaard called the God-relationship into the ears of everyone whom he could collar, and even landed himself in jail several times for his antics, and in comparison to Paul, Kierkegaard is a downright timid and timorous fellow. That is all well and good, but Kierkegaard's point is that by now (well, then) eighteen hundred years have passed and the situation had changed considerably. Paul was trying to bring the word to a world where no one was a Christian and which he thought was going to end very soon, perhaps in a few months; so a certain amount of shouting was in order. Kierkegaard on the other hand was addressing a world that was falsely convinced that it already was Christian and that the blood of the apostles flowed freely and generously through its veins. He addressed a world in which, instead of risking martyrdom by declaring oneself a Christian, one could not so much as marry the prosperous butcher's daughter, or even get a decent job, unless one professed profusely that one had been a Christian from the day one was born and perhaps even earlier. And as for lacking temerity, Kierkegaard's conscience was so delicate on this point that he even went so far as to criticize the Apostle Paul himself, whom he otherwise deeply admired, for the "selfish urge" of "acquiring adherents." The Apostle, he explained, was not the Christ and not above criticism.[6]

For all this, Kierkegaard deployed the resources and strategies of deconstruction, of this complex and astonishing arsenal of pseudonyms and signed works, of humor and irony, of texts written with the left hand and without right hand knowing what the left was doing, of relatively straightforward discourses with an edifying purpose and astonishingly imaginative works of art like *Either–Or* and the whole outpouring of the "aesthetic" productions. Kierkegaard was trying to make room for the decision and decisiveness of what he called "the poor existing individual" which he did by way of constructing a text that was marked throughout by undecidability. He described this as a matter of holding a text before the individual as a possibility, for whose actualization the individual was singularly responsible and in such a way as to make his own position obscure.

Blunt Reading

There are admirers of Louis Mackey, writing in the wake of Mackey, who go very far in this direction and who would draw Mackey along with them. The late Roger Poole rightly admires Mackey as one of the first people with the sense to read Kierkegaard as a *writer* and as a writer who deployed all the textual strategies that were later theorized by deconstruction in order to make sure that his texts floated in the air of undecidability and did not land heavily and, as

Poole likes to say, "bluntly" in our lap.[7] Poole warned against what he called "blunt reading," for example, in reading *Either/Or*, the Either (the aesthetic) is bad, the Or (ethics) is good, and we are told forthrightly, as directly as possible, that we should choose the good and eschew the bad. End of story, next book, please. As Poole points out, the entire book is a pseudonym, including the ethical *Or* and, as Mackey points out, in the "Ultimatum" at the end, the position of the Judge is overthrown as so much vainglory. Ethics is pride. *Either–Or* is neither–nor.

Poole takes with deadly seriousness the admonition signed in Kierkegaard's own name in "First and Last Declaration" that "there is not a single word by me. I have no opinion about them except as a third party, no knowledge of their meaning except as a reader, not the remotest private relation to them," and then goes on to ask the readers please to cite the name of the pseudonyms, not his own name, whenever they cite a passage in the pseudonymous books.[8] There is not a single word by Kierkegaard! Therefore, Poole concludes that none of the pseudonyms represent Kierkegaard's own view." It might very well be that the "real" author of these books is a complete skeptic, that he/she does not believe a thing, that the aesthetic, the ethical, and the religious are all failures, all equally futile passions, that there is no way to control the free play of signifiers in these texts, to police the pseudonymous works with the veronymous works, to stabilize their free play by means of the more reassuring figure of Søren Kierkegaard as a man of Christian piety. Kierkegaard's *Journals* is not a book that tells us how to read his other books but just another book. Indeed, even were we to turn to the veronymous works, and even to the *Journals*, what we would find is not a transcendental signified, an Archimedean point upon which everything can be balanced, but more texts, more writing, more undecidability, more posturing. After all, Kierkegaard was like most geniuses a genius who knew he was a genius, and he was acutely aware when he wrote his journals that was writing for the ages, not for himself – or, what amounts to the same thing, that he was *writing*.

I regard the view that Poole takes (it had been worked out once before by Josiah Thompson), a view which would lead Mackey all the way down the primrose path of deconstructive dalliance, as first of all *structurally possible*, that is, it is in principle necessary to hold as a structural matter, that such might indeed be the case, that the letter does not reach its destination, and the author of these books is a complete skeptic. It is structurally necessary that the positions expressed in these texts be auto-deconstructing, self-destabilizing. But I reject the stronger version of this thesis that it is *structurally necessary*, viz., that *none* of the views expressed by the pseudonyms are Kierkegaard's or, what is more to the point, that none of the views developed by the pseudonyms are views by which we should be seduced, solicited, enticed. Were that the case, the reading would close down the undecidability and cut off anything said in the aesthetic mouth of the pseudonym from any possible truth. What Kierkegaard wants is to let these opinions float freely in the space of undecidability. He wants to deprive them of their *authority*, not of their *truth*, and hence to provoke readers into deciding for themselves, into taking responsibility for themselves, into choosing out of the resources of their own inwardness and God-relationship. As Joel Rasmussen argues, when Kierkegaard said he had not the least relation to these views except as a "third party," that is, as a reader, Rasmussen argues, he leaves open the possibility that Kierkegaard's own view would "sometimes and in certain respects agree with those of the pseudonymous authors, just as they also often disagree," just as any reader sometime does and sometime does not agree with any author. [9]

Affirmation

That brings me back to the point of what I call Danish deconstruction, an expression which tries to maintain the space between Kierkegaard and Derrida. For me, and I dare say for Derrida and Mackey, deconstruction is first, last, and always affirmation, but it is an affirmation without being positive. The affirmation lies in a desire, an undeconstructible desire, for what Derrida, deploying a Levinasian expression, calls the coming of the wholly other. Were the affirmation that drives deconstruction removed, were what Derrida does not hesitate to call the "love" of the undeconstructible that animates deconstruction withdrawn, then deconstruction would become pointless, destructive, self-destructive. But there is no single, untranslatable form in which this affirmation can take shape, no single or privileged space in which it can take place, for once that desire is expressed, once it is given positive content and positive formulation, once it is posited or constructed, it becomes deconstructible. That does not undo the work of taking a positive position, such as Christian faith, but it does describe its difficulty, the conditions under which it must labor, the quasi-transcendental conditions, for the very conditions that make such positive faiths possible also make them impossible, that is, delimit them and expose their contingency and instability.

I do not believe that there is any credible reading of Kierkegaard's texts which confirms the extreme skepticism of Poole's reading. I say Kierkegaard's texts, since I have not the least inside information to pass along about the inner heart of the man, about Søren, whom I have never met and could not and would not psychoanalyze even if I had. He might in his heart of hearts have been just a scheming ambitious writer who did not believe a thing and was just trying to sell books, a task in which he succeeded only after his death. I have never beheld his heart of hearts. Indeed, James O'Donnell has recently suggested something not entirely unlike that about St. Augustine![10] I restrict myself to the texts, in which I find a subtle, passionate, intensely self-conscious, and lively faith in God and in Christ expressed with an almost perfect fidelity to what Derrida calls the auto-deconstructibility of the text.

There is always a creative tension built right into this alliteration that I love, "Danish deconstruction," the tension between Kierkegaard, the Christian Socratic, the man of Christian faith, and Derrida, the slightly black and Arab Jew who quite rightly passes for an atheist, who is no less a man of prayers and tears. The tension is *not* between a Christian believer and a skeptic, between a religious man and an irreligious one. The tension is between two kinds of faith, two kinds of religion, two forms of passionate inwardness. Kierkegaard's faith was cast in the *positive* terms of Christian revelation, of a positive revelation, in a determinate historical religious tradition, where there is a name that is above every name, at the sound of which every knee should bend, a positive form that for Kierkegaard was final and untranslatable. Derrida's faith is an affirmation that resists any such positive, final, and untranslatable form; Derrida's faith is an affirmation without positive revelation, without the *determinacy* of a determinately Christian or Jewish or Biblical faith. There is no final, definitive, or determinate form for deconstruction's affirmation, no untranslatable name at the sound which every knee should bend. But for all that deconstruction is no less passionate, no less a passionate inwardness, no less what Derrida himself calls the "passion of non-knowing," a "passion for *the* impossible." Indeed, inasmuch as here the objective uncertainty has reached a certain fever pitch of non-knowing, one might even – were one unwisely to be drawn into trying to arrange a competitive match between Kierkegaard and Derrida – venture the idea that the passionate inwardness was even deeper or higher or more passionate. That is why what Derrida once called, speaking of others, a "religious without religion," the non-dogmatic doublet of the confessional religions, applies no less to deconstruction.

Louis wrote to me in 1998 that while he loved the early Derrida, he had no taste for the later writings. That saddened me greatly and so I rushed off to him, by special delivery, a copy of my *The Prayers and Tears of Jacques Derrida,* a book that was in a certain way an attempt to bring to a head the argument that was set forth in "Slouching Toward Bethlehem." For it was in that seminal article that Mackey made clear that deconstruction was cut to fit a determinate faith like Christianity, upon which it produced deeply salutary, salvific effect, inasmuch as it protects Christian faith (or any faith) against itself, against its own worst tendencies, by reminding it of the mediacy and contingency of the terms of its faith in the Mediator. In *Prayers and Tears* my idea was to complete Mackey's project by showing that he was prophetically right about Derrida, who had in his later writings swerved in the very direction of a certain symbolic Bethlehem that he called the pure messianic. In the later writings, deconstruction emerges as infinite affirmation, as a practice driven by the irreducible energies of faith, the unflagging power of hope, the irreducible strength of love, in short, by the undeconstructible desire expressed by the *viens, oui, oui,* which are practically, *verbatim,* the penultimate words of the New Testament, even as the journey toward Bethlehem constitutes its opening episode.

Notes

[1] "Slouching Toward Bethlehem: Deconstructive Strategies in Theology," *Anglican Theological Review*, 65, 2 (1983): 255-272.

[2] Mackey has taken the title for this article from an unnerving poem by William Butler Yates, "The Second Coming" (1921).

[3] *Kierkegaard's Writings*, XXII, *The Point of View for my Work as an Author* and *Armed Neutrality*, trans. and ed. Howard and Edna Hong (Princeton: Princeton University Press, 1998), 495.

[4] John Updike wrote the preface to a separate edition of *The Seducer's Diary*, trans. Howard and Edna Hong (Princeton: Princeton University Press, 1997).

[5] *Kierkegaard's Writings*, XII, Vol. 1, *Concluding Unscientific Postscript to the "Philosophical Fragments,"* trans. and ed. Howard and Edna Hong (Princeton: Princeton University Press, 1992), 619.

[6] *Kierkegaard's Writings*, XXIII, *The Moment and Late Writings*, trans. and ed. Howard and Edna Hong (Princeton: Princeton University Press, 1998), 181–82, 341.

[7] Roger Poole, *Kierkegaard: The Indirect Communication* (Charlotteville: University of Virginia Press, 1993).

[8] *Concluding Unscientific Postscript*, 626–27.

[9] Joel Rasmussen, *Between Irony and Witness: Kierkegaard's Poetics Of Faith, Hope, And Love* (New York: Fordham University Press, 2005), 6–7.

[10] James J. O'Donnell, "Augustine's Unconfessions," *Augustine and Postmodernism: Confessions and Circumfession*, eds. John D. Caputo and Michael Scanlon (Bloomington: Indiana University Press, 2005), 212–21.

METHODOLOGICAL POSTMODERNISM: ON MEROLD WESTPHAL'S OVERCOMING ONTO-THEOLOGY

[In *Faith and Philosophy*, Vol 22, No. 3 (July 2005): 284-96]

Abstract: I characterize Merold Westphal's synthesis of Christian faith and postmodern philosophy as an "epistemological" or "methodological," postmodernism, one that sees postmodern thought as describing certain limits upon human understanding while leaving open the question of how things are in the nature of things, that is, how things are understood by God. Postmodernism (unless it waxes dogmatic) is not denying God, but only that we are God. In a characteristically postmodern way, Westphal has found it useful to limit knowledge in order to make room for faith, in the tradition of Kant, where these limits are historical and linguistic rather than ahistorical and a priori. In the second half of this paper, I advance the notion that postmodernism cuts deeper than epistemology and makes questionable certain features of the self and God.

One of the joys reserved to us who have chosen to do philosophy in a continental rather than an analytic mode is that reading Merold Westphal is a part of our regular diet. This is not to say that analytic philosophers of religion are not invited to the same banquet. As a matter of fact, if you look closely at Westphal's style, and you had not been tipped off in advance as to the sort of things he usually writes about, you might be a little puzzled about how to classify him. He is far too clear to be continentalist and far too witty and interesting to be analytic. He writes a kind of sensible American prose, a little like William James, perhaps. He seems to have decided simply to ignore the distinction between obscurantist continentalese and the withering aridity of analytic philosophy's unnatural untalk, neither of which sound like a language that any earthling could ever actually speak. He walks calmly beneath the fire that is exchanged overhead between these two warring parties and simply talks sense without sacrificing substance. What a perfectly novel idea – it is astonishing that no one has thought of it before! It is also very courageous because, in making himself clear, he has deprived himself of the philosopher's handiest and readiest line of defense against a serious objection, "but that is not what I mean!" That line is true enough as far as it goes inasmuch as most of the time we do not know what these philosophers mean but only hoped that in criticizing their position we would hit upon something that they did mean, like poking a stick down a hole to see if there is anything alive down there. But Westphal goes out of his way to expose himself to the hazards of being understood.[1]

[285] Methodological Postmodernism

Overcoming Onto-Theology is filled with judicious appraisals of postmodernist thinkers like Nietzsche, Derrida, and Foucault, defending them against the extreme distortion and demonization (176 ff.) to which they are subjected by both the Christian and the secular right. Against such misguided critiques he shows that postmodernism need not take the form of a denial of God or religious faith but need simply "make it clear that we are not God." (187). The demand for absolutes on the part of the Christian right is, he says, in one of his keenest observations, a "flight from incarnation," from the concession that we are linguistically and historically embodied users of signs. This flight is ironically "carried out in the name of the Word who became flesh and lived among us." (188)

I take Westphal to be defending a post-modern-day post-Kantianism. We get a good insight into his general philosophical orientation in the essay on Kant that appears midway through this collection. Westphal is defending Kant against the charge of Alvin Plantinga and the "Christian Realists" that Kant has nothing to offer Christians – or worse that Kant is going to take something away from them. That is because Plantinga charges Kant with feeding lines to those secular subjective humanists who threaten to steal God's good world right from under our nose, turning created stuff into epiphenomenal fluff, turning the world that is a sign of God into a frivolous play of signifiers, and turning truth into illusion. I myself grew up with that argument, where it was forthcoming not from Reformed Epistemologists but from equally anxious Thomistic Realists, two groups which today are forming something of an alliance, as Westphal also notices (105).[2]

Against this, Westphal replies, rightly I think, that Kant's position is fundamentally Christian, or at least theistic, because everything in Kant turns on distinguishing The (capitalized) Truth from truth, that is, the world as it is known by God (noumenally) from the world as it is known by us (phenomenally). Kant is not denying all creatures great and small but simply saying that you can't deny that "in the absence of human cognition, the world as apprehended by human minds would disappear," which is after all a tautology (97). We human beings do not get to occupy the divine standpoint but have to settle for a created one. Seeing the world on Kant's view, says Merold, is like seeing things on an old black and white TV set, where it is only God who gets to see the real game being played in the colorful real world. Back in the early 1950s we were all very grateful to watch the World Series in black and white, because without it we could not see the World Series at all. So we lived within its limits, while regarding seeing the real Series in color as a Regulative Ideal to be asymptotically approached, which is rather like what Kant is saying. God, on the other hand, does not have to live within any such limits. So we should not be ungrateful. The conditions under which we have access to the world at all are simultaneously the conditions which limit our access. Nor should we despair; from the fact that we must settle for (uncapitalized) truth, we cannot conclude that there is no Truth, no more than from the fact that the jury is hung, that the defendant was neither guilty nor innocent (100). Or from the fact that our knowledge is not divine we are not rashly to conclude that [286] there is no divine knowledge. Or, once again – and this I think is a Leitmotif of Merold's work – as Johannes Climacus says, from the fact that the world is not a system for us, it does not follow that it is not a system for God. The truth is, there is no Truth (for us), but that does not mean there is no Truth – period, flat out, simpliciter, *schlechtin*. Or, as Westphal says, "only some mushrooms are poisonous" (100). *Différance* does not imply that there is no God, but only that we are not God. The finitude of our knowledge does not spell trouble for the infinity of God's being. Our knowledge does not "lose its relativity and its finitude by being about God, any more than we become purple by thinking about grapes" (172).[3]

Westphal would have us guided by two principles, each of which constitutes a Warning Against Arrogance, the first against Philosophical Arrogance, the second against Theological Arrogance (272). The days of Absolute Knowledge, or Absolute Monarchy, or Absolute Authority, are over in philosophy and the philosophers would do well to lend an ear to the "other" that is theology, to listen to the words of the Scriptures, for example, by which Kierkegaard and Levinas, to name two very good examples, have been profoundly instructed.

Philosophy has learned a great deal about "existence" and the poor existing individual from the one and a great deal about the "wholly other" and the critique of autonomy from the other. The great mistake of philosophy is to confuse its own concepts with the things themselves, for which the shock of biblical alterity is an irreplaceable antidote. But by the same token, the days of Absolute Knowledge, or Absolute Monarchy, or Absolute Authority, are over in theology as well, where we must take care not to convert our theologies into idols, images of ourselves, of our preconceptions, and of our personal politics. The great mistake of theology is to confuse God with the church, theology, or religion, for which postmodern hermeneutics is an irreplaceable antidote.

That careful, sensible, relentless sorting out of the limits of our human point of view from a possible unlimited divine point of view goes to the heart of what I am calling Merold Westphal's "methodological postmodernism." The "postmodern" signifies the most recent and felicitous way of casting the finitude of human understanding, which means that for Westphal postmodernism is a continuation of Kant by another means, viz., by following a pluralist rather than a universalist model of human finitude (103). The "methodological" signifies that these limits are not substantive, that is, that they do not at all impose limits on how things are, which means for Kant, for Johannes Climacus, and for Westphal, how God knows them. This methodological postmodernism is to be opposed to a secularizing or reductionistic postmodernism, which is a dogmatic position that concludes that our limits are also the world's limits, or God's. "God, *s'il y en a*," is how a latter day Derridean might put it. And there is nothing about postmodernism to say that there is not a God, unless you twist postmodernist epistemology into a metaphysics, or postmodern method into a dogmatic substance, which would brush quite against the grain of post-modernism itself, which claims to have sworn off the metaphysics of presence once and for all.

When all is said and done, postmodernism for Westphal is hermeneutics, and hermeneutics has an epistemological status as a description of [287] the possibility and limits of our knowledge. I would only make a terminological point here, which is that it is significant that Gadamer opposes "hermeneutical" consciousness to "epistemological consciousness," the latter being for Gadamer a foundationalist inquiry that turns on a strict subject/object distinction (128), but I will come back to epistemology in the final section of these remarks. All contemporary hermeneutics is radical for Westphal[4] and this because it has broken with the aspiration for ahistorical objectivity, which is the form the Copernican revolution takes for us (170). Hermeneutics is the contemporary historical-linguistic version of the Copernican revolution, which reconciles itself to the idea that we see things from the point of view of our linguistic and historical situation. This differs from Kant's version, where our point of view enjoyed timeless, supra-historical, and pre-linguistic universality, which means that his post-Kantianism has a post-Hegelian twist. Postmodernism for Westphal is a post-Hegelianism for poor existing spirits, a project that, as Keith Putt has shown, has been significantly impacted by Paul Ricoeur's "post-Hegelian Kantianism."[5]

But finitude, Kant and Hegel are not the whole story. From a religious point of view, postmodernism fills in the details about our fallen nature and makes plain the distance that separates us from God, which can be attributed not simply to finitude but also to sinfulness, which gets us from Kant and Hegel to Kierkegaard. Kant teaches us that human understanding is irreducibly finite, but "Hegel helps us to see that it is worse than that. Human understanding is not timeless, unchanging, and universal. It is always some contingent, particular point of view, shared by a certain group of people at a certain time." (155) But Hegel should have stuck to making that point instead of allowing himself to lay the audacious and self-congratulatory claim to a capitalized Reason which unites all possible perspectives within the Divine Totality, which has pitched its tent in Prussian departments of philosophy. After Hegel is the "story of Hegelians without the absolute," above all, for Merold Westphal, Kierkegaard, who thinks there is an absolute perspective but that it is, alas, not available to us, and Nietzsche, who thinks there is no such thing at all.

Allow me to cite the single passage from *Overcoming Onto-Theology* which, in my view, expresses perfectly the spirit and the substance of this book, and which formulates a point of almost perfect convergence between Merold Westphal's project and my own work in postmodern religious theory. In this passage, Westphal is saying something nice about Derrida and deconstruction – which is not the only reason I have chosen it. For "Derrida" and "deconstruction" you can very easily substitute "postmodernism" generally. He is discussing "the possibility of appropriating postmodern insights in the service of a Christian interpretation and critique of contemporary culture." Westphal writes:

> Deconstruction is the denial that we are divine. At the heart of the metaphysical tradition Derrida sees a Heracliteaphobia...a flight from flux and flow as endemic to the speculative impulse of Greek and Hellenized Christian thought, a flight rooted in anxiety in the face of a world...too changeable to be under our control. The longing for [288] Absolute Knowledge, which presents itself as the love of Truth, is less a desire to submit one's

thought to the way things are than a desire to compel the world to submit to our conceptual mastery. The attempt to bring a halt to the play of the world or the play of our structures of signification is the attempt to find a location for our own discourses out of that play that is primarily, but not exclusively, the flow of time. This is a theological issue because the identity of Thought and Being, that is both required and promised as Absolute Knowledge, is one of the classical definitions of God...Metaphysics is the not terribly subtle desire and demand to be God: and deconstruction is the continuous reminder that we are not God. In fact, it claims, we cannot even peek over God's shoulder. (189)

Deconstruction is the continuation of Kantianism by another means, by a quasi-transcendental rather than a straightforwardly transcendental means. Deconstruction serves as a permanent reminder that our theologies, our churchly institutions, and the word of God are always couched in human terms, a point on which Derrida and Karl Barth are very much in agreement (192-93):

> We do not become God by purporting to base our discourse on divine revelation. Nor are we anything but confused when we act as if our attempt to point to the Absolute somehow made our point absolute. This confusion is perhaps the great temptation of Christian intellectuals. And there stands St. Jacques, working his hardest to protect us from Wormwood and Screwtape. (193)

The Christian Right puts us in the untenable position of having to choose between relativism and playing God (196), and Derrida protects us from that. You do not have to go all the way to laying claim to the divine standpoint, to being God, to avoid relativism, no more than you need to commit suicide in order to lose weight.

Kant points out the limits of our finite minds (the hermeneutics of finitude or creaturehood) when they are working properly, while the Protestant tradition from Luther to Kierkegaard points out that they rarely are (hermeneutics of suspicion)! (178, 182) That is also an argument familiar to me from my earliest years when I, like most everyone else I knew, was a Thomist. St. Thomas, we would say, was describing the natural man to which the more Augustinian types among us, who were very much in the minority (until I came to Villanova) would reply, "but there is no natural man, we are all fallen." That is why Catholics call St. Thomas the "angelic" doctor, because he was capable of such serene, detached, undisturbed and Cherubinic argumentation, and that is why what St. Thomas said was often so very positive and hardly ever grim. Having never been lured down the primrose path of sensuality, he was never led to say that sexual love is made in the dark (he may not even have known that!) because it is so shameful, which alas, Augustine, love him though I do, did say. Now assuming that from a strictly phenomenological point of view, we cannot really use the theological idea of "sin," we can say that what the tradition [289] from Augustine to Kierkegaard has seized upon is the way that the human heart can corrupt our best laid plans, that there is no such thing as a disinterested consciousness, or pure cognition, that the darkness of our desire, the darkness of our hearts, can corrupt the possibility of pure cognition and undermine the pretense of disinterested judgment, a point also noticed by Freud and Nietzsche. We can at least use the hermeneutics of suspicion to explain what theology calls sin and make of it something of a commentary on Paul (182). If the Thomistic perspective is angelic, the Augustinian-Kierkegaardian perspective is certainly not diabolic, but simply sensitive to the "human, all too human" (192), having drunk deeply from the well of human darkness. From Kierkegaard's point of view Thomas was like the Greeks, a little too beautiful. The constraints on the human condition described by hermeneutics squares with revelation not if we think that revelation means human apotheosis, being lifted out of the human condition and up to the third heaven to see God face to face, but if we think that revelation means divine kenosis, that God "kenotically enters our world and speaks to us under the conditions of our encavement," which means "to see in a mirror dimly" (174-75).

Something about Derrida

I have two series of remarks to make about this wonderful book, the first concerning Derrida, the second about the possibility of what I will call a more radical postmodernism.

Merold Westphal's book contains in general a model treatment of Derrida, exemplarily sane and well balanced, which I would recommend to anyone. I would offer only two refinements.

After referring us to one of Westphal's guiding texts from the *Concluding Unscientific Postscript*, Climacus's observation that while reality is not a system for us it very well may be for God, Westphal says that Derrida goes on to simply assume that God does not exist and that there really is no such thing as the word of God. Derrida's atheism is not a hypothesis, he says, but more or less dogmatic; for Derrida the truth of atheism goes without saying. There I beg to differ. Deconstruction is not only the denial that we are God; it is also the denial that we would ever have the authority to deny that there is a God. For Derrida,

God is at the top of the list of things that deserve to wear the little epaulet *s'il y en a* on its shoulder. It is not true that Derrida is an atheist, but it is true that he associates himself with atheism. I think that if he were pressed to give reasons for that association they would be more or less psychoanalytic, but this atheism, such as it is, is very much monitored by his notion of undecidability. While Westphal would certainly prefer that Derrida associate himself with theism, I think that Derrida's atheism seems to me to be exactly the sort of atheism that Westphal should approve of, if *per impossibile* he must approve of any, and that Derrida's formula of "rightly passing for" an atheist might have been penned by Johannes Climacus himself, who like Derrida hesitated to say he is – in this case – a Christian, but who said that he was trying to become one. That I think means that in the meantime the most Johannes Climacus could hope for was to "rightly pass" for a [290] Christian, which seems to me a splendid formula for anyone who wants to rightly pass for any such and such.[6]

But if Westphal thinks that Derrida is an atheist, he also thinks that he is a natural law theorist, and this on the grounds of the resistance that Derrida puts up to reducing the law to positive law, his insistence that positive laws are always deconstructible in the name of undeconstructible justice. This is a lovely essay that is one more sharp and shiny nail in the coffin of those who, even at this late date, are still confusing themselves with the notion that Derrida is a relativist. We deconstructionists very much appreciate the generosity of this Westphalian peace treaty, with the attempt to make us respectable, but on this point it is perhaps better that we decline the kind invitation to join the majority party, or at least to state clearly the terms on which we accept. Deconstruction is like the loner cowboy hero who, after having chased the outlaws out of town, can never accept the generous invitation from the townsfolk to make himself respectable and plant his roots there. He always has to ride on into the setting sun. So here's the qualification. "Justice" does not supervene upon positive law because it is a law of nature for Derrida, and that is because justice is not transcendent but transcendental, and again, it is not a transcendental Ideal, but a quasi-transcendental non-ideal. Justice is the sheer open-endedness of the promise that is inscribed in words like "justice" or "democracy," promises that are never delivered upon or realized in any actual law or democracy. "Nature" would imply some kind of natural reality or essence or being and that brushes against the grain of Derrida's anti-essentialism. He is continually unmasking the claims of convention to be nature (226), but not in the name of a positive idea of nature. Another way to see this is to see that it is not nature, which implies universality, that is being suppressed by bad laws, but singularity. Let us take the case of homosexual rights. Derrida does not think that homosexual rights rest on nature, but on singularity, on the right to be different, to push against the limits of what the majority calls nature, so it is more like the right to be "unnatural," thank you very much. Justice is more likely to be found where something is being denounced as "unnatural." Nature would always mean somebody's present or determinate idea of nature, however ideal. In deconstruction as soon as someone opens their mouth about "nature" (the ninety-nine), the idea of "justice" will send us off in search of what this idea of nature has omitted (the one hundredth lost sheep).

Unless of course – and here's my proviso – by "nature" you just mean "singularity," and you are saying that the "nature" of human beings lies in their "singularity," which would be a lot like saying the "the 'essence' of Dasein lies in its 'existence.'" Or it would be like Kierkegaard's remark in *Works of Love* that if one upright individual cannot do the opposite of what another upright individual would do under the same circumstances, then the God relationship – which is one to one – would be abolished.[7] If every human being would be judged by a universal criterion, then everything would be completed in our public secular social life. Then everything would be easy and empty, having removed the depth that comes of the one-to-one relation with God. We are all equal, but all equally different, before God, like so many points on the circumference of a circle, all [291] equidistant from the center, yet each point with its own defining, singularizing, uniquely proper one-to-one radius to the center. Derrida's idea is like that, but without God or nature. The most you could get him to say is that our nature is to invent new ideas of what our nature is and never to accept any fixed or present idea of nature. Any such idea would always be as Westphal says "perennially penultimate" (228), at best but a temporary pause in human history where we stop to catch our breath and tally up the results thus far and at worst a barrier to innovation. Contrary to what Westphal claims, for Derrida one cannot "articulate the idea of a higher law to which every human code is answerable in a conceptual framework not constituted (or constricted by those ideals)." (224). Not because there is nothing higher than these human codes, but because what is higher cannot be articulated and certainly cannot be articulated in any conceptual framework, past, present, or future. Justice is not a future present ideal. It is the inarticulatable, unforeseeable, unconceptualizable, unframeable open-endedness of any code of law, past, present, or future, to what it is leaving out, to what is "to come" (*à venir*). Justice is the 100th odd sheep who wanders off, while natural law is the 99. Perhaps my objection to Westphal's idea is that it is rhetorically wrong. There is more juice in saying that Derrida is not a Natural Law theorist but an Unnatural Law theorist, not a Legal Positivist but a Legal Affirmationist. Not a

249

Seventh Day Adventist but a Legal Adventist, by which I mean an *à-venir*-ist, one who affirms the coming of the other. Or even a Legal Messianist, by which I mean a Messianist without a Messiah who actually shows up, one who prays and weeps for a justice to come, which is always to come, whose very idea is to come, as long as we are in the soup of time and history and language.

More Radical Postmodernism

But leaving Derrida aside, I have a concern about the "methodological" or "epistemological" in Westphal's postmodernism, or indeed about any "methodologism" or "epistemology."[8] Postmodernism for Westphal is a post-Kantian epistemology in which we postmoderns have found our way of denying knowledge in order to make room for faith. Now we know that what happens in Cartesian methodological doubt is that after subjecting everything to methodological doubt, what ends up being clear and distinct to Descartes is nothing other than the finite soul substances, the finite material substances, and the infinite creator God, that is, all the principal furniture of pre-critical medieval metaphysics. And we know that after Kant subjects God, the soul, and the world-totality to critique, what ends up being restored in the second critique as objects of practical faith is nothing other than this same God, soul, and immortality of pre-critical Rationalism. In Descartes and Kant, the old metaphysics is not false, it was just hasty or precritical, and the way things were in the old metaphysics ends up being reasserted but now in critical garb instead. In a similar way, the upshot of Merold Westphal's postmodern delimitation of onto-theology is that, when all is said and done, we are free to believe everything that onto-theological arguments, in all their clumsy woodenness and misplaced absoluteness, were getting at. We are perfectly free to believe in the God of [292] metaphysical theology: that God is an infinite eternal omnipotent omniscient creator of heaven and earth. Onto-theology is overcome by being postponed and chided for being so precipitous, presumptuous and impatient to shuffle off these finite, mortal and temporal coils. What onto-theology is talking about comes true in eternity, but here in time we should make more modest proposals. Postmodernism is the methodological requirement of the day, enjoining epistemological modesty and hermeneutical patience, but at the end of days, when this methodological veil is lifted, classical metaphysical theology steps on to the stage, wholly unable to suppress a bit of an "I told you so" smirk on its face. "We told you so," metaphysical theology says, wagging its finger at us postmoderns, "the world really is a system! We told you!"

My chief objection concerning *Overcoming Onto-Theology* is that it turns on a classical and classically Greek metaphysical distinction between time and eternity, even as it evokes a parallel distinction between an epistemological self and a noumenal world (and hence between epistemology and some sort of ontology). So I would like to press Westphal a little harder in the direction of what I might call a more robust postmodernism, or what I usually call a more radical hermeneutics, where these distinctions are not so settled. I am pushing a little harder on three things that Westphal and I hold in common. (1) The notion of undecidability is permanent; it is first, last and constant, and faith does not somehow lift us up above undecidability. Westphal affirms this idea but I think this point cuts a little deeper than he does. (2) Westphal claims that postmodern critique shows us how deeply linguistic and historical conditions bleed into and shape our beliefs and practices, and that that is what makes all hermeneutics radical. That is true, but I want perhaps to squeeze more juice (or blood) out of that than does Westphal. (3) Westphal's guiding notion is that we would turn postmodern critique into a metaphysical dogmatism if we tried to use it to say that Christian faith, or any faith, is false or illusory. True, but I think that this is one of the lesser or weaker implications of postmodernism, constituting a thin postmodernism, and if it is a radical hermeneutics, it is not a very damn radical hermeneutics (138), because it is content to "make room" for faith, that is, to save the name of faith by making it "safe."

Let me sketch out or adumbrate the pressure that I would thereby apply to three ideas – that of faith, of the self and of God – in which Westphal and I share a common interest.

Faith. In a way, Westphal's epistemological or methodological appropriation of postmodernism proves too much. This "free to believe" approach makes too many things safe. There are very few things that one could actually prove to be false or illusory. Postmodern critique does not prove that eternal recurrence is false, or reincarnation, or that we cannot commune with the spirits of the dead through a medium who is a regular on the Oprah Winfrey Show, or a host of other beliefs. There is nothing in Derrida that could silence Shirley MacClaine. There are a lot of things that we treat as more or less perfect nonsense even though we can't prove them false. We are free to believe quite a lot of things. But that point aside, the main idea behind postmodernism as regards faith is not so much to make faith safe as to give us a shocking and salutary [293] reminder of the contingency of our beliefs; it is not out to prove their relativity but to exhibit their radical contextuality. Postmodern critique insists – but I do not hear this in Merold Westphal – that there is an undecidable fluctuation among what I am doing when I engage Christian beliefs and practices and what someone else is doing by engaging Jewish or Islamic or Hindu beliefs and practices, and someone else by engaging beliefs and practices that are not overtly "religious" at all. One way to be equal before God is to say that when I affirm the name of God I also admit that the constancy of the name of God goes under many names.[9] Or, as Kierkegaard said, if one upright individual cannot do the opposite of what another upright individual would do under the same circumstances, then the God relationship – which is one to one – would be abolished.[10]

In the spirit of Karl Barth, Westphal quite rightly warns us that our theologies and our churches can become idols, images of ourselves, not pathways to God. But I take that to imply not simply that, in a kind of standard form Gadamerian hermeneutics (as opposed to a more radical one), the essential truth of Christian faith can be expressed in many ways no one of which is definitive. It also means, in what I would call a more radical hermeneutics, or a more robust postmodernism, that faith itself takes many forms, Christian and non-Christian, religious and non-religious, with or without Christianity or biblical religion, with or without religion, so that one finds oneself radically non-privileged. (It is a little presumptuous, e.g., for Rahner to call the others "anonymous" Christians.) To fess up to the radical hermeneutical situation is to fess up to the radical translatability of what one cannot simply call "divine revelation." For there are many such revelations. One can speak of God's revelation in the Lord Jesus or in Lord Vishnu, of God's revelation in the Torah, or in the Prophet, or even God's revelation in the death of God, which means that the kingdom of God has come down from heaven to reveal itself in and empty itself into the form of the love of peace and justice on earth. Postmodern faith means one holds one's faith in earnest and with a certain irony, knowing that were I situated elsewhere I would be equally earnest about something entirely different.

In the radical hermeneutical situation, the truth is, none of us knows The Truth or has broken through to the Secret, to the Absolute Secret. There is no way to settle the undecidable fluctuation among the several faiths, or between the several faiths and a non-religious view of things. In other words, postmodern critique does not merely deny knowledge in order to make room for faith, but it bleeds into faith itself, and without relativizing it, without reducing it to an arbitrary fancy, recontextualizes it, so that the terms of our faith are struck with a certain contingent, contextual, and symbolic sense. Postmodernism is stronger stuff than a methodological buffer in time that makes room for faith in the eternal. Everything about postmodernism implies that the languages of the several faiths are what the young Heidegger called "formal indications" of something I know not what, that these several discourses signify something whose Secret I cannot probe. Something is getting itself said in these several faiths, I know not what. Is it some dark unconscious desire? Some evolutionary impulse that has surfaced in an odd way? Or the voice of God drawing me mysteriously down dark corridors to Godself? *Je ne sais pas.* I [294] do not know. It is not even a matter of knowledge.

Self. Next, as regards the self, everything about postmodernism implies that we do not know who we are, *quaestio mihi factus sum*, that at best we can "rightly pass" for a believer or a non-believer. Every time I say *"credo"* there is a voice within me that contradicts that faith and insists it does not believe a thing. Even so, those who say they disbelieve or do not believe must confess that they are haunted from within by another voice, one that fears that unbelief has forever closed itself off from the depth of things, from a wisdom both ancient and beautiful. "I" am a multiplicity of voices competing within me so that what I call the "I" is at best a shorthand for the one who does the talking, like a committee chairperson who speaks for the committee and gets to put his own slant on things and who in the process conceals how much dissent and how many competing voices there are back on the committee. Being at odds with ourselves is not so much part of being a self, or something we just have to put up with; it is pretty much what we mean by a "self," whereas a dull mono-vocal settled self-identity is pretty much what we mean by a post.

God. Finally, while it is minimally true that postmodernism need not take the form of a denial of God, but "makes it clear that we are not God" (187), it is also making a more radical invitation than that. To begin with, it shows us how exposed we are to the possibility that no one is God, including God, that even God is not God, that the name of God goes under other names. It does not dogmatically proclaim that the name of God reduces to other names, but it exposes us to that endless translatability. Postmodernism is not simply an epistemological way to delimit human knowledge here in time in order to make room for the world as it is eternally known by God; it shows us more mercilessly how exposed we are to the possibility that the world is not known comprehensively by anyone and that no one knows us we are here. It does not dogmatically proclaim that, but it exposes us to that. Deconstruction is not only the continuous reminder that we are not God (189) but it is the claim that the name of God is endlessly translatable into other names, like justice, and that we are in no position to stop this fluctuation.

To be sure, as Westphal says, the finitude of our knowledge does not mean that there is no infinite knowledge, but postmodernism exposes us more radically to the possibility that nothing is infinite, that God is otherwise than infinite, otherwise than omnipotent and omniscient, and that the discourse of metaphysics is wrong-headed. Postmodernism is not simply a caution sign held up before onto-theology, telling it not to speed, that the highway to God up ahead is still under construction, warning it that this is still the church militant and the church triumphant is reserved for another time. It is not saying that the main lines of onto-theology are more or less right but it is none of our business now, in this temporal vale of tears, to try to get a such conceptual handle on eternal things. Postmodernism issues a more radical invitation to theology to think God non-metaphysically: to think God outside the metaphysical categories of finite and infinite, time and eternity, sensible and supersensible, body and spirit. One finds this in current attempts to think God not as pure actuality (*actus purus*) or a necessary being (*ens necessarium*) but as "the impossible," or to rethink the idea [295] of divine omnipotence. What is interesting about this is how closely the invitation issued by postmodernism to redescribe God in non-metaphysical terms can converge with a more Scriptural way of thinking about God. Postmodern theology is closer to the way Abraham Heschel described the God of the Scriptures as a God of pathos, in defiance of Hellenistic metaphysics, than to the way Kant delimited knowledge in order to make room for faith in classical metaphysics.

In short, it is perfectly true that postmodernism proves that we are finite but it does not prove that nothing is infinite; or that it proves that we are contingent, but not that nothing is necessary; or that we are temporal but not that nothing is eternal. But to settle for that is to cash in one's chips and leave the game too early, while the night is still young. When postmodernism's game really gets going far into the early hours of the morning, it exposes our faith to an irreducible plurality of faiths, and our voice to a multiplicity of voices, both within and without. Moreover, it does not simply contend that the settled categories of metaphysics have been stored up for eternity but are not available for use here in time. Rather, postmodernism exposes us to the possibility and the prospect that things are otherwise than we thought. Postmodernism is an invitation to think in terms that are otherwise than temporal or eternal, otherwise than finite or infinite, otherwise than possible or necessary. In so doing, postmodernism does not undermine faith but makes more emphatic the extent to which faith is really faith.

Je ne sais pas. Il faut croire.

Notes

[1] This exchange was part of a panel at the annual meeting of the Society for Phenomenology and Existential Philosophy in Boston, in November 2003, on Merold Westphal's *Overcoming Onto-*

Theology: Toward a Postmodern Christian Faith, Perspectives in Continental Philosophy, No. 21 (New York: Fordham University Press, 2002). All page numbers in parentheses in the body of this article are to this book.

[2] For a discussion of Catholicism and postmodern philosophy see John D. Caputo, "Philosophy and Prophetic Postmodernism: Toward a Catholic Postmodernity," *American Catholic Philosophical Quarterly*, 74:4 (Autumn 2000): 549–568. Reprinted in *John D. Caputo: Collected Philosophical and Theological Papers*, Vol. 3, *1997-2000: The Return of Religion*, ed. Eric Weislogel (John D. Caputo Archives, 2021), 273–89.

[3] Take the example of the *causa sui*. Westphal does not want to deny that God as the creator *ex nihilo* is indeed the uncaused cause of the world, but his methodological postmodernism tells him: 1) that is not anything one could establish by a conclusive argument, 2) even if one could pull off such an ontotheological feat that is not all that God is. That would get us only to some sort of energy source for the universe, and not bring us into a religious relationship to God, which is the God to whom we pray (175).

[4] Here Westphal is putting it to me, very politely, I would say, for having written two books entitled respectively *Radical Hermeneutics: Repetition, Deconstruction, and the Hermeneutic Project* (Bloomington: Indiana University Press, 1987) and *More Radical Hermeneutics: On Not Knowing Who We Are* [296] (Bloomington: Indiana University Press, 2000).

[5] Keith Putt, "The Benefit of the Doubt: Westphal's Prophetic Philosophy of Religion," *Journal of Cultural and Religious Theory*, Vol. 3, No. 3 (August 2002). www.jcrt.org

[6] See Mark Dooley's interview with Jacques Derrida, "The Becoming Possible of the Impossible: An Interview with Jacques Derrida," in *A Passion for the Impossible: John D. Caputo in Focus*, ed. Mark Dooley (Albany: SUNY Press, 2003), 32. Dooley asks Derrida (I put Dooley up to it!) why Derrida says he "rightly passes for an atheist" instead of just saying "I am" an atheist. See Derrida, "Circumfession: Fifty-nine Periods and Periphrases" in Geoffrey Bennington and Jacques Derrida, *Jacques Derrida* (Chicago: University of Chicago Press, 1993), 155.

[7] *Kierkegaard's Writings*, XVI, *Works of Love*, trans. and ed. Howard and Edna Hong (Princeton: Princeton University Press, 1995), 230.

[8] Remember that Gadamer objected to "epistemological consciousness" because it divided the subject from object while "hermeneutical consciousness" emphasized their fusion or solidarity in "being-in-the-world."

[9] Derrida, "Circumfession," 155.

[10] Faith is not a univocal term. There are many faiths, each of which has its own validity and integrity, and this because God is God, and we are all equal before God. But to be equal before God means God does not give privileged access, or a privileged revelation to some people that is denied to others. Each revelation is special or unique, but none is privileged; everyone enjoys equal if different access, which means that there are multiple accesses.

18

JENNINGS'S DECONSTRUCTION OF CHRISTIANITY: ON PAUL AND DERRIDA

[Delivered on November 20, 2006, in Washington D.C., at a "Semiotics and Exegesis" session of the Society of Biblical Religion, in a book panel on Theodore W. Jennings, Jr., *Reading Derrida / Thinking Paul: On Justice* (Stanford: Stanford University Press, 2005). Previously unpublished.]

In deconstruction one sets out to show that a given belief or practice, a given text or institution contains something that it cannot contain, that it contains something uncontainable, which it is the task of deconstruction to release or emancipate. If that is so then in *Reading Derrida / Thinking Paul* Jennings undertakes nothing less than a deconstruction of Christianity, for his argument is that Paul is just such an uncontainable element, one which the Christian tradition, both institutional and theological, has labored mightily and all too successfully to contain. The book offers both a comparative study of Paul and a deconstructive performance, a deconstruction of the Christian containment of Paul and emancipation of the uncontainability of Paul. He simultaneously draws Paul out of what he calls the "confessional/ecclesiastical ghetto" (1) of Christianity into the wider circle of what Derrida calls "religion without religion," even as he draws Derrida into the open-ended circle of a certain Christianity as someone who has caught the flavor of a certain Christianity. On this point he and I are comrades in arms, and I have found *Reading Derrida / Thinking Paul* as instructive as a reading of St. Paul as it is a thinking of Derrida (158) even as, in correcting a misreading of Paul, he also corrects a misreading of Derrida. I will remark first on the parallels Jennings builds between Derrida and Paul and then on the deconstruction of Christianity, which I take to be the point, or the punch, of the book.

1.
The book is substantively centered around the word *dikaiosyne*, which normally is taken to mean to be counted or accounted righteous, in the right and, ever since Augustine, has been taken to mean being right before God, right in God's eyes, with the accent on the private rightness of the inner heart, not social justice

in the outer world, and on orthodox belief, not transformative justice (5–7, 40). Following the lead of Mexican liberation theologian José Porfirio Miranda, Jennings flatly rejects the Augustinian reading and stresses the justice (*dike*) in justification, making things right in the streets, not interior "righteousness." On this reading, Paul does not mean being made or counted just *in interiore homine* even as the world is going up in flames around us, but real-world other-directed economic and social justice, feeding the hungry, lifting up the poorest and most defenseless people in our society. Paul is thus seen to be interested in a new politics, a new social and political order (126). It is to buttress this reading that Derrida is called upon. The argument is driven by a central proportionality between Derrida's distinction between justice and the law and Paul's distinction between grace and the law, a relation of relations, a is to b as c is to d.

Derrida distinguishes justice in itself, if there is such a thing, which is not deconstructible, and the law, the body of positive, historical laws that, having been constructed in the first place, are constitutively deconstructible. Justice without the law is ineffectual; laws without justice are terror. Laws have real force, but justice has only an appeal. Laws must be deconstructible in order to make room for the appeal of justice. If the law were not deconstructible, the law would be a monster, could never be appealed or repealed, never made to respond to the peal of justice. The distinction is not an opposition because the law ought to be just and justice the law. We seek the convergence in what Jennings calls the "between" (27) of justice and law, which is impossible, *the* impossible, what we hope for with a hope against hope, like hoping for a Messiah who is always promised but never shows up. Justice "is" not, but it solicits us from beyond being, like a ghost or a specter, a *revenant* or an *arrivant*. Laws on the other hand do exist. They have the weight of being, the force of law, and accordingly they run the risk of violence and serving the interests of the powerful. But whoever thought life is not risky? Jennings stresses this point of force, coercion, or violence as the crux of the heterogeneity of law and justice, and that is all too true. A more upbeat way of distinguishing them is to say that while justice belongs to the sphere of messianic or prophetic hope, laws belong to the sphere of "judgment," the skill of application in the urgency of the concrete, having the insight and the heart to hear the appeal of justice that calls out from the singularity of the situation. That is what Derrida calls the three aporias of law in "The Force of Law," a point where he is not far from what Gadamer calls "hermeneutics." My reason for adding this will become plain in a moment.

While Derrida is addressing the problem of democratic life at the turn of the second millennium, the situation with which Paul comes to grip is radically different, but his solution is oddly analogous. Paul, who lives in the Roman empire, is puzzled about what has become of the order of the "law" – which he had faithfully observed in the first half of his life – now that the Messiah has come and introduced, not a new law, but a new order, the order of grace beyond the law. This has been given to us through and in and as the coming of the Messiah, which is also – and this is the thrust of the political reading – the grace that brings justice. Paul does not think the law is evil, but he does think it has become obsolete, having been trumped by the new order of grace. More precisely, Paul does not think that the contents of the law, or its big moral law prohibitions, at any rate – of fornication, idolatry, murder and stealing (Gal. 5:19-21) – are obsolete in the sense that we are now free to ignore them; these prohibitions are "holy, just and good" (Rom. 7:12). But he does think that the "mind" we should have in conforming to the law, the spirit or motive behind leading law-abiding lives should be different. Even when laws are just, the law itself has been trumped. We should have the mind of the Lord Jesus, the spirit of grace, the freedom of the children of God – not the mind of the law itself, not the mind of what Derrida would call the "law of the law" or what Kant would describe as the will not simply to conform to duty but to act from the motive of duty itself. Instead we should act with the mind of the Messiah, with the spirit of grace. That is why Paul thought that some laws, which Jennings likes to say are endemically "religious," like circumcision or dietary laws, are highly deconstructible, that is, they may serve a purpose in one context but prove to be an obstacle in another context.

The middle term that links justice in Derrida with grace in Paul is the "gift." For both writers, justice is founded on or made possible by the gift (85). For Paul, justice is a gift we did not earn; it does not come in exchange for anything we did. That compares with Derrida who says that the real passion of life is found beyond "exchange" or "economy," where we get x in return for doing y, in a new order which is the passion of the gift. Justice in Derrida is not a good investment made with a reasonable expectation of return or restitution but an an-economic expenditure without return.

I think Jennings is quite right about this but I would like to explore an interesting difference between Paul and Derrida on the way justice is indeed founded on the gift – one that I am not sure that Jennings points out. I offer this as a way to complicate the picture Jennings is drawing and as the stuff of further reflection, not with any intention of rebutting it. In Derrida justice is the *gift we give* by making an expenditure without return on behalf of the other, whereas in Paul grace is the *gift we are given*, for we "receive the abundance of grace (*charitos*) and the free gift (*doreas*) of justice" (Rom. 5:17). We have received it, as Jennings puts it, by "the having come of the messiah" (64) and we have done nothing on our part to deserve this gift. In Derrida's analysis of the gift, justice calls to us and solicits the gift from us. We are thus stationed on the side of the giver of the gift, under the demand made by justice to give beyond our resources, to do everything and then to do more, to give what we do not have. But in Paul, we are stationed on the side of the recipient, of being unable to bring about what is God's doing, of being given something "unmerited and unmeritable" (52), something that we could not even imagine to be possible. In Derrida, the impossible means the impossible place we must go; in Paul, the impossible means the impossible grace we have been given.

    That is an important point, I think, because of the political reading of Paul that Jennings is pursuing. Real life political justice is something we must do, a requirement to take personal action, and that seems a much better fit for the gift of justice in Derrida's sense, the gift we are expected to give, and it does not sound much like a gift we are given without any possibility of making it happen ourselves. The gift as something that is done to us, some gift that happens to us but is not our doing, sounds more like being right in one's heart even though the outer world around us is all wrong. Even if it is more than inner righteousness, whatever it is, such a gift does not sound like economic justice. In Derrida, justice is never given, it is always coming and we are always already called upon to give without return, in an infinite or asymmetric responsibility for the other, the call we are under to make justice, or hospitality, or forgiveness happen. In Paul, justice is the gift that in these latter days has been given to us in Messiah Jesus.[1] But if so, the world has continued in its bloody course and the demands of social and political justice have gone unmet. In short, in Derrida, justice is an unconditional claim but it does not exist; in Paul, God does indeed exist, so that God and the justice of God that is given in Messiah Jesus, the new creation, the new reality of grace, seem quite compatible with the ongoing existence of social and political injustice.

    There is another way to put the same point. In Derrida, justice has appeal but it does not have force; the law has all the force (police, jails, judges, etc.). In Derrida, "justice is weak" (70-71). In Paul on the other hand the law once had force but now it no longer does because that force or power now belongs to justice/gift/grace. Derrida is interested in the singularity of the hermeneutical situation in which ethical judgment is made – to which the universality of the law always and structurally does violence. Paul does not seem as interested in that as in emphasizing that even if the law were infinitely respectful of the singularity of the situation, and even if one were blameless before the law, even if one were not a literalist but judicious in one's observance, it would be to no avail, for the sphere of the law as such has been trumped or left behind by the new order of the grace of Messiah Jesus. Derrida is interested in how the weak peal of justice can interrupt the strong programmability of the law, how its soft voice can disturb the powerful tendency of the law to predetermine and subsume singular and exceptional situations, for the crown of justice settles on the head of the exception, which is what appeals to us for recognition and response. Paul is less interested in the aporia of universality/exceptionality than in a different aporia: how the law itself, even if it is applied judiciously and is respectful of exceptions, has *lost its force*, for the only force able to produce justice now is grace, let us say, the power of grace, the power of the gift, for the weakness of God is stronger than the strength of men, and the "weakness of God" is only "apparent" (70). The law used to have force and Paul followed it and was blameless before it (Phil. 3:6); unlike Luther, Paul was not wracked with guilt. But now that Messiah Jesus has come, the law lacks the power to make us just. As Jennings points out, in Derrida, the Messiah/justice is yet to come; in Paul, the Messiah has already arrived (93). In Derrida, justice or the gift has no force, only a weak appeal, and it is – rather like Bonhoeffer's view – we who must give it force or actualize it, because justice in itself, if there is such a thing, cannot do anything, cannot make or account anyone just. In Paul, grace is the power of God in Messiah Jesus, and it can do plenty – it can "actually somehow produce justice (Rom. 3.26)" (40), or "make just the one who has the faithfulness of Jesus" (3:27) (107), while the law which once had the force to do that has it no more. In Derrida, justice is a call that solicits us to make something happen, which never quite does; in Paul, justice makes something happen, which actually has happened, for "they are now made just by divine grace (*charis*) as a gift (*dorean*) (3:24)."

I think there is a tension or complication here that Jennings needs to address.

I should add that it is important to see that from the start, on Jennings's accounting, Paul has in mind in Romans, if not in Galatians, not only the Mosaic law but Roman law (43-44), that Paul was commenting on the powers that be in both the Temple at Jerusalem and the imperial throne in Rome, which we should bear in mind in reading the letter to the Romans, where "tact" (62) dictates that Paul tone down some of the stronger criticisms he had earlier made of the law in the letter to the Galatians. The unjust execution of Jesus makes a mockery of the administration of justice under Roman law, which governed under the horrendous but effective rule of public crucifixion, which worked in a Foucauldian way: a public display of unusual cruelty to make a vivid impression on the general population and impress upon them the need to obey the law. Thus the violence of the law, which is what demands its deconstruction, is made manifest in the cross. That conservative Christians today would support the death penalty is, thus, a very peculiar turn of events, given that the injustice of the death penalty is a central event in Christianity (66-67). I will leave it to New Testament historians to adjudicate that as an historical claim, but as a philosopher I can say I do think it is a sound move. If the law of Moses has lost the power to make us just, surely that applies, *a fortiori*, to Roman law.

2.

The scope of Jennings's argument, what I have called the deconstruction of Christianity, is made plain in his conclusion where he comes out swinging. We must wrest Paul free from the "clutches of his ecclesial and dogmatic jailers" (157), from the "ghetto of ecclesial self-confinement" (163) – that seems frank enough – who are responsible for silencing the question of justice in his work and turning it into a doctrine of individualizing and inner justification, the indispensable mediator of which is the institutional church, thereby excusing themselves from the sphere of social and political justice.

Along with this political, liberating (liberation) Pauline theology Jennings raises the question of hospitality, or cosmopolitanism as regards what Jennings calls "the messianic hope for all humanity" (164), or universal salvation, which is a problem that arises once again from this crucial difference between Derrida and Paul. For Derrida, the Messianic event is essentially and structurally "to come," going back to a Rabbinic tradition mentioned by Blanchot in which the Messiah never actually shows up in the flesh but serves rather as the figure of hope, the very form of expectation. For Paul, on the other hand, the Messiah has already come, in the flesh, and his crucifixion and resurrection are the galvanizing center of Paul's life, which is the theme of the event in Badiou's *Paul*. In Derrida, without some idea of messianicity, or the pure "messianic," we are locked into confessional exclusivism, at risk of a theological imperialism which absolutizes the actual appearance in the flesh of the Messiah in some particular historical form that is clearly unavailable to countless other people born in other times and places. "Instead of an open-ended and essentially border less sociality of expectation, it [Christianity] has become an institution with carefully policed frontiers." (164) To the extent that the pure messianic becomes a concrete messianism, the future becomes the filling in of a pregiven ideal and that "abolishes the very idea of the 'to come,'" its character of absolute futurity (168). To meet this demand Jennings suggests a twofold inside/outside: both a Derrida within a certain Christianity and a certain Christianity that has been forced to situate itself outside Christianity, a point that was made by in various ways by Kierkegaard, Altizer and more recently by Vattimo. The essence of Paul, and by implication then the essence of Christianity, on Jennings's account, occupies a place outside "Christianity," constituting a Christianity that Christianity cannot contain, an affirmation that resists and twists free from Christianity doctrinal and institutional architecture.

My own suggestion, which I do not at all propose as a competitor to Jennings's, but as a supplement or a graft to his exciting book, which I regard as a comrade in arms, is to embrace the non-existence of "justice" in Derrida and to embrace a distinction between the "event" of Christianity and its real or objective existence. To do this I return to the theme of hauntology in Derrida, a theme Jennings himself also singles out (37-39). Derrida is interested in the several ways the seeming solidity of presence (ontology) is disturbed by demi-beings, by the presence/absence of the ghost (hauntology), of the *revenants* and *arrivants*, whose role in breaking up presence is the key to justice. Now the New Testament is filled with well-known ghosts – with angels, resuscitated bodies, empty tombs, and the transfigured and risen body of Jesus, over which there presides the ghost of a memory, the memory of a man shrouded by the fog of history, the memory of Jesus, to which we should also add, in the present context, the memory of Paul. The memory of these two men, who may or may not have met each other, constitute what Johann Baptist Metz would call "dangerous memories," posing a danger as they do to the priestly institutions that have authorized themselves to police these memories, not least a danger to the orthodoxy that has drawn itself into a tight defensive circle, like a fort fortified on every side, which is the *munis* in *communio*.

For a very long time now I have been haunted by the ghost of Jesus, by the ghost of a question that keeps asking itself in me again and again – not "what would Jesus do?" but "what would Jesus *think*?" What would he think if he could see the history of this Holy-Trinity-cum-Virgin-Birth-cum-Chalcedonian-Nicean-Constantinian-Catholic-Protestant-history-of-the-persecution-of-his-Jewish-people thing called "Christianity"? My suspicion is that he would scratch his head, wrinkle his brow, look over his shoulder to see if there is someone else standing behind him, and ask, in a state of genuine bewilderment, "are all you people talking about *me*?" I wager that Jennings has been haunted by the same question about Paul.

Because while Jesus and Paul are *revenants* who disturb the history of Christian theology with dangerous memories, they are no less *arrivants*, that is, figures of the open-ended and unforeseeable future toward which Christianity points, with which Christianity is related in the mode of a future anterior something that "will have been." On my accounting, the uncontainable thing that Christianity contains goes under the name of the "event," the event or complex of events that stirs within the preaching and the sayings of Jesus and within the letters of Paul, the event of a radical and paradoxical kingdom, of the most amazing reversals, of a kind of sacred anarchy that consists in forgiving the unforgivable, loving the most unlovable, indeed loving one's very enemies, of offering hospitality not to the friend but to the stranger, in believing what it has become impossible to believe, in hoping against hope, the very scene that Jennings sketched for us under the name of radical justice. Those are indeed determinate loves and hopes, nurtured by the determinate memories of Jesus and of Paul that are lodged in determinate texts and institutional memories. But this is also at the same time a ghostly scene, turned toward an *arrivant* in a more indeterminate and open-ended expectation of an absolutely unforeseeable future. We are haunted by the ghost of something of which what we here today call by the determinate names of Christianity, Judaism, Islam, or by the generic but also very specifically Western word "religion," will have been antecedent states. Of this ghost we say, or we are asked to say, full of fear and trembling and wary of the risk, "come."

For this gift of giving us much to read and to think about Derrida and Paul we owe Jennings all our gratitude. How can we ever repay him?

Notes

[1] Jennings himself reflects this ambiguity when he says that according to Paul "all humans are summoned to justice and *all receive, or are intended to receive, or actually will receive*, the gift of justice and life." (124, italics mine)

ON BEING CLEAR ABOUT FAITH:
A RESPONSE TO STEPHEN WILLIAMS

[In *Books and Culture: A Christian Review*, Vol. 12, No. 6 (November/December 2006): 40–42]

[40] I wish to thank Stephen Williams for his thoughtful and articulate response to *On Religion*. He raises questions that go to the heart of what I was proposing and I am grateful for the opportunity to respond. When he describes the point of my work is to argue that religion provides "a messianic space" that gives our search for justice "its deep dimension, power and, perhaps, meaning," he expresses sensitively what I am trying to do. He and I are agreed that love and justice go to the core of religion and about the danger of religious exclusivism. But he is worried that I have dogmatically made it impossible for there to be a "clear revelation," by which I think he means one that is clearly true to the exclusion of others. So he argues for an exclusively true revelation – the Judeo-Christian one – but without exclusivism, without pride and arrogance. That prompts a suggestion concerning the conditions under which a just and loving God might reveal Godself truly in just one time and place. Still, we cannot expect that even that revelation would be "universally clear," because human beings are as prone to flee the light as to seek it.

I begin with the point about "dogmatic skepticism," namely, claiming definitely to know that we cannot know certain things: "John Caputo says that *no one* can know [41] whether or of what kind God may be." The emphasis falls on the "no one:" you or I might be skeptical about knowing this, but to claim to know that no one can know it is dogmatic. If "knowing" whether or what God may be means that valid philosophical arguments to this end have been or will be forthcoming, then I am guilty. But, like almost all philosophers from Kant to the present, religious and non-religious, I have perfectly "good reasons," principled ones, for arguing that attempts to sail that far beyond experience by way of speculative argumentation inevitably run amuck, which also explains why these arguments enjoy acceptance only among people of faith.

I would not call this view "dogmatic" except in the technical sense that I hold it to be true, which I do.

I would put a different emphasis on this sentence: "no one can *know* whether or of what kind God may be." I argue that our understanding of God is guided by *faith*, not knowledge in a "standard form epistemological sense." (I will clarify in a bit why I use this phrase.) But I make a living promoting the religious side of "post-modernism." *On Religion* is a (slightly popularized) argument that the days of dogmatic metaphysical theism *and atheism* are over (see especially chapter 2) and that postmodern means post-secular. So, my delimitation of our *knowledge* of God comes by way of making room for faith. I make everything turn on the "love of God" and on determining just what that love could mean.

Williams continues, "But let us consider what that implies. Let us assume, *ad hominem*, the intelligibility of the traditional Judeo-Christian notion of God." I accept this assumption. The text continues – but with my italics: "On Caputo's account of things, no one is justified in claiming to *know* that such a being exists." I agree.

Williams concludes: "That means that there is no clear revelation of or by such a being. For if there had been such a revelation, someone, somewhere might be justified in claiming to *know* that such a being exists. No one is so justified; therefore, there has been no such revelation."

I deny the implication. From the fact that we cannot *know* God's existence I conclude the very opposite, viz., that clear – for me, vivacious and vigorous – religious revelations are just about the only way somebody, somewhere can come around to holding that God exists. From the reality of such a revelation I conclude that someone would be justified, not in *knowing* but in *having faith* that such a being exists. Many people, in many places, are so justified, and therefore there are many revelations, each with a characteristic clarity cut to fit its time and place. I so much support the idea of revelation that I prefer more rather than fewer revelations. The main way most people come to God, come to affirm their belief in God, is through revelation, through one religious revelation or another, through settling themselves inside one religious tradition or another and letting it shape their lives.

One comes to God, one comes to faith in God, one comes to adopt a religious point of view, by settling into a historical community of faith, a religious form of life. But there are *multiple* religious forms of life, each with its own unique "clarity" – each is a vigorous, persuasive, and living tradition (although for me the deepest things always retain a rich ambiguity). The mistake is to think that one of them is exclusively true, which is no more convincing to me than saying one culture or one language is exclusively true. So when Stephen

Williams proposes that one may doubt there is one exclusive revelation either because there is no God to do the revealing, or because God is unable to do such a thing or because God just doesn't want to, then I would say, given these options, that God does not want to because it would buy God too much trouble with his other constituencies. St. Paul spent his life struggling with this. First God (who is impartial) made the Jews his people of choice, but then he sent Jesus, whose grace trumps the law, so what is going on? I think Paul's best solution is in Romans 9-11 when he says that God is not defeated, that everyone and everything (*ta panta*) are saved, but please don't ask him how. O how rich and unsearchable the ways of God. The healthiest religious forms of life from my point of view always figure out some way to say things like this, sometimes just slipping it in (hoping it will not grab too much attention from the conservative donors). They find a way of building a kind of wormhole to the other faiths that say things like being circumcised or uncircumcised make no difference, or whoever loves is born of God, or other generous and expansive things like that.[1]

At their best, these forms of life nourish the life of faith while also encouraging the reflective clarification of faith (they have and seek "intelligibility," *fides quaerens intellectum*), but they are not exclusively true as to the "determinate" particulars of their narratives, which do not translate into "knowledge" in the standard form epistemological sense.

Why? My argument is that a determinate religious revelation – a set of framing beliefs sustained by faith – however clear, constitutes a revelation just in case you actually *have faith* that something is being *revealed* to begin with. You have to believe (that is, see only in part or through a glass darkly, [1 Cor 13:8–12] that is, *not so clearly* in the epistemological sense) *that* it is a revelation in order to count the particulars of what it says as clearly revealed. What is revealed to the faithful is a revelation only in function of their faith that this *is* a divine revelation. The items revealed are the fruit of a tree of faith. What we see (however clearly) is a function of what we do *not see* clearly, but only darkly. That means that a religious revelation should be distinguished from a revelation in a standard form epistemological sense, where we see more straightforwardly (more clearly). For example, under the headline "Deep Throat Revealed," the May 31, 2005, *Washington Post* reported that Mark Felt had revealed that he was indeed Deep Throat, the secret contact who supplied the crucial clues in the Watergate case. When all the principals involved in the case confirmed that Felt was the man, that was a clear revelation in the standard form epistemological sense. That was a matter of making public information that had previously been concealed, thereby causing the rest of us to pass from ignorance to knowledge about the matter in question. We came to know what we did not previously know. Many people had suspected Felt but they did not know. Now they do.[2]

But the same thing cannot be said to happen when Islam teaches that it was from the Dome of the Rock of that Mohammed ascended into heaven, or when Luke "reports" (Barth) a conversation between an angel named Gabriel and the maid Miriam of Nazareth about the virgin birth of Jesus, or when Joseph Smith reveals that he received the Book of Mormon (along with the glasses needed to translate it into English) from an angel named Moroni, or when a Lakota Indian shaman reveals that Inyan, the Rock, is the first in existence and the grandfather of all things, and Maka, the Earth, is next in existence and the grandmother of all things.[3] The only people who think that anything was "revealed" clearly to them by these narratives are the ones who live within and embrace these religious traditions. If they did not previously have such a religious faith, then they now believe something that they did not previously believe. But they do not come to "know" anything more than they did before, not in a standard form epistemological sense. [Ed. Note: *the following sentence was cut from the printed version:* The *Book of Revelation* is a book of revelation only if you believe it, and what is revealed in the standard epistemological sense by the Book of Mormon, the Bible, the Koran, or the Lakota oral tradition to someone who does not have a religious faith that it is a divine revelation is relatively limited.]

Now I do not regard this as bad news for religion and revelation but as a way to keep them honest (clear – about *themselves*). I argue against confusing religious faith, or revelation, or religious witness (testimony), with *knowledge*.[4] [Ed. Note: *the following sentence was cut from the printed version:* All the faith in the world, all the testimony given to faith (many different people have died for many different things) does not turn religious faith into knowledge. Of course, it does not make such faith bogus, either. I have no hard inside information to pass along about communications with an angel named Moroni or another named Gabriel or that Maka is not the grandmother of all things. It is enough for me that these revelations are not "knowledge" in a standard form epistemological sense.]

I am furthermore arguing that the slippery slope from religious faith to knowledge in the standard form epistemological sense is dangerous and it will make it difficult to avoid the exclusivism that both Stephen Williams and I reject. When people forget that distinction, when they do not keep uppermost the coefficient of "faith" (seen in part, darkly) that is attached to revelation, they are – on their best days – led to look with a certain benign tolerance or civility upon those who do not share their faith, or to describe them as "anonymous" members of their own faith, or even think to themselves that such people are not inclined to seek the light. My guess would be that we have no good reasons to doubt that the odds for seeking the light and fleeing the light are about the same for religious believers and for people who believe other things, that the distribution of good faith and bad faith among both groups is about the same. But on their very *worst* days, and this is the side of religious revelations that gets all the headlines, when they forget this distinction, they might be induced to slam an airplane into the side of a tall building, or to torture or imprison people who do not share their faith-now-[42] become-knowledge. So I spent some time in *On Religion* in trying to talk people off the edge of that slope, in not making that leap from faith to knowledge.

Next, in addition to being dangerous, I am also arguing that thinking about religious traditions and religious revelations as making epistemic claims to be exclusively true, hence as providing us with "knowledge" in a standard form epistemological sense, just does not put their best foot forward. So when Stephen Williams switches from the interrogative to the suggestive, he proffers a kind of four-step *cur deus homo?* that the Incarnation was a fairly felicitous way for God to negotiate the straits imposed by an exclusive revelation. My favorite part of this account is the conclusion, when he offers a little apology that this should not be viewed as offering a remedy for a divine predicament and that in the end this portrait is not worthy of God. I agree. Even fair-minded suggestions like this to minimize the damage of holding to an exclusive revelation of the truth suggest only that we are following the wrong scent and not thinking rightly about revelation, which ought not to catch us up in such a conundrum.

What then *are* religious revelations ultimately about? They are centrally made up of important religious narratives that shape their lives of the faithful in that tradition; they are formative not informative. They don't reveal (or "report") secret bits of information to us – like the identity of Deep Throat – about the transactions of angels but they imaginatively embody a form of life. Religious narratives are told and retold, chanted and danced in liturgies, meditated upon and depicted in art, taken to heart, interiorized and ultimately translated into existence, into a way of living, which is where they have their pay off. Mormon religious life, like Christian life, consists in energetic works of love and non-violence, even as Lakota life moves within a zone of absolute respect drawn around the natural world from which we high-tech polluters, *über*-consumers and urban sprawlers have a great deal to learn.

Are they true? Yes. But we are thinking about their "truth" in the wrong way if we take them as supplying clear knowledge in a representational theory of truth. Their truth – and this is what I think *vera religio* comes down to – comes in the way of the fruitfulness of the form of life to which they give rise, which they both shape and embody. Their truth comes in the way of a living truth, of *facere veritatem*, of a truth that we should make happen in our lives, just the way music does not exist in a score but in the playing. In the sphere of religious truth, it makes perfect sense to say, "I am the way, the truth and the life." It would make no sense for Aristotle, Euclid, or Einstein to say that, but it makes perfect sense to have Jesus say it. For the life of Jesus – behold the birds of the air, Father, forgive them, blessed are the peacemakers, and all the rest – is paradigmatic of the way you do things in this form of life, otherwise you are deceiving yourself and others if you say you are a follower of Jesus. Jesus provides a clearly powerful and powerfully clear embodiment of what we mean by God.

Now it is in this sense that these narratives do indeed supply a certain "knowledge," an understanding, not in the standard form epistemological and representational sense of reporting information about conversations with angels and other supernatural events that merely mortal historians of the first century could never have uncovered, but in the sense of "knowing-how" and "understanding-as." They provide those who inhabit these narratives with a way to think about and view things, instructing them in a certain art of life, attuning them to the rhythms of birth and death, joy and sorrow, from just that distinctive point of view.[5]

This view of religious truth also leads me to conclude that the theism/atheism cut is not the deep divide in human affairs, since lots of people lead lives of energetic love and peacemaking (the Kingdom of God) but are not Christian or religious in the conventional sense ("religion without religion"), while lots of card-carrying Christians or religious people lead scandalously unevangelical and irreligious lives precisely in the name of religion. True religion is a matter of truly making something happen in your life, not signing on to certain propositions or acquiring knowledge not otherwise available to human beings.

That is why Derrida's notion of a pure and *indeterminate* "messianic" faith is so important to me. This Derridean faith is not one more confessional faith (or "determinate messianism"), Derrida's personal entry in the competition of confessions which Derrida promotes. Derrida is not recommending that we resign our present confessional affiliations and sign on to a new faith. Rather, he is attaching a certain coefficient of epistemic instability to the determinate confessional faiths in the name of *faith itself*. It is his way of visiting upon the "faithful" in the particular confessions a reminder that if they were born at another time and another place they would very likely claim to "know" something quite different based upon a quite different "revelation." Derrida's pure messianic faith does not undo the confessional faiths or concrete revelations; it just reminds them that faith is faith, not knowledge. His faith is a "confession" — one that in my view has even more teeth in it than Augustine's — that we do not *know* in any deep way who we are, or who God is, or what is what, *quaestio mihi factus sum*. But, secondly, like Augustine's beautiful confessions, his confession comes as a word of encouragement (*viens, oui, oui*) for our neighbors (since God already knows everything that Augustine could ever cough up) to confess in the sense of profess, *confiteor*, to have faith, to put one's faith in something, even if I do not know exactly what, even if I do not *know* what. *Je ne sais pas; il faut croire.*

I confess, I do not know in some deep way who I am or what lies before me, although of course, like the next chap, I have certain (deconstructible) ideas about these matters. As often as I visit the local cemetery, I cannot quite make out what the dead are saying to me, what they who have passed this mortal threshold now know, if they know anything at all. They will not pass along their secrets, intervene in my disputes, tell me who is right and wrong, or add anything to what they have already said or done or written. So I am left to put my faith in certain well-worn words, like love and justice and, perhaps faith itself, in what they promise, and in texts that say that God is impartial, and that God is love and *whoever* loves is of God.

As a final note, when Stephen William protests that after all "There may well be some decidable things around here," he suggests that Derrida's notion of "undecidability" leaves us unable to decide anything. But for Derrida, undecidability is the condition of possibility of genuine decision. The opposite of "undecidability" is not a decision but decidability, that is, programmability or formalizability (Derrida has taken this word from Gödel), so that if things were "decidable" a computer program could do the job for us. You wouldn't need good judgment, just good software. The first really strong account of what Derrida means by undecidability is Aristotle's notion of *phronesis*, the power to discern what to do in the shifting tides of singular circumstances where hard and fast rules don't hold up. Undecidability requires a kind of "meta-phronesis" cut to fit our more cosmopolitan "postmodern" situation, where we nowadays have trouble coming up with even the general schemata that Aristotle thought were supplied by the local polis and its *phronimos*. Without undecidability, our lives would be routinized, run on automatic pilot, relieved of the stress and strain of decision making.

But above all, without undecidability, we would be bereft of faith. For faith is faith just in virtue of the fact that we do not in some deep way know what is what and that we must accordingly put our faith in certain promises, in certain hopes and dreams, praying and weeping that they come true, all the while confessing that there are many ways to dream, many forms of life, many determinate religious traditions. I agree that undecidability is an unnerving magister in the art of life, but it is a salutary one, because undecidability keeps us honest (lucid, "clear"). Undecidability functions like a great equalizer, as if it were God's impartiality here on earth. It does not undermine our decisions but ensures that we decide free from the illusion that we have been hard wired up to being itself or given some privileged access to the really real or that, lifted above the fray by the hook of faith, we have been given some "knowledge," of which, we regret to say, others less fortunate than us have been deprived.

Notes

[41] 1 That is a good example of an "auto-deconstruction": the way something that tends predominantly to draw itself into a closed circle also, circumspectly, breaches the circle and opens itself to the outside. The most menacing structures are the least auto-deconstructive; the most fruitful structures are the most auto-deconstructive.

2 In saying this I am not renouncing "hermeneutics." I reject the idea of presupposition-free uninterpreted facts of the matter. I am just saying that knowledge in the standard from epistemological sense proceeds from publicly shared and inter-subjectively confirmable interpretive presuppositions while religious revelations do not.

3 See Mark Hoolabaugh, "Lakota Celestial Imagery: Spirit and Sky," copyright 1997 at http://faculty.normandale.edu.

4 I have only so much faith in the distinction between faith and knowledge because my deeper aim, based on my views about hermeneutics, which I do not have time to develop here, is to weaken that distinction and to distinguish between the different sorts of faith that are constitutive of knowledge in the standard form epistemological sense and faith in the narrow sense of religious faith.

[42] 5 These traditions cultivate penetrating insights into things – like forgiveness – that arise from adopting a particular religious point of view, not because they are vehicles of supernatural disclosure, but because they engender *periti,* experts, people deeply practiced and experienced in their form of life.

BOOK REVIEWS

REVIEW: GOD AS OTHERWISE THAN BEING

[In *Journal of the American Academy of Religion*, 73:1 (March, 2005): 276-278]

God as Otherwise than Being: Towards a Semantics of the Gift. By Calvin O. Schrag. Northwestern University Press, 2002. 157 pages. $27.95.

[276] The most recent book of Calvin Schrag, long one of the most eminent American philosophers in the continentalist tradition, is a significant contribution to the growing field of continental philosophy of religion. This exceptionally clear and well-argued book, which helpfully brings together a great deal of what is happening in recent continental religious theory, pursues a three-fold movement: beyond beings to Being, beyond Being to the Good, and finally, beyond the Good to the Gift.

(1) *Beyond beings to Being.* Schrag first seeks a way beyond the God of metaphysical theism (God as the highest being, as the cause of other beings) by recourse to Tillich, for whom God is not a being beyond or beside beings, and hence not a personal being at all, but being-itself, a move Tillich clearly made under the influence of Heidegger (15-16). The personal God of classical theism is an anthropomorphism who is impaled on age-old dilemmas of the problem of evil (see Spinoza). The other alternative to classical theism – the atheisms of Nietzsche and Freud – are rejected by Schrag as reactive positions that do not explore what is happening in the idea of God in a sufficiently affirmative way.

(2) *Beyond Being to the Good.* But for Schrag God is not just otherwise than beings (Tillich) but also otherwise than Being-itself, lying beyond, not only metaphysics and epistemology, but also theism and atheism. The resources for this claim, the basic claim of the book, are found in three sites: (a) the later Heidegger (Heidegger III), who moved past Being to that which gives Being, *Ereignis*, which is the first appearance of the "an-economics of the gift." (b) Jean-Luc Marion, for whom God is not Being but, in classical Neoplatonic style, a superlative *hyperousios*, more eminent than Being whom Being itself never reaches. (c) Levinas, who represents the most radical position of all, for while

Heidegger's "gods" are creatures of the poets, and while Marion's God belongs to a classical Christian Neoplatonism, Levinas strikes out on the altered ground of ethics as otherwise than being and knowledge. Levinas describes the responsible subject faced with the neighbor who comes toward [277] us in the trace of God (a predominantly prophetic idea of God which needs to be complemented by a priestly and sacramental sense of concrete embodiment).

(3) *Beyond the Good to the Gift.* But even this ethical re-envisioning of God is insufficient, for taken to the end the relationship to the neighbor exacts an impossible and an-economic responsibility, what Schrag calls the "fitting response" demanded by the concrete situation, which is the gift of unconditional love (*agape/caritas*) beyond ethical duty. Now the dialogue partner shifts from Levinas to Derrida's analysis of the gift and especially to Kierkegaard. For the gift lies beyond the ethical as such, in the properly religious stage, by which Schrag means to resist the tendency of a certain version of postmodernism (Nietzsche, Foucault) to estheticism. The gift is not anything we "own" (or first possess in order then to give) but something over which we are stewards, which is paradigmatically true of our relationship to nature, which does not belong to us but rather we to it. God is thus to be thought within or perhaps even as the horizon of the gift. God's presence in the world is neither that of the realized eschatology (Hegel), nor the constant deferral of the arrival of the kingdom of God in Levinas and Derrida, but what Schrag calls a "preenacted eschatology," a partly realized eschatology, in which the kingdom has not fully come but begun to come. The transcendence of God is the transcendence of the gift, which is its unconditionality, which is nonetheless immanent to our quotidian economies. We acknowledge a gift not by a return gift (economy of remuneration) but rather – following Stephen Webb – a continuation of the gift by giving to a third one farther down the chain, so that the recipient is transformed by the gift into a giver (without returning anything to the original donor). One acknowledges an unconditional gift by attesting to it. The ethical returns, not as *nomos*, but as transfigured or transvalued by the gift; economies or rights and duties remain, but they are punctuated by gifts and ongoing giving, an "asymmetrical reciprocity" not an exchange. We move about in the acknowledgment of a gift that precedes us. God gives the power of giving, the ongoing participating in giving, enhancing the gift. Beyond *philia*, which is a reciprocal arrangement among equals, in which it would be irrational to befriend one's enemy, Schrag takes up Kierkegaard's exposition of the Christian concept of non-preferential *agape/caritas* extended to the "neighbor," rich or poor, friend or enemy, scrutinized by Kierkegaard in *Works of Love* (Harper, 1962). The kingdom of God is manifested in the workings of the gift as the

works of love. Love is action. The gift is what comes to mind in the wake of our inquiry into the God without being. We began questioning about the meaning of God and have ended up thinking about the gift (142-43).

This provocative and well-written book raises several interesting questions.

(1) Is this to be understood as a "death of God" theology where God has died but lives on in the "gift"? Is God to be thought *within* the horizon or the semantics of the gift, or has God *become* the horizon or the semantics of the gift? Tillich is the father or grandfather of a certain amount of radical theology, [278] and philosophers of religion like T. J. J. Altizer, Mark Taylor, and Charles Winquist took their cue from Tillich's theology of culture to argue that the transcendent God of classical theism has died but lives on by having been transformed into culture, transferred to what Deleuze would call the plane of immanence. Taylor locates this living-on in Las Vegas and Times Square, in the neon lights of the casinos along the Strip and in the NASDAQ board – which is a completely virtual "stock exchange" – flashing on Time Square. That is the esthetic death of God. Now it is perhaps not widely noticed that Levinas is also a philosopher of the death of God. Levinas is no less convinced than Nietzsche of the death of the God behind the scenes, the death of the two worlds theory inherited from the Greeks and perpetuated in Christian Platonism. Levinas is no less proposing a displacement of religion in the classical sense not however by art and virtual reality (Taylor) but *by ethics*. The kingdom of God is to be realized not in the Magic Kingdom but by an ethical or moral kingdom of ends. The death of God for Levinas is justified not as an esthetic phenomenon but as an ethical one. The trace that God leaves behind is invisible, not visible, not the invisibility of an electronic or virtual world but the moral invisibility of the face that commands. Is this the next step in the death of God theology, that God dies by living on – beyond esthetics and ethics – in the gift? That we do not give gifts to *celebrate* the Incarnation, but rather giving gifts *is* the Incarnation?

(2) If so, how does this position differ from Irigaray's (and from her critique of Levinas), in which the transcendent God of Love has become an immanent divine milieu of love? Love is the medium in which we (should) live our lives. It is not a transcendent entity but immanent force which overcomes the subjectivity of autonomous agents and sweeps the lovers into each other's arms. In the divine milieu of love, lovers are not to be conceived as monadic agents or subjects issuing intentional acts of love, but as moments swept up in a powerful and immanent force. Is this the same account in which "God" has become the "divine" and the divine is love (love is divine)? Or how does it differ from Vattimo's transcription of God into love?

(3) By the same token, how does this account relate to the concrete confessional faiths? Is this the theory that philosophically demystifies concrete cultural-religious practices like prayer or churchgoing? Or alternatively, if someone has nothing to do with the confessional faiths and does not "believe in God," but leads a life of "gifting," has one on this accounting entered into an authentic relationship with "God?"

(4) Finally, is this transcription of the idea of God as the God of love into the semantics of the gift in the end too narrowly Christian? Does it apply to conceptions of God outside the Biblical tradition? Is it possible to transcribe God in terms that are "otherwise than the gift"? Should that be the title of Schrag's next book?

REVIEW: *BEING GIVEN: TOWARD A PHENOMENOLOGY OF GIVENNESS*

[In *Journal of the American Academy of Religion*, 74:4 (December 2006): 986–989]

Being Given: Toward a Phenomenology of Givenness. By Jean-Luc Marion. Trans. By Jeffrey L. Kosky. Stanford University Press, 2002. 375 pages. $27.95

[986] We can all be very grateful to the work done by Jeffrey L. Kosky for this superb translation of Marion's *Étant donné* (1997). Marion is not an easy read in the French. While not an experimental and avant-garde writer like Derrida or Irigaray, his sentences are intricate, elusive and difficult. The very titles of his books are often – like this one – multi-leveled word plays. He is a tantalizingly subtle reader of other texts, especially of Descartes, on whom he is an international authority, making everything turn on the finest nuances, and an equally crafty and sophisticated expositor of his own views. So it is a daunting charge to get all this into English. Kosky, who is an experienced translator of Marion and did graduate work with him at Chicago, has done a splendid job.

Marion is the central figure in the new phenomenology in France, a group of Catholic thinkers working in the phenomenology of religion. Their work, which is being steadily translated into English, is an important part of the turn toward religion in recent continental philosophy, a movement that can be traced back to Levinas. Marion's project is to extend phenomenology beyond the garden variety and quotidian phenomena upon which human reason can get a decent grip that preoccupied traditional (especially Husserlian) phenomenology. These "handicapped" phenomena (321) pale in comparison with the more overwhelming phenomena – like the work of art, the experience of love or an historical event like the Holocaust (or maybe "nine-eleven") – phenomena that we have trouble conceptualizing and objectifying, that land on us and take us by surprise. The latter he calls "saturated phenomenon," which he presents as a radicalization of Husserl's principle of "givenness" – to accept phenomena just as they give themselves from themselves. The expression arises from a clever critique of Husserl for compromising this principle. By confining himself to "meant intentions" that are never completely "fulfilled" (I know what "Budapest" means but I have never "seen" it), Husserl neglects richer phenomena whose fulfilling givenness overwhelm or "saturates" their intentions (or concepts).

[987] The saturated phenomenon par excellence is the God of mystical theology, to which we were earlier introduced in *God without Being* (1976), the first major work of Marion to appear in English. That book reached an unapologetically apologetic (theological) conclusion – the only way to overcome the God of metaphysics and find the truly divine God is mystical theology. Since then, Marion has regained his confidence in philosophy, but of a specifically non-metaphysical sort – phenomenology – and has set about expounding his work as a rigorous phenomenology. If the only way to be true to God was to abandon philosophy for theology in *God without Being*, now the only way for philosophy to be true to God is to abandon metaphysics for phenomenology. Beyond that, the only way for phenomenology to be true to phenomenology itself is to take up saturated phenomena – like God. This is not without its critics. In *The Theological turn in French Phenomenology*, the late Dominique Janicaud complained that phenomenology here has become imperious, having been hijacked by theology and forced to serve theological purposes beyond its methodological limits.

The account of the saturated phenomenon is presented in a trilogy of which *Being Given* is the centerpiece. The stage is set for the analysis by *Reduction and Givenness* (1989), where Marion works out an innovative theory of the "three reductions" by means of a micro-reading of Husserl and Heidegger. "Givenness" is the translation of *donation*, which is the French translation of Husserl's *Gegebenheit*. In French and English, "donation" (like "creation") can mean either the act of giving (or creating) or the donation (or creation) that results from the act. So the obvious translation of *donation* into English is "donation." But Marion himself prefers "givenness," because this Anglo-Saxon word is true to Husserl's German term, but this cuts off the double movement of the word. Kosky's decision is made in part to respect Marion's wishes (341 n117) but, while this is true to the German, it obscures what Marion is up to. The force of *donation* (in French or English) is to make of *Gegebenheit* an agency or "self" that is actively doing something, a dynamic power and not merely the state of being given. In Husserl, one attaches an asterisk to a phenomenon to signify a change in status (*Gegebenheit*), but in Marion *donation* is a star in its own right. In Husserl, givenness itself does not do anything. Indeed, there is no givenness itself and it has no self. Marion's fundamental claim is that it – *donation* – does.

The three reductions, which are rehearsed in Part I of *Being Given*, follow the rule: so much reduction, so much givenness. This means: the more the constricting horizons and inhibiting conditions that are imposed upon phenomena by the ego or the subject are removed (reduced), the more givenness is released or freed up. The first set of constraints to be removed are those imposed by the transcendental subject (Descartes, Kant and even Husserl). The range of given phenomena cannot be confined within the limits of an "object" constituted by a "subject." The breakthrough beyond objectivity was made by Heidegger in *Being and Time*, but Heidegger's breakthrough was purchased at the cost of imposing a higher or finer set of conditions, in virtue of which the given is confined to appearing within the horizons set by "Dasein" and "Being." Only the final reduction, beyond both objectivity and being, removes every condition, subjective or ontological, and allows the given to appear absolutely, unconditionally, [988] purely in its givenness. The third reduction moves beyond the given *being* to being *given* as such.

Marion has been accused of having a theological purpose here – by redescribing every being as a given, he has turn beings into gifts where every good gift is from God. He responds In Part II of *Being Given* that he is doing the opposite: he is not describing the given as a gift, but the gift as a given. Furthermore, he shows that one of the forms the gift can take is to appear without a giver, as happens when someone receives a gift from an anonymous donor. This is carried out by means of a well-publicized debate with Derrida on the pure gift. For Derrida, as soon as a gift is manifest as a gift, it begins to annul itself by taking away from the recipient (who is indebted) and enhancing the donor (who is praised for being generous) and setting in motion the circle of exchange (repaying the gift). Marion accepts this analysis but maintains that it does not eliminate the gift as such, but only the economy of exchange (81), whereas the true gift should be inscribed in the field of givenness, which is defined by the aporias of gifts without visible gifts or givers. Defenders of Derrida respond that that was exactly Derrida's point.

After identifying certain features of the saturated phenomena – they land on me, surprise me and bring me up short (Book III) – the analysis shifts to an elaboration of the four kinds of saturated phenomena. These are rather loosely derived by overturning or overflowing the four kinds of transcendental conditions of judgment in Kant's First Critique. (1) The event: conceived somewhat like the fog of war (228), the historical event overwhelms any particular horizon or concept meant to capture, comprehend or grasp it, so that all we can do is multiply horizons to try to grasp it (quantity); here is the place of hermeneutics within the field of givenness. (2) The idol: the work of art, like a painting, which stops our intentional gaze in its tracks and floods or inundates it with so much color, form, atmospherics, depth and subtlety that no analysis can do it justice or articulate its content; it is "unbearably" bedazzling (quality). (3) Flesh: the lived immediacy of the flesh, which feels itself and is contracted to itself, is self-saturating (in pleasure or pain, for example). Called by Michel Henry "auto-affection," flesh can never be conceptually articulated in words; the flesh is absolute or absolved (according to relation). (4) The icon: here the look the ego sends out to an object is thrown into reverse by the look that comes to me from the other person, so that I myself am seen not seeing, and the eyes of the Other who sees me are not seen things but invisible and her face "irregardable" (according to modality) (taken from Levinas).

Things get testy when Marion introduces a fifth "possibility," in which all four modes of saturation are combined in one, thus redoubling saturation or saturating an already saturated phenomenon. This is called "revelation" (uncapitalized), a formal philosophical category in which the divine appears. The "example" he uses is the "visible Christ" (236 ff.). Mindful of Janicaud's criticisms, this is introduced not as "datum of Revelation," capitalized, which requires Christian faith, but as a purely phenomenological essence or possibility, like a literary narrative. The Christ takes the prophecies by surprise (event), his transfigured body is unbearable to the disciples (idol), his flesh is tortured and crucified, and he [989] regards or calls his followers who are seized by his gaze (icon). This is the form a divine Revelation would take, if ever there were one, and who is to say that God could not choose such a possibility for himself?

All that remains is to describe the "gifted" (*adonné*) which is how Marion describes the successor to the transcendental subject and to Dasein (Book V). Very much like what the later Heidegger calls "thinking," the role of the gifted is not to constitute what gives itself but to provide a place for its showing, to bring it into manifestation and give it words. The gifted receives the given by surrendering to it, and by surrendering to it, it receives itself in turn. As such the gifted does not have being but a vocation, having been called all along and in advance by a call that it never heard. The call can be answered and witnessed to, but that is all we know of the call, for it cannot be identified without dominating and distorting it. Is it God who calls, or Being, or the Other? Who knows? Only faith would allow us to call it God.

The third volume of the trilogy, *In Excess (De Surcroît,* 2001) elaborates the four plus one kinds of saturated phenomena.

Corrigenda: p. 23, l.4: *reiner*, not *reined;* 206: "*According to Relation,*" not "*Without Relation*"; 278, l.1: dependent, not dependant.

REVIEW: THE EROTIC PHENOMENON

[In *Ethics*, vol. 118 (October 2007): 164–68]

Marion, Jean-Luc. *The Erotic Phenomenon*. Trans. Stephen E. Lewis. Chicago: University of Chicago Press, 2007. Pp. 230. $35.00 (cloth).

[164] Jean-Luc Marion is the leading figure in a movement of French Catholic phenomenologists said to have taken a "theological turn." This expression, coined by the late Dominique Janicaud, was a complaint, not a compliment. Janicaud meant a swerve, as in driving off the road, even a kind of hijacking of phenomenology by an overriding theological agenda. But the speed with which *The Erotic Phenomenon*, published in France in 2003 (*Le phénomène érotique: Six meditations* [Paris: Grasset, 2003]), has been translated is testimony to the interest American philosophers and theologians have shown in Marion, who divides his teaching between Paris and the University of Chicago. Every important work of Marion, including his studies of Descartes, which have earned him a reputation as one of the leading Cartesian scholars of the day, has now been translated. Marion is famous for the idea of what he calls the "saturated phenomenon," which is inspired by his study of Christian Neoplatonic mystical theologians like Gregory of Nyssa and Pseudo-Dionysius the Areopagite. The idea is a heresy within Husserlian phenomenology. Husserl maintained that the act of meaning or intending an object is fulfilled only to the degree that the object intended is actually given (having never actually visited "Moscow" in person, this is for me a relatively empty intention). The notion of complete fulfillment remains an ideal only approximated asymptotically.

Marion proposes the reverse. Over and above these "poor" phenomena described by Husserl, there are phenomena of such overwhelming givenness or overflowing fulfillment that the intentional acts aimed at these phenomena are overrun, flooded – or "saturated." While it is a debated point whether such phenomena could be accommodated by a more generous reading of Husserl's idea of an intentional act, Marion has provided a rich and seductive account of several such phenomena, beginning with the work that first earned him international standing, *God without Being* (trans. Thomas Carlson [Chicago: University of Chicago Press, 1991]), which described a God given in the excess of love not "contaminated by being." This idea of doing "without being" owes something both to Levinas, according to whom the ethical demands of the other person draw me out of "being" (self-interest), and to Christian Neoplatonism, where being is what is created while the good is why it was created. Marion's proposal was hotly contested in Catholic circles, because it departed from the mainstream position of Thomas Aquinas that God is subsisting being itself, but no less in [165] phenomenological circles, where the idea that God could be given as a phenomenon in experience was understandably controversial. In a later book, *Being Given* (trans. Jeffrey L. Kosky [Stanford, CA: Stanford University Press, 2002]), arguably his *magnum opus*, Marion described four categories of saturated phenomena: the confusion of a great historical "event," the bedazzlement of the "idol" (work of art), the intense flush of self-feeling "flesh," and the "icon," the face of the other person who sees me without being seen; the idea of divine revelation is there placed in the special category of what he calls the "doubly saturated" phenomenon.

Having devoted many pages to the mystical experience, the face and the work of art, Marion here takes up the saturated phenomenon of flesh by way of its most striking expression, the erotic phenomenon. The choice of topic is less surprising than it might seem. Not only is there is a long-standing analogy between mystical and erotic experience, but the idea that God (who is without being) has become "flesh," is the central teaching of Christianity. That implies that flesh can do without being, a proposal that Marion defends in the present study. By denying "being" of flesh in the present book – and one would have to keep count of the different senses "being" has for Marion, who in each case comes out for what is "beyond" or "without" being – Marion means that flesh is neither an "object" constituted by a subject (Husserl's transcendental reduction) nor a being that deals concernfully with the world, as in *Being and Time* (Heidegger's ontological reduction). That one might characterize "being" more generously and thereby circumvent this need to do without being is another of the debatable points raised by Marion's work. Objects and beings together make up the "world," but in the life of flesh the world is suspended (in a "third" more radical phenomenological reduction), which lets the phenomenon of "flesh" appear. Marion is continuing the work of Michel Henry, another student of Catholic mysticism and an elder statesman of the movement spearheaded by Marion, for whom flesh means "auto-affection."

Flesh is not the body doing (Heidegger) or aiming at (Husserl) something, but flesh feeling itself feel.

Erotic flesh is not only a striking example of flesh for Marion but its primal phenomenon, the point at which flesh is awakened as flesh. This again is food for a debate as Marion seems at times to underestimate the sense in which flesh is equally awakened by pain. He even denies that the body in pain is flesh, a suggestion on which I suspect he will find little agreement (119, 177). His argument or exploration is broadly Cartesian, or perhaps counter-Cartesian, constituting a kind of "erotic" or "amorous meditations" as a counterpoint to Descartes's epistemic *Meditations*. Instead of starting with the cogito's search for epistemic certainty, Marion starts with the lover's search for assurance of being loved, and instead of the cogito's well founded certainty in the veracity of God, love is assured by the God who is love and who became flesh. Indeed, the Christian God is the perfect and unique *sens* – the singular sense and unique direction – of the erotic phenomenon (§42). Is this not unvarnished theology, as Janicaud complains? While Marion would concede that this conclusion in a robust form is only available to Christian Revelation, he does think that a phenomenology of the erotic phenomenon can lead us up to the point of seeing [166] the possibility of such a Revelation and that, were such a Revelation to take place in actual fact, phenomenology shows that it would make perfect sense.

The argument proceeds in several steps elaborated in six "meditations" in which we are invited to meditate along with Marion on the "things themselves," without the distraction occasioned by the mention of proper names. Of course, this expression "the things themselves" alludes to Husserl and Heidegger, so Marion is not trying to make a mystery out of his debt to numerous authors from the early Church Fathers to Heidegger. But the controlling analogy of the book is to Descartes *Meditations*, which is already detectible in the subtitle of the book as well as in the titles of individual meditations (or chapters), which employ the Cartesian syntax (Of God, that he exists…Of the Flesh, That it is Aroused). That makes it somewhat puzzling that the French subtitle of the book is omitted in the English translation. One can be grateful to translator Stephen E. Williams for an excellent job of rendering Marion's very nuanced French, but one would like an explanation of that decision.

The "erotic" phenomenon, while certainly a phenomenon of flesh, is an amorous phenomenon, a phenomenon of love (*amour*), not of sexual self-gratification. Having heard from Marion in the past about *agape*, in this book he has turned to *eros*, and in such a way – this is part of its argument, in fact – as to skew any hard distinction between the two. The meditations proceed by

287

placing a series of questions in the mouth of the lover, the first of which is "does anyone out there love me?" (3). The opening movement in Descartes's *Meditations*, which issued in the certainty of the cogito's existence, is thus replaced with the search for the assurance of being loved. Of what use is it simply to exist? Sheer being is a vanity of vanities, a Parmenidean plenum without articulated sense, a pure *de trop*. Being is redeemed only by love, whence the first question is not whether I exist but whether I am loved (16-22). Nor can I love myself – I am no *causa sui*. With what surprise could I overtake myself to break the boredom of being (44–46)? The first question proves too self-centered. It presupposes that I will not love until I am assured that I am loved, that my love will not go unrequited. This requirement of reciprocity blocks the emergence of the erotic phenomenon, which necessitates a second and more fertile formulation: "can I love first?" (71-72) Now the lover means to offer love as an expenditure without return, to give love as a gift without demanding that love be requited. In what Marion calls the "advance," the lover takes the initiative and puts him or herself at risk, and even does so in the blind, without knowing whether his own love is true or whether it will be truly returned. I am not sure of being loved, but I have the higher assurance that I love without return, or at least would love to so love. If at least I love to love, even if I fail to love truly, then I love (as in *si fallor sum*).

The lover's advance is met with love's response, "Here I am," a phrase Levinas use to signify ethical responsibility to which Marion assigns an erotic role (106-107). Here I am – please "come" (131), a word with both eschatological and erotic charge in both French and English. Bodies make contact in space and offer one another resistance, but when my flesh meets the flesh of the other, the other withdraws, makes room for me, and invites me into hitherto forbidden places. The two fleshes "cross" and give each other flesh in a movement of "crossed" (mutual) deep erotic passivity. I come to feel myself as flesh in feeling [167] the other to whom I am giving flesh, even as I feel the other feel me and give me the flesh I cannot give myself (117-20). This crossing reaches a glorious climax, the climax of bodies turned into flesh, blazing with orgasmic glory like the eschatological glory of the body of the risen Jesus (127), almost "immaterial" (135). But such glory as the orgasm gives is intermittent, reaching a peak and then a fall, a "suspension," at which point flesh subsides and the sway of the world is reasserted. That means that the erotic rhythm requires "repetition," in which the lovers again and again take temporary leave of the irremissible world (134).

At this point the lovers are assured of their love only intermittently, just as the cogito knows its own existence each time it thinks this thought "I think, I am;" and just as Descartes required the veracity of God to ground this proof more firmly, Marion sets out in search of a comparable anchoring of love. In Meditation V, bearing the very Cartesian title "Concerning Lying and Truthfulness," Marion analyzes the possibility of deceit, bad faith and ambiguity that beset the lovers. What is to stop the one from deceiving the other, or even deceiving him or herself, or simply not knowing his or her own mind? At best, each lover assures the other that the love the other gives is received as true, which brings these meditations to their third and final question, "do you love me?" (189), the answer to which is "you loved me first" (215). Given that the lovers' mutual assurances are as fragile and fallible as their being is mortal and finite, Marion, following Levinas, turns to the child, to give their love phenomenality, durability, and stability (196–97). But that, too, is only a provisional solution, for the child does not return to the parents as their validation but sets off as an independent form of life; neither do children return the gift of life to their parents but pass it on in turn to their own children (203–205).

So the instability of the lovers' situation is still unresolved. But they have sworn each an "eternal" oath, to love beyond being – the lover goes on loving even after the beloved has died – with a resolve that is irrevocable, having made an "eschatological oath" before eternity, unto God, *à dieu*, whom the lovers call upon as the eternal witness to their love (211–12). (There is an obvious objection to this crucial move: "eternal" means they vow to love each other "forever," "until death do us part," for as long as they both shall live, but nothing says that they will live on forever.) So too I now know how to love myself, not directly, but as one whose lovableness is affirmed by the other who loves me. Still more importantly, it is no longer true that this "I love, I am loved" is true only intermittently, only as often as flesh meets flesh, but now it is enduringly, stably true, resting upon the foundation of eternal love. In the final section of the book (§42), Marion argues that the three kinds of love differentiated in the tradition are but variations on the unique sense of love, erotic love, for friendship (*philia*) bears all the features of erotic love minus sexual enjoyment, even as we have seen that *eros* is no less self-renouncing than *agape*. That means that even God, who is agapaic love, and who gives his love flesh in Christ, burns with erotic love hyperbolically, more perfectly, without intermittence. God is the unique sense and direction (*sens*) of erotic love, and it is indeed from God that we first learned of this love, which is why erotic love borrows so much of its language from mystical love (and not the other way around; 149).

The book is what we have come to expect from Marion: challenging, subtle [168] and nuanced analyses, dazzling formulations that are the despair of any translator, a provocative and original philosophical genius. But however fascinating and concrete these analyses, they will not lay to rest the anxieties of his critics. Phenomenologists in the Janicaud style will continue to see this course of meditations as steered from the start by a theological *sens*. But considerations of phenomenological method aside, one wonders in the end whether the Cartesian allusion is not too strong, whether the attempt to situate the intermittence and repetition of the lovers' condition within the loving arms of eternal love is not to do too much. Why not concede that as a phenomenon love is irreducibly finite, fragile, and unstable, a risk taken by lovers whose mortality and lack of eternal assurances is what makes their love so precious? The lovers fear that this night may never be repeated, or if it is, that someday the repetitions will simply cease and dissipate into entropic dust, and that is the reason they embrace each other so tightly. It may be there is more to love than that, that something eternal has loved us before we love, but if so, that is a faith one holds in the face of phenomena that give us no assurance about that.

INTERVIEWS

23

EMMET COLE INTERVIEWS JOHN D. CAPUTO

[In "Emmet Cole Interviews John D. Caputo," *The Modern Word* (May 16, 2005). This interviewed was originally published at: http://www.themodernword.com/features/interview_caputo.html, but it is no longer available online.]

> *In formulating my confrontation with Heidegger in terms of Heidegger's exclusion of the "jewgreek" I use the expression Derrida has borrowed from James Joyce....*
> *Heidegger would have gotten very different results if his perspective were the history of power instead of the poetics of truth. Or indeed if he had chosen to heed other temples besides the ones at Paestum, or other poets than Hölderlin, if, for example, he had actually listened to Trakl instead of making him say what he must have meant! Or if he had listened to James Joyce, e. e. cummings, or Mallarmé.*
> –John D. Caputo, *Demythologizing Heidegger*, 6, 28

The Modern Word: We have all been warned against creating entries for encyclopedias. So when a book suggests the possibility of a signpost like this one:
<Derrida, Joyce, Caputo>
<Joyce, Caputo, Derrida>
<Caputo, Derrida, Joyce>
The Modern Word's natural response is to follow the labyrinthine way suggested by the sign, rather than create a scene by declaring this or that to be the case. This invariably becomes a search for both origins and destinations, the maker of the sign and the place it points to.

The labyrinth has been kind this time – sometimes it is cruel and indicates only dead-ends and signs without substance. This time, the labyrinth directed us straight to the maker himself, John D. Caputo, author of the opening gambits (but not *as such*) above, distinguished philosopher, writer, and thinker.

After Derrida, Caputo makes use of the term "jewgreek," a fictive phrase in which extremes are said to meet, but one within (and outside of) which much else of great consequence occurs.

You and I, for example.

From Joyce through Derrida to Caputo there runs a filament – jewgreek – which is intriguing to Joyceans and philosophers, not just because of its genealogy, but because of its destination. As to where that destination lies, it is surely not a single site or a particular place, but our very selves.

* * *

Emmet Cole: The first-name John appears on the spine of your books, yet I have found instances in, let's say, less formal environs (including your initial email reply to my request for an interview, for example) of a different first-name – Jack. Is John the author and Jack the man? Which is your proper name? Which is the proper name?

John D. Caputo: You had no way to know this, of course, but that is a very deep question for me, touching upon my whole destiny (if I have one!). Everything is at stake in this question. My "proper name" is John. As you well know, one of the central theoretical problems in what Derrida calls "deconstruction" is the *impossibility* of the proper name; if it were possible, we would not be discussing this question of my name. But for me the name "John" resonates with nuns, with religious sisters. I think of being a small child in grade school, terrified of those black-and-white figures that hovered over me, like angels of terror, delegates of heaven and hell, of dark powers and vast cosmic forces. I'm sure they were unselfish and very good women, but some of them, I think, were teaching grade school because they loved God, not us. At any rate, they scared the daylight out of me – and they called me "John," where everyone else, my family and my friends, called me "Jack." So my world divided between John/Jack, the outside hostile "world"/the familial and familiar. All my life everything "official" and impersonal went under the name of "John." When I began to publish, I used "John D.," which was meant to build a wall as high as possible around that scared little boy back in grade school that I am (was/will always be).

What gives this question added depth for me has to do with Jacques Derrida. In 1989 Jacques Derrida published a journal, a kind of quasi-Jewish slightly atheistic *Confessions* that clearly alluded to St. Augustine's *Confessions*, in which he revealed that his name is actually the American name "Jackie." (Incidentally, St.

Augustine's homeland, ancient Numidia, is modern day Algeria, and Derrida lived as a child on the *Rue St. Augustin*.) "Jackie" is also a feminine name, the familiar form of Jacquelyn, in French (and English), which among many other things suggests a kind of miscegenation (*cousin/cousine*) of which he would approve. It was a popular custom among Algerian Jews in the 1930s to name their children after American movie stars, and "Jacques" was named after Jackie Coogan, a child star who had appeared with Charlie Chaplin. When Derrida first began to publish, he decided he could not use a name which seemed ridiculous, so he followed the phonic flow from Jackie to Jacques, although of course "Jack" is the nickname for John/Jean. So it turns out that we have the same name, and one of my most bitter-sweet moments was when, shortly before his death, Jacques signed his last letter to me "Jackie." Jacques/Jack was torn by the same tensions; we suffer from the same anxieties! As my work makes extensive use of deconstruction, I wrote in one of my books, "I do not know where to draw the line in this game of Jacks." I cannot remember sometimes whether he said something, or this was a way I put something he said, or I just said it "myself" (if there is one.) We could spend this entire interview on this question, because in one way or another everything is there.

Cole: I ask because the pairing of author and man resonates with the pairing of philosopher and ethical actor, which resonates with Greek and Jew. May I call you John Jack in honor of this attractive proposition?

Caputo: That would please me greatly. In fact, it would touch my soul. That would also be, in a certain way, Rousseau's name, who also wrote a famous *Confessions*. We could cover everything we have to say under this distinction.

Cole: John Jack, I never fail to recommend *Demythologizing Heidegger* (or *How to Recover from Reading Heidegger*, as I call it) to those with an interest in the great German, especially those I suspect may be susceptible to falling under the sway of his bewitching prose. I may prescribe *Demythologizing Heidegger* as medicine, but what were your intentions in writing it?

Caputo: I wrote it as a medicine for those who were susceptible to the sway of his bewitching prose. (Did you say that I did? Is your middle name "Jack"?) You are exactly right. In the de-Nazification hearings that followed WW2, Karl Jaspers, the much-respected German philosopher and contemporary of Heidegger – Jasper's wife was Jewish and barely escaped the camps – was asked about "what to do" with Heidegger, who was at the least a fellow traveler of the Nazis. Should he be relieved of his position, deprived of his pension, etc.? In answering this question Jaspers said that he thought that Heidegger's relationship to his students was "unfree." He meant Heidegger was a spellbinder, a word wizard, so that while Heidegger was constantly appealing to us to "think," the effect he often produced was thoughtless acolytes who simply processed behind him, chanting words like *Ereignis, physis, aletheia*. One of Heidegger's "discoveries" was that Being qua Being speaks only Greek and then, as a supplement and only when it is necessary, Being uses German, which is the spiritual kin of Greek. Heidegger confided to us, that his French friends – surprisingly, there was actually a groundswell of support and admiration for him among the French after the war, including Jean-Paul Sartre – confided to him that when they want to "think," they have to switch to German! Presumably, when they want to make love, they stay with French. I think they also dine in French, although Heidegger does not go into these, presumably ontic, matters. This so-called "spiritual kinship," of course, is a function of the retardation of the German language. Because of the political disarray of Germany before von Bismarck, the language did not modernize as quickly or as thoroughly as other modern languages, and so did not complete the process of substituting word order for endings. That is why it is still highly inflected and, for that reason, is grammatically more like Greek and Latin. Now as Derrida said, all of this would be extremely funny were it not so dangerous. It is not only a ridiculous thing to say, but it is dangerous, a ruse in which a vicious nationalism and an enormous political stupidity and blindness makes its nest. This was in many ways a rehearsing of a myth that began with Winckelmann about *Germania*, the place where everything Great and Greek and Originary finds its modern home. Of course, that gives the German people its calling, its vocation, its mandate to lead the West by whatever means necessary out of the darkness, a darkness which Heidegger thought had settled in an especially deep way upon the United States and the Soviet Union, between which Heidegger thought – this was really as much political insight as Heidegger's "thinking" (*Denken*) could muster – there was not a dime's worth of difference. The Nazis could never figure out what their revolution had to do with Heraclitus, but they were glad to have a famous philosopher on their side and glad to hear that "the Greeks" were also on their side.

At a certain point, after many years of studying Heidegger quite faithfully – I even wrote to him, once – I just could not stand this stuff any longer and I decided to lay out my case. So I am a kind of Heideggerian apostate and that is how the acolytes treat me. But do not misunderstand me. I do not want to lynch Heidegger or dismiss him. I was myself in the beginning – this was my first "research program" as they call it in academicese – deeply interested in the convergence between what he called "thinking" (and the thinking that "called" him, as he said in a well-known book called in English *What is Called Thinking?*) and the late medieval mystical tradition whose peak I myself would locate in Meister Eckhart, in whom the young Heidegger had a serious interest. Heidegger made many important breakthroughs about poetry, metaphysics, and technology, and he opens the space within which continental philosophy in the second half of the twentieth century takes place. Those who want to simply jettison him go too far. But he has a dark side; he is a spell binder, with an unhealthy oracular voice, telling a too simple and highly elitist and Romanticized story, and he has a tendency to produce not thought but epigones who simply incant what he says, who divide the world up into those who are inside and those who are outside their little esoteric world, and who translate his books into no known language, certainly not English.

Cole: James Joyce is mentioned a couple of times (sufficient to warrant this exchange, of course) in "Demythologizing Heidegger." How did "James Joyce" – a proper and mighty name if ever there was one – find its way to the tip of your pen?

Caputo: Through Derrida, and I pursued Derrida's texts on Joyce in *The Prayers and Tears of Jacques Derrida* even more than in *Demythologizing Heidegger*. Before Derrida, I had not made any special effort to get to know Joyce beyond what any literate Anglophone would know. Even under the prodding of Derrida I have not become competent in Joyce, which as you know was the first thing I said to you when you approached me about this interview.

Cole: You mention Joyce as a representative of a "jewgreek" perspective – an alternative voice that might have saved Heidegger from himself, specifically his totalizing tendencies. First, what does the term "jewgreek" represent? But also, what saving qualities does it hold?

Caputo: This famous Joyceanism requires a little background. In 1964, Derrida wrote a now classic article on the relationship of the Jewish philosopher Emmanuel Levinas to Edmund Husserl (the founder of "phenomenology"), whom Levinas deeply admired but criticized, and Heidegger, whom Levinas not only criticized but detested (he had lost most of his family in the Holocaust). In this article, one that helped make both Derrida and Levinas famous, Derrida who up to a point is defending Heidegger and Husserl, refers to them as these "two Greeks," by which he meant philosophers, heirs to the style of thinking both founded by and still today largely derived from what was started by the Greeks, especially Socrates, Plato and Aristotle. That was said to differentiate them from Levinas, the Jew who was also a philosopher, the philosopher who was trying to expose philosophy itself to its "other," to another voice, one that had its roots in the biblical tradition, where God is "wholly other," and especially in the prophets, who call for justice. This is an ancient distinction, one that goes back to the discourse to the Greeks about the unknown God that Luke attributes to Paul, and to Tertullian's famous question, "what does Athens have to do with Jerusalem?" Now a crucial part of the Heideggerian "myth of Being" is a myth of monogenesis, that the "West" is a Greek creation, which means that everything Jewish and Christian is a distortion of its originary essence, a "fallenness" from Greek primordiality. Levinas hated this, and rightly so. As Derrida says, Levinas was trying to interrupt this monologue or soliloquy of philosophy with itself, to push philosophy beyond itself, to widen philosophy's circle, the result of which would be a new and very radical version of what Levinas called, in the language of Greek philosophy, "ethics." The result would be not anti-philosophy but philosophy radicalized by biblical ethics, not a philosophy of "Being" (Heidegger) but of what is "otherwise than Being" (Levinas). What Levinas intended, and this was the "saving" element he was introducing, was to break up the hegemony of the paganism and aestheticism that is represented by Heidegger's "Being" and to insist upon the central fact of ethics and human suffering. Remember the Holocaust.

Now when Derrida comes to the end of this brilliant article, and he wants to summarize what he is saying, to encapsulate it, to give us a way to remember this extremely careful and complicated analysis, he turns to James Joyce. Are we Greeks? (Beauty, truth.) Are we Jews? (Prophetic justice.) Are we one before the other? Can we even say "we"? We live in the difference between the two, Derrida answers, in the space that opens up between them, the space called (Western) "history." Is this "between" to be understood as a Hegelian synthesis of Greek and Jew (something that Levinas would profoundly contest, for that synthesis would "assimilate" the Jew)? Or it another kind of relationship, less a synthesis than an odd "coupling." Then Derrida says – this is the final line – "what is the meaning of the *copula* in this proposition from perhaps the most Hegelian of modern novelists: "Jewgreek is greekjew. Extremes meet."

Now I leave it to you, or to what Derrida calls the academic Joyce industry, to explicate what that text means for Joyce…

Cole: In *Ulysses Gramophone*, Derrida writes of his fear of addressing Joyce experts, the Joyce industry. I do hope you don't feel the same way, I can assure you that I am neither expert nor particularly industrious.

Caputo: I feel less fearful hearing you say that. Then let me tell you what this means for Derrida, which is also what I have in mind whenever I use it. It refers to the irreducible complexity of what we call too simply, as if there were one, "society," "tradition," "history." It refers to the illusion of monogenesis; it is a name, an emblem, for pluralism, polymorphism, polygenesis, and for prophetic justice. (Back to Jacques's name: we do not know what his proper name is or whether it is masculine or feminine.) It is a name for no proper name, no simple identity that is identical with itself, and hence a name for hospitality and welcoming the other. I say it is an emblem because, in itself, it too, like any name, is immensely limited, since it excludes, right off, and very fatefully today, the Arab, the Palestinian, the non-European, not to mention the African, the Asian. Let us say that "Jewgreek is greekjew" means what St. Paul says, when he says, "there is neither Greek nor Jew, male nor female, master nor slave." It is a name for the non-exclusionary. Not the encyclopedic assimilation of differences into a higher unity but the simultaneous patchwork peaceful co-existence of differences, which is not a bad way to describe what is today called "postmodern."

Cole: However, I couldn't help noticing in the same work, that at one point Derrida asks, "What right do we have to select or interrupt a quotation from *Ulysses*?" There's a certain illegitimacy, Derrida observes, in such an appropriation. Placing aside proprietorial questions, questions of Joyce's ownership of the text, how do you justify spinning Joyce's thread into your own work? What kind of connection is established when a philosopher draws on fiction?

Caputo: I should begin by saying that, in the particular case of Joyce that we are discussing – in another text I myself made use of Joyce's "The Dead" – I am drawing less on fiction than on Derrida, who is drawing on fiction. Still, the question stands. I would say two things. First, the reinscription of a text from fiction in a philosophical text should derive from a reading that also observes the classical protocols, that has worked very hard at reconstituting the sense of the text, its original language, its context, etc. Only then will this reinscription be productive and not simply capricious. But reinscription is both necessary and inevitable; texts do not have a meaning so much as they have a history. It will be done anyway, so let us do it well. Secondly, philosophy should turn to literature for instruction, not illustration. Philosophers often "use" literature as an "example," to "illustrate" a point that has been independently established by philosophy. That is dabbling with literature. I think philosophy must submit to literature, be humbled by it, and allow itself to be taken by it to a place that, left to its own resources, it cannot go. That is also how I feel about biblical texts, and what Levinas was saying to the philosophers: here is a voice you have not heard before. Incline your head, hear it well.

Cole: The qualities you attribute to the jewgreek perspective seem to me to have a lot in common with the values of experimental fiction, especially in virtue of the fact that experimental fiction does not privilege any archê-typal mode or manner of writing. Do you agree that the spirit of experimental writing has much in common with the term "jewgreek," especially in as much as it consists of marks and erasures and is a call to the particular?

Caputo: I answer this question only on the condition we both agree that I am completely incompetent to answer it, as I have not studied experimental fiction. But it is a tradition of long and venerable standing for philosophers to answer questions about which they have no competence. Sometimes they even get lucky and say things that are actually right. But what strikes me first about your question is that the answer must be yes if only because Derrida is himself an avant-garde and highly experimental *writer*. If you look at the simple typography of *Glas*, with a line down the middle dividing two different texts, one about Hegel, one about Jean Genet, and the little windows inside both columns with still other continuous texts; or the "love letter" format of *Postcard*; or the autobiographical text of "Circumfession" running at the bottom of the page of a book up above "about" "Derrida," etc. All of those inventions constitute so many experiments aimed at establishing what he called the "end of the book," the delimitation of the claim of the book to be a little, or even a big, encyclopedia, which tells the whole story with a beginning, a middle and an end, in a clean edition, with nothing spilling over the margins. These techniques are all so many ways to draw a zone of absolute respect around the singular, the unclassifiable, that which resists enclosure within one genre. That is also why Derrida has so deeply scandalized the professional philosophers, the philosophy industry, who rend their garments when they read his texts. I take that back. Most of them never read his texts – but they rend their garments anyway, based upon what they read about deconstruction in *Time Magazine*.

Cole: Experimental fiction descries inner (and outer) logic, and delights in self-consciously subverting its own logic. How do you think this relates to the jewgreek equation?

Caputo: We could, if we took enough precautions, let this formula, "jewgreek," be a stand-in or emblem for all these effects, the point of which would be to produce a new reading. Such deconstructive "subversion" is what Derrida is always talking about, and it is what his books *do*. In a certain sense, when the young Derrida read James Joyce, he must have felt what Harold Bloom called the anxiety of influence; he must have wondered what there was left for him to do. Of course, there was always a certain ambiguity of Joyce for Derrida, both a glory and a weakness. Joyce's greatest work was the unfolding, the embodiment, the enactment of deconstruction, that is, the exhibition of the labyrinthine weavings of language, the uncontainable dissemination of the play of differences. But the ambiguity of Joyce for him, his criticism of Joyce, was that he saw this huge and rhizomatic sprawl of differences as a Hegelian gesture, an attempt to encompass everything, to write an encyclopedia.

Cole: One key element of your project in "Demythologizing Heidegger" is justice. Can you explain what you mean by the term justice and why you think it is undeconstructible? How does justice avoid becoming another archê if it is always already inviolable?

Caputo: This is something that religious thinkers have always understood but it took Levinas to instruct the philosophers about it. In the classical — let us say "Greek" — concept of justice, justice is blind. A just law is a universal principle that applies equally to all, that contains no proper names (proper names again!). When politicians write laws that in reality only apply to one person, although their proper name is never used, we call that corruption or political influence. But on the concept of justice that I advocate, justice has to do with only proper names, by which I mean that justice has to do with the singularity of each one of us, precisely in our singularity. The Book of Justice would be then the Book of Proper Names, or what Levinas calls the "Judgment of God," for it has to do with what befits each one, even the least among us, in the singularity of their heart and mind. It would be like a map that is so perfect that it is the same size as the region of which it is the map. That perfect map, of course, would be a perfectly useless map, and impossible. That is why we distinguish justice, which is *the* impossible of which we dream, from the "law," which tries to be as just as possible while remaining in its blinded schematic condition. Now I say this is a more biblical model than a Greek one, more "Jew" than "Greek," because it has to do with the one lost sheep, not the ninety-nine safe in the fold; the lost coin; with the secret in our hearts that is known only to God; with counting every hair on our head, counting every tear. These are biblical models of justice, not to be found in Plato or Aristotle or John Rawls, who also favors blindness (the veil of ignorance).

Now, on this accounting – and I think you are right to push me on this – every law that we write will be deconstructible, that is, an imperfect instantiation of justice (someone always gets ground under by a law), but justice in itself, if it exists, is not deconstructible. But the point is that it does not exist, at least not as such; it is the undeconstructible of which we dream, a productive fantasy. It is a dream but it is not an *arche*. It does not provide determinate instruction like an *arche*. It is not a program to follow, a pattern to repeat, a model we can see, something that can be applied or approximated or approached asymptotically, but what Derrida at a certain point did not hesitate to call a "messianic" expectation of something unforeseeable.

Cole: You are, of course, well-known as a theologian...

Caputo: ...let us say a philosophical theologian, or a philosopher of religion. I was trained in philosophy and spent my whole life in the philosophy department at Villanova University. I confess that I have recently gotten religion, that is, I have moved to the Religion Department at Syracuse University, where I have been given the opportunity to spend the last phase of my teaching career peddling my wares among people who actually know a thing or two about religion. It is like a philosopher of science who moves to a physics department. When I speak about religion there, I feel like a fellow in one of those old cowboy movies who raises his hat on a stick to see if someone is going to shoot at it...

Cole: Apologies. Although you are unknown as a theologian, your words cause me to wonder whether the concept of jewgreek, as you employ it, is a component part of a postmodern Christology? That is, part of an attempt to discover a post-secular model of Christ. How does the term "jewgreek" relate to the Christian concept of Jesus as Word made flesh?

Caputo: Once again, given enough precautions, we could say that this is indeed just what it is. I have a new book entitled *The Weakness of God* that will be out sometime in 2005. This will be my most theological statement, philosophical-theological, that is, and here I speak of something I call a "sacred anarchy" – I take special note and heartily approve of your use of "Joyous Anarchy." There is tradition of "Christian Anarchy," in Jacques Ellul for example. By this expression I mean that the divine favor rests on the one who is out-of-power and authority (*archè*), the left out and left over; on weakness, not power; on the last, not the first; on the lost, not the safe. That I think is the philosophical lesson to be learned from meditating the life of Jesus, and what it means for God for take the form of flesh. If Jesus spoke Greek instead of Aramaic, if he had an urban and Greek instead of an Aramaic, rural and biblical imagination, if he uttered propositions instead of telling parables, if he used the Greek word "ethics," then my prediction is that such an ethics would be an "anarchical" one, where the real meaning and force of the "teaching," *Torah*, or the "law," the alpha and the omega of the Torah, to speak a little jewgreek, would be that the mark of God lies on the face of least among us, the an-archical. I wax a little heretical in this book by extending this anarchy to God's own being, which I want to maintain is marked by weakness not strength, which is emblematized in the Crucifixion. There is something like this in Moltmann, but there I think it is still consistent with the orthodox teaching of omnipotence, whereas I am not so sure that I am orthodox.

Cole: *Ulysses* ends with a fleshy affirmation of Molly's particular existence, a "Yes" that is committed to the indeterminateness and chaos of the flesh. This reminds me that in every moment, we are, according to the meaning of the phrase under discussion, first and foremost, Jews. Yet the phrase "jewgreek," *qua* philosophical signifier, is Greek. Is there any need or way to escape universalizing Greekness, open to philosophers, novelists, and friends?

Caputo: There is no way to stop speaking Greek if we use this in the widest sense of the gift of the inherited philosophical framework handed down to us by the Greeks, and it would be ungrateful of us to try. But there are many ways to interrupt this voice, to disturb its hegemony, to loosen its grip, to expose it to its other. That is what deconstruction does all the time, and that is what is emblematized by this word "Jewgreek," upon which we have been meditating. The aim is not to destroy "the" Greek or "the" philosophical but to widen its circle, to disturb any attempt to close the circle, keep it open to the surprise, to what it does not and cannot see coming, which is what makes life interesting. That being said, we are all Jews, we are all Greeks, not to mention all the other things we are, not to mention that we cannot quite say "we." We can say *oui*, but not we. Not we, we, but *oui, oui*. Yes, I said, yes. Molly's absolutely magnificent hymn, her Mollyian if not quite Marian *Magnificat*, yes, I said yes, let it be, let it happen, let it come, that is what deconstruction *is*: yes, to the coming of the other ("coming" having in English a happy polyvalence that is missing in French). Derrida says again and again, yes, that deconstruction is affirmation, yes, welcoming the other, yes, and that yes is yes only if it is repeated, *oui, oui*. When at a wedding, the bride and groom say yes, "I do," well, we don't know if they do. Maybe they do, maybe they don't. We will find out, and it will take a lifetime of repetition to find out.

Cole: I reminded that we are first and always Jews again, for I wish I could shake your hand to thank you for this interview. However, my email software doesn't yet extend me such luxuries.

Caputo: Do not be nostalgic. There is no pure origin. The Heideggerians complain about technology and want to replace technology with the "hand," with the things that are handmade, which they say are primordial and originary, and they look down upon the world-poor animals who they say have no hands, poor things (so let's eat them!). (I do not even mention his notorious remark about Hitler's hands.) But an amusing anecdote: as I mentioned above, when I was a young man I wrote to Heidegger and, *mirabile dictu,* I actually got a response – but, will you believe, it was typewritten!! I should have seen then that the whole thing had to be demythologized! Now, do not misunderstand me, I am not against hands, but I say yes to technology, and I think you do, too, and yes to email, which has allowed us to extend a hand to each other and made this exchange possible. This is the whole problem of the *pharmakon* in "Plato's Pharmacy," which I was recently rereading, but we cannot take this up here.

Cole: Please accept this lonely termination instead.

Caputo: I am not alone, and I will say a little prayer that you are not either, but I thank you very much for your questions, which were probing and provocative and, as we Americans say, quite a handful.

IN MEMORIAM

24

RICHARD RORTY (1931-2007): IN MEMORIAM

[In *CrossCurrents*, Vol. 57, No. 3 (Fall, 2007): 434–38]

[434] Richard ("Dick") Rorty died at the age of 75 on June 8, 2007, of pancreatic cancer, the same illness to which Jacques Derrida succumbed in 2004. Rorty's daughter, who seems to have inherited her father's ironic wit, said that this must be what comes of "reading too much Heidegger." The first contact I had with Dick Rorty was back in the mid-1970s, when I, a young department chair, invited him to speak at Villanova University. It was the "and now for something different" part of the philosophy department's annual lecture series. I thought it would be a good idea to hear a Princeton "analytic" philosopher – this was before *Philosophy and the Mirror of Nature* had appeared – do a critique of metaphysics, the department at Villanova having been centered around the metaphysics of Thomas Aquinas from its very beginnings. Rorty delivered an interesting critique of metaphysics which didn't sound as much like "analytic" philosophy as it sounded like Heidegger. When I brought this up at dinner afterwards, he deadpanned me as only he could and said, "that's where I got it." We all laughed – and then a few years later *Philosophy and the Mirror of Nature* appeared and changed the landscape of American philosophy. He wasn't kidding.

The next exchange was in the 1980s when I began reading what he actually had to say about Heidegger, and decided he was getting it wrong. This is one of the elemental mistakes to make in reading Rorty, to worry about the exegetical correctness of his readings of the great philosophers. We don't need Rorty for that; [435] we already have assistant professors coming up for tenure. So I wrote an article in which I criticized his views of Heidegger and sent it to him. I explained that Heidegger was not just relativizing the "vocabularies" that philosophers came up with in their own times, that to whatever extent he did seem to be doing that, it was all part of a larger, deeper (Rorty did not like that word) meditation on the history of Being in the West and the deepest (there it is again!) sense of Being's "truth." In typical fashion, he wrote me a gracious reply, thanked me for pointing all that out, and said that I had shown him what was upbeat (the skeptical part) and was downbeat (the "deep" stuff) in Heidegger and that would be "useful" to him in the future. Later on, I also took exception to what he said about Derrida, that Derrida was not just making fun of the great philosophers but he had an important philosophical project of his own. His response to that was equally gracious. Again, he did not contest what I said about Derrida but only mused that at those times when Derrida stopped making fun of philosophical theories and started developing positive philosophical theories of his own, Derrida was just having a bad day. After those early exchanges, I got it. We maintained contact over the years and became friends. Unlike a good many other people, Dick Rorty was the kind of person whom you could befriend with a criticism. He always listened to what people objected to, went along with what he could, and parted company with them at the point he thought they were getting too "philosophical," too inclined to proclaim the Truth of What There Is, as if they had been sent into the world to inform the rest of us about how it is with Being or Truth. We all have a great deal to learn from the good humor and equanimity he displayed in the face of the storm of criticism set off by the controversial positions he struck.

I said it is mistaken to judge him by the usual exegetical standards, because he was not an exegete, but a philosophical genius in his own right, doing what geniuses in any discipline do, drawing upon the resources that he found in several different places to forge a view that was uniquely his own, the one that bears the name "Rorty." A good many of the people who can get Heidegger or Derrida, or Wittgenstein or Dewey "right" have not much to add on their own. Rorty, on the other hand, redrew the map of American philosophy, in no small part by his ability to draw upon so many different sources, crossing the boundaries between "analytic" and "continental" philosophy – his first heresy which made life at Princeton difficult for him – and between philosophy and literature, the insights of which he also treasured. He did not think that there was some special method or professional skill called "philosophy" that could unlock [436] the secrets of human life, nor did he think that "science" was the successor goddess to philosophy. He held simply that there were different vocabularies tailored to different jobs whose merit was strictly limited to their success in getting the job done, "Truth" being an unnecessary compliment we pay to successful vocabularies. He thought that insight into our condition was a matter of scattered insights gathered here and there, no less in literature than anywhere else, and that the most that "philosophers" could do is put out the fires whenever the flame-throwers of "Truth" or "Being" (in caps) showed up on the scene. He belonged to a tradition of philosophers who made a living out of criticizing philosophy – he once said philosophy is a discipline in search of a subject matter – which always means philosophy as it had been practiced up to now. The result was to forge a new philosophical view that emerged from a kind of philosophy-against-philosophy, an anti-philosophical philosophy, but the kind of critique that does not do philosophy in but turns it around and gives it new life. That is exactly the sort of thing that people like Kierkegaard, Nietzsche, Heidegger, Derrida, and Wittgenstein themselves were doing. "Post-analytic," "post-modern" were words used to describe him. I am sure he was post-something or other. He was impatient with the academy – as well he should be – and impatient with the business as usual of philosophers who, as he said, read unreadable papers at one another at their professional meetings and counted *that* as their service to the wretched of the earth.

In all this, he became something of a celebrity, a public intellectual, better known to a wider public than any top ten professional philosophers you want to name combined, which only made the professional philosophers even madder at him. He made it plain to analytic philosophers that, beyond being technically precise, it is necessary to say something of interest to the human condition, and to the continental philosophers that, beyond taking up issue of existential interest, it was necessary to make sense and not feel fulfilled by making everything oblique, paradoxical, confusing and confused. To their disadvantage, both groups consider his example beneath them. One of the reasons Rorty became so much more important than his sometimes colleagues trapped inside the standard academic disciplines was his complete mastery of the idiom of American English. His was not the Queen's English, Americans trying to sound like British dons, nor was it the barbaric English of Americans who thought there was some virtue in sounding like a bad English translation of Heidegger or Derrida. This was the real thing, a dead-on musical ear for the cadences, the rhythms, the resources, the idioms, the unpretentiousness, the humor of [437] American English, and no one was better at it than was he. His sentences danced with clarity and dry wit, and he managed to combine originality with readable and entertaining English prose in a way that we have not seen since William James. Nothing was compromised by this stylistic clarity. His sentences were chiseled, sharp, witty – and groundbreaking. No one since Kierkegaard and Nietzsche has had this same capacity to make a conceptual breakthrough with a joke. Well, maybe Derrida, but Derrida is devilishly difficult to understand and Rorty is eminently readable. And the establishment, where both wit and conceptual breakthroughs were in short supply, fumed.

For most of his life, he bristled (quietly) if you brought up religion, which he thought started more fires than it put out, but towards the end he began to reconsider his views. Instead of saying that he was against religion, he quipped, he should have been content to say he was merely anti-clerical. There is nothing wrong with religion – were it not for religious people. In this he had good biblical precedent, going back to Jesus and the prophets. Any religion would have been proud to have nurtured someone of his honesty, modesty, and capacity for self-criticism. But beyond modesty, he had a passion for social justice and the well being of the disadvantaged, a passion that was in his blood – his parents were admirers of Trotsky and his maternal grandfather was Social Gospel theologian Walter Rauschenbusch. It was this "prophetic" passion that links him with what is best in religion. One of the great embarrassments to the religious establishment is the way it gets shown up by people like Rorty, people with a prophetic passion for justice who do not swallow a word of what the establishment peddles under the name of divine revelation, someone whose love of the least among us, which is the sum and substance of the law and the prophets, goes along with complete disbelief in "religious" doctrine. Once again, I think that what is going on in Rorty's (typically Enlightenment) suspicion of religion forces us to rethink religion and redefine it along more ortho-practical lines, which is largely what Rorty would have called "pragmatism."

Rorty was fine with feeding the hungry in the name of Jesus, if that's what it took to get you to feed the hungry. Whatever it took. But he was not sure what it would take to get academics away from their computers and actually do something to reduce human misery. For him, it was all a matter of being a man of the left, with as little philosophical, theological, and ideological baggage as possible, thank you very much. He enjoyed reading people who talked funny, like Derrida or Heidegger, which for the most part he regarded as a creative way to reinvent ourselves, just so long as we did not attach any deep metaphysical import [438] to such talk. But he especially wanted the left to get its act together, to get the job done in the streets, among the poor and the dispossessed, to get past personal dignity issues, to which of course he had no objection, and to move on to the more intractable social justice issues. And he wanted religion to look more like Martin Luther King or Desmond Tutu than Jerry Falwell. He wanted the left to stop alienating the American mainstream, and in particular blue collar working people, by bad-mouthing the United States, which was to court the current political disaster from which the left in the United States is still digging itself out. While the New Left was devising clever schemes to take over the English department, he quipped, the Right – both secular and religious – was busy taking over the country.

Rorty was a native American genius, a master of our language, a practitioner of a home-grown Yankee hermeneutics, who taught us to check our inflated speculative vocabularies at the door in order to get a close up look at the human condition in all its unadorned splendor.

Acknowledgments

Our thanks to the various publishers for permission to reproduce these materials, the source of which is acknowledged at the beginning of each entry.

Our thanks as well to Paul Caputo, M.F.A., for the design of the cover and for his considerable help and advice in preparing the copy for print.

More from John D. Caputo Archives

Previously published:

Collected Philosophical and Theological Papers:
Volume 1 – 1969-1985: *Aquinas, Eckhart, Heidegger: Metaphysics, Mysticism, Thought*

Collected Philosophical and Theological Papers:
Volume 2 – 1986-1996: *Hermeneutics and Deconstruction*

Collected Philosophical and Theological Papers:
Volume 3 – 1997-2000: *The Return of Religion*

Collected Philosophical and Theological Papers:
Volume 4 – 2001-2004: *Continental Philosophy of Religion*

For more information:
For links to podcasts, videos, recorded lectures, interviews, and more, visit:
johndcaputo.com
Follow John D. Caputo – Weak Theology on Facebook:
www.facebook.com/John.D.Caputo

Made in United States
Cleveland, OH
01 March 2025